AMERICAN JEWRY:
PORTRAIT AND PROGNOSIS

AMERICAN JEWRY

Portrait and Prognosis

Edited by

David M. Gordis and Dorit P. Gary

The Susan and David Wilstein

Institute of Jewish Policy Studies

Library of Congress Cataloging-in-Publication Data
American Jewry : Portrait and Prognosis / edited by David M. Gordis
and Dorit P. Gary.
    p.   cm.
    Includes bibliographical references.
    ISBN 0–87441–634–5
    1. Jews—United States—Social conditions. 2. Jews—United
States—Identity. 3. Judaism—United States. 4. United States—
Ethnic relations. I. Gordis, David M. II. Gary, Dorit P.
E184.J5A537 1997
305.892′4073—dc21   97–10912
                                                 CIP
                                                 r97

Published by Behrman House, Inc.
235 Watchung Avenue
West Orange, NJ 07052

Manufactured in the United States of America

Contents

Introduction

David M. Gordis

The Socratic admonition to "know thyself" has been adopted by the American Jewish community with an extra dimension of seriousness since results of the disturbing and disorienting findings of the 1990 National Jewish Population Study began to reach the larger public. Initial reactions were predictable: hand-wringing and keening in some quarters; denial and debunking in others; "I told you so" triumphalism in still others. It was only after the first flush of shoot-from-the-hip reaction that careful study and analysis of the findings and the beginnings of further research and careful reflection began. The papers that make up this volume are part of this more thoughtful and deliberative process of self-understanding which has begun in earnest in the Jewish community. The compendium is not absolutely comprehensive in bringing together all that can already be said concerning the subjects dealt with. Nor do we presume to provide total coverage of the significant subjects touched upon in the survey which merit concentrated attention from the community. Rather, this volume lays out the landscape of contemporary Jewish life in its many dimensions and constitutes an agenda for Jewish policy planning for the coming decades.

This is a brave new world, Jewishly speaking. The icons of the last half century of Jewish public life have either disappeared or are so far on the way to being transformed that they are virtually unrecognizable. A new set of issues has emerged along with a new vocabulary. "Jewish continuity," for better or for worse (or, perhaps, for better and for worse) has moved to center stage in Jewish planning and programming. Its meaning is not always clear: Are we concerned about the continuity of Jews or of Judaism? In other words, does continuity refer to the survival of Jews as people or does it connote the continuing relevance of Judaism as a religion or culture? Judaism cannot survive as a living entity without Jews. Can its people survive as Jews without Judaism? What can—and should—be the content of Judaism and Jewish life in an age when the overwhelming majority of its members have abandoned a literalist or fundamentalist Judaism? How can that content be transmitted at a time when conventional family structures hardly exist, and when schools appear to be failing to teach values of any sort? These are among the most obvious questions American Jews must now ask about their future.

An underlying theme of many of the papers in this volume, beginning with the demographic findings themselves, is that it is now much harder to describe Jewish difference, and that lines of demarcation between Jews and others are becoming more permeable. What are the implications of these changes?

In early May 1994 the hearts of many were warmed by the story of a teenage girl from a New York Hasidic family who became detached from her classmates during a school field excursion. After being lost overnight and raising fears for her survival, she was found safe and sound the following day. Little Suri Feldman at first did not respond to her rescuers' calls because she was praying and could not interrupt her recitation of the *Amidah* or silent devotion. Reflecting on the happy story a day or two later, a friend suggested that it was "these Jews" who were preserving Judaism, and that without them and their predecessors Jews would have disappeared.

The story is relevant here because the questions now arrayed before the Jewish community relate directly to my friend's observation. Is he right? Within the Jewish community, increasingly loud voices assert that the price of Jewish continuity is more emphatic physical, social, and intellectual separation from the larger society in which Jews live and clearer rejection of its norms. The greatest challenge to Jewish survival, they say, is that Jews are becoming too much like everyone else. In order to ensure that Jews continue to be Jews we must set out, as a community, to ensure that Jews are different. By implication, at least, the content of the difference is less important than the difference itself.

Are they right? Is the price worth paying even if we are willing to pay it? What kind of Judaism will emerge from this self-imposed isolation? Should Jews now undertake to be different in order to survive, or is it important that we survive in order to be different?

It really is time for American Jews to get serious about being Jewish in America. Reliance on an Israel-based agenda, i.e., organizing American Jewish public life around issues of political and economic support for Israel, a convenient but always questionable strategy, is becoming increasingly obsolete and ineffective. This agenda was founded on the assumption of Israel as an economic basket case and a political pariah. Happily and increasingly, Israel is neither. The peace process has broken down its isolation. American Jewish philanthropy is marginal as the Jewish state makes giant strides towards economic self-sufficiency and strength. Israel no longer depends as heavily on a powerful American Jewish establishment to extract political support from a grudging Administration and Congress. Even in its prime, the Israel agenda served as a distraction from the fundamental issue of American Jews: What does, can, and should it mean to be Jewish in America? Israel certainly belongs on the agenda of American Jewry, but it can no longer be the fulcrum around which Jewish public life revolves. Israel will not sustain Jewish life and culture in America.

The second traditional pillar of American Jewish public life, anti-Semitism and the need to confront it, also remains a significant item of Jewish concern. Continued vigilance is required, in response to manifestations of anti-Semitism in the United States—particularly from within the African-American community—in Eastern Europe, and in other areas of the world. But this issue, too, can no longer effectively occupy center stage on the agenda of the American Jewish community. At worst, it is a marginal phenomenon. Despite our acute sensitivity, anti-Semitism hardly enters into the lives of the vast majority of American Jews. The term itself has become a catch-all phrase covering a range of disparate phenomena, some serious and some trivial, including religiously based animosity, teenage pranksterism, intergroup conflict, economic competition as well as extremist xenophobic rhetoric. Even retaining the label "anti-Semitism" to refer to the range of anti-Jewish manifestations does not transform these phenomena into anything more than matters of marginal concern. American Jews must come to realize that anti-Semites will not create Jews; only Jews will. We must face the fundamental questions: What kind of Jews do we seek to create? How does the community go about creating them?

This book presumes to be both descriptive and prescriptive. It analyzes the data of the 1990 National Jewish Population Survey along with other data and attempts to translate them into a portrait of American Jewry. It seeks to point the way to planning for a continuity of Jewish life. The portrait raises a fundamental question about the planning. Is the prognosis so bleak that any efforts to alter it are futile? A number of the authors represented here would admit to pessimism over the future, even if they do not advocate surrender. Others are cautiously more optimistic. None are Pollyannish in their optimism. One is reminded of the pessimist's description of an optimist as one who believes that the future is uncertain. Only the historian of a later generation will be able to render judgment whether pessimism or optimism was justified. But despite the sober realism in the assessment of the challenges facing American Jewry that these chapters convey, the underlying thrust of this book is optimistic. The contributors to this volume aspire to objectivity and are dispassionate in their scholarship; they are not without passion for the object of their study. They are profoundly committed to the future of Jewish life. The enterprise of deepening the community's understanding of itself aims to build for the future, and the chapters proposing directions for planning and programming imply the usefulness of these efforts and the promise of their potential success.

No observer of American Jewish life can fail to be struck by the variety of modes of living and connecting Jewishly which have evolved in this unique setting. The challenge to define "who is a Jew" is not only for demographers and statisticians, but also confronts religious, educational, social, and communal leaders who need to understand the nature of their respective constituencies and plan for them. Halakhic, ideological, economic, and social issues need to be addressed. A variety of definitions and parameters has emerged in different quarters and for different purposes. This is unavoidable, for ultimately the identity of an individual is forged within, and the large majority of American Jews draw from a broad palate of Jewish and general cultures in shaping their personal identity. A useful way of formulating the question of Jewish continuity is: Will large numbers of American Jews continue to assert their Jewish identity and infuse it with content and meaning? Identity is created both by the adoption of the vocabulary, values, disciplines, mores, and "textures" of the group, and by developing a sense of differentiation from those outside the group. A minority of American Jews would argue for restricting the palate, for excluding non-Jewish cultural elements from the components of the identity of American Jews. That will not work for most American Jews who aspire to be part of the larger society in which they live. A clear picture emerges from the pages of this volume, and that picture is one of a highly educated but Jewishly ignorant community. The issue appears in bold relief: a Jewishly ignorant and uninformed community cannot draw on the elements of Jewish culture in the shaping of its own identity, since for them Judaism is, by and large, a closed book both literally and figuratively. The challenge to American Jewry, and the one to which this book is directed, is to find ways to include significant elements of Jewish religious culture and civilization on the palates from which American Jews create their personal identities.

Since the appearance of the Population Survey the Jewish community has begun to deal with the issues it raised energetically and constructively, and that is encouraging and hopeful. In sum, this book will contribute to Jewish life if it elicits neither pessismism nor optimism, but realism, in clarifying the challenges, and suggesting new directions for the community to follow in the coming millennium.

In conclusion, it is a pleasure to acknowledge with appreciation the partnership which the Wilstein Institute established with the Council of Jewish Federations in sponsoring the conference at which most of the papers in this book were originally presented in an earlier form. In particular, I wish to thank Professor J. Alan Winter who served as a research associate at the Council of Jewish Federations, and provided editorial assistance in the early stages of work on this book. While my Wilstein Institute associate Yoav Ben-Horin and I were responsible for much of the conceptual formulation of the initial conference and of the book, the extensive and detailed work of collaboration with individual authors and editing the book was the work of my co-editor, Dorit Gary, Director of Publications of the Wilstein Institute. To them, and to all the authors and scholars whose work makes up this volume, my thanks and those of the Wilstein Institute of Jewish Policy Studies.

PART ONE

Demographics

1

Toward Understanding American Jewry

Sidney Goldstein

Concern about the health of American Jewish life, and particularly Jewish population trends in the United States, has expanded beyond the professional interests of rabbis and of a comparatively small number of specialists in demography and sociology to become part of a general and spirited debate over the Jewish experience and future in America. What is more, the tone of the debate has gone well beyond neutral and scientific discussion to embrace such distinctions as "pessimists" and "optimists," "assimilationists" and "transformationists."

Some hold that American Jewry is progressively weakening demographically as a result of low fertility, high intermarriage, greater dispersion, and assimilatory losses (e.g., Schmelz and Della Pergola, 1988). Others argue that the demographic issues are of marginal importance; that the issue is not how many Jews there are or will be, but rather the quality of Jewish life (e.g., Goldscheider, 1986). In their view, concerns about population size, growth, fertility, and migration represent misplaced emphases; the critical concerns should focus on Judaism, Jewish culture, Jewish education, the perpetuation of Jewish communal institutions, and the linkages between the American Jewish community and Israel. It is argued that the changes in the substance and style of Jewish life present no serious threat to the survival of American Jewry, that we may, in fact, be entering or may already be in the midst of a transformation to a new Golden Age. Indeed, Irving Greenberg (1991) has proposed that world Jewry stands at the brink of a new era in Jewish history, one that may rival the Biblical and Rabbinic periods in its impact and challenges. From this perspective, it is the shift from powerlessness to power which has changed the basic condition of the Jewish people, with lay people and Jewish communal professionals emerging as the leading group of the Third Era.

The gaps between these views are wide, the emotions are strong, and unfortunately, to date, the evidence needed to assess the validity of the different perspectives remains limited. What they all implicitly share, I believe, is a recognition that the size, mobility, location, composition, and modernization of the Jewish population greatly affect its social, cultural, and religious viability, whether this is judged by the ability to support an educational system, organize religious life, maintain a Jewish marriage market, or provide sufficient density of population to insure a network of interaction among Jews and a sense of community. In short, all are realistic enough to recognize that in order to have Judaism, we must have Jews, and the right kind in the right places.

On the Jewish scene, quality and quantity are inexorably linked in a complex fashion. We must, therefore, be concerned about both, and about the connections between them. The need to do so is certainly exacerbated by the impressive success of American Jews in their struggle over the last century for acceptance into the larger American society. Jews have reached new heights in educational achievement and occupational choice as well as far greater freedom in selection of place of residence, memberships, friends, and spouses. Together, these changes help explain associated demographic features such as later age at marriage, low fertility, more intermarriage and divorce, and high mobility. The major question is the extent to which they have contributed to the weakening of American Jewry, and especially the ties of individual Jews to the Jewish community.

Such concerns over the vitality of the community are coupled with a growing recognition that facts rather than speculation and myths should be the basis for planning for the future. They have led to the initiation and development of various efforts to assess ourselves as the basis for identifying problems, measuring needs, and making decisions about facilities, services, funding, community relations, as well as religious, social, and cultural activities.

The issues are intensified because the American Jewish community has evolved into a national Jewish community, judged demographically both by the increasing proportion of the population that is third, fourth, and higher generation American, and by the extensive dispersal of the population across the United States. Yet, even while migration has helped produce the national community by redistributing the population among regions, it has also, through its selective character, helped to insure the maintenance of fairly sharp differences among localities. Local populations differ on such criteria as age, occupation and education, generation status, and extent and type of Jewish identification. Thus, the very development of a national community occurs simultaneously with the perpetuation and, in some cases, even exacerbation, of the unique features of local Jewish communities (Goldstein, 1987). In the process, individuals, both movers and stayers, develop familial, social, and economic networks that span the nation, reenforcing the national character of the community.

The greater opportunities afforded individual Jews in their economic and social activities have introduced greater complexity into the structure of the organized community. They are making it much more difficult to provide for individual social, psychological, economic, and health needs while concurrently trying to enhance the strength of Jewish identity. Moreover, the concurrent existence of a national and a large set of local communities means that we must take both levels into account in planning for the future. Indeed, to plan for one without recognizing the existence of the other is to overlook a key to the effective functioning of the community's agencies, nationally and locally. Planners must help to ensure continuing opportunities and stimuli for individuals and families to maintain their Jewish identity and ties to the larger Jewish community regardless of where they live or how often they move (Goldstein, 1990).

The Search for Data[1]

The importance of a national perspective and recognition of the multiplicity of interactions between the national and the local communities have, in turn, reenforced the need for demographic, social, and economic information at both levels. Since separation of church and state has precluded a question on religion in the United States census, we have no core of information about those who identify themselves as Jewish by religion. We have, therefore, had to look for alternate sources of data and usually to rely on our own efforts and ingenuity to create the types of information we need for assessment and planning purposes (Kosmin, Ritterband, and Scheckner, 1988; Goldstein, 1988).

A variety of alternate sources have been tapped or developed. But unfortunately most have had limitations for an analysis of American Jewry. Omnibus sample surveys directed at the general population, such as the Gallup Poll, seldom include more than a few hundred Jews and often considerably fewer, so that the number of Jews is inadequate for in-depth assessment (Fisher, 1983). Aggregating the results of several years of such surveys helps to overcome the small-numbers problem, but raises new problems related to comparability of information from year to year and to possible changes in attitudes and behavior over the interval encompassed by the surveys.

Use of census data on country of birth, and in recent censuses on ancestry, on the assumption that those born in Russia are largely Jewish, runs the risk of error due to lack of exact comparability between birthplace or ancestry and Jewish identity (Lieberson and Waters, 1988). Information on Jews identified by the census as Yiddish speakers at home or while growing up are also subject to serious bias because of sharp age differentials in the use of Yiddish (Goldstein, 1985). Moreover, the value of this and other approaches based on ancestry will likely decrease as the origins of the American Jewish population change and as more and more Jews are further removed from their immigrant ancestors.

The same concern applies to use of distinctive Jewish names (DJNs) as a way of identifying and estimating Jews in the population (Kosmin and Waterman, 1985). The value of this approach is also increasingly seriously impaired as the rate of intermarriage rises, especially as more Jewish women intermarry and take the "non-Jewish" names of their husbands (even if their husbands convert); even an Orthodox Melissa Callahan is not easy to identify as Jewish on the basis of name alone.

Local Jewish communities have increasingly recognized that to be effective their planning programs must be based on comprehensive, accurate assessments of the population (Levin, 1984). Through these surveys we have learned much about ourselves. Yet our knowledge is incomplete. Since first undertaken, the surveys have varied considerably in scope and quality. Various local surveys relied upon different questionnaires, varying sampling designs, and diverse tabulation plans. The result has been differential coverage of the Jewish population. The absence of standardized methods and definitions (including definitions of who was to be counted as a Jew) made it difficult and sometimes impossible to compare findings across communities, either to obtain a better understanding of a particular community or to obtain insights into the national Jewish community.

Recognizing the problems of coverage and variation in quality among local studies, the Council of Jewish Federations (CJF) undertook the first National Jewish Population Survey in 1970/71 (NJPS-1970/71). The national sampling design relied on a combination of local Jewish Federation lists of Jewish households and standard area probability methods to insure representation of Jewish households not included on lists (Massarik and Chenkin, 1973). Housing units of the combined list and area samples were screened for Jewish occupants. Three criteria were employed to identify Jews: whether any of the occupants had been born Jewish, had a parent who had been born Jewish, or regarded himself or herself as being Jewish (Lazerwitz, 1978).

In all, a national sample of 7,179 units was identified, with at least one member meeting one of the three criteria. Once weighted, this yielded an estimated national Jewish population of 5.4 million Jews. After adjusting for housing units whose religion could not be ascertained and for biases resulting from area sample cut-offs, the total estimated population ranged between 5.6 and 6.0 million (Lazerwitz, 1978). Of the persons identified as Jewish by one of the three criteria, 97.3 percent were born Jewish and were still Jewish at the time of the survey, 1.2 percent were born Jewish but no longer considered themselves Jewish, and 1.5 percent were not born Jewish but were reported as Jewish at the time of the survey (Massarik, 1977). In addition, 6.4 percent of all members of the sampled households consisted of persons neither born Jewish nor currently Jewish. These were largely the non-Jewish spouses of Jewish household members or the children of mixed marriages who were not being raised as Jews. As Massarik concluded, "Interpretations of the Jewish population must therefore give careful attention to the number of persons living in Jewish households and the number of members who specifically meet clear criteria of Jewishness. Failure to do so can lead to quite discrepant estimates of the total Jewish population" (Massarik, 1977, p. 119). Undoubtedly this caveat has even greater importance in the 1990's.

NJPS-1970/71 was a milestone in the development of American Jewish demography. Unfortunately, the exploitation of its rich data was limited, so that the full value of the survey for understanding the Jewish population was not realized. Nonetheless, the experience gained in both implementing that survey and in trying to utilize the results has served American Jews well.

In the 1970's, few local community surveys were initiated because the national survey was seen as obviating the need for new ones. Since 1980, however, about 50 Jewish communities, including most larger ones, have undertaken local surveys. Some have already done so twice and a few, like Boston, have done so three times. Even though cumulatively these surveys have encompassed approximately three quarters of the total U.S. Jewish population, questions were again raised about how well they represented the Jewish population as a whole and, in the case of some surveys, about the quality of coverage.

In the absence of another NJPS in the early 1980's, but with keen recognition of the need for national assessments of the Jewish population, individual groups and scholars have attempted to develop national samples. Steven Cohen has been in the forefront of such efforts with the studies he has undertaken for the American Jewish Committee. A number of these earlier surveys (Cohen, 1983a, 1983b, 1985) employed samples based on distinctive Jewish names derived from lists of persons affiliated with a wide range of Jewish organizations or activities. Whether a sample based on such lists of affiliated or identified Jews is representative of the entire adult Jewish population and especially of those at or near the margins of the community remains questionable, as Cohen (1987) himself recognized.

In more recent surveys, a stronger effort has been made to achieve less biased coverage by relying on a different base for developing the sample. A Consumer Mail Panel of 200,000 households developed by a marketing and survey research firm contained 4,700 households which had been identified as containing at least one member reported as currently Jewish. Based on the total sample, a demographically balanced subsample (based on region, income, population density, age, and household size) was developed containing over 2,000 Jewish households. The data collected suggest that this sample "succeeded in reaching a slightly larger number of marginally Jewish respondents" than did the earlier samples based on distinctive Jewish names (Cohen, 1987; see also Cohen, 1991). However, both the self-selective character of participants in the panel and the fact that the sample presumably reflects current religious identification, and therefore misses individuals who do not report themselves as currently Jewish by religion, necessarily raise doubts about the representativeness of such samples of the full array of persons currently and formerly Jewish. As Cohen (1987:91) himself stresses, "There is no completely satisfactory way to sample American Jews nationwide, and no single method yields a representative group at a reasonable cost."

Planning for NJPS-1990

This situation presents a major challenge to any effort to undertake a national assessment of the Jewish population. In preparing for a possible new CJF national survey, it was a challenge that had to be met by taking advantage of the vast improvements in sampling and survey procedures since the 1970–71 NJPS was undertaken, the experience gained from the large number of local Jewish community surveys completed since then, and the more limited efforts to collect national data. Moreover, the much stronger professional credentials in recent years of the planning and research staffs—at local Federations, the CJF, and other national agencies—as well as the availability and commitment of a substantial number of Jewish scholars interested and often experienced in studying the Jewish population, means that there is both a greater appreciation of the need for data of high scientific quality and a far greater potential for employing the most sophisticated methods to obtain such data and using them effectively for analytic and planning purposes.

Recognition of the need to correct problems of comparability among local surveys and to design better sampling methods and a core questionnaire that could be used both locally and eventually in a national survey had led to the creation of the Federation's National Technical Advisory Committee on Population Studies (NTAC) in 1984 and of the Mandell L.

Berman North American Jewish Data Bank (NAJDB), founded in 1986 through the cooperative efforts of CJF and the Graduate School and University Center of the City University of New York.

Greater standardization of concepts and methods and fuller exploitation of the data from local surveys by NAJDB have allowed better and more comprehensive assessment of both the local and the national situation in the 1980's. Yet, exclusive reliance on local community studies has failed, and will continue to fail, to meet the needs of a comprehensive evaluation of the national situation. Not all communities undertake studies or do so within the same period. As a result, gaps exist in our knowledge of the situation in medium and small sized communities; also, it may be dangerous to compare or aggregate the results of surveys undertaken in different communities more than a few years apart. Moreover, the key role that migration plays in affecting local characteristics, as well as national distribution, requires national data with information covering both in- and out-migration from different types of communities.

Operating through the concerted efforts of NTAC and NAJDB, planning for a 1990 National Jewish Population Survey was initiated in the late 1980's. The decision to undertake the survey coincided with strong interests worldwide in launching a "world census" of Jewry parallel to the 1990 round of censuses being undertaken by national governments. The October 1987 World Conference in Jewish Population, in which over 20 countries were represented, concluded that a stocktaking of world Jewry was imperative as the basis for obtaining information for future study and action in the Jewish population field.

The Field Survey

In late 1988, CJF's Endowment Committee and its Board of Directors both approved undertaking a 1990 National Jewish Population Survey in the United States. Organization of the study was the responsibility of NTAC. In close consultation with Federation planners, it designed the core questionnaire. With assistance from a number of national sampling experts, several of whom serve on NTAC, and following consultation with a number of survey companies, it developed a sample design that was intended to insure the widest possible coverage of the Jewish population, encompassing all type of Jews, ranging from those strongly identifying themselves as Jewish, at one extreme, to those on the margins of the community or even outside it, at the other; it sought to include born Jews who no longer considered themselves Jewish and the non-Jewish spouses/partners and children of Jewish household members, as well as other non-Jewish members of the household.

To achieve both comprehensive representation and the collection of the desired information specified in the questionnaire, following receipt and review of proposals from a number of survey firms, CJF commissioned the ICR Survey Research Group of Media, Pennsylvania, to collect data in a three-stage national telephone survey. The first stage involved contacting a random sample of 125,813 American households using computer-assisted telephone interviewing. Since the universe of Jewish households was not known, the first stage involved sampling households representing all religious groups in continental United States, as well as secular households, in order to identify the Jewish households among them.

This initial screening was carried on as part of the twice-weekly nationally representative omnibus market research surveys conducted by ICR. One thousand households were contacted in each of 125 successive rounds over the course of the period April 1989 to May 1990. Each household was selected using a random digit dialing (RDD) methodology; within each cooperating household, an adult respondent was chosen using the last birthday method to insure random selection. The overall procedure allowed for an equal probability of Jews to be selected from every state (except Alaska and Hawaii) and from all sizes of locations so that a national profile could be obtained. Representation of Alaska and Hawaii was incorporated into the national sample in the third stage of the survey.

In addition to traditional census-type questions on socio-demographic, economic, and household characteristics, the screening survey asked "What is your religion?" Only 2.2 percent of the respondents refused to reply to this question. One by-product of this phase of the study was a unique profile of religious identification and of denominations in the United States. The responses provide the largest contemporary data set on American religious adherence. The results of this first stage were publicly announced in April 1991 and received wide dissemination in the press, including front page coverage in *The New York Times*.

To insure the comprehensive coverage desired in NJPS for current and former Jews, additional questions were included in the first stage screening phase for those not identified as Jewish on the basis of the question on current religion. Whereas in the general screening question respondents only had to answer for themselves, the follow-up questions required that respondents provide information both on themselves and on other members of the household. Three follow-up screening questions were successively directed to all respondents who did not identify themselves as Jewish by religion: (1) Do you or any one else in the household consider him/herself Jewish? (2) Were you or anyone else in the household raised Jewish? (3) Do or did you or anyone else in the household have a Jewish parent? A positive answer to any of these questions qualified the household for initial classification as "Jewish." Experience with these additional screening questions demonstrated the complexity of the self-ascription process for the Jewish population.

This procedure, using multiple points of qualification, more than doubled the unweighted sample of identified "Jewish households." It added households in which respondents reported themselves as Jewish by criteria other than religion. It also added "mixed" households, which included respondents who had either indicated they had some other religious identification on the religious screening question or had even initially refused to answer. The four screening questions identified 5,146 households containing one or more "qualified" Jews.

Over the course of a year, a panel of potential respondents was thus created to be used in the summer of 1990 as the basis for an intensive assessment of the socio-demographic, economic, and identificational characteristics of the American Jewish population. To requalify potential respondents, and to minimize loss to follow-up between the initial screening and the in-depth survey, 2,240 members of the 5,146 Jewish sample identified in the early months of the screening survey were recontacted. This inventory stage, or stage two, took place in the months before the final interview. During this procedure, a number of potential respondents dropped out of the survey sample due to changes in household composition or disqualification upon further review.

The third stage, the in-depth survey, was conducted during the 10-week period between May and July 1990. Consistent with the original goal of obtaining about 2,500 completed interviews, 2,441 households of those qualified in the two earlier stages were interviewed. The extensive questionnaire prepared by NTAC for in-depth assessment of the American Jewish population—including their socio-demographic and economic characteristics, and a wide array of attitudinal and behavioral variables related to their Jewish identity—was used. It is the data obtained from these 2,441 households, encompassing 6,514 individuals, that constitute the final sample for NJPS-1990.

The Complexity of Jewish Identity

The results of both the screening phase and the in-depth interviews attest to the validity and importance of the view that conceptual and measurement concerns should not only enter into the initial sample selection process but also into the analytical process. The complexity and fluidity of the contemporary American Jewish community is clearly demonstrated by the survey findings.

Of the 5,146 households that qualified initially as having at least one Jewish member, just under half qualified on the basis of religion, just over one-third as having an ethnic Jew, five percent on the basis of some member having been raised Jewish, and another 12 percent on the basis of at least one member reporting a Jewish parent (Goldstein and Kosmin, 1992). Clearly, any survey that restricts its identification of the Jewish population to those reporting being Jewish by religion would therefore run the risk of excluding a substantial part of the total population of Jewish religio-ethnic identity.

Moreover, among the 5,146 households that were initially screened as being eligible for the in-depth survey, only 3,665 of the respondents themselves qualified as being Jewish under one of the four criteria (only 57 percent of them on the basis of being Jewish by religion). The other 1,481 qualified because members of the household other than the respondent met one of the criteria employed in the screening phase. This situation reflects the large number of households whose members are of mixed religious/ ethnic identification.

Only 57 percent of American Jewish households are composed entirely of Jewish persons. That so many households are religiously and ethnically mixed is largely due to the sharp increase in mixed marriages in the last several decades, from 26 percent in 1965–74 to 52 percent since 1985. In addition, a number of households contain a person raised as a Jew or one of Jewish parentage who no longer regards himself or herself as Jewish, and whose children are therefore not reported as Jewish under any one of the four criteria. Indeed, the substantial numbers of households falling into the mixed category (27 percent) and into the residue group, which contains no one who is currently Jewish (16 percent), attest to the increasingly complex character of American Jewish households, as well as the challenges of identifying and measuring the Jewish population.

One might question whether individuals should be counted as part of the Jewish population if they do not regard themselves as currently Jewish, even though born of one or two Jewish parents or raised as Jews, particularly if they currently report identification with another religion. The answer to this depends, of course, on the religious and sociological perspectives adopted and on the use for which the analysis is being undertaken. The great advantage of NJPS-1990 is that we have the information concerning these persons and now have the option of including or excluding them, depending on the purpose of the analysis. Assessment of their behavioral characteristics with respect to Jewish practices should provide a more definitive answer to how they should be classified sociologically and demographically, as well as what factors may explain their current status with respect to Jewish identity. Unless we know how many are in each category, including those on the margins and those who have left, we cannot realistically design programs to maintain the strength of the community, to hold on to those in it—especially those on the margins—and to attract back those who have opted out.

Extension and Exploitation of NJPS-1990

Two other features of NJPS-1990 are worthy of mention. The first relates to the efforts NTAC undertook to develop a Consortium of communities which would undertake surveys, at their own expense, approximately at the same time as NJPS-1990, and which would employ as much as possible the same basic sample design and core questionnaire. Such an arrangement was motivated by recognition that, while the size of the national sample can adequately provide reliable insights into the characteristics of the national Jewish population and allow comparisons by region and community type, it is not large enough to permit in-depth assessment of individual communities, with the possible exception of New York. While the idea of the Consortium was quite favorably received, financial and logistic considerations restricted the number of participating communities. That they include New York and Chicago and such smaller communities as Columbus, Seattle, and South Broward County, Florida, should greatly enhance the richness of our insights into American Jewry in 1990, both nationally and locally, and also the opportunities we have for evaluating methodological aspects of the various surveys.

The second major feature of NJPS-1990, and one which sharply distinguishes it from the NJPS-1970/71, is the extensive attention paid from the early stages of the study to the uses to which the data will be put analytically and for planning purposes. A sub-committee of NTAC developed an agenda for disseminating the findings. Beginning at the 1990 General Assembly, and following it through major news releases, the findings have been publicized in leading newspapers (sometimes even the front pages), on national TV, and on radio. A number of papers have already been presented at professional meetings; more are scheduled. Moreover, a number of scholars and planners, many of them leaders in their field, are authoring individual monographs on specific aspects of the study; these are to be published as a series by State University of New York (SUNY) Press. Clearly, the results of the survey will be widely exploited and disseminated, thereby enhancing their value for planning purposes.

Illustrative Findings

A few selected key findings of the NJPS-1990 can illustrate the kind of
contribution it is likely to make to our understanding of American Jewry.
The survey estimates that there are 3.2 million households in the United
States containing one or more persons who are Jews or former Jews, using
the four criteria cited earlier. These 3.2 million households contain 8.1
million persons; another 80,000 Jews living in institutions and 20,000
Russian immigrants estimated to have arrived after the survey was initiated, raises the total estimated population to 8.2 million. Of these, 5.5
million constitute a "core Jewish population" (the 4.4 million reporting
themselves as Jewish by religion and the 1.1 million classified as secular or
ethnic Jews). Another 625,000 persons were born of Jewish parents or
raised as Jews but belonged to a non-Jewish religious group in 1990
(210,000 of them as the result of apostasy). Their inclusion in the Jewish
count raises the total to over 6.1 million. The resulting range of population
estimates, from a low of 5.5 million to a high of 8.2 million (if all persons—
those currently Jews, those of Jewish descent, and gentiles—in the 3.2
million households are included), with intermediate variations, depending
on who is counted as in or out, attests to the complexity of the definitional
and measurement problems, and the resulting difficulties in ascertaining
clearly the actual size of the Jewish population.

Moreover, we must remember that the information is derived from
respondents and therefore reflects subjectivity on two levels: firstly, respondents applied their own interpretations to the questions; secondly,
they replied in terms which were personally meaningful. In short, they fit
themselves into constructs and categories in terms of their own understanding, experience, and environment, rather than official ideology of
movements and organizations, even if the results often reflect inconsisten-
cies between their behavior and normative expectations. As frustrating as
this complexity may be for analytic purposes, the resulting set of classifica-
tions of religio-ethnic identity undoubtedly reflects the situation more realistically than earlier evidence. It provides the opportunity to better understand the Jewish community in the United States and to confront the
challenges that such complexity creates as we move toward the twenty-first
century.

The value of NJPS-1990 for understanding the Jewish community, and
particularly its increasingly national character, is further illustrated by:
information on the changing regional distribution of the population; the
ways that the Jewish population differs regionally in attitudes and behavior
affecting the extent and character of Jewish identification; and the role of

migration in affecting the regional redistribution of the population as well as ties to the community.

When NJPS-1970/71 was undertaken, 64 percent of America's Jews lived in the Northeast, and 17 percent in the Midwest. Today, accordingly to NJPS-1990, the percentage of core Jews living in the Northeast has declined to only 44 percent, and that in the Midwest to 11 percent. In contrast to 1970/71, the percentage in the South has risen dramatically from eight to 22 percent, and that in the West from 11 to 23 percent. Jews have clearly come to span the nation. For the first time, according to NJPS-1990, more Jews are living outside the Northeast than in it. Yet, the regional data point to considerable variation, both in socio-demographic composition and in Jewish identity. For example, the Northeast remains strongly Jewish, if judged by a variety of indicators of Jewish identity, including the rate of intermarriage. The West, on the other hand, has the highest proportion of secular Jews. Thus, the development of a national society is occurring simultaneously with perpetuation, and in some cases perhaps exacerbation, of the unique features of regional and local communities.

That population movement is related both to the development of the national society and to differentiation in regional characteristics is suggested by initial review of NJPS-1990 data on migration. In 1990, only one-fifth of all adults (age 18 and over) in the core Jewish population were living in the same city/town in which they were born. Ten percent were immigrants from abroad; almost half (46 percent) had changed state of residence since birth, and an additional one-quarter had moved within their state of birth.

That high mobility is a strong feature of American Jewish life today is further evidenced by data showing that 43 percent of the total adult population was living in a different house in 1990 than just five years earlier, in 1985. One in 10 had changed state of residence in this short period. Eleven percent had changed city or town of residence within the same state. These rates of inter- and intra-state migration were even higher for young adults. Like Americans generally, Jews are engaged in extensive movement as they try to take fuller advantage of the wide array of educational, occupational, and environmental opportunities available to them. How such mobility affects their ties to the Jewish community and their individual Jewish identity, and how their identity affects their mobility behavior, is one of the promising lines of inquiry that fuller analysis of NJPS-1990 data will allow. In so doing, the factors contributing to the increasing complexity of the Jewish population structure and to the development of a national community should become clearer. The resulting insights should lead to alternative ways to cope with the problems associated with these changes.

Uses of NJPS-1990 and Future Research

Based on experience with community studies and the NJPS-1990, it is clear that a national Jewish community has evolved that requires national assessment. Such a profile is essential in order to help national and local Jewish organizations plan for the future. The initial NJPS-1990 findings already document the complexity of the national Jewish population and the extent to which and ways in which this complexity varies across the nation. They confirm the high level of mobility of American Jews and the key role that migration plays in affecting both the size and the composition of local communities and regions. They suggest, too, the necessity for creating organizational linkages among the communities of origin and of destination, to help insure the continued Jewish identity of the migrants themselves and the continued vitality of the communities they are leaving and entering.

The national profile developed on the basis of the 1990 survey also provides crucial information for use by local communities as a standard against which to measure their own populations. They will thereby be able to better understand the dynamics of local change and to assess the ways in which local history and structure help to explain unique features of the local community. In addition, local communities will be able to use the national profile to identify those patterns which all communities may share because of the common life-styles that have come to characterize some aspects of Jewish life, regardless of where one lives, and to anticipate the directions in which the local community may change as indicated both by national developments and by the past experiences of other regions and communities.

Such a national profile will also allow comparison of Jewish life in America with that in Israel, Europe, Latin America, and elsewhere, once comparable data are collected in other national surveys. The adoption, with minor modification, of the core questionnaire developed by NTAC for use in the United States by other national surveys will enhance their value for comparative assessments. The results of all these surveys should provide a firmer basis for formulation and evaluation of policies to cope with the demographic changes and challenges faced locally, nationally, and internationally, particularly in areas of concern related to the strength of Jewish identity and the vitality of the community.

Concurrently, we must recognize that completion of NJPS-1990, and of the large set of analyses and monographs which are in process, represents only a beginning toward our fuller evaluation of American Jewry and toward the fuller use of research findings for sound planning. We cannot afford to sit back and relax simply because we have such a rich set of data in hand. Conditions continue to change, and these changes need to be frequently, if not continuously, monitored and assessed. Moreover, the data from NJPS-1990 will undoubtedly raise as many questions as they answer, and so we must go on finding answers to our new questions.

We need more information than an omnibus survey such as NJPS-1990 can provide on such groups as the aged, the intermarried, the mobile segments of the population, single parents, the disabled. An omnibus survey can indicate the prevalence of such groups and provide some insights into how their characteristics are related to other factors. However, in-depth assessment requires studies directed at specific problem areas, and having enough cases involving the particular variable being researched to allow meaningful evaluation. The same can be said for issues which were of peripheral interest in 1990 when the survey was designed (for example, languages spoken at home), but which may merit future research attention. A major by-product of a study such as NJPS-1990 is that the analysis itself points to important new questions, the answers to which cannot be obtained from the survey itself.

Furthermore, we cannot rely on a single-round population study as the basis for planning indefinitely into the future. Outdated concepts and data may be of even less value than no information, especially when change is rapid and affects key aspects of community life, such as the character of Jewish identity, marriage, the family, population distribution, or community stability. Reliance on NJPS-1970/71 for gaining insights into Jewish life in the United States in the 1980's and 1990's would certainly have been risky and ill-advised. At best, it provided a standard against which results from community studies could be compared to identify changes since 1970. The speed with which changes in basic concepts and in socio-demographic structure and processes can occur, and their serious implications for community planning, argues strongly for regular surveys at reasonable intervals, certainly no longer than 10 years apart.

At the same time, methods must be developed that will allow us to exploit most effectively a variety of data sets that can be used to monitor changes in the inter-survey period. Particularly in the age of the computer, fuller and more careful use of Federation lists, birth and death records, school enrollment statistics, city directories and telephone books, and information from records of moving and utility companies, can all provide rich insights on what is happening to the population in the post-survey period.

The emphasis given in this volume to the results of NJPS-1990 should not detract from the continuing need for local community studies. As stressed earlier, development of a national society is occurring simultaneously with perpetuation and perhaps even exacerbation of the unique features of regional and local communities. Clearly, it is at the local level that most of the services are provided, and that the facts essential for planning such services are most needed. Therefore, collection and evaluation of data at the local level must be a continuing part of our strategy to more fully utilize research as the basis of planning and to integrate local and national research as the basis of our efforts to link more meaningfully the local and national communities.

A concerted effort to maintain follow-up contact with respondents in NJPS-1990 as well as in specific community surveys would also be valuable. Especially with computers making record matching and maintenance quite feasible, it seems irresponsible that stronger efforts have not been made by the Jewish community to develop data bases for evaluation and planning. I very much hope that in the months and years ahead both NTAC and NAJDB can jointly and increasingly turn their attention to assessing the value of these varied sources of information and to developing methods and manuals for using them, even while they continue in their efforts to enhance comparability among community surveys. Before long, it will also be time for them to begin planning NJPS-2000.

We have achieved much in a relatively short time. Nevertheless, we still face a long list of research and planning tasks that will challenge our expertise and our imagination. This has been an exciting time in the history of Jewish demography. We have already successfully met a number of the challenges that confronted us when we first began to talk about a national survey. Our experience with the survey, whose successful completion resulted from the close collaboration of researchers and planners, augurs well for the future. The information we have helped to generate and which we are now beginning to analyze in our joint efforts will, in turn, help to establish a more effective basis for improving the quality of Jewish life in the United States and insuring the continued strength and vitality of *Klal Yisrael* and of the values it treasures.

Note

1. Material related to the background and design of NJPS-1990 can also be found in Goldstein, 1992.

References

Cohen, Steven M., *Content or Continuity? Alternative Bases for Commitment*, New York, American Jewish Committee, 1991.

———, *Ties and Tensions: The 1986 Survey of American Jewish Attitudes Toward Israel and Israelis*, New York, American Jewish Committee, 1987.

———, "The 1981–82 National Survey of American Jews," in *American Jewish Year Book*, Vol. 83, Philadelphia, Jewish Publication Society, 1983a.

———, *Attitudes of American Jews Toward Israel and Israelis: The 1983 National Survey of American Jews and Jewish Communal Leaders*, New York, American Jewish Committee, 1983b.

Fisher, Alan M., "The National Gallup Polls and American Jewish Demography," in *American Jewish Year Book*, Philadelphia, Jewish Publication Society, 1983.

Goldscheider, Calvin, *Jewish Continuity And Change*, Bloomington, Indiana University Press, 1986.

Goldstein, Sidney, "Profile of American Jewry: Insights From The 1990 National Jewish Population Survey," in *American Jewish Year Book*, Volume 92, New York, American Jewish Committee, 1992.

———, "Jews on the Move: Implications for American Jewry and for Local Communities," *Jewish Journal of Sociology*, Volume 32, (June, 1990), pp. 5–30.

———, "A 1990 National Jewish Population Study: Why and How," in *A Handle on the Future—The Potential of the 1990 National Survey for American Jewry*, Reprint No. 4, New York, North American Jewish Data Bank, CUNY Graduate Center, 1988.

———, *Demography of American Jewry: Implications for a National Community, Parsippany Paper III*, New York, Council of Jewish Federations, 1987.

———, "A Further Assessment of the Use of Yiddish in Rhode Island Households," *Rhode Island Jewish Historical Notes*, Volume 9, (November, 1985), pp. 209–219.

Goldstein, Sidney, and Barry A. Kosmin, "Religious and Ethnic Self-Identification in the United States 1989–90: A Case Study of the Jewish Population," *Ethnic Groups*, Volume 9 (1992).

Greenberg, Irving, *Perspectives: A CLAL Thesis*, New York, National Center for Learning and Leadership, 1991.

Kosmin, Barry A. et al., *Highlights of the CJF 1990 National Jewish Population Survey*, New York, Council of Jewish Federations, 1991.

Kosmin, Barry A., Paul Ritterband, and Jeffrey Scheckner, "Jewish Population in the United States 1987," *Counting Jewish Populations: Methods and Problems*, Reprint No. 3, New York, North American Jewish Data Bank, CUNY Graduate Center, 1988.

Kosmin, Barry A., and Stanley Waterman, "The Use and Misuse of Distinctive Jewish Names in Research on Jewish Populations," in *Papers In Jewish Demography*, U.O. Schmelz and S. Della Pergola, eds., Jerusalem, Institute of Contemporary Jewry, Hebrew University, 1985.

Lazerwitz, Bernard, "An Estimate of a Rare Population Group: The U.S. Jewish Population," *Demography*, Volume 15 (August, 1978), pp. 389–394.

Levin, Lester I., "Federation and Population Studies," in *Perspectives in Jewish Population Research*, Steven M. Cohen, Jonathan Woocher, and Bruce A. Phillips, eds., Boulder, CO, Westview Press, 1984.

Lieberson, Stanley, and Mary C. Waters, *From Many Strands: Ethnic And Racial Groups In Contemporary America*, New York, Russell Sage Foundation, 1988.

Massarik, Fred, "The Boundary of Jewishness: Some Measures of Jewish Identity in the United States," in *Papers in Jewish Demography*, U. O. Schmelz, P. Glickson, and S. Della Pergola, eds., Jerusalem, Institute of Contemporary Jewry, Hebrew University, 1977.

————, and Alvin Chenkin, "United States National Jewish Population Survey: A First Report," in *American Jewish Year Book*, Vol. 73, Philadelphia, Jewish Publication Society, 1973.

Schmelz, U.O., and Sergio Della Pergola, "Basic Trends In American Jewish Demography," in *Jewish Demography Papers*, New York, American Jewish Committee, 1988.

Sidney Hollander Memorial Colloquium, *The Emergence of a Continental Jewish Community: Implications for the Federations*, New York, Council of Jewish Federations, 1987.

2

Demographics and Geography

Barry A. Kosmin

The results of the 1990 National Jewish Population Survey (NJPS) reflect the fast-changing and increasingly complex society of contemporary American Jews. Its major finding is that Jewishness as a concept is undergoing change today on both an individual and a collective level. This is, in part, a continuation of a historical process that has been under way for two centuries as Jews have tried to come to terms with full participation in modern societies populated by Christian majorities.

Based upon a large and representative sample of American Jews, the survey tries to understand what being Jewish means to individuals, and how they manifest their Jewish roots.

Jewishness is hard to define today because it is multi-faceted: there are different Jewish populations for different purposes. How one views what makes a Jew—religious belief and practice or descent and biology—obviously affects one's opinion of how individuals enter or leave the group. In theory, a faith community is open to those who want to believe and practice, including converts, expels and disavows, heretics, and both those who deny the existence of the God of Israel and those who adopt another belief system. This approach holds that being raised as a Jew is more important than biological descent. Reform Judaism adopted this approach as its standard for membership, whereby it is irrelevant whether the Jewish parent is the mother, and converts are welcome.

The nationality principle is linked to biological descent. From this perspective, even the Jewish *neshuma* is seen more as a product of nature than nurture. If Jews are a descent group, than it is both difficult to join or leave the group. If Jews are a nationality, they can be like Frenchmen or Hungarians of any or of no religion. They still remain Jews. Most systems of nationality and citizenship operate on the principle of paternity, where membership is bestowed through the father, by using his family surname. However, the maternal line has governed membership in Judaism since the days of Nehemiah, which creates more problems.

All this intellectual baggage is significant today for two reasons. First, there is no consensus as to which membership criteria are paramount. Even within the religious camp there is pluralism, and *halakhic* criteria no longer operates for all synagogue groups. Second, what was largely theoretical 40 years ago, and affected only a few cases, affects hundreds of thousands of people today due to vast increases in intermarriage over the last two decades.

So who does the man in the street regard as Jewish? Is it Ruth Goldberg whose mother is Lutheran and father is Jewish, or Sean McCarthy whose mother is Jewish and father Catholic? What do the Jewish grandparents of both think? Who is most likely to be solicited by the Federation campaign or invited to join B'nai B'rith?

The NJPS adopted self-definition as its criteria for Jewish identity. This is a socio-psychological base that enables different groups in the Jewish community to decide who is to be included or excluded from the community according to their own agenda or mandate. However, it must be recognized that there are different meanings to the term "Jew" in contemporary America. One man's Jew is literally another man's gentile. This confusion in identity is reflected by the responses in the survey itself and the public reaction to this social reality.

How many Jews there are in the United States depends on answering the question of "Who is a Jew?" In the absence of communal consensus on clear-cut definitions, the boundaries of the population will remain unclear and permeable. The task of the social scientist is to present the social reality with all of its problematic issues.

Apart from the pluralism of the Jewish people, what else did the survey reveal? From the demographic standpoint, it confirmed much of what was already assumed. Marriage is less frequent, and entered into later, than in the past. Jewish women do not have enough children to increase the population, but the nuclear family is still the focus of biological reproduction. Few cases of out-of-wedlock births were reported, and teenage pregnancy is not an issue. However, the overall pattern of household composition has changed. Nuclear families containing husband, wife, and children are only a small minority. Households where everyone is Jewish and the couple are in their first marriage are even rarer. The average size of the all-Jewish household is 2.2 persons. Jews have the smallest proportion of households containing children of almost any population group in the U.S. Conversely, Jews have very large numbers of single people living alone (young singles, older never marrieds, divorcees, and widows).

Unfortunately, the lack of clarity regarding Jewish identity carries over into the home. For analytical purposes the report identified three types of households: Entirely Jewish, Mixed, and ones with No Core Jews. Again, there are other possibilities using different criteria.

The survey revealed an American population with all that it implies. Even today's grandparents are overwhelmingly American-born. On the other hand, the population is far from being composed of average Americans. The Jews are too old, too well-educated, too liberal, too secular, too metropolitan, too wealthy, too egalitarian, and too civic-minded to be normal Americans when compared to the overall U.S. population. In fact, American Jews look like Scandinavians, sociologically speaking.

One particularly interesting finding is that despite the large-scale migration to the South and West, the heartland of American Jewry remains the Northeast. Judaism does not appear to prosper once it leaves the old metropolitan cities of the East. Among the growth areas, the West is home to the largest group of secular Jews and the South has the largest group of those who converted to other religions. Geography makes a difference. Finding out why it makes a difference will require research to determine whether it is differences in life-styles, generation in the country, regional cultures, levels of concentration of population, or all of these factors and many more that erode Judaism.

The survey process was constrained by practical considerations. It was a telephone survey, requiring that questions and answers be both short and factual, and it placed an emphasis on behavioral aspects of Jewishness and on questions which could be answered immediately without resorting to any records. By necessity it asked one adult to report on the other members of the household, so answers were constrained by how well that adult knows the backgrounds of the others, such as grandmother's years of Jewish education or a nephew's donation to the Jewish Federation campaign. The choice of a random adult and not necessarily the head of the household provided us with a more accurate and sobering picture of social reality than most local surveys. The cost was that the respondent was not necessarily the most Jewishly aware or knowledgeable member of the household, and some information was inevitably lost.

This also raises the need to differentiate individual from household data. Not only did we discover Core Jews in households which they identified as Christian in terms of overall denomination, but we also found other anomalies. For example, different types of Jews reside together so that many household practices are, in effect, a negotiated compromise. What first appears contradictory, such as Jews with no religion eating strictly kosher and reporting themselves members of an Orthodox household, are merely reflections of wider societal trends whereby American concepts of

individualism and personal autonomy have affected even traditional households and families.

A number of social and demographic trends serve to undermine the
informal intergenerational transmission of Jewish culture which operated
in the past. The increasing geographical dispersal of the population, combined with changes in the household composition and the makeup of
families, all tend to undermine the dense network of familial, neighborhood, and ethnic ties which strengthened group cohesion. Today, formal
communal institutions have to fill the gap left by the *zaydes*, aunties, Jewish
neighbors, and Jewish storekeepers, who no longer live in daily contact
with most of the younger generation of American Jews. Moreover, formal
institutions not only have to replace these sources of Jewish cultural information, but they also have to offset the influences of gentile friends, neighbors, and grandparents who are part of the lives of many younger Jews.
This is in addition to the negative forces, from a traditional Jewish perspective, associated with a seductive consumer culture and the homogenizing
forces of the media.

There is also the question of when the inclusion of the peripheral Jewish
or gentile population makes sense. It would be inaccurate and unhelpful to
exclude gentiles from analyzing household composition, since it would
exaggerate the number of one-parent families. The same logic applies to
economic and occupational data. Gentile sources of household income
cannot be excluded without making the data meaningless. Other cases
involve close judgment calls as to the relevance or the inclusion or exclusion of certain sections of the total population. An assessment of what
constitutes the "population at risk" may well involve ideological assumptions, but that is inevitable.

The NJPS data reflect what and where the *Yiddisher massn* are today in
America. It is only if we recognize and accept them for what they are and
"where they are at" that we will be able to begin to move them in the
direction we want.

3

Measuring the Quality of American Jewish Life

Calvin Goldscheider

A series of community studies over the last decade, culminating in the 1990 National Jewish Population Survey, has produced an enormously rich body of evidence on the Jewishness of American Jews, their religious and communal activities, ritual observances, and the content of their Jewish identities, including: Jewish education and organizational affiliations, attendance of religious services, support for Jewish charities, and identification with the state of Israel. As a result, we now know more about the behavior, attitudes, identity, and values of contemporary American Jews than Jews anywhere, ever before in history.

Nevertheless, there is a feeling that something is missing: aspects of Jewishness or Judaism do not seem to be fully captured by our surveys; and the data available fail to reveal important, perhaps critical, dimensions of the Jewishness of American Jews.[1] Many Jewish leaders—including rabbis, Jewish professionals, as well as lay persons, and some social scientists—often deny that the quality of Jewish life can be measured with data obtained from surveys. They argue that Jewish quality involves primarily the personal, idiosyncratic, inner dimensions of Judaism and Jewish expressions, the Jewish "soul" or Jewish "heart." These "inner" aspects are elusive and are poorly revealed in the statistical data that we employ. They are joined by policy persons who have had difficulty using data from survey research as a basis for planning, and have not been able to connect the data from surveys to the decisions that need to be made for enhancing the quality of Jewish life.

Indeed, the policy implications of our research findings are often unclear, in large part because we have not identified what determines Jewish quality in the American Jewish community. I will argue that the sources of these determinants have been examined at the individual level, while policy is designed to shape Jewish quality by focusing on building and strengthening institutions such as schools, families, Jewish community centers, synagogues, Jewish homes for the aged, etc. Until we examine the linkages of these community and institutional contexts to the quality of Jewish life, our understanding of continuities and changes in the American Jewish community will be limited and our policy and planning will not be effective.

I start from a different set of premises about the nature of Jewish quality, its measurement, and analysis. My position is that the patterns of Jewishness that are real are measurable. While we have collected extensive data on the quality of Jewish life, we need to focus on the institutional and communal contexts that shape variation and change. As we re-conceptualize the determinants of Jewish quality, we shall need to connect institutional and survey data, and identify new types of data to be collected to fully capture the community contexts that determine individual expressions of Jewishness.

Since our interpretation of every sociological aspect of the Jewish community reflects our assessment of Jewish quality, we need to specify explicitly what it means. The value of examining the demographic structure, stratification, and family patterns of Jewish communities is that we can then link them empirically to the quality and continuity of the Jewish community. We therefore measure quality in order to assess the meanings of Jewishness and Judaism in America, as well as to interpret the impact of the demography and the resources available within the community on American Jewry. So the first, and the most critical, task in the analysis and interpretation of the rich data collected in the 1990 NJPS, and in parallel community studies carried out in the last decade or so, is to face more directly the issue of the quality of American Jewish life. This paper focuses on one central theoretical and methodological issue: How can we use national and community surveys to advance our understanding of the quality of American Jewish life?

One response to the limitations and frustrations of using surveys to clarify the quality of life of American Jews, and the difficulties of studying the deeper meanings of the Jewishness and Judaism of American Jews, has been to add more detailed questions about religious practices to our surveys. Thus, for example, in addition to obtaining information on the standard dimensions of Kashrut and synagogue attendance, we have added new questions to the 1990 NJPS on fasting on Ta'anit Esther, celebrating Purim carnivals, and Yom Ha'azmaut (although it is not clear why these were chosen, and not questions on fasting on Tisha B'Av or on the use of Mikvah or Sha'atnez). There has also been an attempt in some surveys to move beyond questions about religious ritual to include questions on belief in God, revelation at Sinai, feelings about the Bible and the importance of the Torah. These questions have some inherent value in describing the beliefs and religious identities of a select number of American Jews. However, few would argue that they have the potential to add much to our understanding of issues concerning the quality of American Jewish life. Indeed, the skeptics say that you cannot capture beliefs about God in a telephone interview or about Judaism by asking more questions in a survey. So adding in-depth questions in surveys may not be the most helpful solution to the difficulty of obtaining an accurate assessment of quality.

Another response to the dilemma of gaining insight into the quality of Jewish life has been to challenge the survey method of obtaining information. The argument is that since surveys cannot capture the depth associated with the quality of Judaism and the details of Jewishness and Jewish identity, we need alternative methods that probe the deeper meanings of Jewish quality. If one cannot capture God in a community study or a national survey, then perhaps God can be found in a "focus" group with Jewish elites, selected Federation executives, or rabbis; perhaps, the argument goes, we should do anthropological research as a basis for an analysis of Judaism and Jewishness in America.[2]

There are clearly elements of Jewish life that community and national surveys cannot capture, and alternative methods are useful in adding new insights into the analysis of American Jewish life. However, small, intensive focus groups are hardly representative of the broader American Jewish community, even if they are insightful and thought-provoking; detailed multi-houred interviews with several dozen respondents are not likely to represent anyone but the interviewees. The value of the focus group is to clarify concepts so that they can be included in representative surveys. Small, local, qualitative studies complement the larger national survey but can never be adequate by themselves. These methodological strategies must be linked systematically with representative surveys to portray a more complex and integrated picture. Otherwise, we end up with more questions on our surveys, more focus groups, and more data, yet we seem to know less. As we begin to analyze the results of the latest survey of Jewish life, the most extensive, carefully designed, national survey on Jews ever conducted in the United States, my initial question returns: How do we capture and measure the quality of American Jewish life—of Judaism and Jewishness—toward the end of the twentieth century, and can we do so by using these survey data?

To begin to address this issue, we start by specifying a theory of Jewish life in America that will tell us whether we need new questions for surveys and new methods of data collection, or whether existing surveys can serve as a basis for useful understanding of Jewish quality. In particular, I shall stress the value of integrating community level factors within our conception of the determinants of Judaism and Jewishness. Community is the context that shapes the personal expressions of Jewish quality: The ideas of Judaism and the content of Jewishness cannot be evaluated without attention to the contexts within which they occur.

I think that we currently have an enormous wealth of information, not everything we want but enough to keep researchers busy until new, perhaps unforeseen changes in community life require another survey. We have asked most of the questions that really matter for indicating the quality of Jewish life among individuals; we need to analyze what we have collected and supplement the survey data directly and systematically in order to understand new features of American Jewish life. These will facilitate the development of policies that could enhance the quality of Jewishness and Judaism. As we begin to analyze the rich lode of recently available data, we must plan to supplement it even before we have digested the results. New data collection efforts, along with coordination among a variety of data sets available, need to begin, in order to avoid missing another critical window of opportunity. The value of the 1990 NJPS, both for evaluating the quality of American Jewish life and for designing policies to enhance and deepen that quality, needs to be spelled out clearly, so that we can know what to expect from the data for analyses and interpretations and creative policy applications.

Our understanding of the American Jewish community and our policies to enhance the quality of Jewish life have often been trivial because our conceptions of Jewishness and Judaism have been limited to a focus on individuals. Moreover, we have failed to fully and systematically analyze the extensive data that we collect and have therefore failed to translate the cultural, social, historical, and social meanings of Jewishness and Judaism into goals that are the targets of policies. The lack of translation of conceptions about Jewish life, particularly its communal and institutional dimensions, into analysis has led to ad hoc policies, some of which are insightful and may work. However, they are almost never based on the data we collect. We have become better at suggesting policies than implementing them and better at implementing policies than at evaluating their long-term effects on the quality of American Jewish life.

Nothing is more practical than good theory. Jewish communal policies, whether national or local, have rarely been derived from surveys. There are good reasons why we hardly ever use survey data for policy formulation. First, policies and their implicit ideologies often tell us what to ask, so survey data too often reinforce our policy preconceptions. Second, policies are hardly ever informed by evidence but are largely shaped by politics at the institutional level. Third, survey data are rarely analyzed in any depth. Almost always the data have been described too superficially and incompletely to be the basis of policy analysis and planning. So we are either constrained by prior conceptions and theories, or we have not exploited the data we have collected at great expense.

Judaism and Jewishness: Re-conceptualization and Measurement

Let us consider briefly the dominant themes that have informed the analysis of data on the quality of American Jewish life by considering the focus of some research on Jewish identity. The social psychological approach emphasizes Jewish identity in terms of individual attitudes and beliefs as measures of Jewish quality. It is inadequate until it places the individual within a community context. In large part, the social psychological approach simply uses Jewish identity as a substitute concept, another indicator of the Jewish quality issue, and hence only restates the issue at the individual level. In my view, the Jewish "identity" of individuals emerges from context, from social structures of the community. Therefore we must examine Jewish identity within those contexts directly. Most importantly, Jewish identity focuses on the individual level and relates to the personal internalization of Jewish values and norms. Since Jewishness and Judaism are only partially individual-oriented, a focus primarily on Jewish identity will miss critical dimensions of the quality issue. Issues of contexts and community networks become the basis of continuity, not an individual identity abstracted from context.

Some have argued that cultural or religious ideological factors have been critical in the maintenance of Jews over the centuries. Among these cultural factors, religion, i.e., Judaism, has been, and must continue to be, the basis of American Jewishness. As a result, our surveys have attempted to measure aspects of the "religion" and religiosity of American Jews. Others have argued that social interaction and community cohesiveness are the basis for the continuity in the Jewish community, in contemporary America as in the past. The emerging social and cultural networks have great potential for communal developments and for the redefinition of Jewish culture and politics in a secular society. We need to merge these two arguments, not treat them as alternatives. Our re-conceptualization of Jewish quality involves the linkage between the cultural content of Jewishness and the contexts within which they occur, connecting the multiple ways that Jewish quality is expressed within the structures, institutions,

and communal networks that reinforce Jewishness over time from generation to generation.

To label the focus on Jewish culture or structure as reflecting the views
of optimists and pessimists, or to group one as emphasizing "content"
versus "form", is to seriously misstate the arguments and to personalize
and trivialize fundamental theoretical differences about the nature of Jewish quality. At issue, I think, are different conceptions of people and
society and thus of Jewishness in American society. It is these conceptions
that need to be integrated, so that culture and attitude, religion and identity are linked to structure and context, community and networks.

The American Jewish community is strong in some ways (e.g., institutionally and in terms of financial and human resources), and weak in other
ways (e.g., regular ritual observances, synagogue attendance, and religious
commitments). Israel and the Holocaust have become ideological substi-
tutes for religious ritual, God, and Torah, for example. Commitment to the
survival of the community, without a carefully articulated set of Jewish
values specifying the content of that survival, has become a higher priority
goal than personal piety and textual expertise. Instead of asking what is the
content of the American Jewish community today, the questions should
be: What are the variety of contexts that shape the range of Jewish expressions? How do institutions and social-cultural networks enhance the quality of Jewish life? What has Jewishness been in its historical and cultural
forms so that we can develop analytic models and therefore policies that are
more appropriate for American Jewish life in the twenty-first century?

Two hundred years ago in parts of Eastern Europe almost no women
attended synagogue services and perhaps, more surprisingly, many men
did not attend either. All synagogues may have been filled. However, the
proportion of men attending daily or even weekly services was constrained
by the structure of residential dispersion in Europe and, thereby, by access
to the synagogue. Many Jews lived in rural areas and towns where there
were few synagogues and hardly enough men for a regular *minyan*. Attending services required access as well as desire—structure as well as values.

Not many people were educated Jewishly 200 years ago: there were few
Jewish schools, no adequate Jewish curriculum, and the tutors-teachers
were themselves poorly educated. If judged by partial and anecdotal evidence, these teachers were often more a discouragement to education than
a stimulus to knowledge. Tutors were often hired by households more
distant from the centers of Jewish life, but they were limited to the wealthy
few.[3] Most Jewish men and women in the beginning of the nineteenth
century were illiterate in any language. So at least in terms of synagogue
attendance and the depth of Jewish literacy and Jewish education, we have
come a long way.

Correctly, one could be admonished for presenting such superficial historical comparisons: After all, synagogue attendance and formal Jewish education were constrained at that time by limited resources and by geographic distance, communication difficulties, and enforced Jewish segregation. Those are interesting arguments, since they highlight the centrality of institutions in the development of quality in Jewish life. Similar points—if not resources, then certainly geography and access—can be made about contemporary constraints in parts of the United States and in some metropolitan areas. Think about Los Angeles in the 1950's and early 1960's without the complex array of institutions and networks that characterized the long-settled areas of the Northeast and the impact that more recent institutional developments have had on the Jewishness of this community.

More importantly, synagogue attendance and formal Jewish education are not the major factors in understanding the Jewishness and Judaism of 200 years ago. Religious and social communal components of Jewishness were intertwined in the past and were an integral part of the everyday life of the pre-modern European Jew. That too is an interesting point, since the lesson of history lies not in trivial comparisons over time but rather in helping us raise the critical issue about the role of context in shaping the quality of Jewish life and hence in our ability to measure it adequately. We need to ask: What were the major features of Jewishness and Judaism in the recent past? The answer would rest with the totality of Jewish life, the associational ties and the family-economic networks, the constraints of community, and, therefore, the positive impact of segregation and distinctiveness, the communal and the social, the shared life-style and the values. In short, the total round of activity was intensely Jewish in the past, a pattern that is often used as the basis for examining the transformation that has characterized Jewish communal life for the last 200 years.[4]

The totality of Jewish life in the past was intensive and cohesive, reinforcing the values and shared experiences of individuals and resulting in the continuities over time and across generations. These are the distinctive features of world Jewry. In that historical context, the examination of synagogue attendance, formal Jewish education, and the depth of Jewish knowledge hardly reflect the fullness of this totality. So while religion and religious observances were characteristic of the Jewish communities in Eastern Europe in the past, these cultural features were the outward symbols of a much deeper set of communal and family ties, of shared history and shared socio-cultural location within a Christian society. We should not confuse the outward symbols with the underlying depths of communal attachments. Poverty and anti-Semitism were additional forces that shaped Jewish life in the past but were not the basis of Jewish quality.

Are synagogue attendance and Jewish education the major features of Judaism that have emerged in the American context? The answer is no more and no less than they were valid indicators of the Judaism and Jewishness of 200 years ago. Then, in the past, the social class composition and the occupational and residential concentration of Jews, the institutions and cultural forms that reinforced a sense of distinctiveness were all critical in shaping the social world of the Jews. So it is in America today, even as the form and content have been transformed. What is critical in terms of continuity is context and community.

We can now raise our central question more precisely: How can we use national and local survey data on the Jewish population as a methodological instrument to capture this total round of Jewish communal and religious-cultural activities for American Jews in the contemporary context? How can we determine the extent to which our assessments of the Jewishness of American Jews inform us about the total round of activities that capture the quality of American Jewish life?

The NJPS Questionnaire as Test and Context

What are the forms of Jewishness and Judaism that emerge from the questionnaire of the 1990 National Jewish Population Survey? How does the content of the questionnaire reflect the current conception of Judaism and Jewishness?[5]

Several interesting features of Judaism and Jewishness are implicitly assumed in the survey: Judged by the contents and formulation of the questions, one would assume that the Judaism to be learned about in the survey is a religion of individuals who self identify religiously in terms of denominations and membership. Questions of identification are of critical importance since there is intense interest in the relationship between current denominational identification and that of parents when the respondent was growing up. No other item of religion gets that much "personal" historical reconstruction.

The questions were addressed to one person in the household with less information collected on the Judaism and Jewishness of the other members of the household, and about other family members not living in the household.[6] The key "religious" elements of this Judaism are: observing Kashrut (two questions—on purchasing Kosher meat and on separating meat and dairy dishes); synagogue attendance and membership, fasting on Yom Kippur and Ta'anit Esther, lighting candles Friday night, celebrating Hanukkah, Purim, and Yom Ha'azmaut, participating in a Seder, having a Christmas tree, handling money on Shabbat, and having some feelings about the Bible-Torah (not how many hours one studied or studies Bible, or whether anything about Judaism is known). Questions on Jewish education are rather straightforward and deal with type and years. No attempt is made to address either the quality of instruction received, the amount learned, subjective evaluations of the experience, or the perceived impact on later education and knowledge.

Except for self identification, Judaism in the questionnaire is a household religion based on selected religious rituals that are presumed to be shared by all members of the unit; it is static over the life course, making the assumption that current behavior is indicative of the past and the future. Jewish institutions are important to the extent that people belong to them or participate in them. The presence or absence of institutions and organizations at early points in the life course, the location and access to these institutions currently, or previous associations with them are not relevant. Nor is it important to know whether these institutions are geographically near the family-household or their proximity at earlier stages of the life course. The basic assumption of this "questionnaire Judaism" is that a focus on Jews and their behavior and attitudes will reveal the basis of cohesion of the community. In addition, there is no need for a Jewish community to learn directly about its distinctiveness through specific comparisons with non-Jews.

The constraints of surveys conducted over the telephone are well known. In addition, the survey's budgeting constraints limited the number of questions included. Some issues were omitted not necessarily because they were unimportant but because there was no simple way or consensus on whether or how to ask them; some were asked for selected subpopulations only.

What we miss from the survey is some indication of the role of community and networks, the role of institutions at previous points in time, as we do not have information on the access that people have to these institutions at the present time. We accept the constraints of surveys that are focused on telephone interviews and require us to shape questions that are limited to one respondent for the household. Nevertheless, are we satisfied to read back into the results the contours of the Judaism that the methods we select impose on us? Instead of overemphasizing the limitations of the conception of the questionnaire about Judaism and Jewishness in America, and in lieu of rejecting the survey a priori, let me share some constructive thoughts about the data that were collected. More precisely, let me suggest how to build onto the survey information that will in part allow us to better capture what Judaism and Jewishness in America are about.

Orientations to Measuring
and Understanding Jewish Quality

There are various points of orientation toward issues of Jewish quality that are derived deductively from the nature of Jewishness and Judaism, and not inductively from the survey.[7] Six are listed as a point of departure, to examine their implications in the context of the ways in which the survey of the national Jewish population in 1990 can help us clarify issues related to the quality of Jewish life in America. The lack of attention to these parameters have made our past surveys less useful for policy formulation, and less convincing as a basis for analysis. Specifically, research should be oriented to community, generational continuity, longitudinal study, organizations and institutions, Jewish distinctiveness, and Jewish complexity.

Community

The first aspect of Judaism of critical importance is that it is a communal religion not solely focused on religious ritual. To investigate Judaism and the quality of Jewish life in its religio-cultural dimensions, we must deal directly with the community setting as well as the broader range of social, cultural, and institutional activities of Jews.

The most powerful source of Jewish continuity is, therefore, community, that is institutions and networks. The salience of cultural, religious, and ideological ideas in a social-communal vacuum is not what sustained Jews in the past. However powerful ideas and ideologies were, they always operated in a context. The content of Judaism and Jewishness for American Jews is a combination of religious and ethnic elements, together with important negative supports derived from the European Holocaust, perceptions of anti-Semitism, and Jewish distinctiveness in a Christian society. Whether the lack of a more traditional, well-articulated ideology precludes Jewish continuity needs to be the basis of our research, not asserted as a conclusion.

The importance of community to American Jewish continuity needs to be reflected directly in our measurement of Jewish quality. If community is important in a multi-dimensional way, then it follows that community is a variable that can be stronger and weaker, that changes over time, and varies among different subgroups and in different places. The greater the sources of commonality and interaction among Jews (i.e., networks and connections), the stronger the community. The more the bases of connections—whether they are family, work, social, neighborhood, religion, life-style, or education—the greater the likelihood of reinforcing the cultural, historical, and religious content of Jewish identity. Moreover, the importance of institutions and networks needs to be studied directly, not simply asserted from our theories. Thus, we can examine the circumstances under which community networks reinforce the quality of Jewish life.

Translating the community level emphasis to the Jewish quality dimension means focusing our analysis on residential, social class, family, and household networks. It means that the measurements of Judaism and Jewishness have to focus on communal expressions and not only on "self" identification. These expressions are multi-layered, linking individuals to families, to neighborhoods, to communities, to national and international connections, both ethnic and religious.

The data from the NJPS is structured to allow some of this multi-layered analysis. These include the direct linkage between individuals within households (the employment patterns of co-residents, for example), the linkage between households in neighborhoods, and in communities; the linkage between local and regional data, and national patterns. An emphasis on networks emerges from an analysis of residential and occupational concentration rather than a focus solely on rates of occupational mobility and migration. The limited data of the NJPS on these residential and occupational patterns could be supplemented by local studies, where they are more detailed. This is particularly important since it is likely that these networks operate more at the local than national level. Suggested below are other ways in which the data can be further enhanced through supplementing it with additional network data at the local level. Policies are largely based on this kind of hierarchical and contextual analysis and that should be emphasized in research.

Generational Continuity

Judaism is dynamic in the generational sense—linking the current with the next as well as past generations. In studying the quality of Jewish life, therefore, the examination of the extent of generational continuity becomes critical.

Which aspects of the quality of Jewish life are transmitted generationally? Unfortunately there is little in the NJPS that can examine this at the family level. The relationship between the generations is critical, and unfortunately has been studied only indirectly at the aggregate level. A poor and indirect substitute is to examine age variation. A better strategy is to make systematic comparisons between NJPS 1990 and previous surveys and compare other data sources. We shall probably have to seek more local surveys to supplement the national data. The examination of this dimension should become the highest priority for both the analytic and policy phases.

It follows from the community and generational basis of Judaism that the examination of the quality of Jewish life cannot focus exclusively on Judaism as an individual-based religious system, even though it may have such elements. Community-level data are therefore our primary "independent" variable, those that shape and explain the variation in the measures of Jewish quality. To address the issue of quality, one must therefore link the community to the individual level.

The Importance of Longitudinal Studies

Judaism changes over the life cycle of persons and over the generations. It means different things to younger persons than to older persons; to the married with children than to singles; to those in and outside of families; to women than to men. Over time, communities and neighborhoods change as well. Some age and others are renewed; some grow, others decline in population. Variations in the quality of Jewish life occur in the contexts of these changing communities, their organizations and institutions, their demographic growth and distribution. Individuals, families, and communities are linked together to share different experiences, and thereby change over time.

Attitudes, practices, and beliefs vary over time, both because people at different life stages face different contexts and because times change. Unfortunately, the NJPS data do not provide satisfactory means to disentangle the cohort from the period effects. Changes need to be studied as they unfold. One cannot simply continue to take cross-sectional, static snapshots when examining a dynamic, moving picture. It is necessary to initiate a carefully designed and systematically monitored longitudinal study to probe changes over time for a cohort of young adults. Without longitudinal analysis, we cannot disentangle cause and effect; without knowing cause and effect, our policies and programs will be unable to specify whether they are addressing the problem or the symptom.

At a minimum it is necessary to examine how previous patterns affect later ones and how some environments improve while others detract from Jewish quality. Having never measured successes, the Jewish community does not know which policies work and which do not, and therefore, cannot choose the variety of models that will help shape future policies. (By success I mean, of course, in terms of improving the quality of Jewish life and not in terms of per capita giving to Jewish organizations.)

No subject demonstrates more clearly the need to use a longitudinal approach than intermarriage. We cannot infer either from the rates of intermarriage or from current cross-sectional patterns of identification what the patterns of identification among the partners, or among the children, will be over time. No data set currently available has been designed to examine these processes as they unfold. Despite the continuing concerns expressed by organizations and researchers about the costs of intermarriage, we have not developed adequate national or local data sources to study these patterns. A clear understanding of the Jewish costs and benefits of intermarriage requires a longitudinal design. Unfortunately, the NJPS can clarify the intermarriage issue no better than other studies that are cross-sectional.

The influence of past on current patterns within a person's life course can be examined further by linking past synagogue attendance and subsequent religious and Jewish commitments; seeing how the exposure to Hillel institutions at the college level influences Jewish organizational commitments at a later point in life; and by asking similar questions about the longer term life course influence of visits to Israel, Jewish camps, and Jewish educational experiences. Our truncated, snapshot view of Jewish life has prevented us from considering the differing outcomes of Jewish educational experiences, which vary in terms of the number of years and type of school, for the quality of Jewish life in college, when persons marry and have children of their own.

Organization and Institutions

Judaism has important institutional and organizational components that include local, national, and international religious and communal organizations. These organizations promote social activities, focus on formal Jewish education, and have cultural and religiously oriented objectives.

This parameter of Jewish quality is often treated by viewing organizational and institutional components too narrowly and in individualistic forms. Data concerning the patterns of belonging and organizational leadership, the number of memberships and the extent of knowledge and awareness of these institutions, are collected and examined. However, we have not systematically linked the presence and type of these institutions, and their distribution, to the distribution of population. Consequently, we do not know how the presence of these institutions is connected, if at all, with the quality of Jewish life within their community. Does it matter whether there is a Jewish family service, a Jewish home for the aged, or a Jewish community center? Or if there are five or 25 synagogues? Does playing golf in a Jewish country club or swimming at a Jewish Community Center enhance the quality of Jewish life, intensify shared values and commitments, or increase the social, family, and economic networks that sustain the continuity of the Jewish community? Those questions are not trivial and can be studied by linking, longitudinally, organizational and population based data at the level of community. They focus our attention on the impact of these institutions on the quality of Jewish life for the community as a whole and not only on the programs provided. We often know if people have heard about Jewish institutions and whether they use their services or expect to do so. Still, we have not studied their communal impact, and that is what policy experts need to learn. We should move away from the oversimplified "marketing" approach in the analysis of the importance of Jewish organizations and institutions.

The NJPS would be enhanced enormously if contextual information of this sort was attached to the study's parallel individual and household data. Such organizational data are readily available for most communities. We know how many Jewish institutions—including synagogues—there are and where they are located. These organizational locations can be linked to the zip code addresses at the household level. Together, these newly created data would be most powerful from both policy and analytic points of view; they would allow, for the first time, the systematic analysis of Jewish institutions within the community, their distribution, and their current impact.

The Distinctiveness of Judaism

Judaism means distinctiveness. While influenced by the religious forms of other churches, synagogue and church attendance are not simply interchangeable forms of attending religious services in different religious traditions. Judaism and the synagogue are related to each other in ways that are fundamentally different from the relationship between Christianity (Protestantism or Catholicism) and the church.

The distinctiveness of Jewish communities extends to almost every other facet of their social and institutional lives. Indeed, even as Jews and their communities have been thoroughly assimilated politically and economically as full participants in American society and are, perhaps, at the forefront of many aspects of American culture and society, they live in communities that are distinctive in almost every way—from their continuing voluntary residential and occupational concentration to their educational attainment, organizational and political activities, family patterns, and values. We need to examine this distinctiveness, in all of its forms even as it changes; it is a key component of Jewish continuity and community.

Only a systematic comparison of Jews and non-Jews will reveal the special distinctive qualities of the Jewish community in the broadest sense. While there were reasons behind the focus of the NJPS on an only Jewish sample, there were costs as well, both analytically and in terms of policy.

Many of the issues of Jewish distinctiveness, except at the most superficial level, cannot be satisfactorily addressed.[8]

By examining Jews only, we cannot know whether the patterns that we find are special and reinforce Jewishness, or are common among others who share some—but not all—features of the Jewish community. Our interpretations and policies on Jewish quality issues will also be limited, since it will remain unclear whether what we are observing reflects some aspects of Jewish distinctiveness, and hence some Jewish quality, or the quality that characterizes others in similar economic and social positions.

There are no easy ways around this limitation except through a concerted effort to make comparisons with other available information. The General Social Survey or the U.S. Censuses are of particular help since many of the items in the NJPS parallel data from these sources.

Complexities within a Pluralistic Society

One consequence of considering these aspects of the quality of Jewish life is that it requires a view of Judaism and a Jewishness that is complex, multi-dimensional, multi-layered, and changing. Lone indicators will not capture that complexity; simple descriptions should not be expected to adequately reflect the complexities and diversities within a pluralistic and heterogeneous society. If Judaism is complex, then our measurement and analysis of Judaism must be complex as well. Policies cannot be based on simple descriptions that are at best useful for public relations and politics.

An elementary and obvious point is that our analysis must be multivariate. That point is taken for granted by social scientists and researchers using empirical evidence. Most Jewish community surveys and their reports unfortunately limit analysis to simple distributions and bivariate cross-tabulations. We have hardly done the minimal in analyzing the data, and we certainly have failed to exploit the rich community data sets that we have collected.

At the very least we need to develop more complex models of Jewish life in order to analyze the complexities that characterize the community. For example, we have often found that recent migrants to communities have the weakest institutional links to their new communities. (We rarely ask them about links to the community of origin.) We need to examine whether these links vary by age and sex, length of stay, religious background, and education, in order to detail their community connections. In the past, we often carried out these variable analyses by addressing them in some simple statistically descriptive way. On the basis of these crude findings we often suggested policies of community outreach to newcomers.

More detailed and multivariate modelling might have shown that the low levels of community participation are short-term and may be more characteristic of men than women, so that "outreach" may not be necessary. We need to develop more inclusive models in order to examine the complexities of the quality of Jewish life in systematic ways.

What does this all add up to? We can obtain a clearer picture of the quality of Jewish life through surveys, but we shall have to work at it. It will not emerge "naturally" from the cross-sectional data we have collected. The data will not automatically provide the facts for planning. All data are political, as are data analysis and policy formulation. Nevertheless, the NJPS, along with survey data already collected at the local community level, set up a window of opportunity to begin to systematically examine the major issues involved. If we have not been successful in identifying the quality of Jewish life in America from our surveys in the past, it is a consequence of the limited analytic-theoretical questions that we have asked, not the survey method itself.

All of us, policymakers and researchers, scholars and laypersons, optimists and pessimists, need to address the complex issues concerning the quality of Jewish life. We will evaluate the policy implications of the 1990 NJPS by the extent to which issues of quality are clarified and examined. We can more successfully carry out that goal by linking local communities to the national patterns; by connecting Jewish communities to the non-Jewish context, which for many is their reference group. Current patterns need to be compared to the past; individuals need to be linked to households and neighborhoods; we need to invest in continuous monitoring through longitudinal data collection and to link institutions and their distributions to households and individuals. We need to analyze the data in ways that enable us to make policy judgments about the costs and benefits of diverse Jewish quality issues, and therefore allow us to take the first steps toward enhancing the quality of life of American Jews and their communities.

Community is a context that determines the quality of Jewish life. Policymakers have been justifiably confused by their inability to use data collected in the past as a result of the failure to study contexts systematically. Researchers must meet their policy goals by paying closer attention to theory and to the determinants of Jewish quality in analysis. Institutional and community data must be added to survey analysis so that policy makers can examine the ways institutions can generate a higher likelihood of Jewish continuity.

The research and policy challenges are great, the financial and human resources have already been committed, and the stakes are high for the future of the American Jewish community.

Notes

1. This feeling with regard to Jewish identity was expressed in several papers at a 1989 Wilstein conference. See Gordis, David and Yoav Ben-Horin (eds.) *Jewish Identity In America*, Los Angeles, Wilstein Institute, 1991.

2. Steven M. Cohen in particular has made this suggestion, even though he has, more than others, relied almost exclusively on survey and poll data for the analysis of Jewish issues. See Cohen in Gordis and Ben-Horin, op. cit.

3. See Goldscheider, Calvin and Alan Zuckerman, *The Transformation of the Jews*, Chicago, University of Chicago Press, 1984.

4. Ibid.

5. I think that the underlying conception was developed implicitly without much theoretical forethought, a comment and criticism that is not specific to the formulators of that questionnaire since I was involved in shaping its contents.

6. The major exceptions were questions about spouses and their Jewish parentage or conversion, and questions about the Jewish education of younger persons.

7. I do not want to define the theological or substantive content of American Judaism or American forms of Jewishness, in large part because there is little consensus on the content, i.e., the content is diverse and changes over time. There is little to gain from forcing a common agreement about content that would end up to be too abstract from the lives of most Jews and hence not measurable anyway. Here we specify primarily the parameters within which aspects of the quality of Jewish life should be analyzed. Some earlier attempts in other contexts to broadly consider the quality of American Judaism and Jewishness were made in Goldscheider and Zuckerman, 1984; and in C. Goldscheider and J. Neusner, "Introduction," *Social Foundations of Judaism, 1990*.

8. See the discussion by Calvin Goldscheider, "Including Non-Jews in Jewish Community Samples: Substantive and Methodological Issues" in Cohen, Steven, Jonathan Woocher and Bruce Phillips (eds.), *Perspectives in Jewish Population Research*, Boulder, Westview Press, 1984.

PART TWO

Jewish Identity

4

Being Jewish in America: Religion or Culture

Nava Lerer, Ariela Keysar, and Barry A. Kosmin

A merican Jews today can choose between a religious or a cultural—ethnic group identity. This study[1] explores differences in background which might create such alternative attributions of group identity, as well as areas of behavior and attitudes of the two groups. Following Herberg's (1960) thesis, this study examines the role of Americanization in the formation of the American Jewish collective identity. In addition, it tries to assess the relative importance of factors stemming from historical context and personal socialization.

Rabbinical and biblical literature, as well as gentile authorities, have viewed Jews both as a nation and a religious community. After Emancipation, during the nineteenth century, this fabric of unity began to unravel. In Western Europe, some Jews chose to define themselves solely as a religious group, eliminating the national aspect. In Eastern Europe, particularly in Russia, and also to some extent in the Austro-Hungarian Empire, Jewishness was expressed by modernizers, such as Zionists, who formed a secular national category comparable to the other nationality groups dwelling in the multi-ethnic empires.

The fact that Jews arriving in America encountered a level of tolerance and acceptance unequaled elsewhere created a unique dilemma. On one hand, there was the pressure of acculturation. Jews wanted to join in, speak the language, and be accepted as Americans. On the other hand, they wanted to retain a separate identity within the larger social group (Herberg, 1960; Eisen, 1983). The religious emphasis on Jews as "God's chosen People" only increased the dilemma since it could be interpreted as contradicting the ideology of equality for all peoples. "To abandon the claim to choseness would be to discard the raison d'être that had sustained Jewish identity and Jewish faith through the ages, while to make the claim was to question or perhaps even to threaten America's precious offer of acceptance" (Eisen, 1983, pp. 3–4).

According to much of the historical literature, most first and second generation Jews in America moved toward the secularization of Judaism as a result of their wish to assimilate. The new religious denominations that arose in America tended to emphasize Jewish universalism. The Reconstructionists described Jews as an ethnic group rather than a religious one, while the Reform movement emphasized universalistic values and equality of all Americans. Moreover, Jews as a group with a history of persecution and discrimination supported universalistic and humanistic values and social justice; they are still more liberal than any other group with similar socioeconomic status (Lenski, 1961; Eisen, 1983; Leibman and Cohen, 1990).

One solution for the group survival dilemma Jews faced, was the creation of Jewish communal services and organizations, and the Jewish neighborhood. These enabled Jews to meet each other and express identity in a nonreligious setting (Eisen, 1983). Lenski (1961) found "organizational weakness [in the Jewish community] . . . limited entirely to religious association. In fact, the vigor of Jewish communalism more than compensates for the weakness of religious association" (p. 319). By and large, the wider American society looked with favor upon the operations of Jewish communal institutions within a quasi-religious framework and the adoption of religious symbolism to advance their purposes.

Eisen (1983) argued, however, that third generation Jews in America returned to religion as an expression of their identity as a result of the Holocaust, the persistence of discrimination and anti-Semitism at home, and the fact that nearly all other religious groups in the U.S. maintained their religious identity and expected Jews to do the same.

The emergence of the state of Israel is an additional factor which has shaped American Jewish identity, especially after the Six-Day War in 1967. The attachment of many Jews to Israel has become a major source of involvement in Jewish communal life (Cohen, 1991; Liebman and Cohen, 1990; Eisen, 1983). Their work on behalf of Israel's economic and political future reflects an impulse towards the ethnic-national identity desired by the secular European modernizers.

Thus, Jews in twentieth-century America are heirs to three traditions: the pre-modern religion-nation; the Western modernizers who defined themselves as a people with a distinct religion who maintained the nationality of their host country; and East European modernizers who defined themselves as a secular nationality on the basis of Yiddish or Hebrew language and culture. Though American Jews are largely of East European stock, they live in a society similar to Western Europe, a society of unitary nationality but with multiple religious groups. Since any self-definition must take into account the historic memory as well as the contemporary reality, Jewish self-identification is problematic.

Furthermore, Jews are considered members of one of America's three great faith groups. Yet as our data show, Jews are far more secular in their observance than Protestants or Catholics. But America has also allowed for the voluntary construction of another variation of the national option suited to modern pluralistic societies. This comprises ethnic identities based upon national descent groups—hyphenated Americans with special cultural traits.

The Data

The present study is based upon a subsample of 621 currently Jewish adults drawn from the 1990 National Jewish Population Survey (Kosmin et al., 1991). They consist of respondents to the Jewish Identity Module administered to one-third of the overall Jewish sample who also qualified as "Core Jews."[2] Whereas 80 percent of these respondents reported their current religion as Jewish, the remainder considered themselves Jews but had no religion or described themselves as Agnostics or Humanists.

Two alternative group identities were specified, based upon respondents' replies to four questions concerning whether being a Jew in America today means being a member of a religious, ethnic, or cultural group, and whether it is a nationality.

In addition, the NJPS questionnaire contained 22 questions about issues of religious behaviors, community social behaviors of a non-religious type, attitudes towards Judaism, intermarriage, politics, emotional attachment to Israel, and charitable contributions. These variables have been incorporated into the study.

Results

Despite the fact that being Jewish is widely perceived by social scientists and the general American public as pertaining to Judaism as a religion, the situation appears to be different within the contemporary Jewish population. Whereas 47.3 percent of the study's respondents agreed that Jews in America today constitute a religious group, 52.7 percent disagreed and chose instead one or more of the ethnic, cultural, and nationality options.

Only 4.8 percent replied that being a Jew in America today means being a member of a religious group only, while denying the existence of other factors. It is of particular interest to note the inconsistency that despite the fact that 80 percent of interviewees reported their religion as Jewish, about half of these cases then denied that to be Jewish in America means to be a member of a religious group.

Socio-demographic Characteristics

The two halves of the sample, those with the religious group preference and those with the cultural-ethnic-national group preference, were compared on a range of variables that pertain to their socio-demographic background, religious upbringing, current religious behaviors, community behaviors, and attitudes. The socio-demographic variables included: age (over vs. under 50), gender, education, generation in the United States (first and second vs. third and fourth), and the four census geographic regions (Northeast, Midwest, South, West). The results show (see Table 4.1) that while women are evenly divided between the two preference groups, men tend to view Jews in America as an ethnic-cultural group more often than a religious group. Those over 50 tend to regard Jews less as a religious group than younger people, who are split evenly between the two options. First and second generations in the U.S. are less likely to view Jews as a religious group than the third or fourth generations.

TABLE 4.1

Socio-Demographic Characteristics by Jewish Group Identity

	% NON-RELIGIOUS PREFERENCE	% RELIGIOUS PREFERENCE
Male	55	44
Female	50	50
Under 50	50	50
Over 50	59	41
1st, 2nd generation	57	43
3rd, 4th generation	50	50
Northeast	50	50
Midwest	49	51
South	56	44
West	57	43
No College	54	46
College education	51	49
Total	53	47

Geographic region of residence is clearly related to one's view of the meaning of being a Jew in America: respondents in the West and in the South are far less likely to favor religious identity as their Jewish group preference. A different pattern is found in the Northeast and Midwest, where the two identity groups are evenly distributed. Among those with no college education, more choose a non-religious option rather than a religious one. However, among those with at least a college education, both options are equally chosen.

The findings in Table 4.1 show that young people who are Americanized lean towards the religious group preference, more than those who are closer to their European roots, who show an ethno-national preference. However, the regional findings contradict and offset this trend. The West, for example, which is home to many young Jews and to many third and fourth generation Americans (Kosmin et al., 1991), favors the non-religious options. These crosscutting trends necessitate further analysis in order to explain the interrelationships of the socio-demographic characteristics.

Demographic Factors: Interrelationships

The interrelationships between five socio-demographic characteristics (age, gender, level of education, generation in the United States, and census region), two religious factors, and the likelihood of choosing a religious option versus the cultural-ethnic-nationality option are shown in Table 4.2. An analysis of the interaction of age and generation shows that there is no generational difference among respondents younger than age 50. Among Jews older than 50, those who are third and fourth generation Americans were more likely to include religion in their group identity than younger ones.

Two religious background variables were added to the subsequent analyses, including parents' religious denomination and the respondent's exposure to Jewish education. Jewish education was found to be a highly significant factor. Those who did not receive any Jewish education are 14 percent less likely to regard the meaning of being a Jew as belonging to a religious group.[3]

The effect of the parents' denomination is similar to that of Jewish education: The differences among those raised in the three main branches of Judaism, namely, Conservative, Orthodox, and Reform, are rather small, while those raised in secular homes have different views. However, this last group is based upon a small sample of only 38 respondents.

Further analysis[4] shows that all those who belong to the Orthodox, Conservative, or Reform Jewish denominations are distributed between the identity groups in a similar way. Of the Orthodox respondents, 59.4 per-

TABLE 4.2
*Multiple Classification Analysis: Jewish Group Identity
by Socio-demographic and Religious Background*

GRAND MEAN = 0.49

VARIABLE	N	EFFECT
Gender		
Male	263	− .02
Female	291	.02
		− .04★
Jewish Education		
Yes	421	.03
No	133	− .11
		− .12★
Age		
Under 50	363	.03
Over 50	191	− .06
		− .09★
Generation		
1st, 2nd, foreign	219	− .05
3rd, 4th	335	.03
		− .07★
Education		
Up to grade 12	90	.06
College junior	121	− .02
College senior	165	.02
Post graduate	178	− .03
		− .07★
Region		
Northeast	273	.01
Midwest	67	.08
South	106	− .00
West	108	− .07
		− .08★
Parents' denomination		
Conservative	189	.03
Orthodox	115	− .02
Reform	162	.01
Secular	38	− .21
Other religion	50	.05
		− .13★

Multiple R = 0.253
★ Partial correlation ratio

cent identify with the religious preference group, slightly more than the 53.8 percent of Conservatives and 52.3 percent of Reform. In contrast, 75.5 percent of the secularists, who do not identify with any Jewish religious denomination, say that the meaning of being a Jew is not membership in a religious group. In other words, the secularists are less than half as likely to choose the religious group identity option as are Jews who identify with a denomination.

Structure of Attitudes and Behaviors

The purpose of this section is to explore the actual attitudes and behaviors related to Jewish identity. Although they cannot be viewed as explanatory variables, it is important to explore the way the differences between the two preference groups are displayed in everyday life. These variations were recorded by respondents in their answers to questions on their Jewish practice and identity. Therefore, our next step was to examine the structure of these items using factor analysis.[5]

In all, the analysis identified five factors or scales. The first scale, Cultural-National, is a mixture of attachment to Israel and involvement in communal Jewish life in the United States. It contains the following items: celebration of Israel's Independence Day, subscribing to Jewish magazines, contributing to Jewish charities, visiting Israel, strong emotional attachment to Israel, and belonging to Jewish organizations other than synagogue. This scale seems to measure active involvement in all non-religious aspects of Jewish life. Such non-religious aspects of Jewish life were described by Woocher (1986) as "civil Judaism"; it includes philanthropic activities, membership in Jewish organizations, and is not affiliated with religious denominations. As might be expected but still worthy of note, "civil Judaism" appears to be strongly related to an emotional attachment and commitment to Israel. Thus, Jewish nationality and the cultural non-religious commitment aspects of Jewish identity seem to be interrelated.

The second scale, Traditional Religious, is composed of items pertaining to religious behavior and attitudes. It includes identification with Jewish denominations, adherence to traditional and regular religious in-home rituals such as the lighting of candles on Friday evening and keeping a kosher home, the belief that Torah is the word of God, and an opposition to intermarriage. This scale seems to represent a traditional Jewish religious outlook, which also involves opposition to intermarriage, belief that the Torah is the word of God, and adherence to the more private "religious" rituals. The same pattern is reported by Cohen (1991), who found that only the most religious American Jews keep kosher and light Friday candles.

TABLE 4.3
*Factor Loadings of the 22 Jewish Behavior and Attitude Variables
Using VARIMAX Rotation*

	FACTORS				
	1 CULTURAL NATION	2 TRADITIONAL RELIGIOUS	3 MAINSTREAM	4 ETHNIC NETWORK	5 SYNAGOGUE MEMBER
Items					
Membership in Jewish organizations	**.62**	.07	.13	.12	.20
Jewish charity	**.51**	.08	.28	.20	.16
Emotional attachment to Israel	**.50**	.28	.19	.1	−.21
Jewish magazines	**.48**	.12	.22	.08	.12
Celebrate Israel's Independence	**.41**	.30	.15	.05	.16
Visiting Israel	**.41**	.17	.07	.14	.07
Kosher meat	.12	**.61**	.09	.17	.08
Religious denomination (Orthodox-secular)	.28	**.57**	.22	.15	.00
Torah word of God	.04	**.55**	.04	.01	
Friday candles	.24	**.48**	.21	.17	.38
Oppose intermarriage	.31	**.41**	.11	.11	.04
Hanukkah candles	.15	.06	**.67**	.16	.17
Passover Seder	.11	.16	**.65**	.07	.22
Importance of being a Jew	.39	.19	**.55**	.18	−.03
Yom Kippur	.28	.29	**.44**	.07	.09
Living in Jewish neighborhood	.17	.15	.11	**.78**	.13
Importance of Jewish neighborhood	.27	.31	.29	**.49**	−.12
Jewish friends	.41	.10	.25	**.45**	.06
Synagogue membership	.40	.06	.33	.05	**.59**
Synagogue attendance	.32	.40	.30	.07	**.36**
Anti-Semitism danger	.13	.09	.20	.07	**.03**
Political attitudes	.04	.24	.07	.24	**.00**

The third scale is Mainstream Religious. This scale appears to reflect the religious behavior of mainstream American Jews and includes the most popular annual festivals followed by all the religious denominations. The items comprising this scale measure the importance of being a Jew as well as participation in the most popular rituals of American Jews such as lighting Hanukkah candles, having a Passover Seder, and observing Yom

Kippur. A similar pattern of differentiation between the three major holidays (Passover, Hanukkah, and Yom Kippur) which are kept by most American Jews, as opposed to the observance of kashrut laws and the lighting of candles on Friday evening by a small minority, was reported by Cohen (1991). Unlike the religious rituals measured by the scale of Traditional Religious which are done in the privacy of one's home as a part of everyday life, the three annual holidays measured by the scale of Mainstream Religious are more social or family events.

The fourth scale focuses on the importance of the Ethnic Network. The items on this scale refer to the number of Jewish friends one has, how Jewish one's neighborhood is, and to the importance of living in a Jewish neighborhood. Thus, this scale measures whether one lives in a close-knit Jewish network, including one's neighborhood, or in a non-Jewish environment in which most people in one's social network are not Jewish.

Differentiating Between the Preference Groups

The fifth scale consists of only one item, Synagogue Membership.[6] Statistical analysis[7] (see Table 4.4) shows that when all other variables are taken into account, Synagogue Membership is the most important discriminator between the two preference groups. Respondents who are synagogue members are more likely to see Jews as a religious group. The Cultural Network scale, which reflects a combination of "civil Judaism" and nationalism, is the second best discriminator although its predictive power is quite weak.[8]

All the religious variables are good predictors of what identity group an American Jew will belong to. Synagogue membership is the best predictor among the religious variables. However, the other religious variables—the

TABLE **4.4**

Standardized and Structure Coefficients
of the Jewish Behavior and Attitude Variables

PREDICTOR VARIABLES	STANDARDIZED COEF.	STRUCTURE COEF.
Cultural-National	− .506	.255
Mainstream Religious	.239	.636
Traditional Religious	.321	.632
Synagogue Membership	.672	.790
Synagogue attendance	.190	.611
Political affiliation	.250	.377
Anti-Semitism	.136	.248

Canonical Correlation = .30   Eigen value = .096
Wilk's lambda = .91
Chi-squared = 49.169 DF = 7
Chi-squared significance = .00000

Traditional Religion scale, the Mainstream Religious scale, and synagogue attendance—are good predictors as well. Thus, the difference between the religious and the cultural-ethnic groups, not surprisingly, has a lot to do with the degree of display of religious behavior. Fear of anti-Semitism hardly discriminates between the two preference groups (see Table 4.4). Political attitudes have a weak relationship to the perception of Jews as a religious group.

Conclusions

The high level of secularization among American Jews is reflected in the fact that fewer than half include religion in their definition of what it means to be a Jew, and only a tiny number believe its meaning is solely that of being a religiously based group. Religious background was found to be more important than socio-demographic variables in explaining differences between respondents from the two different groups. The number of generations in the United States, suggested by Herberg (1960) and Eisen (1983) as crucial in propelling individuals towards a religious identity, was found to have an effect only on respondents older than age 50, who were also third and fourth generation American Jews. The number of American-born ancestors appears to have no affect on younger respondents. In contrast, socialization, as reflected by Jewish education and parental religious denomination, seems to affect the way respondents perceive the meaning of being a Jew in America. Those who had some religious upbringing, received Jewish education, and were brought up in a Jewish religious denomination, were more likely to mention religion as a part of a Jewish group identity.

Whether people's definition of what it means to be a Jew in America is a reflection of their own personal identity or of the way they were socialized to regard Jews in general was investigated by exploring the relationship of the definition to their behavior. Those who define being a Jew as being a member of a religious group are, indeed, more inclined towards religious expressions of Judaism in their own behavior and attitudes. Furthermore, synagogue membership and attendance, irrespective of denomination, inclines people toward affirming the religious group basis of a Jewish identity. One reason for this finding may be expressed in Greeley's (1963) argument that attendance at religious services, a key measure of religiosity, is a way to form primary groups, which in turn provide norms and role images for their members. These norms and images serve to unite members under a religious doctrine. In any case, the results do show that a high degree of religiosity is related to the view that to be a Jew means to be a member of a religious group. Thus, respondents show a consistency between their personal attitudes and views of the meaning of being a Jew. Moreover, this relationship is found across denominational lines. There are religious Orthodox, Conservative, and Reform Jews who all regard themselves as members of a religious group and focus their behavior around their respective synagogues.

Furthermore, although certain annual festivals such as Passover and Hanukkah, and to a lesser extent Yom Kippur, have been transformed from religious rituals into group ceremonials by many American Jews, the scale of Mainstream Religion, which measures celebration of the festivals, distinguishes those who see the meaning of being a Jew in religious terms from those who see it in secular terms. Thus, it may be that these holidays still carry a religious meaning for most respondents, despite a lack of correlation with the more traditional religious practices.

Nevertheless, there seems to be a consensus position among American Jews, irrespective of the inclusion of religion in their definition, that to be a Jew is to belong to an ethnic or cultural group. Most respondents, even those who think that to be a Jew is, in part, to be a member of a religion, agree that to be a Jew is to be a member of a cultural group. However, in view of the relatively weak predictive power of the Cultural-National scale and the fact that religious variables are stronger predictors, an overriding consensus appears to emerge among American Jews. Part of what it means to be a Jew in America entails membership in secular, Jewish organizations, support of Jewish charities, and attachment to Israel.

Moreover, while respondents' categorization of "Jews in America" reflects past experiences, especially religious upbringing, these categorizations are not mere abstractions. They are expressed by actual individual behavior. For example, there is a difference in religious practices between those who opt for a religious notion of what it means to be a Jew and those who do not. However, it should be stressed that we depict a general pattern which fits only 65 percent of the respondents. That is, while many of them behave in a way consistent with their notion of what it means to be a Jew, others behave less consistently. Not all respondents who mentioned religion as part of what it means to be a Jew are personally religious. Paradoxically, some of those who did not mention religion adhere to Jewish rituals and practices in their personal behavior.

Most American Jews subscribe to a secular—ethnic, cultural, or national—notion of what it means to be a Jew. Most also accept a liberal theology and secular values. Some perceive their own Jewish identity and that of "American Jews" as also consisting of an additional religious dimension. Others do not. In view of the fact that 48.5 percent of respondents identified their religion as Jewish but ignored the religious aspect of

Judaism when responding to a question concerning the meaning of being a Jew in America, it might well be that the concept of "being a Jew" is ambiguous, even for many Jews.

These findings also raise other important questions. Does religious identity mean one thing to Jews and another to the general public? If Jews do not agree among themselves on the inclusion of religion in the meaning of being a Jew, both on the personal and social level, is there any other way in which they maintain their Jewish identity? In particular, how do those who do not engage in religious rituals and practices and do not belong to a synagogue remain part of an organized "Jewish" community, if they do? Do they have other ways to manifest their personal commitment to being Jewish? Do the "religious" and "secular" Jews meet and merge when dealing with issues most of them agree on, such as support for Israel and contribution to Jewish charity?

One possible answer to these questions is that by denying the religious nature of being Jewish the majority are essentially denying the power of traditional religious authority, the rabbinate, over both their own individual behaviors and over the group as a whole. In asserting a cultural base for the Jewish group, they may be endorsing Mordecai Kaplan's view of the Jewish people as an "evolving civilization" (Kaplan, 1934). From Kaplan's perspective, American Jews constitute neither a religious nor an ethnic group in the conventional sense; instead they stress a notion of Jewish peoplehood whereby authority lies within the populace. They endorse a religion with few transcendental trappings and a form of nationality without the complications of a separate civil society.

In contemporary America, such a compromise position translates into a cultural identity on the one hand and an ethnic identity on the other. If such is the case, it is no wonder that 70 percent of respondents supported various combinations of the ethnic-cultural identity options, which bring together the two bifurcated modern Jewish collective identities, the religious and the national. Such an ethno-cultural duality may reflect the efforts of contemporary American Jews to reproduce the cohesive premodern group identity of religion-nation in an acceptable, modern, consensus. Such a definition of what it means to be Jewish aims to meet both external American demands and internal Jewish needs. At the same time it marries the remote biblical concept to the more recent European heritage of American Jews.

Whether this kind of "Kaplanesque" solution is acceptable to Jews with strong religious feelings is not clear. Instead, two subcultures within the American Jewish population might be emerging: One expresses its social identity by belonging to religious entities, while the other searches for an ethnic or cultural substitute. The latter group, however, does not have a readily available social outlet within the infrastructure of the American Jewish community. Their personal Jewish identity may lack the reinforcement of social organizations. Consequently a link between personal and social identity may be missing. Such a lack of support on the collective level might make people less committed to their Jewish identity. Moreover, a lack of social support would make it harder for them to transmit their cultural identity across the generations. Since many do opt for a secular or cultural notion of what it means to be a Jew in America, it behooves the organized Jewish community to find a way to support them, lest they and their descendants ultimately lose their Jewishness, a loss that can only hurt the chances of Jewish survival in America.

Notes

1. Revision of a paper presented at the American Sociological Association annual meeting. Cincinnati, Ohio, August 1991.

2. The "core Jewish" category excludes respondents with a Jewish background but who currently follow another non-Judaic religion.

3. See Table 4.2, the MCA Table, where the deviations from the grand mean are given for each category of the explanatory variables.

4. Based on cross tabulation of respondents' current denominational preference by group identity option.

5. Factor analysis is a sophisticated statistical technique for analyzing the relationships among the correlations of a large number of variables. Here the analysis using the Maximum Likelihood Method revealed five factors with eight values greater than 1.0. The 22 items on behavior and attitudes mentioned above and their loading on each of the five factors (using VARIMAX rotation) are presented in Table 4.3.

6. The four scales were checked for reliability using Cronbach's alpha. The Cultural-National scale has reliability of 0.74 (adding the Jewish friends item which has a loading of 0.40 on this factor, does not add to the scale reliability, while it is important in the Jewish environment scale and is included there); the Traditional Religious scale had an alpha reliability of 0.71; the Mainstream Religious scale had an alpha reliability of 0.79; and the Ethnic Network scale had an alpha reliability of 0.69. It should be noted that all scales received high reliability scores and therefore can be used in further analyses. The single item or the fifth factor has a loading of 0.40 on the Cultural National factor and .33 on the mainstream religion factor. Its factor loading on the fifth factor is much higher (0.59). Three items are not included in the five factors. One is synagogue attendance (1 = never, 5 = every week), which has almost an equal loading on four out of five factors (ranging from 0.30 to 0.40). The second, political affiliation (1 = very liberal, 5 = very conservative) does not seem to belong with all the other items, which are specifically Jewish. This item was included in the factor analysis, however, because of the large emphasis in the literature on the liberal and universalistic characteristic of the Jewish culture in

America and the tendency among a large proportion of American Jews to display a liberal political outlook. Lastly, the feeling that anti-Semitism is a danger in America (1 = strongly disagree, 4 = strongly agree), which again was mentioned in the literature as an important part of Jewish identity, had low loadings on all factors.

7. The four scales and all the other items which were part of the factor analysis were entered in a discriminant analysis in which the two identity groups are the dependent variable. However, statistical analysis not reported here showed the advisability of dropping the Ethnic Network scale from the discriminant analysis. When the Ethnic Network scale is dropped from the discriminant equations, the other variables discriminate 64.5 percent of the cases as opposed to 65.1 percent when the network scale is included.

8. It is, however, a "negative" discriminator, that is, when all other variables are controlled for, respondents who scored high on the Cultural Network scale were somewhat more likely not to regard Jews as a religious group. It should be emphasized, however, that this variable had a relatively small structure coefficient: while second, it is still not a particularly strong predictor.

References

Berger, Peter L. and Thomas Luckmann, *The Social Construction of Reality—A Treatise in the Sociology of Knowledge*, New York, Anchor Books, 1967.

Cohen, Steven M., *Content of Continuity? Alternative Bases for Commitment: 1989 National Survey of American Jews*, New York, The American Jewish Committee, 1991.

Eisen, Arnold M., *The Chosen People in America*, Bloomington, Indiana University Press, 1983.

Greeley, Andrew M., "A Note on The Origins of Religious Differences," *Journal for the Scientific Study of Religion*, Volume 3(1), 1963, pp. 21–31.

Herberg, Will, *Protestant, Catholic, Jew: An Essay in American Religious Sociology*, Garden City, New York, Doubleday, 1960.

Kaplan, Mordecai M., *Judaism As a Civilization: Toward a Reconstruction of American-Jewish Life*, New York, Macmillan Company, 1934.

Kosmin, Barry A., S. Goldstein, J. Waksberg, N. Lerer, A. Keysar, and J. Scheckner, *Highlights of the CJF 1990 National Jewish Population Survey*, New York, Council of American Jewish Federations, 1991.

Lenski, Gerhard. E., *The Religious Factor: A Sociological Study of Religion's Impact on Politics, Economics, and Family Life*, Garden City, New York, Doubleday, 1961.

————, *The Religious Factor: A Sociologist's Inquiry*, New York, Doubleday, 1961.

Liebman, Charles S. and Steven M. Cohen, *Two Worlds of Judaism: The Israeli and American Experiences*, New Haven, Yale University Press, 1990.

Woocher, Jonathan, L., *Sacred Survival: The Civil Religion of American Jews*, Bloomington, Indiana University Press, 1986.

5

Jewishness Among the Intermarried

Egon Mayer

Neither shall you make marriages with them: Thy daughter shalt though not give unto his son, nor his daughter shalt thou take unto thy son. For he will turn away thy children following Me, that they may serve other Gods.

Deuteronomy 7

These simple words of the Torah are among the clearest of the relatively sparse textual sources for the age-old Jewish aversion to interfaith marriage. There are two striking features of this ancient Biblical prohibition. One is that it is embedded in a relatively rational explanation. The other is that it conforms quite neatly to both Jewish historical experience and modern, universalist social science theory.

While most of the commandments and prohibitions of the Torah are either given without reason or couched in reasons that are difficult to comprehend, the prohibition against marrying outside the Jewish fold is given in the context of the prohibition against idolatry. The legislator, wanting to insure the continuity of the faith and the people, expresses a common parental concern. The wrong marriage partner can lead one's children from the path one wishes them to follow. The text either assumes that one's own Jewish sons or daughters would not be as effective as the sons or daughters of the Canaanites in attracting their mates to their own people or that even successes are not worth the probable risk of at least occasional failure. Better marry within the tribes of Israel.

In his seminal analysis of the fate of ethnic and religious minorities in the U.S., Gordon (1964) comes to rather similar theoretical conclusions about intermarriage as the Torah—though without the element of prohibition.

Entrance of the minority group into the social cliques, clubs, and institutions of the core society at the primary group level inevitably will lead to a substantial amount of intermarriage . . . The price of such assimilation is the [inevitable] disappearance of the ethnic group as a separate entity and the evaporation of its distinctive values. (80–81)

Most other students of Jewish interfaith marriage, from the playwright Israel Zangwill, who extolled its virtues in his classic *The Melting Pot* (1909), to the much less sanguine Julius Drachsler (1921) and Arthur Ruppin (1940), to the influential Eric Rosenthal (1960, 1963) have also accepted as given that the assimilation of the Jew is the natural, inexorable by-product of exogamous marriage.

The record of modern Jewish history has further fueled the most lachrymose view of intermarriage. For example, Todd M. Endelman writes (1990:6),

It does not take a professional knowledge of Anglo-Jewish history to realize that scores of once prominent Jewish families ceased to be Jewish between the eighteenth century and World War II. . . . The departure of these families, once the pillars of the Jewish establishment, indicates that radical assimilation was not an extraordinary event, a phenomenon on the periphery of Jewish life, but rather a common occurrence, eating away at the maintenance of group solidarity.

As explained in greater detail elsewhere (Mayer, 1989), the taken-for-granted embeddedness of Jewish intermarriage research in assimilation theory has resulted in a rather singular focus upon the *causes* of intermarriage—with the tacit assumption that a better understanding of its causes might lead Jewish parents and the Jewish community to work more effectively to prevent their children from marrying gentiles, thereby fulfilling the commandments of the Torah.

The publication of the first National Jewish Population Survey in 1970 ushered in a new era of concern about intermarriage, both on the programmatic and research fronts. Its finding that the rate of intermarriage among the then recently marrying first wave of the post-War baby-boom generation had climbed to approximately 33 percent sent shock waves of alarm throughout the organized Jewish community. It triggered new calls for redoubled efforts at intermarriage prevention through more effective Jewish education. However, it also raised some previously unasked questions about just how effective the Jewish community's approach can be. Is it possible, some asked, that no amount of Jewish admonition or lamentation might be sufficient to stem the tide of interfaith marriage? Since Jewish parents in the modern world no longer selected the prospective mates of their sons or daughters, as the Torah had envisaged, would it still be possible to engineer—if not control—Jewish mate selection so as to prevent intermarriage?

In the absence of encouraging answers to these questions the focus of Jewish intermarriage research took a radical turn in the mid-1970's when the American Jewish Committee commissioned me to undertake a series of studies which would look not for the *causes* but rather for its *consequences*.

Implicit in the shift of research focus was the recognition that despite the prohibition in the Torah and the age-old Jewish aversion for intermarriage, perhaps not all cases ought to be tarred with the same feather, and that not all the consequences of every intermarriage are equally bad for Jewry. Perhaps, an effective Jewish communal response to intermarriage is not exhausted by programs that seek to prevent it—particularly as they have been noteworthy for their general ineffectiveness—but, rather, it may require that the community attempt to address the consequences of intermarriage in a way that would be more beneficial to the Jewish community; possibly even to the interfaith families involved.

It is that new focus, born of the findings of NJPS 1970 and of the pioneering research efforts of the American Jewish Committee studies of the late 1970's and '80's, which frames the analysis of the 1990 NJPS.

The Thesis

Contrary to the image of intermarriage portrayed in the Torah, and contrary to much of the Jewish historical experience, Jewish intermarriage in modern America does **not** represent the terminus of Jewish identity. Rather, it constitutes an accelerating factor in a multi-generational process of assimilation. Whether that process ultimately culminates in the disappearance of the Jewish heritage in particular families or not depends considerably upon prior factors shaping the strength of Jewish identity and upon the ability of the Jewish community to lend support and reinforcement to weakened Jewish identity. How it might do so will be discussed in the concluding section of this study.

The Sample

The overall methodology of the 1990 NJPS has been amply discussed elsewhere by Kosmin (1991). Therefore this brief methodological digression is offered merely as a reader's guide to the sub-sample of the larger sample, which comprises the data base of this particular study.

In order to understand the possible consequences of intermarriage upon various aspects of Jewish life, the present study focuses principally upon those who are currently married and are in their first marriage. Elsewhere

(Kosmin, Lerer, and Mayer, 1989; Keysar, Kosmin, Lerer, and Mayer, 1991) we have reported upon the complex relationship between intermarriage and remarriage. That subject is intentionally excluded from the present analysis. All the ever-married are included only for the purposes of assessing the impact of intermarriage upon marital stability.

Though seemingly a somewhat esoteric technical matter, this sampling restriction underscores the point that to understand the possible impact of intermarriage upon various aspects of Jewishness it is necessary to distinguish it, as much as possible, from other family circumstances, such as divorce, widowhood, or remarriage.

Thus, this study compares intermarried Jews with in-married Jews, all of whom are currently in their first and only marriage. The former are respondents who indicated that they are now Jewish and/or were born and/or raised as Jews, and are now married to someone who is not Jewish. The latter are identical to the former in all respects, except that they are married to someone who is Jewish.

The Comparative Perspective

The comparisons to be analyzed focus primarily upon those items of the 1990 NJPS questionnaire that are suggestive of the impact of intermarriage upon the Jewishness of individuals and families, and upon the Jewish community. Clearly, there are numerous other dimensions upon which one might wish to compare the two groups, as was done recently by Evan S. Nelson (1991), that do not fall within the present frame of analysis. To a limited extent, the comparison also focuses on two demographic impacts: marital stability and Jewish population composition. Except for these two demographic outcomes, the focus here falls upon Jewish behavior, child-rearing, belonging, participation, and identification.

Demographic Processes

The NJPS of 1970 initially reported that American Jewry consisted of approximately 5.4 million Jews living in about two million households—which also included about 430,000 non-Jews. Successive re-evaluations of the survey have determined that the American Jewish population remains somewhere between 5.5 and six million persons. Its overall growth is slightly diminished by low fertility—probably even less than what is required for zero population growth (ZPG)—but counterbalanced by immigration.

Among the most dramatic findings of the 1970 study was that pertaining to the changing composition of the Jewish family due to intermarriage, i.e., marriage between persons of Jewish parentage and upbringing and persons of non-Jewish parentage and upbringing, as shown in the table below.

Table 5.1 reveals the abruptness of change in Jewish marital selection starting in the early 1960's. While the percentage of Jews marrying a person of non-Jewish origins had remained relatively constant from the early 1940's to the end of the 1950's, it nearly doubled, quite suddenly, from the end of the 1950's to the mid-1960's, and nearly tripled from the mid-1960's to the early 1970's, when the first NJPS was concluded.

It is instructive to note, too, that the percentage of non-Jewish spouses who converted to Judaism had fluctuated from a low of around three percent in the 1940's to a high of 26 percent in the mid-1950's and around 23 percent in the early 1970's. This last statistic is of particular significance because it lends numerical support to the common observation of the early 1970's that the American Jewish community was experiencing an influx of "new Jews," that is converts or "Jews-by-choice," as many preferred to be called.

It is true that intermarriage had been historically associated not only with religious and cultural disloyalty but also with Jewish demographic erosion. However, the trends of the early 1970's raised for the first time the realistic possibility that, at least in the American cultural context, inter- marriage might also produce a large population of converts—with pro-

TABLE 5.1

Percent of Jews Married to Non-Jews by Year of Marriage
(Source: NJPS, 1970/Schmelz & Della Pergola)

Year	Percent	NON-JEWISH SPOUSE CONVERTED?	
		Yes	No
Before 1924	1.7	0.3	1.4
1925–29	2.6	0.5	2.1
1930–34	3.4	0.4	3.0
1935–39	3.9	0.5	3.4
1940–44	5.9	0.2	5.7
1945–49	6.5	0.3	6.2
1950–54	5.1	0.6	4.5
1955–59	6.6	1.7	4.9
1960–64	11.6	1.7	9.8
1965–71	29.2	6.7	22.5
Overall	8.1	1.3	6.8

found implications not only for Jewish demography but for Jewish religious life and culture as well.

Unlike the 1970 study, the 1990 NJPS employed a national probability sample of more than 110,000 U.S. households selected by means of random digit telephone dialing. This method completely avoids any selection biases inherent in organizational lists or "Distinctive Jewish Surnames." Respondents thus contacted were asked to indicate their religion, whatever it might be. In addition, they were asked a series of questions about their own religious background as well as about the backgrounds of other members of the household. As a result of its more sophisticated methodology, the study ultimately found that about four percent of those contacted had some Jewish ancestral connection. Of these respondents 2,441 agreed to participate in the study.

On the basis of this method, the 1990 NJPS found that there are 3.2 million households in the United States today which have at least one person who is of at least some Jewish parentage. Put another way, there are about a third as many more households in 1990 with at least one person of Jewish parentage than there were in 1970.

Given its more precise sampling methodology and its more encompassing selection criteria, this latest NJPS was able to identify not only more households with a Jewish connection but also a much richer variety of ways in which people could be counted as part of the American Jewish population.

As in the 1970 NJPS, intermarriage continues to be the critical variable illuminating the transformation of the American Jewish population. Indeed, probably no other trend in the population has continued to change as rapidly and with such potentially profound consequences as the incidence of intermarriage.

A closer look is provided by Figures 1 and 2. Figure 1 shows that in 1990 only about 69 percent of all married Jews had a spouse who was born and/or raised Jewish too. About another four percent were married to a convert or "Jew-by-choice," and approximately 27 percent were married to non-Jews. As seen in Table 5.1 above, in 1970 the NJPS found that only about eight percent of the married Jewish population had a spouse who was not born and/or raised Jewish.

Figure 2 provides a graphic illustration of the quickening pace of intermarriage in the 20 years since the 1970 NJPS, which helps the reader understand why the overall proportion of intermarriage has risen from eight percent to 31 percent.

Figure 2 indicates that the proportion of born and/or raised Jews marrying a person of the same background has slid from 89 percent among the segment of the population that married prior to 1965, to 69 percent be-

Currently Married Jews-by-Birth
By Religion of Spouse

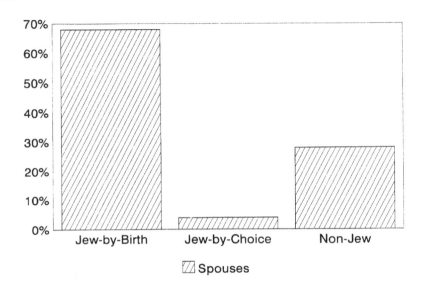

Spouses

Jewish Out-Marriage Pattern
% of Jews who "married out" in all, first, and second marriages

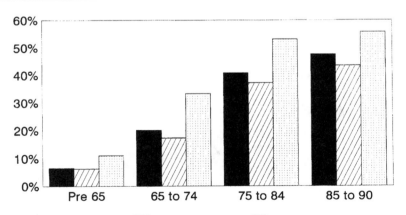

■ All marriages ▨ First marriages ▢ Second marriages

By year of marriage
Jewish = Person born or raised Jewish

71

tween 1965–74, to 49 percent between 1975–84, and further still to 43 percent among those getting married since 1985.

Incidentally, it might be noted that while the 1970 NJPS found the intermarriage rates of marriage cohorts prior to 1965 to be well under 10 percent, the 1990 NJPS found that about 11 percent of that population segment had intermarried. The reason for this discrepancy is probably explained, at least in part, by simple random variation from one sample to another. But, it is probably also due to the more accurate sampling and screening methodology of the later study.

One inevitable consequence of the rise in intermarriages is the commensurate growth in the numbers of people, both adults and children, who are of mixed parentage. As can be seen below, in Figure 3, less than five percent of Jewish adults over the age of 75 are of mixed parentage. But, that proportion has grown steadily throughout the first half of the century, so that among those between ages 18–24 about 35 percent are of mixed parentage.

The progressive growth of the adult (over age 18) population of mixed Jewish parentage has continued inexorably among children under age 18. The entire survey sample included a total of 1,433 children under the age

Jewish Parentage of Respondents
By Age 18+

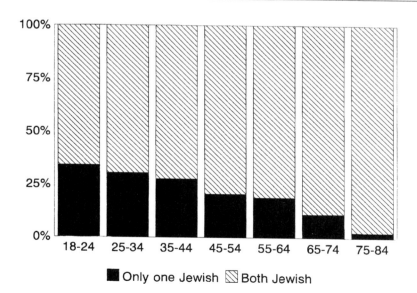

of 18 in 825 households. Table 5.2, below, describes the religious composition of the parental couple in the households where these children live. This particular table reflects responses from households that include terminated marriages and remarriages as well as first marriages.

As can be seen in Table 5.2, in 1990 only a minority (42 percent) of children under age 18 lived with a parental couple that is constituted of two Jews married to one another. Thirty-one percent lived in mixed households and another 15 percent lived in a household where neither member of the parental couple is Jewish. Presumably, the latter are children of formerly intermarried couples who have divorced: the gentile mother obtained custody and then remarried a gentile.

Among single parents, the high probability of remarriage, coupled with the great likelihood of an intermarriage, further increases the likelihood of children being raised in a mixed household even if they were born to two Jewish parents. Perhaps, the most important consequence of this last trend is its apparent "snowball" effect. The adult children of mixed parentage are far more likely to intermarry themselves than are their counterparts who have two Jewish parents. Table 5.3, below, illustrates this finding, while also demonstrating the absence of a significant difference between those of mixed parentage whose mother was Jewish and those whose father was Jewish.

TABLE 5.2
Religious Composition of Parents of Children Under Age 18

Single-parent Jewish	12%
Both parents Jewish	42%
Father Jewish	17%
Mother Jewish	14%
Neither parent Jewish	15%
	100%

TABLE 5.3
Religion of Respondent's Spouse
By Jewish Parentage of Respondent

RELIGION OF SPOUSE	WHICH PARENT IS JEWISH		
	BOTH	MOTHER	FATHER
Jewish-by-upbringing	68	6	5
Jewish-by-choice	4	3	3
Not Jewish	28	91	92
	100	100	100
N =	250	32	37

Though based upon a relatively small sub-set of the total survey sample, Table 5.3 suggests that the intergenerational influence on the likelihood of intermarriage is a significant contributor to its progressive growth.

In addition to fueling the growth in the proportion of children of mixed parentage in the population, intermarriage has also added disproportionately to the incidence of divorce among Jews. When one looks at the everdivorced respondents and compares the distribution of those Jews who were ever intermarried with those who were ever married to other Jews or to Jews-by-choice, the first group constitutes 42 percent of the whole, the second is 53 percent, and the third is five percent of the whole.

An analysis of the total weighted sample found that the religious backgrounds of the spouses of ever-married respondents were distributed as follows:

Spouse born/raised Jewish	65%
Spouse Jew-by-choice	3%
Spouse not Jewish	32%
N = 2.6 million married Jews	

The comparison of the distribution of the ever-married and the everdivorced by the religious background of spouse indicates, yet again, the oft-noted finding that intermarriages are more divorce-prone than endogamous marriages. Although in-married respondents are 65 percent of the ever-married population they are 53 percent of the ever-divorced population. By contrast, the intermarrieds are 32 percent of the ever-married population but comprise 42 percent of the ever-divorced. Respondents who were married to Jews-by-choice or Jews-by-choice who were married to born/raised Jews comprise just three percent of the ever-married population but five percent of the ever-divorced.

Comparative Jewishness: The Public and the Private

Typically, Americans in general, and American Jews in particular, express their identification with voluntary groups and the norms and values those groups represent through public acts of affiliation, participation, and monetary contribution, as well as through private acts, feelings, and attitudes.

The first set of comparisons presented below focuses upon the most objective and external, hence public, expressions of identification as reflected in affiliation with synagogues, other Jewish organizations, and contribution to Jewish charities. On each of these issues the survey ascertained a simple "yes" or "no" response.

I. Synagogue

(a) Affiliation

TABLE 5.4

Is Anyone in Household Currently a Member of a Synagogue,
By Type of Marriage
(Percent)

	MARRIAGE TYPES		
	BJ–BJ	BJ–JBC	BJ–NJ
Yes	57	72	9
No	43	28	91
	100	100	100
N =	619	67	361

Legend: BJ–BJ = both spouses Jewish by upbringing
BJ–JBC = one spouse a Jew-by-choice
BJ–NJ = one spouse not Jewish (intermarriage)

(b) Attendance

TABLE 5.5

Frequency of Synagogue Attendance, By Type of Marriage
(Percent)

	MARRIAGE TYPES		
FREQUENCY	BJ–BJ	BJ–JBC	BJ–NJ
Never/Rarely	33	19	71
Holidays	33	36	21
Monthly	20	37	6
Weekly	14	8	2
	100	100	100
N =	612	67	260

II. Organizations

TABLE 5.6

Is Anyone a Dues-Paying Member of a Jewish Organization,
By Type of Marriage
(Percent)

	MARRIAGE TYPES		
	BJ–BJ	BJ–JBC	BJ–NJ
Yes	27	19	1.4
No	73	81	98.6
	100	100	100.0
N =	197	21	142

As Tables 5.4, 5.5, and 5.6 show, the overwhelming majority of the inter-married affiliate neither with synagogues nor with other Jewish organizations. It is somewhat surprising that within the affiliated minority more maintain ties with synagogues rather than with other Jewish organizations. One might have thought that since intermarried are more likely to be "secular" than "religious," they would opt for organizational rather than synagogue affiliation. It is also instructive to note that more inter-marrieds attend a synagogue, at least sometimes, rather than belong to one.

Affiliation by way of membership affirms a willingness to be counted within the collectivity of one's particular group. As such, it reflects a measure of certainty about ties to a group, a willingness to shoulder its burdens as well as to share in its joys and triumphs, and a desire for some continuity of one's social ties to others in the group. The glaring difference between the affiliation patterns of the in-married and the intermarried no doubt reflects underlying identificational proclivities as well.

III. Contributions

In contrast with affiliation, which may be a relatively strong expression of identification for some, Table 5.7 looks at the pattern of contribution to Jewish charities.

Table 5.7 further illustrates the significant difference between the in-married and the intermarried as regards participation in the life of the organized Jewish community. The intermarried are only a third as likely to contribute to a Jewish cause or charity than in-marrieds. On the other hand, when compared to the previous two tables, Table 5.7 also suggests that Jews in interfaith households are far more likely to make a contribution to a Jewish cause or charity—which involves a relatively lower level of commitment—than to formally affiliate. Why more are apparently willing to give than to join is a question whose answers might shed important light on the meaning of various forms of Jewish belonging and shades of Jewish identity.

In the sections that follow, focus shifts from public expressions of Jewish identification to private ones. Among these are holiday observance in the home, personal practices, beliefs, and attitudes.

IV. Holidays

The 1990 NJPS questionnaire ascertained whether or not the Jewish holidays of Passover, Hanukkah, and Purim are observed and whether or not

TABLE 5.7

Has Anyone in Household Contributed to a Jewish Charity,
By Type of Marriage
(Percent)

	MARRIAGE TYPES		
	BJ–BJ	BJ–JBC	BJ–NJ
Yes	76	73	24
No	24	27	76
	100	100	100
N =	621	67	361

the weekly Shabbat is celebrated by the lighting of candles Friday night. Table 5.8 summarizes the percent of respondents who indicated that these holidays are observed in their homes at least sometimes in some fashion.

Table 5.8 demonstrates, yet again, the oft-noted popularity of Passover and Hanukkah, even among the intermarried. To be sure, it also underscores some robust differences between the in-married and the intermarried, particularly when it comes to the celebration of the weekly Shabbat. It is also instructive to note that a Christmas tree can be found in 13 percent of homes with spouses who are both Jewish by upbringing, 37 percent of homes in which one of the spouses is a Jew-by-choice, and in 87 percent of intermarried homes. In short, the pattern of holiday observances suggests a rather mixed picture among the intermarried. The majority mix celebrations of Passover, Hanukkah, and Christmas in their annual calendar.

In sharp contrast with the observance of popular holidays, the observance of kosher meat consumption is found among fewer than five percent of the intermarried households. However, it is also found among just nine percent of households in which a Jew-by-upbringing is married to a Jew-

TABLE 5.8

Respondents Indicating Home Observance of Jewish Holidays
By Type of Marriage
(Percent)

HOLIDAYS OBSERVED	MARRIAGE TYPES		
	BJ–BJ	BJ–JBC	BJ–NJ
Passover	91	97	60
Hanukkah	87	100	58
Purim	33	58	13
Shabbat	56	75	16
N =	614	67	361

by-choice, while it is found among 30 percent of households where two Jews-by-upbringing are married to each other.

V. Personal Observances

While the observance of holidays reflects upon the identity of the home and family, Jewishness is also reflected in personal behavior and attitudes. Table 5.9 summarizes the pattern of personal observance as measured by fasting on Yom Kippur, refraining from handling money on the Shabbat, and fasting on Ta'anit Esther. These three indicators were used in the survey as telltale measures of more pervasive patterns of personal observance of the complex system of Jewish ritual. As before, this table is designed to show variation between the two types of in-married and the intermarried.

Perhaps, the most striking fact about Table 5.9 is that 27 percent of the intermarried report fasting on Yom Kippur. To be sure, that is a far smaller percentage than those fasting among the in-married. However, as one of the expressions of Jewish identification, it registers a relatively higher percentage of affirmative responses than nearly any other measure listed in previous tables. As such, it suggests that the holiest of the Jewish High Holidays continues to have a holding power over a substantial minority of the intermarried.

Perhaps, one contemporary secular equivalent of Jewish religious observance, at least for a great many American Jews, is acts on behalf of Israel, such as donating money, showing political support, and visiting the Jewish state. Subscribing to and reading Jewish periodicals is yet another way that many have expressed their attachment to the culture of the Jewish folk. Table 5.10 describes the pattern of these expressions of Jewishness among the groups that are under comparison here.

It is evident from Table 5.10 that the intermarried are far less likely to express their sense of Jewish identification in the two secular forms indicated—by visiting Israel and subscribing to Jewish periodicals—than are the in-married.

To further tap the social-secular dimension of Jewish identification, Table 5.11 focuses on the residential choices of respondents: whether or not they live in a "Jewish neighborhood."

Tables 5.10 and 5.11 indicate that the great majority of the intermarried are more likely to be socially isolated from the Jewish community than those who are in-married. Perhaps, these data reflect the intentional choices of the intermarried to be less connected to the Jewish community. Yet, at the same time, the data surely suggest that any effort to retain the

TABLE 5.9
Respondents' Personal Jewish Religious Observances
By Type of Marriage
(Percent)

	MARRIAGE TYPES		
RELIGIOUS OBSERVANCES	BJ–BJ	BJ–JBC	BJ–NJ
Fast on Yom Kippur	66	73	27
No Money on Shabbat	16	8	4
Fast on Ta'anit Esther	7	1	1
N =	620	67	361

TABLE 5.10
Respondents' Personal Jewish Secular Observances
By Type of Marriage
(Percent)

	MARRIAGE TYPES		
SECULAR OBSERVANCES	BJ–BJ	BJ–JBC	BJ–NJ
Visited Israel 1 or +	41	25	9
Subscribes to J Pdcls	42	40	8
N =	620	67	361

TABLE 5.11
The "Jewishness" of Respondents' Neighborhoods
By Type of Marriage
(Percent)

	MARRIAGE TYPES		
JEWISHNESS OF NEIGHBORHOOD	BJ–BJ	BJ–JBC	BJ–NJ
Very/Somewhat	43	31	16
Little/Not at all	57	69	84
	100	100	100
N =	611	67	355

connection between the intermarried and the organized Jewish community has to range much more widely than efforts at maintaining contact with the in-married.

VI. Attitudes

Many Americans, Jewish and gentile alike, find a sense of religious and/or ethnic identity in a worldview which is generally expressed in subjectively held attitudes. In order to measure this dimension of identification the survey questionnaire included a number of items to which differing responses may be said to reflect differing patterns of Jewish identification. These items included the following:

(1) How important would you say that being Jewish is in your life?
(2) How important is it to you that your neighborhood have a Jewish character?
(3) Would you agree or disagree that when it comes to a crisis Jews can only depend on other Jews?
(4) How emotionally attached are you to Israel?

While, as shown in Table 5.12, the in-married continue to differ significantly from the intermarried on the four attitudinal items, much as they differ on all other items of comparison, it is interesting to note that 59 percent of the intermarried affirmed that "Being Jewish is important or very important to me." It is equally noteworthy that nearly a third prefer to live in a "Jewish neighborhood." Whatever the psychological or ideational content of these attitudes, they clearly do not reveal a straightforward march toward Jewish oblivion.

TABLE 5.12
*Percent of Respondents Expressing Positive Jewish Attitudes,
By Type of Marriage*

	MARRIAGE TYPES		
ATTITUDES	BJ–BJ	BJ–JBC	BJ–NJ
1. Being Jewish	92	95	59
2. Jewish neighborhood	62	60	31
3. Depending on Jews	51	43	21
4. Attached to Israel	44	29	12

VII. Child-Rearing
(a) Adult-children

Ultimately, whatever form Jewish identification takes in the life of individual Jews, be they intermarried or not, its test of significance for the
continuity of the Jewish people is determined by whether they raise children who will identify as Jews. As was shown in Fig. 3, the percentage of
adults who are of mixed (Jewish-gentile) parentage has grown steadily over
the past 60 years.

The section that follows examines the possible impact of intermarriage
upon the prospects of Jewish upbringing in the subsequent generation.
The first step in that analysis is to look at the Jewishness of adult respondents who themselves are the products of intermarriage. There are a total
of 159 cases in the sample about whom information was available, as shown
in Table 5.13.

As this table indicates, adults who are of mixed Jewish-gentile parentage
are far less likely to identify as Jewish by religion than are those who are the
children of two Jewish parents. Conversely, many more of the former than
the latter are likely to respond to a question about their own religious
identity as "other or none." One important question about this pattern is
the meaning that respondents attach to "other or none." As was shown
earlier, in Table 5.8 for example, a high proportion of the intermarried
celebrate such Jewish holidays as Passover and Hanukkah. It would appear
that a sizeable proportion of those people may not regard themselves as
Jewish by religion, yet remain attached in some respects to Judaism
through their families.

Coincidentally, Table 5.13 also belies the conventional wisdom that
Jewish mothers who are intermarried are more likely to produce Jewish
children than are intermarried Jewish fathers. There is some indication
from the data that Jewish mothers are likely to try harder.

Responses to a question inquiring about whether the respondent did or
did not receive any formal Jewish education are summarized in Table 5.14.
It should be noted that this table refers to the experiences of adult survey
respondents regarding their own Jewish education. A subsequent section
will focus separately upon what respondents reported about how they are
raising their own children.

Whether the great majority of adults who are of mixed parentage did not
receive any formal Jewish education because of an absence of desire on the
part of their parents to provide it or because of a lack of sufficient opportunity remains an open question. In any case, the net results of the comparison are quite clear. Other indicators, listed in the table below, also

Egon Mayer

TABLE 5.13
Current Religious Identification of Respondents
By Jewishness of Parents
(Percent)

| | WHICH PARENT IS/WAS JEWISH | | |
RELIGION OF RESPONDENT	BOTH	FATHER	MOTHER
Jewish	88	30	31
Catholic	—	7	14
Protestant	1	9	17
Other/None	11	54	38
	100	100	100
N =	529	81	78

TABLE 5.14
Did Respondent Receive Any Formal Jewish Education,
By Jewishness of Parents
(Percent)

| | WHICH PARENT IS/WAS JEWISH | | |
	BOTH	FATHER	MOTHER
Yes	82	26	32
No	18	74	68
	100	100	100
N =	529	81	78

describe a greatly diminished sense of Jewishness among the adult children of the intermarried, as compared with their counterparts whose parents are both Jewish.

As a partial explanation of these differences one might surmise, quite simply, that two parents of the same religious/ethnic background are likely to be at least twice as effective in imparting a sense of their joint heritage to their children than a parent acting alone. What other explanatory factors might be at work will have to be determined by further research.

By now the major thrust of Table 5.15 is hardly surprising. Far fewer of the adult children of mixed parentage express a sense of their Jewishness than is the case for the children of two Jewish parents. However, what does stand out is the relatively high proportion (52–58 percent) who maintain that "Being Jewish is Important" to them. The majority of respondents of mixed parentage appear to attach a subjective significance to the Jewish portion of their identity, even when they do not express it in more substantial behavioral terms. Thus, one question that remains is whether that

TABLE 5.15

Percentage of Affirmative Response to Questions
Indicating Jewish Identification By Jewishness of Parents

	WHICH PARENT IS/WAS JEWISH		
INDICATOR OF JEWISHNESS	BOTH	FATHER	MOTHER
Belongs to Synagogue	41	9	10
Close Friends in Israel	31	14	18
Mostly Jewish Friends	44	12	9
Jewishness Important	85	52	58
Attends a Seder	86	45	46
Hanukkah Candles	81	36	34
Fast on Yom Kippur	58	26	15
Subscribes to J Pdcls	31	10	10
Been to Israel	36	5	9
N =	529	81	78

subjective significance is of such nature and priority that it might be responsive to Jewish communal outreach.

(b) Younger Children

The previous section has looked at the consequences of child-rearing in the lives of adult respondents. In this final descriptive section, the focus shifts to the reported child-rearing practices of respondents with respect to their own children under 18. First, and foremost, Table 5.16 looks at what religion parents ascribe to their children.

What Table 5.16 suggests most clearly is that most intermarried families have not chosen sides. While a large minority have chosen to raise their children as Jews, Catholics, or Protestants, the majority have either opted for some syncretic alternate of their own design or simply have not chosen to raise their children in any religion. Whether this large group in a sort of gray area is treated as a "loss" to the Jewish community or simply an opportunity to be explored is largely a matter of perspective.

It is instructive to note, as shown in Table 5.17, that while the majority of the in-married are providing their children with some type of formal Jewish education, less than 10 percent of the intermarried are doing so.

It should be added that of the intermarrieds described in Table 5.17, 12 percent indicated that their children are receiving some type of non-Jewish religious education. That figure taken together with the nine percent who are receiving some type of Jewish education suggests that nearly 80 percent are not receiving any type of formal religious education.

TABLE 5.16

In What Religion Are Children Raised,
By Type of Marriage

RELIGION	MARRIAGE TYPES		
	BJ–BJ	BJ–JBC	BJ–NJ
Jewish	91	100	21
Catholic	—	—	15
Protestant	—	—	10
Other/none	9	—	54
	100	100	100
N =	235	42	218

TABLE 5.17

Are Children Receiving Formal Jewish Education,
By Type of Marriage
(Percent)

	MARRIAGE TYPES		
	BJ–BJ	BJ–JBC	BJ–NJ
Yes	60	67	9
No	40	33	91
	100	100	100
N =	235	42	218

Descriptive Summary

The 17 tables and several graphs presented thus far clearly indicate a much weaker sense of Jewish identity among the intermarried and their children than is found among Jews who are married to other Jews and their children. There is, however, also a fair indication of certain residual ties to Jewish identification among the intermarried, such as subjective feelings about the importance of one's Jewishness, certain holiday practices that can be enjoyed with one's family, and even a desire on the part of many to live in Jewish neighborhoods that are not nearly as attenuated as more formal religious and organizational ties.

The two questions that remain to be addressed in this report are: (a) To what extent can one attribute the differences between the in-married and the intermarried to the fact of intermarriage itself? and (b) What can the Jewish community do to retain and strengthen the connection between itself and interfaith families?

Explaining the Differences Between the In-married and the Intermarried

It should be readily apparent that none of the differences among the three comparison groups on the items of behavior, affiliation, or attitude described in the preceding tables can be regarded as solely the by-product of intermarriage. Indeed, it is entirely possible that some of the differences are merely circumstantial, resulting from factors not looked at in the present study.

With this concern in mind 11 independent variables were identified as having some possible influence on the differences between the groups. First among these, of course, was the question of (a) whether or not a respondent was intermarried and in a first marriage. The other independent variables included:

(b) the year in which respondent got married
(c) whether respondent had just one or two Jewish parents
(d) in what branch of Judaism was respondent raised
(e) whether respondent was male or female
(f) how much Jewish education respondent received
(g) what was highest academic degree received
(h) age of respondent
(i) whether there are children under 18 in household
(j) how many of respondent's grandparents US-born
(k) whether respondent had Bar/Bat Mitzvah

These 11 variables were entered into a series of regression equations that treated various of the indicators of Jewish identification as outcome, or dependent variables. That statistical procedure has provided a glimpse into the relative influence of intermarriage, in combination with the other factors, upon the variety of Jewish identity outcomes that were examined in previous tables. Table 5.18 provides a brief outline summary indicating which of the above-listed independent variables have proven to be significantly related to the observed differences between the in-married and the intermarried.

From this somewhat cryptic table it is possible to discern that, in fact, intermarriage (a) is an important source of influence upon most measures of Jewishness, even when other possible factors are controlled for. However, in no case is it a single source of influence. Indeed, in every instance it acts together with the branch of Judaism (d) in which the respondent was raised. To a greater or lesser extent, for each of the six outcome variables outlined above, it also acts together with such background factors as: the

TABLE 5.18

A Summary of Statistically Significant Relationships
Between Selected Independent Variables and the Differential
Expressions of Jewishness Between In-Married and Intermarrieds

(*Indicates Statistical Significance*)

SELECTED	ELEVEN INDEPENDENT VARIABLES										
OUTCOME VARIABLES	A	B	C	D	E	F	G	H	I	J	K
Synagogue belonging	*	*	ns	*	ns	ns	ns	*	*	ns	ns
Synagogue attendance	*	ns	ns	*	ns	*	*	ns	ns	ns	ns
Been to Israel	ns	ns	ns	*	ns	ns	*	ns	ns	ns	ns
Jewish rituals index	*	ns	ns	*	ns	ns	ns	ns	*	*	ns
Communal partc index	*	ns	ns	*	*	ns	ns	ns	ns	ns	*
Jewish attitudes	*	ns	ns	*	*	ns	ns	ns	ns	ns	ns

year in which respondent got married (b); age of respondent (h); and whether there are children in the household (i).

Interestingly, the only background factor that appears to have no significant influence on the Jewishness of respondents, when all other sources of influence are controlled, is whether they were born to two Jewish parents or one. Other background variables that proved to have relatively small influence on outcome variables are Jewish education and whether respondent had a Bar or Bat Mitzvah. In short, it would seem that influences from one's family of origin and from the nature of one's current family were the most important in shaping one's Jewishness. Formal educational influences played a less important role.

Implications for Policy:
Toward a New Agenda of Jewish Survival

The great growth in the numbers of intermarrieds poses an unprecedented challenge to the modern American Jewish community. Will American Jewry survive the demographic revolution that is now being wrought upon it by intermarriage? And, will it retain its organizational strength and cultural vitality into the twenty-first century despite the transformation of the Jewish family? It must, and I believe it can survive. To do so we must think beyond the debates now raging in response to the challenges of intermarriage. We must embark on a new strategy of communal survival that differs sharply from the strategies of the past.

In the past century, the central challenges to Jewish group survival have been framed by pogroms, the Holocaust, the rebirth of the State of Israel, and the salvaging of remnant Jewish populations in beleaguered lands. Each of these challenges has been met with the outpouring of extraordinary amounts of political creativity and voluntary group activity on the part of America's Jews.

However, the successful meeting of these challenges has conditioned the Jewish community to deal with its problems by essentially reactive, defensive measures. These are not likely to serve us well in the decades ahead. Needed are more pro-active, culturally and even politically assertive measures that have been rather foreign to the Jewish style in America.

The Traditional Survivalist Agenda

From the dawn of the liberal era in late eighteenth and early nineteenth century Europe, the majority of Jews opted for social, religious, and cultural adaptability as a strategy for group survival. The operative slogan for the Jewish *modus vivendi* was "Be a Jew in your home and a citizen on the street." As part of this strategy, liberal Jews argued that Jewish survival is best secured by three factors: tolerance, law, and social invisibility.

Tolerance was tacitly understood to mean a socio-political climate in which gentiles did not single out Jews for any special deprivation simply because of their Jewishness. It was perceived as generalized social amiability, or at the very least a benign neglect of those aspects of personal belief and religious practice that distinguished Jew from gentile.

Laws that protect civil rights and liberties came to be seen as the best guarantee of tolerance. Consequently, Jews as individuals and Jewish organizations became the foremost champions of civil rights and liberal social legislation.

Social invisibility was the Jewish side of this implied social compact. In return for tolerance and even hospitality, most Jews (with the exception of some Orthodox and Hasidic Jews) implicitly agreed not to display publicly their religious beliefs, practices, speech, manner of dress, or anything else that might visibly differentiate them from their gentile neighbors. Such is the strategy of Jewish survival that Norman Podhoretz (1967:27) called the "brutal bargain." It traded the cultural distinctiveness of the **visible** Jew for the entree that the **invisible** Jew might enjoy in the majoritarian society.

Brutal as a bargain or not, there can be little doubt that most Jews believed significant public displays of Jewish religious or cultural distinctiveness would risk the tolerance of their neighbors. Jews would enjoy the benefits of tolerance by "fitting in" with neighbors, and restricting their cultural and religious distinctiveness to the home and the synagogue.

The success of this three-part strategy hinged on one very important assumption: that with the social, political, and economic benefits that flowed from tolerance, Jews could better enjoy and express their own culture in the private domain. This assumption further rested directly on the Jewish continuity of the home.

Yet, even as Jews succeeded in protecting their civil rights through liberal laws and in securing the tolerance and amiability of their gentile neighbors, they became less and less distinctive in their religious beliefs and life-style. Acceptance from the outside, it seems, was increasingly reciprocated by blending from the inside.

Second and third generation children of Jewish immigrant parents understood fewer and fewer of the terms of the "brutal bargain." Their own social mobility experiences placed increasing pressure on young American Jews to become just like their gentile peers. On the other hand, their increasing distance from immigrant ancestors has rapidly attenuated the hold of tradition on their lives. Thus, they have come to take for granted that their lack of Jewish distinctiveness in the public domain should also prevail in the private domain. In this process, Jewishness has become an identity "brand label" in a pluralistic society, with little more distinctiveness of content than the brands of a multitude of packaged goods. As such, its primary purpose, like many brand labels, is to provide a focal point for the reference group identification that is so highly valued in America. Most Jews want to be known as "Jews" so that they are not perceived as people without a group identity. On the other hand, they have no desire to limit their choices in social participation as a result of being Jewish.

One consequence of this transformation of Jewish identity is that as young Jews have entered the free-choice American marriage market, they have found less and less reason to filter out their gentile friends as potential marriage partners. Not only are their friends more like themselves in all respects, save identity label, but the families and homes they plan on forming would also not be distinctively Jewish.

If Jewish parents and Jewish leaders have been distressed about the rising rate of intermarriage, surely one reason is that they have seen the unanticipated consequences of their own survival strategy boomerang in the lives of their children and grandchildren. In short, intermarriage has been one of the inescapable costs of the "brutal bargain." For that reason, efforts to stem its tide have proven generally ineffective.

The private nature of the act, along with the fact that it seems to spring from values such as love, the desire for personal fulfillment, and egalitarianism that are deeply cherished by contemporary American Jews, have made intermarriage a far more difficult challenge than some of the histori-cally more familiar ones that Jews have had to face in their struggle for survival. The familiar strategies of securing Jewish survival not only can-not work with intermarriage, but may even do more harm than good.

With the knowledge gained from more than a dozen years of my own research on intermarriage and from such seminal journalistic accounts of intermarried life as Paul and Rachel Cowan's *Mixed Blessings* (1987), and more recently the works of Judy Petsonk and Jim Remsen (1988), and Susan Weidman Schneider (1989), we now know that intermarriage does not erode Jewish identity and family life in the simple linear fashion that figured so prominently in the alarmist literature of earlier decades. At the risk of exaggerating the influence of these studies, it is probably fair to say that they have helped change the climate of Jewish opinion about intermar-riage, from **outrage** to **outreach,** in just a few years.

Changes in the perception of intermarriage have gradually led to changes in the Jewish communal response to it as well. In 1979, a task force, subsequently to become the Commission on Reform Jewish Out-reach by the Union of American Hebrew Congregations, was created un-der the leadership of David Belin. That institution served as the first modern attempt to alter the course of what seemed just a decade earlier like the inexorable force of American Jewish history.

By the mid-1980's a variety of Jewish outreach programs to the inter-married had begun to be developed in such different institutional contexts as Reform temples, Jewish family service agencies, and Jewish community centers.

Even as outrage against intermarriage and intermarrieds has gradually begun to give way to greater acceptance and to programs of Jewish inclu-sion, new questions have arisen about the possible effect of outreach on Jewish survival. For example, does outreach serve as a legitimation of intermarriage, increasing its likelihood because of the more hospitable attitude of the Jewish community? Does outreach threaten to dilute the Jewish integrity of the community by including Jews-by-choice whose authenticity as Jews is not universally accepted? Does outreach really ex-tend the hospitality of the Jewish community to those who might otherwise not have come in, or does it simply hold open the door to those who were on their way in anyway?

Then, there are questions about the proper methods and objectives of Jewish outreach: Should it be undertaken with the explicit goal of convert-ing the non-Jewish partners in intermarriages? Should it have other goals, such as improving the marital relationship of the couple? Is outreach essen-tially an educational activity, or a missionary one? Is it therapy by another name, carried out by Jews who did not go on to become licensed psychotherapists as so many of their brothers and sisters have done? These questions, in turn, touch on further concerns within the Jewish community such as who is best qualified to deal with the intermarried, and what the appropriate institutional and ideological premises are.

These questions underscore the point that the challenge intermarriage poses for the American Jewish community is not readily resolved by either conversion or outreach. Both of these solutions create further problems. However, the critical questions that have been raised about outreach and conversion thus far have not addressed what I believe is a more fundamental issue: that even successful outreach and widely accepted conversions challenge the Jewish community's tacit assumptions about group survival.

To the extent that Jewish outreach is successful, it must inevitably challenge the Jewish penchant for social invisibility.

Toward a New Agenda of Jewish Survival

As outreach has become an increasingly common response to Jewish intermarriage, it has raised numerous questions of strategy, practice, purpose, and method. Nevertheless, all its current forms have been marked by a number of common features. The various Jewish outreach efforts that have been undertaken thus far are characterized by their common focus on the Jewish "internal agenda," i.e., a focus on Jewish survival issues, and issues of institutional strategy. Furthermore, regardless of sponsorship or purpose, they have concentrated on issues of program curriculum, e.g., Jewish life-cycle and calendar celebration, or on an introduction to synagogue practice and etiquette, personnel and methods of instruction, and qualities of the setting and recruitment. None have addressed the broader question of how outreach relates to the long-standing commitment of most Jews to social and cultural invisibility in the public domain.

If outreach is to succeed, it must confront the question of how Jews as individuals and the Jewish community as an organized entity confront the wider society. That question is not about the techniques of programming, or teaching style, or recruitment. It is not simply about making the "stranger" feel more welcome. Ultimately, that question is about how Jews as individuals comport themselves vis-à-vis their gentile neighbors, and how the organized Jewish community represents itself in the public.

No community can depend solely on the efforts of its most exemplary members for collective survival. It must also develop institutional strategies that bolster the abilities of its ordinary members. Thus, the challenge that remains for the Jewish outreach enterprise is to articulate a new vision of Jewish survival.

I believe that vision must remain committed to at least two of the three principles of the traditional tri-part strategy: that is, to ever broadening the climate of tolerance in society for all cultures, and doing so by strong political advocacy for laws that guarantee civil liberties and social justice.

On the other hand, if Jewish outreach is to have more than episodic relevance to just a few individuals, it must finally reject the posture of Jewish social invisibility that has been the lot of Jewry in the liberal modern world. It must take Judaism as a religion and Jewishness as a culture and civilization public and stake its claim to a fair share of the public's attention. How this is to be done is the challenge that lies ahead for effective Jewish outreach.

Some of the ways that Judaism might be taken more public are suggested by the struggles of blacks and Hispanics to improve their image. The pressures brought to bear in recent years on advertising and media executives, on the publishers of textbooks and educational policymakers, have clearly borne fruit in changing the public image of those communities. Jews might well consider advocating for:

- more positive, identifiably Jewish characters, themes, and images on the major networks (particularly in major urban markets where Jews comprise a significant segment of the consumer population);
- the inclusion of more Jewish cultural content in high school and college textbooks and courses, particularly in the humanities and social sciences;
- the restoration of Hebrew as a language option in high schools and colleges;
- the greater inclusion of Judaica in the holdings of local libraries, in the exhibition schedules of museums, and in the programs of community-sponsored theaters and symphonies;
- greater cultural exchange with Israel and other significant centers of Jewish culture around the world.

What effect these various strategies might have on the actual rate of intermarriage is impossible to predict. They may well have no impact at all. They are, however, likely to enhance the self-image of Jews in ways that are public and accessible to non-Jews as well. As such, they can provide the open door to Jewish civilization through which all who wish to come in may do so.

References

Cowan, Paul & Rachel Cowan, *Mixed Blessings*, New York, Doubleday, 1987.
Drachsler, Julius, *Intermarriage in New York City*, New York, Columbia University, 1921.

Endelman, Todd M., *Radical Assimilation in English Jewish History, 1656–1945*, Bloomington, Ind., Indiana University Press, 1990.

Gordon, Milton, *Assimilation in American Life*, New York, Oxford University Press, 1964.

Kosmin, Barry A., Nava Lerer & Egon Mayer, *Intermarriage, Divorce, and Remarriage Among American Jews, 1982–87*, North American Jewish Data Bank, Family Research Series # 1, August, 1989.

Mayer, Egon, *Intermarriage and the Jewish Future*, New York, American Jewish Committee, 1979.

———, *Children of Intermarriage*, New York, American Jewish Committee, 1983.

———, *Conversion Among the Intermarried*, New York, American Jewish Committee, 1987.

———, *Love and Tradition: Marriage Between Jews and Christians*, New York, Schocken Books, 1989.

———, "Intermarriage Research at the American Jewish Committee: Its Evolution and Impact," in *Facing the Future: Essays on Contemporary Jewish Life*, Steven Bayme, ed., New York: American Jewish Committee, 1989.

Nelson, Evan S., "Psychological Dynamics in Intermarriages," in *The Imperatives of Jewish Outreach*, Egon Mayer, ed., New York, Jewish Outreach Institute, 1991.

Petsonk, Judy and Jim Remsen, *The Intermarriage Handbook: A Guide For Jews & Christians*, New York, William Morrow & Co., 1988.

Podhoretz, Norman, *Making It*, New York, Random House, 1967.

Rosenthal, Erich, "Studies in Jewish Intermarriage in the US" *American Jewish Yearbook*, New York, American Jewish Committee, 1963.

Ruppin, Arthur, *The Jewish Fate and Future*, London, The Macmillan Co., 1940.

Schmelz, Uziel O. and Sergio DellaPergola, "The Demographic Consequences of U.S. Jewish Population Trends," *in American Jewish Yearbook*, New York, American Jewish Committee, 1983.

Schneider, Susan Weidman, *Intermarriage: The Challenge of Living With Differences*, New York, Free Press, 1989.

Sklare, Marshall, "Intermarriage and the Jewish Future," *Commentary*, Volume 37 (4), (April, 1965), pp. 46–52.

———, "Intermarriage and Jewish Survival," *Commentary*, Volume 43(4), (March, 1970), pp. 51–58.

Zangwill, Israel, *The Melting Pot*, New York, The Macmillan Co., 1909.

6

Intermarriage, Assimilation, and Social Structure

Bruce A. Phillips

Introduction

The most discussed findings of the 1990 National Jewish Population Survey (NJPS) are those concerning the sharp rise in intermarriage in America, usually interpreted by the press, the organized Jewish community, and sociologists as an indication of the eventual assimilation and disappearance of American Jewry. Milton Gordon, for example, in his landmark work *Assimilation in American Life* (1964) described intermarriage as the final stage of assimilation for a minority group.

An alternative to the assimilation model is the social structural model, which "explains social life—the forms of people's associations—in terms of such structural features as size, number, and crosscutting boundaries of groups" (Blau, Blum, & Schwartz, 1982, p. 45). The key concept in this model is "constraint": Individual choices (including marriage) are constrained by social structural factors which affect the availability of partners and the likelihood of meeting them (Blau, Beeker, & Fitzpatrick, 1984a; Blum, 1985). I have shown elsewhere, for example, that the rate of intermarriage is affected by the size of the Jewish community (Phillips, 1989). The rate of intermarriage is higher in Milwaukee than in Chicago, only a hundred miles way. The Jews are more geographically concentrated in Milwaukee than in Chicago, which should lead to easier availability of Jewish mates and tend to create more pressure to adhere to community norms of endogamy (Phillips & Weinberg, 1984), but there are 10 times as many Jews in Chicago as in Milwaukee, and thus the intermarriage rate is lower.

If social structural constraints even partly explain Jewish intermarriage, then it is not the product of Jewish assimilation exclusively. In this study intermarriage is analyzed as the result of a complex interrelationship between both assimilation and social structural constraints. Before Jewish communal policy concerning intermarriage can be effective, it must take these complexities into account. This study is a step in that direction.

Methodology

The data presented here come from the 1990 National Jewish Population Survey (NJPS). Specifically, this study analyzes information provided about the current and previous marriages of respondents and their spouses. Given the complexity of the issues examined here, three questions must be carefully addressed: who is a Jew; what is a marriage; and what constitutes an intermarriage?

Who Is a Jew?

The National Jewish Population Survey took a "wide-angle" picture of American Jewry. A series of five questions in the NJPS questionnaire allowed respondents to explain in what way they are Jewish: Religion of birth, religion raised in, Jewish lineage, conversion, and Jewish self-identification.

In order to classify the broad scope of Jewish identities captured in the NJPS, four categories of Jewish self-definition are utilized in this analysis. The first category is *Born Jewish-Religion Jewish*. These are persons who were born and/or raised Jewish and consider themselves Jewish by religion. *Secular Jews* were born and/or raised Jewish, but identify with no religion. These two categories taken together comprise what I call "conventional Jews." Non-conventional Jews are similarly comprised of two categories: persons of *Jewish descent* who do not identify as Jews (in most cases they were raised in another religion); and *Jews who practice another religion* but nonetheless identify as Jews.

Some people refer to these two different categories as "core" and "marginal" Jews, respectively, but I prefer "conventional" and "non-conventional," which are more neutral terms. By far the most common category (Table 6.1) is "Jews by religion" (67.4 percent). Less common are secular Jews (14.6 percent), Jews who practice other religions (10.0 percent), and persons of Jewish descent who do not themselves identify as Jewish (5.1 percent).

Jews by Choice are the final category of Jewish status used in the NJPS,

TABLE 6.1
*Jewish Self-Definition of
Ever-Married Respondents and Their Spouses*

Jewish Self-Definition	Number of Cases Unweighted		Number of Cases Weighted[1]		Weighted Percent
	Ever Married Respondents	Married Spouses	Ever Married Respondents	Married Spouses	Respondents & Spouses
Jew by Religion	1279	671	1195	584	67.4%
Secular Jew	250	89	285	102	14.6%
Jewish Descent[2]	111	3	131	3	5.1%
Other Religion[3]	204	0	264	0	10.0%
TOTAL	1844	763	1875	689	100.0%

[1] The Weighted N adjusts the original weights used in the NJPS so that the total number of weighted cases will be approximately the same as the total number of unweighted cases.

The NJPS data were weighted to accurately reflect the distribution of American Jewish households. These weights were applied to each marriage in the analysis in such a way as to make the number of weighted cases similar to the number of unweighted cases. Only the number of *weighted* cases are shown in the tables, but these closely approximate the number of *unweighted* cases so as not to artificially inflate statistical significance. Altogether there are 3056 *unweighted* cases, or marriage choices, in the analysis, and 3036 *weighted* cases.

[2] Persons who had a Jewish parent but DO NOT CONSIDER THEMSELVES JEWS. In many cases they were raised in another religion or in no religion.

[3] Persons who practice another religion and BUT STILL CONSIDER THEMSELVES JEWS.

but they are only indirectly included here as part of the definition of intermarriage. The NJPS does include some respondents who are Jews by Choice, but they are excluded from this analysis because they were not born Jews and thus would confuse the analysis of factors that are associated with Jewish intermarriage. They are, however, counted as Jewish spouses in endogamous marriages.

What Is a Marriage?

Respondents in the NJPS were asked about current and/or former spouses. Included here as individual cases, in addition to the respondents, are all current and previous Jewish spouses. In addition to augmenting the numerical base, this approach has expanded the scope of the analysis as well.

Most discussions of intermarriage are based on current marriages only. This technique provides an estimate of the number of intermarriages in a given community and facilitates comparisons among communities or the same community over time (Phillips, 1989; Tobin & Lipsam, 1985). Since divorced respondents are not counted among current marriages, studying only current marriages provides an incomplete picture of the extent of intermarriage.[1] The 1990 NJPS did ask about previous spouses of both divorced and remarried respondents and their mates. To take advantage of the wealth of material on intermarriage included in the 1990 NJPS, the data set used here is comprised of all marriages of Jewish respondents and Jewish spouses, including both intact and dissolved marriages. The data set was constructed as follows:

Current Marriages

A currently married couple in which both partners are Jewish contribute two "cases" to the analysis. The respondent contributes the first case, and the spouse contributes the second case, even though it is the same marriage. The analysis is of two Jewish *individuals* and their marriage choices. An in-marriage consists of two individuals who have both chosen to marry Jews.

A mixed marriage contributes only one case: the respondent (who is always a Jew in the NJPS). Information about non-Jewish spouses is important for a more complete understanding of intermarriage, but that analysis is beyond the scope of this paper.

Dissolved Marriages

Marriages are dissolved by death, divorce, or legal separation (here grouped with divorce). After a marriage has dissolved, the individual may later remarry. The analysis here includes all the dissolved marriages of respondent and spouse for which data were available. Two kinds of dissolved marriages could not be included in the analysis. Because of the complexity of the skip patterns in the questionnaire, no information was collected about previous spouses of currently *separated* respondents[2] nor about the most recent marriages of respondents who were divorced from their second marriages.[3]

Counting Marriages in the Analysis

Students of intermarriage can look at current marriages only, but that leaves out marriages which have dissolved. Marriages that have ended tend to be intermarriages (as will be demonstrated), and thus restricting the analysis to current marriages underestimates the extent of intermarriage. It also means using only data about the respondent, and thus data about Jewish spouses are left out. If, for example, a Jewish male who was raised Conservative is married to a Jewish female who was raised Reform, data are lost about both women and Reform Jews. Since marriage is an individual choice, this study is an analysis of *individuals* rather than marriages: respondents and spouses (if they are born Jews) are both included as individuals.

But what about individuals who have been married twice? Which marriage is used in the analysis? If a person married a Jew the first time and a non-Jew the second time, is that person counted only as an intermarriage? In this analysis both marriages are used, which makes it possible to factor in the impact of remarriage.

This approach takes advantage of the wealth of marriage data collected by NJPS but complicates the terminology. Although data about individuals are used, this is not strictly a study of individuals, since more than one marriage may be used for a single individual. However, using the term "marriages" generally implies that *couples* are being counted. Instead, I introduce the somewhat awkward term "marriage choices." The logic here is that a twice-married person has made two marriage choices. Since the NJPS included both choices in the questionnaire, both are included in this analysis.

A given household in the NJPS can contribute a maximum of four marriage choices to the analysis. This is the case for two Jews who have both been previously married. Here, each Jew contributes the current marriage (two marriage choices) as well each of their dissolved marriage choices (two more marriage choices). Two Jews who are each married for the first time would contribute two marriage choices: the current marriage for the respondent and for the spouse. If one of those two had been previously married, then three marriage choices would appear in the analysis (current marriage for respondent, current marriage for spouse, and the previous marriage of one spouse). A mixed-married household in which the Jew is married for the first time would contribute only the current marriage choice of the Jewish partner (i.e., one marriage choice). The same is true of a currently divorced or widowed Jew who would contribute data only about the previous marriage.

Table 6.2 presents the number of cases or marriage choices contributed to the analysis by each of eight different marriage configurations. The NJPS contained 1,410 married households (see upper left-hand cells of Table 6.2). Of these, 763 were in-marriages, resulting in 1526 marriage choices (763 respondents plus 763 current spouses). Because 288 of the currently married respondents and 94 of the Jewish spouses had been previously married, 382 additional marriage choices are contributed to the analysis. These latter 382 cases are detailed in the first two rows of the third section of Table 6.2, under the heading "First Marriages Which Have Dissolved."

An additional 430 marriage choices are contributed by currently divorced, separated, or widowed respondents (shown in the second section of Table 6.2). Of these, 359 were divorced, separated, or widowed from a first marriage, and another 71 were divorced separated, or widowed from a second marriage. The latter should have contributed both their most recent and their first marriage choices. However, as explained earlier, the skip pattern in the questionnaire did not anticipate so much divorce, and data about the most recent marriage choices of twice-divorced respondents were not collected.

Defining Intermarriage

Given the multiple categories of Jewish self-definition in the NJPS, any definition of what constitutes an intermarriage requires some explanation. As noted above, this analysis includes both "Core" or "Conventional" Jews, as well as "Marginal" or "Non-conventional" Jews. For current marriage choices, an intermarriage is defined as a marriage between any kind of Jew[4] and a spouse who is either: a) a non-Jew (without conversion), or b) a Jew practicing another religion, or c) a person of Jewish descent only who does not currently identify as a Jew. These categories apply only to currently married respondents and spouses because previous spouses were not described in such great detail in the NJPS questionnaire. In the case of previous marriage choices, the respondent was asked only whether the previous spouse was "born Jewish," "converted to Judaism," or was Catholic, Protestant, "no religion", or "other" (Table 6.3).

Respondents are defined as Jews more broadly than are spouses. Respondents who are Jewish by descent or Jews practicing another religion

TABLE 6.2

Number of Marriage Choices by Type of Marriage

Type of Marriage	Unweighted N		Weighted N	
	Ever Married Respondents	Jewish Spouses	Ever Married Respondents	Jewish Spouses
CURRENTLY MARRIED				
Married in 1st marriage	1122	669	1077	597
Married in 2nd + Marriage	288	94	288	94
Subtotal	*1410*	*763*	*1365*	*691*
CURRENTLY DIVORCED, WIDOWED, SEPARATED				
Divorced, separated, or widowed from 1st marriage	359	N/A	414	N/A
Divorced separated, or widowed from 2nd + marriage	71	N/A	79	N/A
Subtotal	*430*	*N/A*	*493*	*N/A*
FIRST MARRIAGES WHICH HAVE DISSOLVED				
1st of Two Marriages & respondent or spouse is currently married	235	78	242	79
1st of Three Marriages & respondent or spouse is currently married	53	16	59	14
1st of Two Marriages & respondent is currently divorced or widowed	70	N/A	77	N/A
1st of Three Marriages & respondents currently divorced, separated, or widowed	1	N/A	2	N/A
Subtotal	*359*	*94*	*380*	*93*
TOTAL	**2199**	**857**	**2255**	**781**

TABLE 6.3

Definition of Intermarriage by Number of Cases

	DEFINITION	UNWEIGHTED N	WEIGHTED N
CURRENT MARRIAGE CHOICES:			
In-Marriage	Spouse is a Born Jew-Religion Jewish, Secular Jew, or Jew by Choice	1508	1353
Intermarriage	Spouse is a Gentile, a Born Jew practicing another religion, or a person of Jewish descent	641	684
DISSOLVED MARRIAGE CHOICES			
In-Marriage	Previous Spouse was Jewish	206	219
Intermarriage	Previous Spouse not Jewish	97	114
FIRST OF 2 OR MORE MARRIAGE CHOICES			
In-Marriage	First spouse was "born Jewish" or "converted to Judaism."	234	234
Intermarriage	First spouse was "Catholic, Protestant, no religion, or other."	170	183
DATA NOT AVAILABLE	A question about the Jewish self-definition of previous spouses was **not asked** of: Currently separated respondents or about the Most recent marriage of currently divorced or widowed respondents who have been married 2 + times	108	133

were counted as Jews, while spouses in these same categories were not. This decision was made as a result of extensive qualitative interviews conducted with intermarried couples in a study subsequent to the NJPS.[5] It became apparent that when "marginal" or "non conventional" Jews marry other "marginal" Jews, they themselves do not consider their spouses to be Jewish.[6] This presents a theoretical problem, but the dual classification schema has no practical impact on the analysis since almost all the marginal Jews had married non-Jews. In only a few cases had a non-conventional Jewish respondent married another non-conventional Jew (Table 6.4). Including Marginal or Non-conventional Jews complicates the analysis but is nonetheless important because it addresses the question of "return marriage." Do Jews who were themselves the products of inter-marriages "return" to the Jewish fold by marrying a Jew or do they repeat their own parents' intermarriage?

Table 6.4 shows they repeat their parents' intermarriage. Persons of Jewish descent and Jews who practice another religion are the most likely to marry non-Jews (73.6 percent and 76 percent, respectively).[7] Born Jews who are Jewish by religion are most likely to marry other Jews-by-religion (71.7 percent). Secular Jews fall in the middle, but more of them have intermarried (53.9 percent) than have in-married (41.4 percent). When secular Jews marry other Jews, they show a slight preference for other secular Jews (22 percent) over Jews by religion (17.9 percent).

The bottom of Table 6.4 summarizes the rate of intermarriage by cate-gory of Jewish self-definition (this is presented graphically in Chart #1). The most mainstream Jews, born Jews who are Jewish by religion, have the lowest rate of intermarriage (18.7 percent). Over half (56.6 percent) of the secular Jews (who identify with no religion) intermarry. The vast majority of Jews who practice another religion and persons of Jewish descent are intermarried (90 percent and 87.6 percent, respectively).

Jewish self-definition is strongly associated with intermarriage. Consid-ered as an effect of Jewish self-definition, intermarriage would result from weakened identity among non-conventional Jews. Persons are thus being consistent with their non-normative Jewish status when they violate the norm of endogamy and marry outside the group. But, it is also possible that non-conventional Jewish self-definition results from the act of marry-ing outside the group. As a result of violating the endogamy norm, inter-married Jews become marginalized.[8] Most of the non-conventional Jews had very weak Jewish backgrounds, which suggests that intermarriage is the result of non-conventional Jewish status. Nonetheless, there are cases in which non-conventional Jewish status could well be the effect of the intermarriage. This cannot be determined directly from the NJPS.

The "bottom line" for policy analysts, however, is that intermarriage

TABLE 6.4
Religion of Partner by Jewish Self-Definition
(All Marriage Choices of Respondents & Jewish Spouses)

	JEWISH SELF-DEFINITION			
SPOUSE IS	BORN JEW RELIGION JEWISH	SECULAR JEW	JEWISH DESCENT	JEW, OTHER RELIGION
Born Jew-Religion Jewish	71.7	17.9	6.5	5.3
Secular Jew	2.3	22.0	5.2	3.7
Jew by Choice	4.5	1.5	0.0	0.0
Jewish Descent	0.0	1.8	2.3	0.3
Christian	16.6	45.7	73.6	76.0
Jew, other Religion	0.7	2.5	0.7	0.0
Non-Christian Non-Jew	0.8	3.9	6.3	4.1
Question Not Asked*	3.5	4.6	6.1	10.6
TOTAL	100.0	100.0	100.0	100.0
Weighted N	2006	448	157	308
Intermarriage Rate Corrected for missing data**	18.7%	56.6%	87.6%	90.0%

* These are second marriages of divorced respondents. The skip pattern did not allow for finding out the religion of previous spouses from second marriages.

**i.e., "Question Not Asked" treated as missing data and not counted as part of the percentage.

CHART 1
PERCENT INTERMARRIED BY JEWISH SELF-DEFINITION

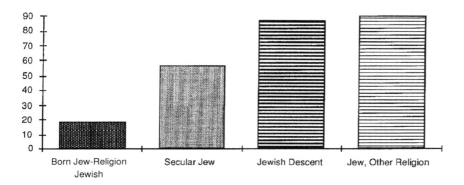

and non-conventional Jewish status are strongly linked. The most conventional Jews (born Jew-religion Jewish) are the most likely to marry other Jews. Secular Jews are more likely than Jews by religion to marry a non-Jew. Secular Jews are less conventional than Jews by religion in the sense that they fall outside the commonly accepted model of "Protestant-Catholic-Jew" as the "three great religions in America." Perhaps because they fall outside the consensus, and perhaps because religion is of no importance to them, they are more likely than Jews by religion to marry non-Jews. Nonetheless, as Chart 1 shows graphically, secular Jews are still much less likely than non-conventional Jews to marry non-Jews. Non-conventional Jews overwhelmingly chose non-Jews as marriage partners.

Intermarriage as Assimilation

Year of Marriage

A strong argument in favor of the assimilation model is the consistent increase in the rate of intermarriage. Table 6.5 presents the rate of intermarriage by year of marriage in four ways: all marriage choices of conventional Jews, all marriage choices of non-conventional Jews, first marriage choices only of all Jews, and all marriage choices of all Jews.

Among non-conventional Jews, as would be expected by now, the rate of intermarriage is 80 percent or higher in every decade. Among conven-

TABLE 6.5

Percent Intermarried by Year of Marriage
Controlling for First Marriage and Jewish Self-Definition
(All Marriage Choices of Respondents & Jewish Spouses)

	ALL MARRIAGE CHOICES			FIRST MARRIAGE CHOICES
YEAR OF MARRIAGE	CONVENTIONAL JEWS	NON-CONVENTIONAL JEWS	ALL JEWS	ALL JEWS
1985–1990	46.5	86.7	53.9	53.8
1980–1984	41.7	81.2	48.1	46.0
1975–1979	41.3	89.8	51.3	51.9
1970–1974	31.6	94.0	43.1	41.6
1965–1969	23.6	94.5	38.0	36.4
1960–1964	22.3	84.5	29.2	29.2
Before 1960	7.1	90.4	16.2	16.0

tional Jews, the rate of intermarriage leveled off somewhat after 1979. This does not mean that intermarriage has slowed down, however. The 1980–89 rates for conventional Jews leave out the intermarriages of younger Jews who have taken on a non-conventional Jews status. Thus, when non-conventional and conventional Jews are combined (Col. 3 of Table 6.5), the intermarriage rates continue to increase by year of marriage.

Taking all marriage choices of all Jews together (first column of Table 6.5), the rate of intermarriage is seen to increase steadily every five years. The largest jumps came between 1960 and 1965 and 1965 and 1970, when the intermarriage rate almost doubled every five years. This same trend holds when only first marriage choices are considered (second column of Table 6.5).

Of special interest are the rates of intermarriage among conventional Jews prior to 1970 because these allow for a check of consistency between the 1970–71 and 1990 National Jewish Population Surveys. Because only conventional Jews were surveyed in the 1970–71 NJPS, the intermarriage rates from the 1964–69 period as reflected in the 1990 study can be used to validate the 1970–71 study. Fred Massarik found in the 1970–71 NJPS that the rate of intermarriage had accelerated significantly between 1964 and 1970 (Massarik, 1974; Massarik & Chenkin, 1973). Because there were not many cases in the sample where the couple married between 1965 and 1971, some researchers questioned whether the rate had really increased so dramatically during this time period (Silberman, 1985). Schmelz and DellaPergola, on the other hand, argued that not only had the rate increased in the late 1960's, it had doubled compared with the period 1960–

64 (Schmelz & DellaPergola, 1983). The 1990 NJPS confirms the assertion of Schmelz and DellaPergola that intermarriage began to rise dramatically among conventional Jews in the mid-1960's. The 1990 NJPS indicates that the individual intermarriage rate increased from 23.6 percent in the 1965–69 period to 31.6 percent in the 1970–74 period.

Generation

Generation is the strongest predictor of assimilation for a minority group (Sklare, 1971). Barring discrimination, the farther a person is from the immigrant generation, the more assimilated into the American mainstream that person will be.

Generation is abstractly interpreted as a measure of Americanization. It is concretely defined as the presence of foreign-born parents and grandparents in the family. Generation is measured by the number of foreign-born parents and grandparents an individual has. Foreign-born persons are "first generation." A child of two foreign-born parents is "second generation." A child of two American-born parents with foreign-born grandparents is "third generation." A child of two native-born parents and three or four native-born grandparents is "fourth generation." A person can also fall between generations. A child of one foreign-born parent and one native-born parent is called "second-third generation." A child of two native-born parents and only one or two native-born grandparents is called "third-fourth generation."

Generation (Table 6.6) is directly associated with intermarriage among conventional Jews (i.e., Jews by religion and secular Jews) and indirectly among non-conventional Jews (i.e., Jews who practice another religion and persons of Jewish descent only). Among conventional Jews, the rate of intermarriage increases with each succeeding generation. First and second generation conventional Jews have very low rates of intermarriage—only about 10 percent. The biggest jump takes place between the second-third and third generations, which suggests that having even one foreign-born parent significantly deters the likelihood of intermarriage. Thus, exposure to the influences of foreign-born parents and even grandparents (who articulate traditional values) reduces the rate of intermarriage.

Among non-conventional Jews, there is apparently no relationship between generation in the U.S. and intermarriage. The rates of intermarriage among non-conventional Jews are above 80 percent in each generation. In fact, there is a very important three-way relationship between generation, Jewish self-definition, and intermarriage. Generation is itself associated with Jewish self-definition: The more advanced the generation, the greater the percentage of Jews who identify in non-conventional ways (Table 6.7).

TABLE 6.6
Percent Intermarried by Generation and Jewish Self-Definition
(All Marriage Choices of Respondents & Jewish Spouses)

GENERATION	ALL JEWS	CONVENTIONAL JEWS	NON-CONVENTIONAL JEWS
FIRST	16.8	10.6	95.1
	N = 239	N = 222	N = 17
SECOND	13.6	10.1	80.3
	N = 722	N = 686	N = 36
SECOND-THIRD	24.8	20.0	100.0
	N = 276	N = 259	N = 17
THIRD	44.1	35.0	90.9
	N = 903	N = 756	N = 148
THIRD-FOURTH	52.7	42.1	89.3
	N = 245	N = 190	N = 55
FOURTH	61.5	45.9	87.5
	N = 399	N = 250	N = 149

CHART 2
PERCENT INTERMARRIED BY GENERATION AND JEWISH SELF-DEFINITION

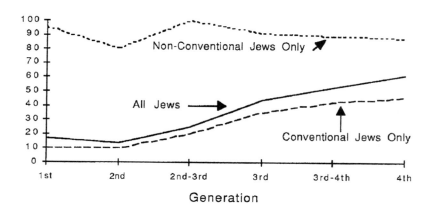

106

TABLE 6.7

Jewish Self-Definition by Generation
(All Marriage Choices of Respondents & Jewish Spouses)

Jewish Self-Definition	First	Second	Second-Third	Third	Third-Fourth	Fourth
Born Jew-Relig Jewish	77.9	86.2	79.0	67.9	49.5	34.8
Secular Jew	12.5	9.0	14.8	15.3	25.6	24.2
Born Jew-Other Relig	6.5	1.7	1.8	10.7	18.7	31.9
Jewish Descent	3.1	3.0	4.3	6.2	6.2	9.1
TOTAL	100.0	100.0	100.0	100.0	100.0	100.0
Weighted N	262	769	297	963	271	469

Only a few percent of first, second, or second-third generation Jews[9] practice a religion other than Judaism as compared with 10 percent of the third
generation Jews, and 32 percent of fourth generation Jews. Altogether, 41
percent of ever-married fourth generation Jews fall into the two non-
conventional categories. Intermarriage is highly correlated with non-
conventional Jewish self-definition.

Generation is indirectly associated with intermarriage among non-
conventional Jews through a generational shift into non-conventional Jewish self-definition. This shift can occur in two ways: the first (and presumably the predominant) pattern is for fourth generation Jews to take on—or
be raised in—a more marginal status and then intermarry. The second is
for fourth generation Jews to adopt a non-conventional status following
marriage to a non-Jew.

When conventional and non-conventional Jews are combined, one finds
a dramatic increase in the rate of intermarriage among Jews whose families
have lived in the U.S. for generations. The rate of intermarriage among
fourth generation Jews (61.5 percent) is more than three times that of the
first and second generations (16.7 percent and 13.6 percent, respectively).
The rate increases with each succeeding generation, including intermediate generations such as second-third (where a person is second generation
through one parent and third generation through another parent).

Again, this represents the convergence of two generational trends:

1) Advanced generation Jews are more likely to adopt a non-conventional Jewish self-definition.

2) Advanced generation conventional Jews are more likely to intermarry.

Chart 3 illustrates the direct and indirect effects of generation on intermarriage. Chart 3 uses shaded areas of variant patterns to represent the
four combinations of Jewish status and marriage type[10] over six gradations
of generational status.[11] The top two areas of the chart represent marriage
choices by Jews of non-conventional self-definition. The top area (dark
shading) represents *intermarriages* by non-conventional Jews. The small
area below that is made up of dark horizontal bars represents *in-marriages*
by non-conventional Jews. The bottom two areas of Chart 3 represent
marriage choices by conventionally identified Jews. The lightly shaded
(dotted) area represents *intermarriages,* and the light horizontal lines in the
lower-most area represent *in-marriages.*

The main visual message is the decline of in-marriages among conventional Jews as the result of two parallel trends: 1) the declining proportion
of conventionally identified Jews in succeeding generations and 2) the
decrease of in-marriage among conventional Jews in succeeding generations. In other words, as generation advances there are fewer conven-

CHART 3
TYPES OF MARRIAGE BY GENERATION AND JEWISH SELF-DEFINITION

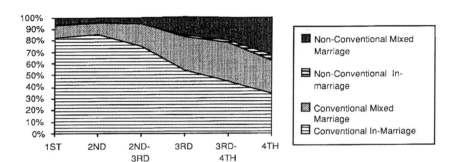

tionally identified Jews, and those who do identify in a conventional way are less inclined to marry other Jews. These two trends are shown at the bottom of Chart 3, where the pattern of thin horizontal lines represents in-marriages by conventional Jews. The next area up (dots) represents mixed-marriages by conventional Jews.

Over the course of the four generations (including two intermediate generations) the proportion of in-marriages by conventional Jews (represented by the height of the corresponding area) decreases steadily. Similarly, the proportion of mixed marriages by conventional Jews increases (as represented by the height of the gray area) up through the third-fourth generation. In the fourth generation, the gray band narrows, representing a slight decrease in the proportion of mixed marriages by conventional Jews. This is not because they are reversing the intermarriage trends. Rather, both categories of non-conventional Jewish marriage choices increase into the fourth generation. The proportion of mixed marriages by non-conventional Jews increases significantly into the fourth generation (i.e., the top area continues to widen). Surprisingly, even the proportion of in-marriages by non-conventional Jews increases from next to nothing to being slightly visible by the fourth generation. In other words, the high rate of mixed marriage in the fourth generation is explained both by a shift to non-conventional Jewish self-definition (of which intermarriage is almost the inevitable consequence) and an increase in intermarriage among conventionally identified fourth generation Jews.

Charts 4a and 4b are "close-ups" of the conventional and non-conventional sections of Chart 3. Chart 4a shows that while the proportion of all conventional Jewish marriage choices declines in each succeeding generation, the relative proportion of mixed marriages among all marriage

CHART 4A
PERCENT INTERMARRIED BY GENERATION AND SELF-DEFINITION
(MARRIAGES OF <u>CONVENTIONAL JEWS</u> ONLY)

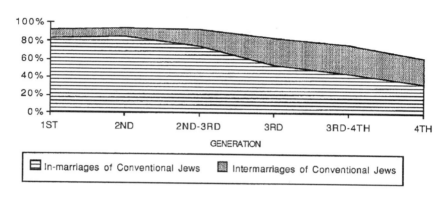

CHART 4B
PERCENT INTERMARRIED BY GENERATION AND SELF-DEFINITION
(MARRIAGES OF <u>NON-CONVENTIONAL</u> JEWS ONLY)

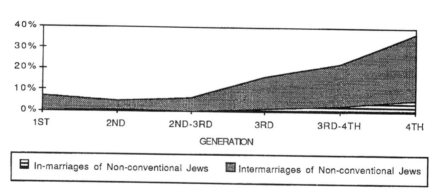

choices by conventional Jews increases (i.e., the shaded band widens as the stripped band narrows through the fourth generation). In other words, even as conventional Jewish marriage choices are decreasing, more of them are becoming mixed marriages.

Chart 4b zooms in on marriage choices among non-conventional Jews. It reveals a dramatic increase in the proportion of mixed marriages by non-conventional Jews among all marriage choices, starting at the second-third generation. This is accompanied by an unexpected (though still small) increase in the proportion of in-marriages by non-conventional Jews. In other words, the proportion of marriage choices by non-conventional Jews increases steadily over generation, and a few of these end up as in-marriages.

Age

The intermarriage trends by age reflect both the intermarriage trends by generation and by year of marriage. The youngest Jews tend to be third and fourth generation as well as the most recently married. It is nonetheless useful to look at intermarriage by age. The youngest age cohorts will be forming the families of the twenty-first century. Age is a way to see what kinds of families these will be, at least in terms of intermarriage.

Even when controlling for generation, intermarriage still increases with age. Chart 5 plots the rate of intermarriage by age controlling for Jewish self-definition, using the data from Table 6.8. Among conventional Jews, the rate of intermarriage increases when passing from older to younger ages and then stabilizes among the three youngest (i.e., under 40) cohorts. This may mean that the rate of intermarriage has begun to level off or it may also be an artifact. Most Jews under 30 have not yet married. Those who have married are also more likely to have in-married. Those who have not yet married will be more likely to marry non-Jews, thereby causing the inter-marriage rate to increase in the youngest age cohorts.

Among non-conventional Jews, the apparent lack of relationship between age and intermarriage is really the effect of generation. Younger Jews are more likely to be third generation Americans or higher (Table 6.9a), and third and fourth generation Jews tend to be young (Table 6.9b). Since Jews of advanced generations are more likely to fall into non-conventional categories (see Table 6.7 above), younger Jews tend to be third and fourth generation and are more likely to take on a non-conventional or a secular Jewish self-definition (Table 6.10). For example, 50.3 percent of Jews under 30 years of age are Jews by religion, compared with 63 percent between the ages of 40 and 60, and 78 percent or more among Jews 60 and older.[12] Thus, younger Jews are very much part of the generational shift into non-conventional Jewish self-definition that is generally associated with intermarriage (Table 6.10).

The "total" column of Table 6.8 incorporates the effect of the generational shift to non-conventional Jewish self-definition among younger Jews. This is presented graphically in Chart 6 using year of birth in place of age.[13] Intermarriage first begins to increase among Jews born just before and during the Depression, starting with the 1926–1930 birth cohort and continuing to rise through the 1936–1940 group. It levels off for the 1941–1945 cohort and then increases again for those born between 1946 and

TABLE 6.8
Percent Intermarried by Age and Jewish Self-Definition
(All Marriage Choices of Respondents & Jewish Spouses)

AGE	ALL JEWS	CONVENTIONAL JEWS	NON-CONVENTIONAL JEWS
18–30	52.3	43.0	85.4
	N = 215	N = 168	N = 47
30–34	52.2	41.4	91.0
	N = 283	N = 222	N = 61
35–39	52.2	45.5	82.8
	N = 375	N = 305	N = 70
40–44	46.6	35.5	94.0
	N = 377	N = 305	N = 71
45–49	36.4	29.2	92.8
	N = 237	N = 211	N = 27
50–54	37.6	22.8	90.0
	N = 161	N = 126	N = 36
55–59	31.4	19.4	95.5
	N = 196	N = 165	N = 31
60–64	20.1	08.1	97.1
	N = 179	N = 155	N = 24
65–69	16.2	11.6	66.6
	N = 236	N = 216	N = 20
70–74	15.3	10.6	100.0
	N = 187	178	N = 10
75 +	10.5	3.6	88.6
	N = 328	N = 302	N = 26

CHART 5
PERCENT INTERMARRIED BY AGE,
CONTROLLING FOR JEWISH SELF-DEFINITION

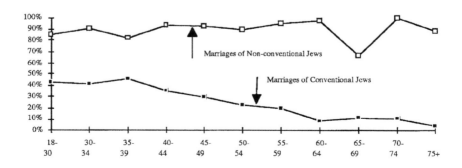

TABLE 6.9A
Generation by Age
(All Marriage Choices of Respondents & Jewish Spouses)

GENERATION	18–30	30–39	40–49	50–59	60–69	70+
1st	4.9	6.1	8.1	7.0	8.3	15.3
2nd	6.5	4.6	8.0	24.1	47.3	63.2
2nd–3rd	4.0	6.2	9.3	15.5	17.1	7.9
3rd	34.0	42.4	48.7	35.1	16.3	7.4
3rd–4th	13.2	14.8	12.7	7.6	3.1	1.0
4th	37.5	26.0	13.3	10.6	7.9	5.1
TOTAL	100.0	100.0	100.0	100.0	100.0	100.0
Weighted N	231	716	677	384	444	572

TABLE 6.9B
Age by Generation
(All Marriage Choices of Respondents & Jewish Spouses)

AGE	1ST	2ND	2ND–3RD	3RD	3RD–4TH	4TH
Under 30	4.3	2.0	3.1	8.2	11.2	18.5
30–39	16.7	4.3	15.0	31.6	39.0	39.8
40–49	20.9	7.1	21.2	34.3	31.9	19.2
50–59	10.3	12.0	20.0	14.0	10.8	8.7
60–69	14.2	27.5	25.5	7.5	5.1	7.5
70+	33.6	47.2	15.2	4.4	2.1	6.3
TOTAL	100.0	100.0	100.0	100.0	100.0	100.0
Weighted N	261	764	296	960	271	467

TABLE 6.10
Jewish Self-Definition by Age
(All Marriage Choices of Respondents & Jewish Spouses)

SELF-DEFINITION	18–30	30–39	40–49	50–59	60–69	70+
Born Jew-Relig Jewish	50.3	60.2	63.2	63.4	78.1	83.5
Secular Jew	27.0	18.6	19.5	17.3	9.0	7.4
Born Jew-Other Relig	17.6	14.8	11.1	10.2	10.4	5.7
Jewish Descent Only	5.2	6.4	6.1	9.0	2.6	3.4
TOTAL	100.0	100.0	100.0	100.0	100.0	100.0
Weighted N	231	716	677	384	444	572

CHART 6
PERCENT INTERMARRIED BY YEAR OF BIRTH: ALL JEWS

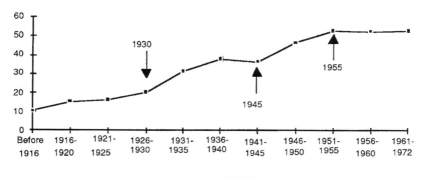

YEAR OF BIRTH

1955. Outside of the leveling off for the 1941–1945 cohort and the uncertain meaning of the slight leveling off of intermarriage among Jews born after 1951, mixed marriage has been on the rise among younger generations for most of this century. The most significant increase occurred during the late 1960's and has continued ever since.

The sense of urgency and alarm present in recent discussions of intermarriage is a reaction to what might be called the "threshold effect" of rising intermarriage rates, 30 percent or less for Jews born before 1945, compared with 40 to 50 percent for those born in the 1960's. Since intermarriage has increased steadily over the years, the phenomenon has become more visible as it has reached "crisis proportions."

Combined Effects of Age and Generation

If age and generation are associated with each other, does this mean that the association between age and intermarriage is an artifact resulting from the overlap between age and generation? Conversely, is age more strongly associated with intermarriage than generation? Both age and generation are related to intermarriage, but the effect of generation is a little stronger (Table 6.10). The same information is presented graphically in Chart 7. The highest rates of intermarriage are among third and fourth generation Jews under 45 years of age (46 percent). The lowest rates are among the first and second generation Jews who are 45 and older. The rates of intermarriage among the younger Jews (under 45) who are first and second

CHART 7
PERCENT INTERMARRIED BY AGE AND GENERATION
(MARRIAGES OF CONVENTIONAL JEWS ONLY)

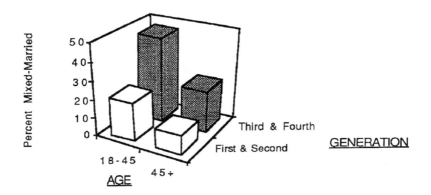

TABLE 6.11

Percent Intermarried by Age and Generation
(*All Marriage Choices of* Conventional *Respondents & Spouses*)

GENERATION COMBINED	TOTAL	18–45	45 +
First & Second Combined	12.5 N = 1241	21.4 N = 217	10.6 N = 1025
Third & Fourth Combined	38.3 N = 1275	46.0 N = 854	22.5 N = 421

generation are virtually the same as the rate of intermarriage among older Jews (45 +) in the third and fourth generations.

The indirect impact is through generationally weakened Jewish self-definition. Third and fourth generation Jews who have adopted non-conventional or "marginal" identities have not become less Jewish; they are acting on the basis of the minimal identity with which they were raised. Most grew up in households that did not practice any religion or in Christian households where one parent was a non-Jew. Given their lack of Jewish background, their marriage to a non-Jew is consistent with their upbringing. There are few compelling reasons for them to seek out a Jewish partner.

In sum, age, generation, and Jewish self-definition are all interrelated. Fourth generation Jews are the youngest and the most likely to be non-conventional Jews. Part of the increase in intermarriage, then, is explained by the propensity of younger, advanced-generation Jews to have assimilated into non-conventional or marginal Jewish identities. Both generation and age remain associated with intermarriage even when controlling for Jewish self-definition.

Among non-conventional Jews, intermarriage rates are extremely high for all age and generation cohorts. Among conventional Jews, the rates of intermarriage increase steadily from 10 percent of the first and second generations, to over 40 percent of the fourth generation. Similarly, the youngest age cohorts among conventional Jews have the highest rates of intermarriage. There is also a joint effect of age and generation. The highest rates of intermarriage are among young fourth generation Jews.

Conclusion

There is strong evidence for the assimilation model. First, succeeding generations of Jews are more likely to be marginal or non-conventional, and thus marry non-Jews out of that weak attachment. Second, conventional Jews who are third generation and beyond are more likely to intermarry than first or second generation Jews. Finally, the rate of intermarriage has increased consistently during the past two decades, especially during the last five years. Nevertheless, assimilation is not the whole story.

Social Structural Factors

Social structural factors may be understood as the inverse of assimilation factors. Assimilation is an internal process in which Jewish identity and distinctiveness weaken with acculturation over succeeding generations. The social structure model, by contrast, is external in emphasis and understands intermarriage in terms of the position of Jews in the larger social structure. It stresses the constraints on the availability of potential Jewish marriage partners created by factors such as gender, remarriage, migration, and educational attainment.

Marriage and Re-marriage

Re-marriage is associated with intermarriage in two ways. To begin with, intermarriages are less stable than in-marriages. First marriage choices to non-Jews are more likely than first marriage choices to Jews (Table 6.12)

TABLE 6.12

Percent Divorced From 1st Marriage by Intermarriage
(First *Marriage Choices of Respondents & Jewish Spouses*)

TYPE OF MARRIAGE	PERCENT DIVORCED	WEIGHTED N
In-Marriage	15.6	1616
Intermarriage	29.1	789

to end in divorce. Overall, the divorce rate among first marriage choices to non-Jews (29.1 percent) is almost twice that among first marriage choices to Jews (15.6 percent). The divorce rate among mixed marriages remains significantly higher than that among in-marriages even when age controls are applied (Table 6.13).

Second marriage choices are more likely to be intermarriages than first marriage choices because divorced Jews are more likely to remarry a non-Jew the second time around (Table 6.14). The rate of mixed marriage among second marriage choices (50.6 percent) is 1.5 times greater than the rate among first marriage choices (32.8 percent).

There are, then, two trends in effect: 1) Intermarriages are more likely to end in divorce than are in-marriages; 2) Second marriage choices are more likely to be intermarriages. Taken together, these two trends produce the following overall picture (Table 6.15): The rate of intermarriage among intact first marriage choices is relatively low (29.8 percent), while the rate of intermarriage among divorces not yet remarried is one third higher (39.6 percent). The intermarriage rate among second marriage choices is higher still (50.1 percent) because it includes Jews who were in-married the first time and have married non-Jews the second time. Put another way, Jews who in-marry tend to stay that way, but those who divorce will most likely marry a non-Jew the second time. Divorce after an intermarriage leads to more intermarriage. Intermarriages are more likely to dissolve and then re-form as intermarriages again. Jews who marry non-Jews often do so twice.

Psychological and social structural theories can both be used to explain the association between intermarriage and remarriage. According to a psychological explanation, an unsatisfactory marriage with a Jew leads to seeking a non-Jew the second time around. Yet the converse is not the case: mixed-married Jews do not seek a Jewish partner the second time around. A social-structural explanation has no such inconsistency because it is based on the concept of "constraint." In-married Jews who remarry will have a harder time finding a Jewish spouse the second time around because there are fewer potential Jewish spouses available. These tend to

TABLE 6.13

Percent Divorced From 1st Marriage by Intermarriage,
Controlling for Age
(First Marriage Choices of Respondents & Jewish Spouses)

TOTAL	18–44	45 +
ALL MARRIAGES		
15.7	14.6	16.3
N = 1608	N = 550	N = 1058
IN-MARRIAGES		
15.7	14.6	16.3
N = 1608	N = 550	N = 1058
INTERMARRIAGES		
28.9	26.9	33.1
N = 787	N = 535	N = 252

TABLE 6.14

Percent Divorced by Marriage Number
(All Marriage Choices of Respondents & Jewish Spouses)

MARRIAGE NUMBER	PERCENT INTERMARRIED	WEIGHTED N
First Marriage	32.8	2405
Second or Third Marriage	50.6	37

TABLE 6.15

Percent Divorced by Marriage Number
and Marital Status
(All Marriage Choices of Respondents & Jewish Spouses)

MARRIAGE NUMBER AND MARITAL STATUS	PERCENT INTERMARRIED	WEIGHTED N
Intact First Marriage	29.8	1655
First Marriage Which Has Dissolved	39.6	750
Second or Third Marriage	50.1	82

be "intermarriages by default" rather than intention. Second, because all marriage choices are counted in this analysis and because intermarriers tend to do so more than once, the overall rate of intermarriage is slightly inflated because some of the intermarriages are the same Jews marrying non-Jews twice. Thus, at least some intermarriages are explained by the social structural dimensions associated with remarriage.

CHART 8:
PERCENT INTERMARRIED BY ORDER OF MARRIAGE
(MARRIAGES OF CONVENTIONAL JEWS UNDER 45)

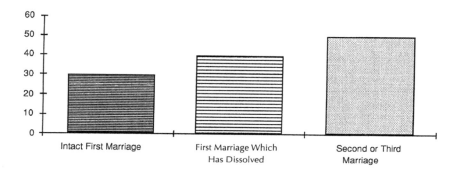

The relative stability of in-marriages seems to be explained by tensions resulting from cultural differences in mixed marriages, which lead to divorce. This intuitively plausible argument has been made by numerous rabbis and parents. More recently, tensions emerging out of cultural differences in mixed marriages have been discussed in depth by Paul and Rachel Cowan in their qualitative study, *Mixed Blessings* (1986). In isolation, this finding is significant but not necessarily surprising. It does, however, at least modify another self-evident truth: mixed marriages are "less Jewish" than in-marriages. The leading research on intermarriage does demonstrate that mixed marriages are *less Jewish* than in-marriages when home observance, communal affiliation, and composition of informal networks are used to measure Jewishness (Medding, Tobin, Barack, & Rimor, 1992; Bayme, 1993). If such differences are strong enough to lead to divorce, then Jews who intermarry may be more strongly identified than is apparent from their behaviors. A detailed analysis of this question is beyond the scope of this paper, and the implications of divorce among mixed-marrieds needs to be further addressed.

Gender

Previous studies have found that Jewish men were more likely than Jewish women to marry non-Jews (Berman, 1968). They did so because they were out in the world more and had greater contact with non-Jews. Most Jews assume that this is still the case. It is therefore surprising to find that there is no longer a relationship between gender and intermarriage among younger Jews (Table 6.16).

TABLE 6.16
Percent Intermarried by Gender, Jewish Self-Definition, and Age
(All Marriage Choices of Respondents & Jewish Spouses)

| | CONVENTIONAL JEWS | | NON-CONVENTIONAL JEWS | |
GENDER	18–44	45 +	18–44	45 +
Male	41.0	17.1	94.0	88.4
	N = 471	N = 675	N = 99	N = 63
Female	41.3	11.0	84.9	91.1
	N = 528	N = 677	N = 151	N = 110

Among ever-married conventional Jews 45 and over, men are almost twice as likely as women to have married a non-Jew. Under age 45, however, gender differences disappear. The accelerated rate of intermarriage among Jewish women is highlighted by comparing the under 45 and over 45 intermarriage rates by gender. The intermarriage rate among ever-married conventional Jewish women increases by a factor of 3.8 at age 45, as compared to a factor of 2.4 among men. The educational gains made by Jewish women have been accompanied by an increase in intermarriage as Jewish women now have the same opportunities to meet non-Jews that Jewish men do. In other words, as Jewish women gain the opportunities that are available to men to participate in the larger social structure, that participation includes marriage to non-Jews.

Migration

Regional Differentials

Intermarriage is associated with migration in various and complex ways. Regional differences are not significant either among non-conventional Jews or among conventional Jews age 45 and older: the rates of intermarriage are above 50 percent for the former and under 20 percent for the latter in all regions. Among conventional Jews under 45, however, there are significant regional differences in the rates of intermarriage (Table 6.17 and Chart 10).

Among conventional Jews under 45, the rate of intermarriage is highest in the West (48.9 percent), followed by the South (43.3 percent); it is significantly lower in the Northeast (38 percent) and the Midwest (31.6 percent). These regional differences are usually explained by selective migration. People with weaker ties to community are more likely to migrate

CHART 9:   PERCENT INTERMARRIED BY AGE AND GENDER
(MARRIAGES OF CONVENTIONAL JEWS ONLY)

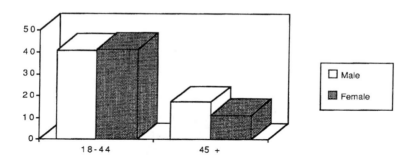

TABLE 6.17

Percent Intermarried by Region of Residence
Controlling For Jewish Self-Definition and Age
(All Marriage Choices of Respondents & Jewish Spouses)

REGION OF RESIDENCE	CONVENTIONAL JEW		NON-CONVENTIONAL JEW	
	18–44	45 +	18–44	45 +
Northeast	38.0	13.3	88.3	84.6
	N = 396	N = 596	N = 56	N = 39
Midwest	31.6	18.9	83.2	88.5
	N = 124	N = 134	N = 53	N = 40
South	43.3	11.6	84.7	95.2
	N = 220	N = 321	N = 58	N = 62
West	48.7	15.9	94.7	89.0
	N = 60	N = 301	N = 82	N = 32

than those with strong ties. The same weak ties that induce migration also explain intermarriage, and thus regional differences would be accounted for by the assimilation model (Cohen, 1983; Berman, 1968). But this turns out not to be the case. The intermarriage rates of migrants and non-migrants among both conventional and non-conventional Jews are almost identical regardless of age (Table 6.18). (Among non-conventional Jews, migrants do have slightly lower rates of intermarriage than non-migrants, but these rates are all over 80 percent.)

Regional differences in intermarriage—particularly in the West—can be explained by two different processes which are evident only at the regional level. The first is selective migration whereby intermarried couples choose

CHART 10
PERCENT INTERMARRIED BY REGION OF RESIDENCE
(MARRIAGES OF <u>CONVENTIONAL</u> JEWS ONLY)

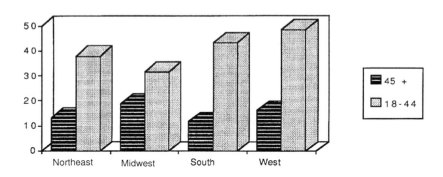

TABLE 6.18
Percent Intermarried by Migration Pattern
Controlling For Jewish Status and Age
(All Marriage Choices of Respondents & Jewish Spouses)

	CONVENTIONAL JEW		NON-CONVENTIONAL JEW	
MIGRATION PATTERN	18–44	45+	18–44	45+
Lives in	42.3	15.5	90.6	95.2
Region of Birth	N = 580	N = 660	N = 161	N = 104
Migrated to	40.9	12.9	84.7	81.9
Current Region	N = 405	N = 664	N = 90	N = 67

the West, and to a certain extent the South, over other regions as their destination. The second process is socialization into regional culture, most notably, growing up in the West.

Selective Migration

Selective migration means that intermarried migrants are more likely than their in-married counterparts to end up in a particular region—the West and South. Table 6.19 compares the regional destinations of in-married and intermarried migrants controlling for age and Jewish self-definition.

The South and West are the most popular destinations for all Jewish migrants because all Jews are participating in the national relocation of population from older regions of residence (Northeast and Midwest). Nonetheless, intermarried migrants are more likely than in-married migrants to move to the South and West. Among conventional Jews under 45 (the two left columns in Table 6.1), intermarried Jews are 1.2 times as likely as in-married Jews to have moved to the West and 1.13 times as likely to have moved to the South. By contrast, in-married Jews are 1.7 times as likely as the intermarried to have moved to the Northeast and 1.3 times as likely to have moved to the Midwest. Thus, migrants with the highest rates of intermarriage move to those regions with the highest rates of intermarriage.

Another way to look at selective migration is to compare "native stayers" with "migrators" from each region (Table 6.20). A native stayer lived in his or her region of birth in 1990. A migrator lived in a region other than the region of birth. Because intermarriage is so prevalent among non-conventional Jews, this analysis is restricted to marriage choices of conventional Jews.

Intermarried Jews born in the Northeast and Midwest tend to migrate out of those regions while in-married Jews tend to stay. Conversely, in the South and West it is the intermarried Jews who tend to stay in their region of birth while in-married Jews tend to migrate out of those regions (presumably to the Northeast and Midwest). What is not known from the NJPS (because it was not asked) is the sequence of intermarriage and migration: do single Jews migrate and then intermarry as a result of that migration, or do they intermarry and then migrate as a result of that intermarriage?

Regional Culture

A second explanation for the higher rates of intermarriage in the West is "regional culture." The individualist culture of the West is corrosive of religious attachments. This phenomenon is true both for Jews and non-Jews. A number of works in religious demography have shown that religious attachment is weakest in the West (Lazerwitz, 1977; Stark & Bainbridge, 1985; Roof & McKinney, 1987; Welch & Baltzell, 1984). The regional culture explanation would posit that Western Jews, like other Western Americans, behave in accordance with their regional culture. Those Jews who have grown up in the least religious region of the country have the highest rates of intermarriage.

The impact of regional culture can be seen in Table 6.21, which compares the intermarriage rate in various regions of birth among conventional Jews, controlling for age. Over the age of 45, the highest intermarriage rates are among Jews born in the West (26.4 percent) and South (23.3 percent)—almost double the rates in the Northeast and Midwest (13.8 percent and 14.6 percent, respectively). Under age 45, conventionally identified Jews born in the West again have the highest rate of intermarriage. Southern-born Jews of the same age do not have a particularly high rate of intermar-

TABLE 6.19

Region of Current Residence
For Jews Who Have Migrated from Region of Birth
by Intermarriage, Age, and Jewish Self-Definition
(All Marriage Choices of Respondents & Jewish Spouses
Who Have Migrated from Region of Birth)

REGION OF RESIDENCE	CONVENTIONAL JEWS				NON-CONVENTIONAL JEWS	
	18–44		45+		18–44	45+
	IN-MARRIED	INTER-MARRIED	IN-MARRIED	INTER-MARRIED	INTERMARRIED	INTERMARRIED
Northeast	18.7	10.8	16.5	17.0	18.6	10.8
Midwest	12.0	9.0	5.6	10.9	14.8	17.2
South	35.0	39.7	41.3	34.7	24.7	43.8
West	34.2	40.6	36.6	37.4	41.9	28.3
TOTAL	100.0	100.0	100.0	100.0	100.0	100.0
Weighted N	239	166	578	86	76	55

TABLE 6.20

Percent Intermarried by Stayer/Migrator Typology
Controlling For Age and Region of Birth
(*All Marriage Choices of* Conventional *Respondents & Spouses*)

REGION OF BIRTH	18–44		45 +	
	STAYER	MIGRATOR	STAYER	MIGRATOR
Northeast	40.8 N = 325	51.2 N = 200	13.6 N = 476	13.9 N = 328
Midwest	31.0 N = 79	40.3 N = 63	17.8 N = 89	12.4 N = 132
South	42.4 N = 69	38.2 N = 32	16.1 N = 46	36.2 N = 26
West	54.8 N = 108	40.7 N = 23	28.4 N = 49	— N = 4
Foreign Born	N/A	18.6 N = 87	N/A	8.3 N = 175

TABLE 6.21

Percent Intermarried by Region of Birth
Controlling For Age
(*All Marriage Choices of* Conventional *Respondents
& Jewish Spouses Only*)

REGION OF BIRTH	18–44	45 +
Northeast	44.8 N = 525	13.8 N = 803
Midwest	35.1 N = 142	14.6 N = 222
South	41.0 N = 102	23.3 N = 72
West	52.3 N = 131	26.4 N = 53
Foreign Born	18.6 N = 87	8.3 N = 175

125

riage compared with other regions. This is probably explained by the "Florida Factor": most Southern Jews were born in South Florida, which has a distinctly Jewish culture heavily influenced by the migration of Jews from the Northeast. In other words, Florida Jews are not so much Southern as they are Northeastern. Growing up Jewish in Miami is different from growing up Jewish in Chattanooga.

The effects of both regional culture and selective migration are presented in Table 6.22. For each region, three groups of conventional Jews are compared, controlling for age: *Native Stayers* (persons born and still living in the region), *Native Leavers* (born in region but living elsewhere in 1990), and *In-Migrants* (living in region in 1990 but born elsewhere). Among conventional Jews over the age 45, no trends are evident. Under 45, the impact of both regional culture and selective migration are apparent. The highest rate of intermarriage is among Western Native-Stayers (54.8 percent). Jews who left the West had a lower rate of intermarriage (40.7 percent) than In-Migrants to the West (45.1 percent).

In the Midwest, Native-Stayers had the second lowest rate of intermarriage over all (31 percent), and In-Migrants also had a relatively low rate of intermarriage (34 percent). Native Leavers from the Midwest had a higher rate of intermarriage (40.3 percent) than both Native-Stayers (31 percent) and In-Migrants to the Midwest (34 percent). Again, these data are consistent both with the regional culture and selective migration models.

Summary

Region, migration, and intermarriage are closely linked in a number of ways:

a) Jews born in the West and South are more likely to intermarry than Jews born in the Northeast and Midwest.
b) Intermarried migrators are more likely to leave the Northeast and Midwest and migrate to the West and South than in-married migrators.
c) The twin patterns of regional culture and selective migration make intermarriage rates highest in the West, followed by the South.
d) In the Northeast intermarriage has gone up substantially, which suggests that regional differences were greater in the past and may be less important now.

Educational Attainment

Education is associated with intermarriage, but the direction of the relationship is opposite that usually expected (Berman, 1968). The old saw in

TABLE 6.22

Percent Intermarried by Migration Pattern

(Marriage Choices of Conventional Jews Only)

REGION	18-44			45 +		
	NATIVE STAYER	NATIVE LEAVER	IN-MIGRANT	NATIVE STAYER	NATIVE LEAVER	IN-MIGRANT
Northeast	40.8 N=325	51.2 N=200	28.5 N=63	13.6 N=476	13.9 N=328	13.2 N=110
Midwest	31.0 N=79	40.3 N=63	34.0 N=44	17.8 N=89	12.4 N=132	22.6 N=42
South	42.4 N=69	38.2 N=32	43.9 N=150	16.1 N=46	36.2 N=26	11.1 N=269
West	54.8 N=108	40.7 N=23	45.1 N=149	28.4 N=49	— N=4	13.2 N=244

Jewish communal life is that, while Jews are proud of their educational attainment as a group, education has not been good for them because when Jewish young people go to college, they become "Universalists," abandon their heritage, and marry non-Jews. The data indicate that this is changing. Among conventional Jews under 45, education is negatively associated with intermarriage: the higher the educational attainment, the lower the likelihood of intermarriage; the lower the educational attainment, the greater the likelihood of intermarriage. The opposite is true among conventional Jews who are 45 and older: those with less than a college education are almost twice as likely to intermarry as those who have attended or graduated college.

These seemingly contradictory trends are encompassed by the tendency of Americans to marry within their levels of educational attainment, which can also be translated as class level (Blau, Blum, and Schwartz, 1982; Mare, 1991). In the past, Jews who were the most upwardly mobile were also the most likely to intermarry. Since Jews as a group have been upwardly mobile, high educational attainment has become the norm among younger adults. Those who have been left behind marry within their own class and thus are more likely to marry a non-Jew. Half of the conventional Jews under 45 who have not attended college intermarry (50.2 percent), as compared with less than a third of those who have attained advanced degrees (30.9 percent). Even with this dramatic association, age is still more strongly associated with intermarriage than is education; intermarriage is higher among younger Jews regardless of education.

Educational attainment is not apparently associated with intermarriage among non-conventional Jews, but there is an important indirect association. As demonstrated in Table 6.24, among Jews under the age of 45, Jewish self-definition is itself associated with educational attainment. The conventional mainstream Jews (Jews by religion) are the most educated: 60.3 percent have graduated college. Secular Jews who are considered conventional but are somewhat outside the mainstream are the next most educated: 56.6 percent have graduated from college. Non-conventional or marginal Jews, on the other hand, are far less educated. Persons of Jewish descent and Jews who practice (and in many cases were raised in) another religion are only half as likely to have an advanced degree, to have graduated—or even attended—college, than Jews by religion: only 27.6 percent of Jews by descent and 23.2 percent of those who practice another religion have completed college.

The direction of causality, if there is any, is unclear. Is marginal Jewish self-definition a cause or a result of lower educational attainment? Without more data about family background this question cannot be addressed. While the answer is beyond the scope of this paper or even the NJPS itself (which did not include questions about inter-generational mobility), the

TABLE 6.23

Percent Intermarried by Educational Attainment Controlling
For Age and Jewish Self-Definition
(All Marriage Choices of Respondents & Jewish Spouses)

EDUCATION	CONVENTIONAL JEWS		NON-CONVENTIONAL JEWS	
	18–44	45 +	18–44	45 +
High School or Less	50.2	10.6	90.1	91.5
	N = 236	N = 591	N = 126	N = 89
Some College	44.4	19.5	85.6	—
	N = 71	N = 48	N = 38	N = 4
Completed College	43.3	15.5	85.4	90.1
	N = 323	N = 303	N = 36	N = 25
Advanced/Prof Degree	30.9	18.3	86.1	—
	N = 333	N = 288	N = 40	N = 13

finding is nonetheless important because it demonstrates a structural association between educational attainment and Jewish self-definition. Since the association between Jewish self-definition and educational attainment applies only to Jews under 45, it is apparently a relationship that has changed over the last few decades. Whatever the reason for their lower educational attainment, non-conventional Jews under the age of 45 do not "fit in" educationally with their conventional counterparts.

Looking at non-Jews by birth who have married Jews underscores the relationship between Jewish self-definition and educational attainment. Non-Jewish spouses who have converted to Judaism (last column of Table 6.24) are a third more likely to have graduated college than non-Jewish spouses who have not (61.3 percent versus 46.5 percent). In other words, the non-Jewish spouses who take on Jewish self-definition have higher educational attainment than those who do not, and even higher than non-conventional Jews as well.

Conclusion

Intermarriage is the result of American Jewish assimilation and the product of social structural factors as well. Intermarriage is not exclusively the result of weakened Jewish identity; it is influenced also by external factors which constrain Jewish marriage choices.

Jewish communal policymakers—be they rabbis, communal leaders, Jewish professionals, or synagogue board members—frequently view intermarriage only as assimilation. However, this study strongly suggests that social structural factors are also involved.

TABLE 6.24

Education Completed by Jewish Self-Definition

Controlling for Age

(All Marriage Choices of Respondents & Jewish Spouses Under Age 45)

EDUCATION COMPLETED	BORN JEW- RELIGION JEWISH	JEW BY CHOICE	SECULAR JEW	JEWISH DESCENT	JEW, OTHER RELIGION	NON-JEW
High School or Less	22.6	27.5	35.4	58.3	45.7	44.7
Some College	7.1	12.2	7.9	14.1	21.0	8.8
Completed College	33.4	36.9	30.5	12.8	15.3	29.6
Advanced/Prof Degree	36.9	24.4	26.1	14.8	17.9	16.9
TOTAL	100.0	100.0	100.0	100.0	100.0	100.0

Our understanding and communal policies regarding intermarriage do not yet reflect the complexity of the factors which affect it. The findings concerning regional culture and selective migration suggest that intermarriage will have a different impact and should be dealt with as a particularly high priority in the Western communities. This study also points to the as yet unrecognized impact of the surrounding culture on Jews. In regions where communal norms in general are weak, Jewish norms will also be weakened.

The relationship between educational attainment, intermarriage, and conversion to Judaism raise disturbing questions about unintended exclusion on the part of the organized Jewish community. At the same time, a number of researchers have commented on the "cost of being Jewish," noting that affiliation increases with income (Phillips, 1986; Winter, 1985). The American Jewish community is properly proud of the accomplishments of its members. It may, however, have to consider ways to enfranchise those who have achieved less and are more "at risk" of intermarriage. It may also have to take more seriously the economic barriers that prevent some Jews from participating in Jewish communal activities.

Notes

1. As will be shown later, the intermarriages are more likely to end in divorce, and thus limiting the analysis to current marriages actually underestimates the extent to which intermarriage has taken place.

The NJPS data were weighted to accurately reflect the distribution of American Jewish households. These weights were applied to each marriage in the analysis in such a way as to make the number of weighted cases similar to the number of unweighted cases. Only the number of *weighted* cases are shown in the tables, but these closely approximate the number of *unweighted* cases so as not to artificially inflate statistical significance. Altogether there are 3056 *unweighted* cases, or marriage choices, in the analysis, and 3036 *weighted* cases.

2. Separated respondents are still legally married, but there is no spouse in the household about whom data could be collected. Since the two partners were not legally divorced, the questionnaire did not ask about separated spouses in the series of questions about "previous spouses," which apply only in the case of divorce.

3. The skip pattern for divorced respondents went back to ask about first marriages on the assumption that this would be the most recent marriage in most cases. The prevalence of twice-divorced respondents was not anticipated when the questionnaire was created.

4. Except for Jews-by-Choice who were excluded from the analysis.

5. This research, funded by the Wilstein Institute, will appear in the near future.

6. For example, one couple consisted of a born Jewish male, married to a female whose own mother was born a Jew but never practiced Judaism herself, and

had married a non-Jew. Although a Jew by halakhic standards, she saw herself only as of Jewish descent. Everyone concerned, including the Jewish husband, the Jewish descent wife, and all the in-laws considered this a marriage between a Jew and a non-Jew.

7. These two categories were almost entirely the product of intermarriages themselves (data not shown). While there are some persons who may have become less Jewish as a consequence of their intermarriage, all of the Jewish descent persons and almost all of the Jews practicing another religion were not themselves raised Jewish.

8. I am indebted to Sergio DellaPergola for bringing this distinction to my attention.

9. To be consistent with the rest of the tables I refer here only to ever-married Jews—the population under consideration. The relationship between generation and Jewish self-definition is true for all Jews in the NJPS, but the exact percentages included here refer only to ever-married Jews.

10. In-marriages by conventional Jews, mixed marriages by conventional Jews, in-marriages by non-conventional Jews, and mixed marriages by non-conventional Jews.

11. 1st, 2nd, 2nd-3rd, 3rd, 3rd-4th, 4th.

12. Again, I am referring here only to Jews who have been married—the group under consideration in this analysis. The statement, if not the exact proportions, would also apply to never-married Jews.

13. Using year of birth reverses the direction of the graph to be consistent with other graphs. Intermarriage now increases with year of birth, rather than decreasing with age.

References

Bayme, Steven, *Intermarriage and Communal Policy: Prevention, Conversion, and Outreach*, New York, No. American Jewish Committee, 1993.

Berman, Louis A., *Jews and Intermarriage*, New York, Thomas Yoselof, 1968.

Blau, Peter M., Carolyn Beeker, and Kevin M. Fitzpatrick, "Intersecting Social Affiliations and Intermarriage," in *Social Forces*, Volume 62 (March 1984a), pp. 585–606.

Blau, Peter M., Terry C. Blum, and Joseph E. Schwartz, "Heterogeneity and Intermarriage," in *American Sociological Review*, Volume 47 (February 1982), pp. 45–62.

Blum, Terry C., "Structural Constraints on Interpersonal Relations: A Test of Blau's Macrosociological Theory," in *American Journal of Sociology*, Volume 91, no. 3 (1985), pp. 511–21.

Cohen, Steven M., *American Modernity and Jewish Identity*, New York, Tavistock, 1983.

Cowan, Paul & Rachel, *Mixed Blessings*, New York, Doubleday, 1986.

DellaPergola Sergio, and U. O. Schmelz, eds., *Studies in Jewish Demography*, Jerusalem, Center for the Study of Contemporary Jewry, 1985.

Gordon, Milton, *Assimilation in American Life: The Role of Race, Religion, and National Origins*, New York, Oxford University Press, 1964.

Lazerwitz, Bernard, "The Jewish Community Variable in Jewish Identification," in *Journal for the Scientific Study of Religion*, Volume 16, no. 4 (1977), pp. 361–369.

Mare, Robert D., "Five Decades of Educational Assortative Mating," in *American Sociological Review*, Volume 56 (February 1991), pp. 15–32.

Massarik, Fred, *Jewish Identity: Facts for Planning*, Council of Jewish Federations, 1974.

Massarik, Fred, and A. Chenkin, "United States National Jewish Population Study: A First Report," in Milton Himmelfarb, ed., *American Jewish Year Book 1973*, pp. 264–306, Philadelphia and New York, Jewish Publication Society and the American Jewish Committee, 1973.

Medding, Peter Y., Gary Tobin, Sylvia Fishman Barack, andMordechai Rimor, *Jewish Identity in Conversionary and Mixed Marriages*, New York, No. American Jewish Committee, 1992.

Phillips, Bruce A., "Los Angeles Jewry: A Demographic Profile," In D. Singer, ed., *American Jewish Year Book*, pp. 126–194, New York and Philadelphia, American Jewish Committee, 1986.

Phillips, Bruce A., and Eve Weinberg, *The Milwaukee Jewish Population Study*, No. Milwaukee Jewish Federation, 1984.

Phillips, Bruce A., and Eve Weinberg, Data Collection Procedures in Random Digit Dialing Screening Studies: Interviewers and Respondents, in Steven Cohen, Jonathan Woocher, and Bruce A. Phillips, eds., *Perspectives in Jewish Population Research*, Boulder, Westview, 1984, pp. 107–118.

Phillips, Bruce A., "Factors Associated with Intermarriage in Three Western Cities," in Uziel O. Schmelz & Sergio DellaPergola, eds., *Papers in Jewish Demography*. Jerusalem, Center for the Study of Contemporary Jewry, 1989.

Roof, Wade C., and William McKinney, *American Mainline Religion: Its Changing Shape and Future*, New Brunswick and London: Rutgers University Press, 1987.

Schmelz, Uziel O., and S. DellaPergola, "The Demographic Consequences of U.S. Jewish Population Trends," in D. Singer, ed., *American Jewish Year Book*, pp. 141–187, New York and Philadelphia: American Jewish Committee and Jewish Publishing Society, 1983.

Silberman, Charles, *A Certain People*, New York, Summit Books, 1985.

Sklare, Marshall, *America's Jews*, New York, Basic Books, 1971.

Stark, Rodney, and William S. Bainbridge, *The Future of Religion, Secularization, Revival, and Cult Formation*, Berkeley and Los Angeles, University of California Press, 1985.

Tobin, Gary, and Julies Lipsam, "Recent Jewish Community Population Studies: A Roundup." in D. Singer, ed., *American Jewish Year Book*, 154–178. Philadelphia, Jewish Publishing Society, 1985.

Welch, Michael R., and John Baltzell, "Geographic Mobility, Social Integration, and Church Attendance," in *Journal for the Scientific Study of Religion*, Volume 23, no. 1 (1984), pp. 75–91.

Winter, Alan J., "Who Can Afford to be Jewish," in *Moment* (May 1985), pp. 36–42.

7

The Educational Background of American Jews

Seymour Martin Lipset

Acknowledgments

This study of Jewish education in America was commissioned and funded by the Mandel Institute for the Advanced Study and Development of Jewish Education in Jerusalem. I am extremely grateful to Mort Mandel, its founder; Seymour Fox, its president; and Annette Hochstein, its director, for the confidence they exhibited in me as well as for useful advice. As will be evident to the reader, the analysis is largely based on the survey data collected by the 1990 National Jewish Population Survey financed by the Council of Jewish Federations and directed by Barry Kosmin. He and the Council have been extremely generous in making the data available. I am indebted to Dr. Kosmin for intellectual advice. I must also acknowledge with gratitude the cooperation of the Susan and David Wilstein Institute of Jewish Policy Studies and its director and associate director, David Gordis and Yoav Ben-Horin, and the Hoover Institution of Stanford University and its director, John Raisian, both of which housed the project as part of their research program.

Finally, I could not have carried out the project without the assistance of three social scientists, much more conversant with statistical analysis than I am; Jeffrey Hayes, now at the University of Chicago, Mordicai Rimor of the Louis Guttman Institute for Applied Social Research in Jerusalem, and John Torres of the Hoover Institution and the sociology department at Stanford. As may be evident from the number of persons and institutions involved, translating data collected for Census type demographic reports for use in a standard survey type bivariate and multivariate analysis did not prove simple and produced a number of false starts.

I trust that this monograph will be of interest and use to scholars of American Jewry and ethnicity, and to practitioners dealing with Jewish educational policy.

Seymour Martin Lipset
George Mason University
March 1994

I. Introduction

The unique aspects of American Jewry compared to other ethno-religious groups fall into five categories: religious behavior, income, demography, politics, and education—both religious and secular. The best effort to document their characteristics, the National Jewish Population Survey (NJPS) of 1990, yields information on all of these matters and much more. The report presented here, one of a series analyzing the NJPS data, focuses on education.

For the NJPS, 125,813 randomly selected persons were asked questions about their own religious preference and that of their household. Altogether, this method produced 2,441 completed interviews, giving information on 6,514 persons in those households. The NJPS sample was then selected from those identified as living in a Jewish household. Interviews were conducted with 2,134 households, providing information on 4,601 individuals. Roughly one-sixth of the respondents were not used for the purpose of this analysis because their responses to various questions indicated that they did not consider themselves Jewish and currently belong to another religion. The Core Jewish Population (CJP) as defined by the demographers who conducted the survey includes Born Jews whose religion is Judaism (BJR), converts who are Jews by Choice (JBC), and born Jews who do not have a religious but a secular identification (JNR). In addition, 84 percent of the CJP had at least one Jewish parent. The data were then weighted through a process which involved using all of the original 125,813 screening interviews.[1] The analysis presented here is based on the weighted sample of the CJP.

A number of stereotypical observations about Jews are confirmed by the 1990 NJPS[2]: Jews are, by far, more well-to-do than the population as a whole and are politically much more liberal. They are also the best educated of any ethno-religious group. Educational achievement has been one of the great prides of American Jewry, and the survey data indicate that it is justified. Among all adults 18 years and over who identify themselves as Jewish in religious terms, just under a third—30 percent—do not have any college education, while just over 50 percent are college graduates. Almost half of these—24 percent—have gone beyond college to some form of post-graduate education. Secular Jews, those who are not religious in any way, are slightly better educated than religious Jews. Only 27 percent have not attended college. It is interesting to note that born Jews who have converted out and belong to other denominations (six percent of the enlarged sample) are less well educated. Over one-third have no college background. The picture is somewhat similar for persons who report Jewish parentage or descent but were raised from birth in another religion.

Other trends regarding marriage and family are also clear. Jews are less likely to marry and do so later than others with similar backgrounds; they have a lower birthrate than other groups in the population; and their rate of intermarriage is high and increasing steadily.[3] Immigration apart, these behavioral traits mean that the Jewish population in America is likely to decline. At the extreme, one demographer predicts a near extinction in the not too distant future. The hope, suggested by earlier studies on intermarriage, that such behavior might actually add to the population, given conversions and Jewish identification of intermarried families, does not seem to be borne out by the 1990 survey. Fifty-nine percent of currently married households are both Jewish, six percent are conversionary households, and 35 percent are mixed-marriage households. Only one-sixth—17 percent—of intermarried Jews have a spouse who has converted. The mates of the rest have remained Gentiles. Since 1985, the majority, 57 percent, of Jews married non-Jews.[4] This compares with 10 percent for those who mated before 1965 and 31 percent for those who wed between 1965 and 1974. As Barry Kosmin et al. note in their preliminary report on the results of the overall study "since 1985 twice as many mixed couples (born Jew with Gentile spouse) have been created as Jewish couples (born Jew with Jewish spouse)."

In addition to the problem that is posed by low fertility for Jewish continuity is the concern that most children with only one Jewish parent are not being raised as Jews. "Only 28 percent of . . . children [in religiously mixed households] are reported as being raised Jewish. Some 41 percent are being raised in a non-Jewish religion." Almost a third—31 percent—are not being given a religious identification.[5] If we look at the full picture, we find that not only has intermarriage doubled but that "just under half of all children in the surveyed households are currently being raised with Judaism as their religion and another 16 percent qualify as secular Jews."[6]

Education is obviously the principal mechanism to socialize succeeding generations into being Jewish and to stimulate adult Jews and Gentile spouses to foster religious and cultural interests in the community. What the Jewish community of the future will look like—occupationally, culturally, and Jewishly—will be, to a considerable degree, a function of both non-Jewish and Jewish education.

This article attempts to understand the determinants and consequences of Jewish education through an exploration of the NJPS data. The first section examines the factors that influence the probability of a respondent securing Jewish training. These factors include gender and age, as well as denominational, generational, regional, and familial background. The second part lends support to the hypothesis that the greater the exposure to Jewish learning, the more likely the recipient is to be involved in Jewish life and the religious community, and to pass the commitment on to his or her children. The conclusions drawn from the bivariate data of these two sections are then given additional credence through multivariate regression analyses. Finally, the paper addresses the future of the Jewish community—its youth. The determinants of Jewish education among the young are evaluated by examining the role of family socioeconomic status, geographic mobility, patterns of religious observance, as well as denominational, familial, and regional background. Again, multiple regression is used to support the contingency table analysis. Those Jews enrolled in college are given particular attention because of the great problems and potential solutions posed by secular education for Jewish continuity.

The concern for Jewish continuity focuses, therefore, on Jewish education as the major tool available to the community to stem the weakening which is taking place. The study permits an examination of the relationship between different types of Jewish education and subsequent participation in—and commitment to—the community. The basic picture is clear: those classified as religious, whether born Jewish or converted to Judaism, are likely to report some form of Jewish education; eighty-four percent of the males and 65 percent of the females do so. The figures, however, drop for those born Jewish but classified as non-religious or ethnic-seculars. Three-fifths—61 percent—of the men and 45 percent of the women said they have had a Jewish education. People who were born and raised Jewish but converted out were much less likely to have had Jewish education (27 percent for the males and 24 percent for the females.)

These findings present us with a classic chicken and egg problem in trying to explain the role of religious education: To what extent do family religious commitments, which themselves might be a reflection of prior education, influence the strong linkages between Jewish education, Jewish identification, and community involvement? Can schooling overcome the lack of commitment of those reared in weakly identified families? No definite conclusion is possible in absence of longitudinal data (information gathered over time from the same respondents), particularly since the decision to educate or not reflects, in most cases, the degree of religiosity in the home. Still, the evidence is congruent with the hypothesis that Jewish education makes a difference.

II. Determinants of Jewish Education for Adult Respondents

Turning to the analysis, approximately 66 percent of the core respondents reported in the 1990 NJPS had, at some point, been exposed to formal Jewish education. Participation has been measured by the type of education received and the number of years completed. The type of education can be differentiated into four groups: 1) full-time Jewish schools including day schools and *yeshivas;* 2) part-time schools that meet more than once a week, mainly in the afternoons; 3) Sunday schools and other once-a-week Jewish educational programs; 4) Private tutoring. There was no question in the survey about attendance at Jewish secular schools, such as those run by the Workmen's Circle. It is not possible to evaluate the quality of Jewish educational programs from the data. The formal Jewish education measures, e.g., types of schooling or years in different educational programs, are dependent variables when analyzing determinants, while, for the next section where the consequences of education are the focus, they serve as independent variables.

Most Jews living in America were not exposed to intensive religious education. More than half of those who ever attended—53 percent, or 35 percent of the whole sample—went to part-time, afternoon programs. The next to largest group is composed of those who had attended Sunday school—28 percent—followed by full-time day schools—11 percent—and private tutoring (eight percent). Almost all of those who have some Jewish education studied for more than a year; only 2.5 percent attended for less than a year. As shown in Table 7.1, 30 percent participated less than five years, and another 36 percent were involved for longer periods, with 15 percent having been in formal Jewish training for 11 years or more.

Given that traditional Judaism places much greater emphasis on men than on women with respect to synagogue observance and religious study, it is not surprising that males are more likely than females to have been exposed to Jewish education (Table 7.2). The former are also more likely to have been involved in the more intense forms of Jewish education. Around two-thirds—66 percent—of day schoolers and 63 percent of the part-

TABLE 7.1
Number of Years of Formal Jewish Education

No. of Years	Born Jews-Religious Jews	Jews By Choice	Ethnic-secular Jews	Total CJP
< 5 years	31	56	20	30
6–10 years	26	4	8	21
11–14 years	8	1	1	6
15 + years	11	2	3	9
Never Attended	25	37	67	33
Types of Schooling				
Day School	13	—	3	11
Part-time/Afternoon	54	14	54	53
Sunday School	27	24	34	28
Private Tutor	5	62	9	8

TABLE 7.2
Form of Jewish Education by Gender (Percent)

	Male	Female	Total
Day School	11	5	7
Part-time/Afternoon	46	25	35
Sunday School	15	22	19
Private Tutor	6	5	5
Never Attended	23	42	33

timers are men. The picture reverses sharply for Sunday School (the least stringent form of training) and somewhat less for private tutoring. Sixty-two percent of Sunday schoolers and 50 percent of the privately tutored are female. To sum up, women are less likely to have been enrolled at all, while those who did so are more likely to have been involved in programs that met less frequently or for less time.

Basically, the same conclusions are reached with respect to the quantity of education received. Among those who received any, men have attended more years than women, although the gender difference diminishes for those who have studied for 10 years or more—17 percent male and 13 percent female. Still, the most noteworthy finding is that within each age group, women are much less likely to have any Jewish education and, if ever involved, to have studied for fewer years than men (Table 7.3).

The same pattern, of course, holds up for the correlates of Bar or Bat Mitzvah ceremonies. It should be noted that the proportion of the denominationally identified who have been confirmed has increased over time,

TABLE 7.3

Years of Attendance by Age, Controlled for Gender (Percent)

	18–19	20–29	30–39	40–49	50–59	60–69	70–79	80+	Row Total
Male									
< 5 years	25	29	34	36	34	38	42	32	35
6–10	25	25	24	29	25	26	14	17	24
> 11 years	15	11	16	18	12	17	19	27	17
Never Attended	36	35	26	17	19	20	24	24	25
Female									
< 5 years	20	25	26	26	29	28	20	21	26
6–10 years	27	22	19	20	21	16	18	8	19
> 11 years	11	10	15	13	9	12	12	27	13
Never Attended	42	43	40	41	37	44	50	44	42

particularly among the younger. The converse is true for the ethnic-secular; only one-sixth of the 18 to 29 year olds among them have been confirmed as compared to two-thirds of the religiously linked. For the core Jewish population as a whole, less than half—46 percent—have gone through the coming of age rite. Confirmants include a majority—56 percent—of the religiously identified birth-right Jews (85 percent men and 27 percent women), compared to 24 percent of the ethnic-seculars (35 percent men and 13.5 percent women).

The fact that younger Jews have been less exposed to Jewish education than the middle-aged is congruent with the evidence that assimilation, particularly intermarriage, has increased. However, the relationship that exists, considering all age groups, appears to be curvilinear. Older and younger people have been less exposed to Jewish learning than the middle generation. Sixty-one percent of the 18 through 29 year olds have been involved in some form. This figure increases gradually to 72 percent for those in the 50 through 59 years old category but then declines to 67 percent for the 60 through 69 year old group, and to 64 percent for those who are 70 years or older (Table 7.4).

Looking at the data in terms of decades, the largest proportion involved in Jewish education for substantial periods is found among those born in the 1930s followed by the war and post-war cohorts, those born in the 1940s. It is impossible to account for this pattern using the available data, but an interpretation may be suggested. The parents of the generations who reached confirmation age during the years that included the coming to power of the Nazis, increased anti-Semitism in the United States, the Holocaust, and the creation of the state of Israel were exposed to very strong stimuli to affirm their Judaism. These events had a positive effect on Jewish identity, activating latent religious loyalties. Logically these events should have led more parents to send their children to Jewish schools. But they were sent disproportionately to the weakest and least effective form, i.e., Sunday school. It may be hypothesized further that as those events and experiences receded into history, the assimilatory forces regained strength.

Socio-political conditions during the school years appear to have had less effect on the type of Jewish education received than on length of time enrolled (see Table 7.5). Across all age or time cohorts, little more than one-third—35 percent—of the respondents report having attended part-time schools. Sunday school attendance is, however, curiously curvilinear. It is greatest for those who were born during the 1930s and 1940s (e.g., aged 40–59 when interviewed), but less for younger cohorts and least for the oldest ones, who partook during the 1920s or earlier. Presumably such a limited form of schooling was less available for the older respondents and

TABLE 7.4

Number of Years of Formal Education by Year of Birth and Age (Percent)

	YEARS OF BIRTH AND AGE						
YEARS ATTENDED	1960–72 18–29	1950–59 30–39	1940–49 40–49	1930–39 50–59	1920–29 60–69	1919 AND BEFORE 70+	ROW TOTAL
1-5 Years	27	30	31	31	32	30	30
6–10 years	24	21	24	23	21	15	21
11–15 years	6	10	7	6	4	3	6
15 + years	5	5	9	12	10	16	9
Never Attended	39	33	29	28	33	36	33

142

TABLE 7.5

Type of Education by Year of Birth or Age (Percent)

Years Attended	1960–72 18–29	1950–59 30–39	1940–49 40–49	1939–39 50–59	1920–29 60–69	1919 and before 70+	Row Total
Day School	9	7	7	6	12	6	8
Part-time/Afternoon	32	36	37	36	36	37	35
Sunday School	17	17	24	23	17	14	19
Private Tutor	3	5	4	9	5	9	5
Never Attended	39	34	27	26	30	35	33
Column Total	21	25	19	10	11	13	100

may have been more disapproved of by families closer to the old country experience. The proportion who went to day school has grown slightly but steadily over time, from six percent for the 1930s cohorts to seven for those who reached school age in the 1940s and 1950s, and nine percent for the youngest cohorts. Thus there has been an increase at the two extremes, those not participating and those attending the most intensive form, day schools. The latter change has particularly involved women.

How does assimilation to American society affect Jewish education? Examining the length of family residence in America provides an answer to this question. The relationship between Jewish education and national origin has been analyzed by breaking the sample into four generations: the foreign-born—10 percent; those born in the U.S. with two foreign-born parents—20 percent; those born here, with at least one parent born here and grandparents who are foreign-born—27.5 percent; and native-born, with at least one U.S. born parent and at least one grandparent born in America—43 percent. The relationship between these "generations" and the types of Jewish education is shown in Table 7.6.

As is evident from the table, those from abroad include close to the largest proportion (37 percent) without any Jewish training and the biggest of those with the most intensive, day school (29 percent). The latter finding may reflect the greater availability of such education in the "old country." One-fifth—20 percent—had attended part-time school. Few, seven percent, went to Sunday School, a form of education linked largely to the Reform movement, which did not exist in Eastern Europe and had a limited membership elsewhere. Clearly, day school attendance falls off steadily with length of generational stay in America, while Sunday school attendance increases.

These findings clearly imply that assimilation pressures are operative. The interplay between generational background and type of training reinforces the assumption that Americanization works against Jewish education. As noted, the foreign-born show great propensity to have attended day school. Not only is it true that American-born Jews are seemingly more assimilated in terms of educational involvements, but logically they

TABLE 7.6
Types of Jewish Education by Generational Background (Percent)

	1ST	2ND	3RD	4TH
Day School	29	12	5	3
Part-time	20	43	46	29
Sunday	7	13	22	22
Private Tutor	7	6	3	6
Never Attended	37	26	24	41

are also less Orthodox. These relationships are reinforced when we relate patterns of school attendance to the third generation, i.e., grandparents. As noted above, those with no grandparents born in the United States are the most likely to have attended day school. More than four-fifths—84 percent—of all day school students do not have a single American-born grandparent. They are also more likely to have gone to part-time afternoon than to Sunday school and are the least likely to report a private tutor or to have no Jewish education. Those who have all four grandparents native-born show the opposite pattern: forty-four percent have not been involved in any form of Jewish education, compared to 26 percent of those with four foreign-born grandparents.

The curvilinear relationship between generation and non-attendance (highest for the first and fourth generations) may reflect two diverse patterns of assimilation. Many of the foreign-born respondents and their parents were reared in cultures which contained large segments of highly religious Orthodox and extremely irreligious radicals.[7] As noted, however, the Population Survey unfortunately did not inquire into exposure to secular Yiddish education. In America, both groups were exposed to cultural pressures to give up the strict requirements of Orthodoxy and adherence to atheistic, irreligious, politically radical doctrines, as they aspired to—or made their way into—the middle class. The more acceptable behavior was Americanized moderate Conservatism for those of Orthodox background and Reform for the scions of secularity.

Whether one is the offspring of an intermarried family or not is an even more decisive factor. The dysfunctional effects of intermarriage on Jewish continuity are clear. The likelihood of receiving a Jewish education is greatest when both parents are Jewish. This is true for roughly two-thirds of the respondents. Four-fifths of them have been to Jewish schools, compared to about 30 percent of those from intermarried families. As noted earlier, relatively few respondents attended day schools, but 93 percent of those who did were from fully Jewish families, while only 48 percent of those who are Jewishly identified—but without any exposure to religious education—had two Jewish parents. Thirty-nine percent of the respondents with intramarried parents continued their studies for six or more years, compared to nine percent of those with intermarried ones.

In religiously mixed families, a Jewish mother appears somewhat more important for educational continuity than a Jewish father. This finding may reflect the fact that Judaism is a matrilineal religion and that in America generally women are more religiously committed and involved than men. Still, as indicated in Table 7.7, only 34 percent of the offspring of intermarried Jewish women had any religious education, a bit more than 27 percent of those whose one Jewish parent was a male.

TABLE 7.7

Intermarriage Effects on Jewish Education (Percent)

YEARS ATTENDED	BOTH PARENTS JEWISH	MOTHER JEWISH	FATHER JEWISH	TOTAL
< 5 years	41	24	19	37
6–10 years	27	8	5	21
11–15 years	7	2	1	6
15 + years	5	—	2	5
Never Attended	20	66	73	31

The denomination of the family of origin is obviously important in affecting the propensity for Jewish education, though by some measures less than might be anticipated. Surprisingly, an identical proportion—20 percent—from Orthodox and Reform families, never had formal Jewish education, while for Conservatives the ratio is a bit higher—23 percent. Those from Orthodox homes, however, exhibited the highest commitment, if type of education is considered: 46 percent attended day school, while 28 percent went to part-time afternoon classes. Over half of them— 53 percent—spent six or more years in a Jewish curriculum. Conservative offspring were much more likely than scions of Reform to have attended day school—12 percent—or afternoon classes—46 percent. Curiously, the children of Conservative families spent fewer years absorbing Jewish learning than those from Reform origins. More than two-fifths of the former— 38 percent—compared with 42 percent of the latter, continued their education for six years or more. Fifty-six percent of those from an ethnic-secular background did not partake of any Jewish education.

Current affiliation produces somewhat stronger correlations, presumably because the level and intensity of Jewish education reflect the degree of religiosity of the respondents. Twenty percent of today's Orthodox report having gone to a full-time day school as compared to less than seven percent of the Conservatives and only three percent of the Reform. Conservatives lead the Reform in proportion of those who have attended part-time school, 50 percent to 34 percent. Conversely, however, those now affiliated with Reform are more likely to have been exposed to the least stringent training (Sunday school)—41 percent—compared to the Conservatives' 16 percent, and Orthodox's nine percent. Not surprisingly, those who have remained Orthodox are much more likely to have had day school education than those who left the denomination. This may suggest that the latter's families were actually much less Orthodox than the former's. In any case, the modal relationships to religious denominations are clear: day school for the Orthodox, afternoon for the Conservatives, Sunday for the

Reform. Not surprisingly, most of those who report some form of secular identification were not involved in any form of Jewish religious education.

The part of the country in which respondents were born also has a clear relationship to exposure to religious teaching. Forty-eight percent of those from the Western states and 34 percent of Southerners had never partaken of any form of formal Jewish learning, compared to 30 percent of Northeasterners and 28 percent of Midwesterners. Those from the Northeast, the oldest region of American Jewish settlement, also show the highest propensity for day school—seven percent—and afternoon school—42 percent—as compared to three percent and 25 percent for those from the South. These results again are congruent with our impressions of the correlates of assimilation: most in the West, least in the Northeast. The foreign-born, it may be noted again, were the most likely to have received a day school education—29 percent—whereas only five percent of the American-born secured such an intensive education.

Considering the different variables—gender, age, denomination, generational background, intermarriage, and region—a clear picture emerges of the factors associated with educational enrollment. The most likely candidate to have received formal Jewish education has the following profile: a male who is foreign-born or has foreign-born parents and grandparents, with practicing non-intermarried parents who raised him in the Northeast and in one of the three major denominations, preferably Orthodox. The more the indicators reflect Americanization, the less chances of having been trained for Jewish continuity. None of these are surprising, and the implications for Jewish continuity are discouraging since all the negative factors are increasing.

These factors were combined in an Americanization scale, comprised of variables such as generations in the U.S., denomination and region reared, and Jewishness of parent. Respondents scored from zero to four. As shown in Table 7.9, the more Americanized one's score, the less exposure to Jewish education.

III. The Consequences of Formal Jewish Education

The previous section related measures of Jewish education to various background variables. This section considers the educational items as independent variables to see how the degree of Jewish training, secured while young, is associated with various adult attitudes and behaviors. The following areas can be hypothesized as consequences of Jewish education: Jewish identity, denomination, synagogue attendance, philanthropy (especially Jewish), involvement in Jewish organizations, intermarriage, attach-

TABLE 7.8
Denomination Raised and Years in Jewish Education (Percent)

YEARS ATTENDED	ORTHODOX	CONSERVATIVE	REFORM	ETHNIC-SECULAR	TOTAL
< 5 years	29	38	38	31	34
6–10 years	30	27	29	7	23
11–15 years	9	6	9	4	6
15+ years	12	5	4	2	5
Never Attended	20	23	20	56	31

TABLE 7.9
Americanization Score and Years of Jewish Education

YEARS ATTENDED	VERY JEWISH	JEWISH	AMERICANIZED	VERY AMERICANIZED
< 5 years	35	45	36	36
6–18 years	29	27.5	19	2
11–15 years	8	5	7	1
15+ years	9	4	3	—
Never Attended	18	18	35	61
Total	10	41	39	10

ment to Israel, attitudes regarding Jewishness, adult Jewish learning, and children's Jewish education. Importantly, it should be noted that what follows are reports of correlations, not of causal processes.

Perhaps the best single indicator of commitment to continuity and the community in the survey is the question "How important is being a Jew for you?" Only 22 percent of those who had never been exposed to any form of Jewish education replied "very important." The same answer was given by 75 percent of those who had been to day school, 68 percent of the privately tutored, 47 percent of the former students at part-time/afternoon classes, and 40 percent of respondents whose training was limited to Sunday school. A strong relationship exists between length of Jewish studies and the response "very important," from 41 percent of those who had five years or less of Jewish education to 70 percent for those who had 11 years or more. It is noteworthy that the 16 percent of the core Jewish population who were classified as ethnic-seculars—over half of whom had no Jewish schooling—were overwhelmingly very low on commitment.

Historically, Jewish life has centered around the synagogue. This is less true in America: as of 1990, 67 percent of Jewish households reported that they are not members. Still, 73 percent of the respondents said that they attend a religious service at least once a year. Only 22 percent participate once a month or more. Fifty two percent attend from once to a few times a year, presumably on the High Holidays, while 27 percent never partake. Synagogue behavior, of course, correlates with religious education. The more involvement when young, the more participation as an adult.

Close to half of American Jews, 48 percent, report that they observe the most serious religious personal obligation, fasting on Yom Kippur. Willingness to do so correlates strongly with type and duration of religious training. Most former day and afternoon schoolers, as well as the privately tutored—70, 59, and 70 percent, respectively—abstain from food on that day. Less than half of those who attended Sunday school—47 percent—fast, while the overwhelming majority—72 percent—of those who never had any Jewish education eat on this High Holiday. As expected, abstaining from food on Yom Kippur correlates strongly with amount of training: from 28 percent for those who never attended religious school, to 52 percent for those who went for the five years or less, to 67 percent for those with 11 or more years education.

To further demonstrate the relationship, a scale was constructed of four so-called "identity" items used in many studies of Jewish commitment. These items are: 1) candles at Hanukkah, 2) candle ceremonies on Friday nights, 3) attendance at Passover seders, and 4) eating Kosher foods. The scale ranges from "very high" (following all four rituals most of the time) to "very low" (never observing any). As expected, the more intense the educational experience of respondents, the higher their score on ritual observance. Close to a fifth, 18 percent, of those who score in the very high category are former day school students. Conversely, only three percent in the very low group have the same background. More than three-fifths, 67 percent, of the extreme non-identifiers lack any Jewish education. Those whose Jewish training is limited to Sunday school are the least likely of the religiously educated to be in the highest identity category: 18 percent are, as compared to 52 percent of those who had been to day school.

The same relationship holds true for the number of years of Jewish education. Close to half, 44 percent, of those with more than 15 years of study are in households which observe all four rituals, while, as noted earlier, two-thirds, 67 percent, of the interviewees without any religious training are not involved in any. The propensity to be totally non-observant correlates in linear fashion with the amount of education: 25 percent for those with no formal Jewish education, 19 percent for one to five years, seven percent for six to ten, four percent for 11 to 15 years, and three percent for those with 15 years or more of formal Jewish education. The ritual observance scale has been disaggregated in Table 7.12 to

TABLE 7.10

*Years of Education and Involvement
in the Synagogue (Percent)*

	Never Attended	< 6 Years	6–10 Years	11 + Years	Total
Member	18	34	44	52	33
Attended Once a Month or More	17	19	28.5	38	22

TABLE 7.11

Type of Schooling and Ritual Observance (Scale) (Percent)

		Very Low	Low	Average	High	Very High	Row Total
Day	Row	5	6	20	17	52	8
School	Column	3	3	6	5	18	
Part-time	Row	6	14	27	28	26	35
	Column	16	31	38	39	40	
Sunday	Row	8	14	25	36	18	19
School	Column	12	17	19	27	15	
Private	Row	4	14	28	26	29	5
tutor	Column	2	4	6	6	7	
Never	Row	25	22	23	18	13	33
Attended	Column	67	45	30	22	20	
Column Total		12	16	25	25	22	100

demonstrate that the longer one attends Jewish schooling, the more likely one is to follow each observance.

The decline of involvement in the Jewish religious community is paralleled by a fall-off in intra-communal social relationships if the popular impression of close ties in the old country, or areas, of first generation immigrant settlement is accurate. Close to two-fifths of the respondents, 37 percent, reported most or all of their closest friends are Jewish. About a fifth, 23 percent, said none or few are, while 41 percent responded "some." As with earlier indicators, the more education, the more Jewish friends (Table 7.13). The data showing most or all are Jewish has, however, fallen steadily over time, from close to three-fifths for those over 65 years old, to below a third for those between 18 and 29 years of age. And as with other indicators of Jewish commitment, informal ties are linked to religious training. Over half, 53 percent, of those with more than 15 years

TABLE 7.12
Years of Jewish Education and Ritual Observance (Percent) (Rows)

YEARS ATTENDED	HANUKKAH CANDLES		ATTEND SEDERS		FRIDAY CANDLES		KOSHER MEAT	
	NEVER	ALL OF THE TIME	NEVER	ALL OF THE TIME	NEVER	ALL OF THE TIME	NEVER	ALL OF THE TIME
1–5 years	21	51	18	47	65	8	59	13
6–10 years	13	61	8	65	54	15	56	13
11–15 years	12	73	11	77	44	25	60	23
15 + years	22	65	12	65	46	30	42	33
Never	48	33	40	31	75	7	65	9

TABLE 7.13
Jewish Friendship and Years of Education (Percent)

JEWISH FRIENDS	< 5 YEARS	6–10 YEARS	11–15 YEARS	15 + YEARS	NONE	ROW TOTAL
Few/None	20	20	18	16	29	23
Some Jewish	41	39	33	30	44	40
Most/All	39	41	49	53	27	37
Column Total	33	23	6	55	33	100

of Jewish education reported most or all of their closest friends are Jewish, compared to over a quarter, 27 percent, for those who never partook in any formal Jewish learning.

Much more important than friendships, of course, is marriage. The most publicized result of the Population Study is that the rate of intermarriage has steadily increased to 57 percent for those wed in the last five years. This is a new development in the history of the American Jewish family. As Egon Mayer points out, the Jewish family has been a remarkably stable institution through much of the twentieth century during which time "Jews continued to marry other Jews, and through the forces of intergenerational continuity, continued to raise children stamped with some inchoate sense of Jewish identity. . . ."[8] Signs of change were revealed in the 1970 NJPS: "What shocked the community was the reported rise in the level of intermarriage from less than two percent of those individuals who had married before 1925, to about six percent of those marrying between 1940 and 1960, to 12 percent of the 1960–64 marriage cohort, to a high of 29 percent of all Jews marrying in the five years preceding the survey."[9]

The 1990 NJPS indicates the pace of change has not decreased. If we consider the entire core Jewish population in the sample, not just the recently married, 61 percent of the respondents report that their first and usually only spouse was born Jewish. Another five percent are married to converts. Of the remaining, 10 percent have Catholic spouses, 13 percent Protestants, six percent "others," and four and a half percent wedded people with no religion. The latter two categories are probably predominantly of Jewish origin.

Once again, the extent and nature of Jewish education correlate strongly with the probability of mating with another Jew. The more Jewish education one has, the less likely one is to marry a non-Jew. Over three-quarters, 78 percent, of those who attended a day school married birth-right Jews, a figure which falls off to two-thirds for both private tutorees (65 percent) and persons educated in part-time school (67 percent), and to 57 percent for Sunday schoolers. Half—50 percent—of interviewees who had no Jewish training wed non-Jewish partners. The full picture is presented in Table 7.14.

The growth in the intermarriage rate reflects current attitudes dominant among adult Jews. The Population Survey inquired: "Hypothetically, if your child were considering marrying a non-Jewish person, would you: strongly support, support, accept, or be neutral, oppose, or strongly oppose the marriage?" Only 16 percent would oppose and six percent strongly oppose such a marriage. One-third would support a child doing so, 47 percent would accept it or be neutral. More religious education only marginally reduces the willingness to accept or support intermarriage, except for those with more than 15 years of schooling, presumably largely dedicated Orthodox. Still, only minorities in each category are antagonistic: 34 percent in the 15 + years group, 23 percent among the six through 10 years one, 15 percent for the five years or less, and only eight percent among those without any formal Jewish education.

The decline in concern for intermarriage is reflected in Jews' preferences with regard to the ethno-religious character of the neighborhoods in which they live. The proximity to Jewish or Gentile neighbors presumably affects the probabilities for marrying in or out of the community. The majority of those interviewed report living in areas which are not Jewish—35 percent, or little Jewish—28 percent. Only nine percent reside in very Jewish districts. The proportion living in the latter falls off in linear fashion by age from those over 60, 15 percent, to the 18 through 29 year old group, eight percent. Many, of course, do not have much choice when their communities lack distinctively Jewish districts as more and more cities do.

The NJPS inquired as to how important the Jewish character of the neighborhood is to the respondent. A majority, 62 percent, replied that it is either not important or not very important, while 32 percent answered that it is somewhat important. Only 14 percent said it is very important to reside in a predominantly Jewish district. Not surprisingly, such feelings strongly relate to the extent and type of education received, much like the behavioral and attitudinal items presented earlier. As reported in Tables 7.15 and 7.16, the longer and more intense the Jewish educational experience, the more people are interested in living among their co-religionists, presumably, at least in part, to facilitate the upbringing and marriage of their children with other Jews. But as we have seen, this is not a major concern of most American Jews. Only 27 percent of those with 15 or more years of religious education said it is very important to live in a Jewish neighborhood, while fully 44 percent did not consider it important.

TABLE 7.14
Type of Schooling and Intermarriage (Percent)

RELIGION OF SPOUSE (FIRST MARRIAGE IF MORE THAN ONE)	SCHOOL TYPE				
	DAY SCHOOL	PART-TIME	SUNDAY SCHOOL	PRIVATE TUTOR	NEVER ATTENDED
Born Jewish	78	65	57	67	50
Converted	1	8	5	3	4
Catholic	6	9	11	5	14
Protestant	3	11	18	19	14
Other	4	3	6	6	9
No Religion	9	4	3	—	7

TABLE 7.15
Importance of Neighborhood Jewishness by Years of Jewish Education (Percent)

		1–5	6–10	11–14	15+	NONE	ROW TOTAL
Not important and not very important	Row	32	22	4.5	4	8	54
	Column	52	51	39	44	62	—
Somewhat important	Row	36	26	6.5	5	26	32
	Column	35	36	33	29	26	—
Very important	Row	30	21	12	10	28	14
	Column	13	13	27.5	26.5	12	—
Column Total		33	23	6	5	33	100

TABLE 7.16
Importance of Neighborhood Jewishness and Type of Jewish Education (Percent)

		DAY SCHOOL	PART-TIME	SUNDAY	PRIVATE TUTOR	NONE	ROW TOTAL
Not important and not very important	Row	5	32	21	5	38	54
	Column	34	48	60	47	62	—
Somewhat important	Row	8	40	19.5	6	26.5	32
	Column	34	36	33	36	26	—
Very important	Row	17	40	10	6	27	14
	Column	32	16	7	17	12	—
Column Total		7	35.6	19	5	33	100

The indicators of sentiments toward the religious background of their children's spouses and neighbors suggest that the walls have been permanently breached, that education alone will not maintain the community.

Nathan Glazer once noted that Israel had become the religion of the Jews. That is to say, it is the major source of Jewish identity or commitment. The findings of the Population Study, however, challenge the assumption that Jews, regardless of their background, are deeply committed to the Jewish state.

The NJPS asked the following four questions: How emotionally attached are you to Israel? How many times have you been to Israel? Do you often talk about Israel to friends and relatives? and Do you contribute to the United Jewish Appeal? (Most of the funds for the latter are collected in the name of Israel's needs.) The responses to the first question clearly suggest that most American Jews are *not* strongly dedicated to the Jewish state. Only 10 percent said they are "extremely attached to Israel," while another 20 percent answered "very attached." The most common response given by over two-fifths—45 percent—was "somewhat," while 25 percent replied they were "not attached." At first glance, the picture looks more positive with respect to the second query, conversations about Israel with friends and relatives. Over two-thirds—68 percent—said they talked about Israel. When the interviewers inquired further, "How often would that be?" giving them the choices of often, sometimes, rarely, or not at all, the interest seems less than implied by the affirmative answers. Only 18 percent of the total sample replied "often." Two-fifths—40 percent—answered "sometimes." A tenth said "rarely," which, when added to the 32 percent in the never category, comes to nearly half, or 42 percent, for both.

Similar distributions of reactions to Israel are reflected with respect to visits to Israel. Only 26 percent of adult Jewish Americans report ever having travelled to the Jewish state. The proportion of those who have done so three or more times is six percent, the same as for those who have visited twice, while 14 percent went once.

These four measures of commitment to—or interest in—Israel clearly correlate with various indicators of Jewishness, such as type of religious involvement and adherence to Jewish ritual. Secular and intermarried Jews are less close to Israel. And as might be expected, attitudes and behavior correlate with educational background. A good majority—63 percent—of those who attended day school report themselves extremely or very attached to Israel (34 percent and 29 percent, respectively). The small group who had private tutoring are a far second in indicating that they are very or extremely attached to Israel, while the part-time students are third and the Sunday schoolers fourth. Almost half of those without any Jewish

TABLE 7.17
Type of Schooling by Attachment to Israel (Row Percent)

	EXTREMELY ATTACHED	VERY ATTACHED	SOMEWHAT ATTACHED	NOT ATTACHED	ROW TOTAL
Day School	34	29	23	14	8
Part-time/Afternoon	11	22	51	16	36
Sunday School	5	24	53	18	21
Private Tutor	13	30	46	11	4
Never Attended	5	10	39	47	30
Column Total	25	45	20	10	100

education—47 percent—said they feel no attachment; only five percent of them indicate extreme attachment to Israel.

The same pattern turns up in the analysis of the other three items—how often Jews visit Israel, talk about the Jewish state, and contribute to the United Jewish Appeal. As can be seen in Table 7.18 below, the more years of education, the more likely a Jew will visit Israel.

And once again, type of Jewish school attended and number of years involved are associated with propensity to engage in discussions about the Jewish state. Three-fifths of those without any formal training rarely or never discuss Israel, while the parallel figures for day schoolers is 23 percent. The proportion who talk "often" is much higher—55 percent—for day schoolers.

Looking at sources of Jewish communal financial support and activity, Jewish education is clearly relevant. Over four-fifths—83 percent—of the respondents in households that contribute to Jewish charities have received formal Jewish schooling. Furthermore, it appears that close to 60 percent of former Jewish school pupils are in households that donate.

The recurrent pattern reported here is reiterated with respect to the background of contributors to the UJA/Federation, as well as to other Jewish charities. More Jews, however, give to the latter, which are not necessarily related to the state of Israel. The more education Jews were exposed to as young people, the greater their propensity to contribute to both types of philanthropy.

And in a similar vein, willingness to belong, and volunteer services, to Jewish organizations correlates strongly with educational history. The range of those who report volunteer activities descends from 29 percent for those with more than 15 years of study to 16 percent for those with less than five years of study, and ultimately to 10 percent for those unschooled in Jewish learning. Similarly, the more intensely educated, the more likely people are to subscribe to Jewish periodicals: 37 percent for individuals

TABLE 7.18
Years of Jewish Education and Visits to Israel (Percent)

	NEVER	< 5 YEARS	6–10 YEARS	11–15 YEARS	15 + YEARS
Never Visited	87	75	67	47	49
Visited Once	7	17	18	22	17
Visited Twice	3	4	6	14	17
Visited Three or More Times	3	4	9	17	17

TABLE 7.19
*Type of Schooling and Propensity to Talk
About Israel (Percent)*

	RARELY OR NEVER	OFTEN
Day School	22	45
Part-Time/Afternoon	41	18
Sunday School	29	20
Private Tutor	29	28
Never Attended	61	7
Total	42	18

TABLE 7.20
*Household Contribution to Jewish
Charities and UJA Federation (Percent)*

YEARS ATTENDED	JEWISH CHARITIES	UJA
< 5 Years	57	38
6–10 years	61	45
11–15 years	65	38
15 + years	65	53
Never	33	21
Total	51	35

with 15 years or more of Jewish education, 21 percent for those with five years or less schooling, and 12 percent for the Jewishly uneducated.

Further, the propensity to continue with Jewish education into adulthood is closely linked to previous attendance and type of former schooling. Even though only 14 percent of the respondents reported attending adult programs during the year before they were interviewed, 78 percent who did so had formal Jewish education. Of the small group who had spent 15 or more years in some form of religious study, 22 percent have continued their education as adults, as have 24 percent for those who were exposed to Jewish education for 11–15 years, and 12 percent for those who had five years or less. Type of education differentiates in the same way. If respondents had attended day school in their youth, they were more likely to be involved in adult Jewish educational programs than were those who had been involved in other forms of schooling. Close to 28 percent of former day schoolers, as compared to 14 and 12 percent of former part-timers and Sunday schoolers, respectively, took part in adult Jewish educational programs.

The results of the 1990 NJPS clearly point up the weakening of American Jewishness. As indicated at the beginning of this study, the combination of assimilation processes (especially growing rates of intermarriage) and a low birthrate have significantly reduced the proportion of Jews in the national population as well as decreased the stringency of the commitment to Jewishness of those who remain identified. Almost one-fifth of the survey respondents report that the denomination in which they were raised was Orthodox, but only five percent identify their current affiliation as such. Conservatives have remained constant at 31.5 percent, while Reform grew from 25 to 35 percent. The proportion who report their family origin or themselves as non-religious or "just Jewish" increased from nine to 14 percent.

The data reported in Table 7.21 emphasize anew the weakening of traditional Judaism and the power of assimilation. Thus, as noted, less than a quarter, 23 percent, of the offspring of Orthodox parents have remained in the same denomination. Conservatives have retained 58 percent, while the most Americanized group, the Reform, have held on to 79 percent. Goodly majorities of the children of the secularized or non-denominational parents fall into similar categories. It is noteworthy that both the Reform and the Conservatives have recruited about one-seventh of their supporters from persons of non-Jewish origins, i.e., converts.

To sum up, the iron law of the "more the more" prevails. The longer Jews have been exposed to Jewish education, the greater their commitment to the community, to some form of the religion, and to Israel. The relationships among type of school attended, attitudes, and behavior reiterate this conclusion again and again. For all items presented above, those who went to day school were much more likely to give the most intensely Jewish responses than respondents who attended part-time/afternoon school. The latter in turn exhibited a higher degree of Jewish commitment than interviewees whose education was limited to Sunday school. It is impossible, however, to conclude from the separate bivariate analyses presented so far

TABLE 7.21

Denomination Raised and Current Denominational Affiliation (Percent)

RAISED	CURRENT	OR	CO	RE	CB	JJ	MX	NR	NJ	TOTAL
Orthodox (OR)	Row	23	46	19	4	7	—	1	1	19
	Col	84	28	10	27	14	—	4	2	—
Conservative (CO)	Row	1	58	26	4	5	—	3	4	32
	Col	4	57	23	38	16	38	23	11	—
Reform (RE)	Row	—	5	79	1	5	—	3	7	25
	Col	—	4	55	11	13	37	15	15	—
Combinations (CB)	Row	1	39	30	17	56	—	2	6	3
	Col	1	4	3	16	2	—	1	2	—
Just Jewish (JJ)	Row	4	6	14	1	63	—	5	6	7
	Col	5	1	3	3	47	—	9	4	—
Mixed J & NJ (MX)	Row	—	—	11	11	—	—	16	63	1
	Col	—	—	—	3	—	—	3	4	—
Non-religious (NR)	Row	—	12	5	—	3	—	80	—	2
	Col	—	1	—	—	1	—	36	—	—
Not Jewish (NJ)	Row	3	14	16	1	6	1	3	57	12
	Col	6	5	5	3	7	25	9	63	—
Column Total		5	32	35	3	10	—	4	11	100

that a Jewish learning experience is the most important causal factor in the processes. Obviously, the religious education a young person receives reflects his or her family values and the character of the community within which he or she lives. Such background factors undoubtedly influence him or her as much or more than what goes on in the classroom. But these variables are interactive, mutually supportive or negating. Clearly, the better (whatever that means) and more intense their training, the more likely Jews are to continue in the faith and community.

The next section utilizes multivariate regression to clarify and support the contingency table analysis in the preceding parts of the paper. Using statistical controls, this approach allows us, on the one hand, to evaluate and compare the different determinants of Jewish education for adult respondents and, on the other, to consider Jewish training as a single independent variable within a larger model of the causes of adult behaviors and attitudes. Basically, it involves holding all variables constant, so that the factors which might have an impact, other than those being tested, are eliminated.

IV. Multivariate Analysis of the Adult Respondents

This section seeks to confirm and further specify the analysis of the determinants and consequences of formal Jewish education. The first part deals with the factors that determine the type and duration of Jewish schooling a respondent receives. Since the purpose is to derive the determinants of enrolling in Jewish educational programs, the factors or covariates logically must be causally prior to the outcome. The second half studies the attitudinal and behavioral consequences of receiving a religious education as measured by a composite Jewish Identity Index.

Data and Variables

The first series of regressions utilizes five different measures of Jewish education as dependent variables: 1) years of formal Jewish training not controlling for the type of education, 2) years of day school, 3) of part-time school, 4) of Sunday school, and 5) of private tutoring. The independent variables for each of these models include denomination (if any) in which the respondent was raised (Orthodox, Conservative, Reform, or Secular), generational background (a four point scale described above), gender (male = 1, female = 0), age, intermarriage of respondent's parents (both parents Jewish = 1, mother Jewish = 2, father Jewish = 3, both non-Jewish = 4),[10] and region born (Northeast = 1, Midwest = 2, West = 3,

South = 4). A variable for respondents who converted to Judaism is added to the final model for private tutoring since adult converts secure this type of education.

The second series of multiple regressions uses as a dependent variable a scale of Jewish identity composed of 18 factors: adult Jewish education, synagogue membership, subscription to a Jewish newspaper, giving to Jewish causes, volunteering to Jewish causes, membership in Jewish organizations, lighting Shabbat candles, Seder, keeping Kosher, having separate dishes, observing Hanukkah, Purim, and Yom Kippur, handling money, Jewish friends, celebrating Israel's Independence Day, giving Jewish education to children, and intermarriage. All factors were transformed into dummy variables and the scale was computed ranging from 1–18. Like the first section, the independent variables include denominational and generational background as well as gender and age. Other variables are: level of secular education achievement (number of years completed), synagogue attendance (scaled 1–9 with 1 representing "a few times a week"), number of trips to Israel (1–3), region born, and income. Five models are generated to observe the different effects of day, part-time, and Sunday school training as well as private tutoring on Jewish Identity.

Hypotheses

The contingency table analysis in the preceding sections has laid out in detail the expectations for the multiple regressions. For the determinants of Jewish education, denominational background should demonstrate a strong relationship with propensity to seek a Jewish education. More specifically, being Orthodox is expected to be an important factor in increasing the number of years of Jewish training, particularly in day school. Conservative and Reform should demonstrate similar but weaker patterns, while being raised in a Secular family should show a negative relationship. All measures of assimilation—intermarriage of a respondent's parents, generational distance from the old country, and age (i.e., younger Jews)—should relate negatively to education. In addition, generational background and age should demonstrate curvilinear trends, as suggested in the above bivariate analysis. Gender (being male) is expected to show a positive relationship. Finally, a conversion should significantly increase the likelihood of having private tutoring.

For the consequences of Jewish education on Jewish identity, we are primarily interested in the hypothesis that training has a positive relationship to identity and that the type of schooling matters (day school having the greatest impact on identity, followed by part-time, and then Sunday school and tutoring). Denomination is again expected to be an important variable in determining Jewish identity. Generation, gender (being male), secular education, and income are expected to produce negative correlations with Jewish identity. With the exception of gender, all of these are indicators of assimilation. This expectation with regard to gender is informed by the larger American pattern of females demonstrating higher levels of religious commitment than males. Age, synagogue attendance, and trips to Israel should show a positive relationship, while region born is expected to be negatively related.

Methods

Ordinary Least Squares (OLS) regression with dummy variables was used to analyze the data. Forced entry multiple regressions were run with independent variables entered according to their order of relationships expressed in the zero-order correlations with the dependent variable.

The following equation was used to estimate all the models:

$$(1) \qquad Y_i - \beta_0 + \gamma_1 D_1 + \beta_1 X_{1\,i} \ldots + \gamma_k D_{ki} + \beta_k X_{ki} + e_i$$

where Y_i is a numerical dependent variable observation, X_{1i} and X_{ki} are fixed independent variable scores, and the D_{ki} are dummy variable regressors. I will comment on the nonlinear forms of the age and generation variables below. Both tables report beta-weights or standardized partial regression coefficients for:

$$(2) \qquad \beta_k{}^\star - \beta_k \, (\delta_x/\delta_y)$$

where $\beta_k{}^\star$ is interpreted as the expected change in Y, in standard deviation units, for a one-standard deviation in increment X_k, holding constant the other independent variables.

Lastly, the e_1 is an error random variable with the same properties as the error in a simple bivariate regression. Errors are assumed to be normally and independently distributed with zero expectations and common variance, δ^2.

Results: Determinants

Confirming the earlier contingency tables, denomination raised played a significant role in explaining both duration and type of formal Jewish education received. Gender also had a consistent impact on the dependent variable. Most important, however, was the extent to which respondents came from fully Jewish families, i.e., whether they were raised in intermarried households. The results from Models [1] through [5] are presented in Table 7.22.

TABLE 7.22

Regression Analysis of Formal Jewish Education Determinants
Dependent Variable: No. of Years of Formal Jewish Education

Variables	Model 1 — Years of Formal Jewish Education Not Controlling for Type of Education	Model 2 — No. of Years of Day School as Formal Jewish Education	Model 3 — No. of Years of Part-Time Formal Jewish Education	Model 4 — No. of Years Sunday School	Model 5 — No. of Years of Private Tutoring
Orthodox	.18*	.35**	.05	.04	−.18
Conservative	.07	−.19	.18	.14	−.25
Reform	.03	−.25	−.05	.41*	−.29
Secular	−.12	−.11	−.18	−.09	−.28
Gender	.08	.21**	.18**	.03	.05
Generation	−.01	−.23	.14	.06	.11
Age	−.06	−.11	−.03	.00	.07
Intermarriage of Parents	−.49***	−.48***	−.58***	−.41***	.04
Region Born	.15**	.00	.02	.22**	.19*
Converted	—	—	—	—	.24*
Constant	4.11***	5.1***	2.4*	.5	−.15
Adjust R^2	.29	.55	.40	.34	.04

Reported results are standardized coefficients. $P < .0001$***, $P < .005$**, $P < .05$*.

In Model [1], where type of schooling has not been controlled for, being Orthodox explains greater variation in the dependent variable—with a standardized coefficient of .18—than being Conservative or Reform (.07 and .03, respectively). Controlling for the type of education, different denominations predictably impact the propensity to obtain different forms of education. For Model [2], being Orthodox has a strong positive relationship with years of day school, while being Conservative or Reform shows the reverse relationship. With a beta weight of .18, being Conservative is a strong predictor of part-time school attendance, relative to the other denomination variables. In Model [4], Reform demonstrates a large positive relationship with years of Sunday school. Finally, a secular orientation is negatively related to all types of Jewish education. These results are not surprising—Orthodox secure the most intensive form of training while Conservative, Reform, and Secular Jews tend to enroll in progressively less rigorous types of education.

The most powerful factor affecting the dependent variable in virtually every model is intermarriage. In Models [1] through [4], the intermarriage variable has betas of $-.49$, $-.48$, $-.58$, and $-.41$, respectively. Clearly, a cohesive Jewish family unit is vital in increasing the probability that a respondent secures some form of religious training.

Gender also demonstrates a clear and consistent relationship with religious education generally. Positive and substantively large betas in each model support the earlier bivariate analysis, which indicated that men are more likely than women to secure training. However, this pattern holds mainly for the more intensive forms of education (day school and part-time), while the gender gap is less apparent in the case of Sunday school enrollment.

Bivariate analyses of the age and generation variables indicated possible curvilinear relationships. This hypothesis was born out for age but not generation. Consequently, the regression results reflect age transformed by the general parabolic curve—

$$(3) \qquad \beta_{age} X_{age}^{1/b}$$

Contrary to expectations, age negatively impacted the likelihood of receiving Jewish education in Models [1], [2], and [3], while this variable had a substantively insignificant beta of .00 in the Sunday school model. Interpretation of these results is difficult. For our purposes, we leave the effect of age on education an open question, only noting that all of the beta weights are small-medium in magnitude and that none achieve statistical significance at $p < .05$.

The original hypothesis regarding generation was neither clearly confirmed or disconfirmed by the results. Generation demonstrated the expected negative relationship in Models [1] and [2], with standardized coefficients of − .01 and − .23, respectively. However, the direction of the relationship changes when predicting years of part-time education and Sunday school. This is understandable since increasing generational distance from the old world would tend to decrease the propensity of Jews to seek the most intensive form of religious training (day school) while increasing, in a relative sense, the likelihood of obtaining less rigorous forms (part-time and Sunday school).

The region variable also had an ambiguous effect on the duration of different forms of Jewish training. The hypothesis regarding the importance of being born in regions of more heavily concentrated Jewish populations and institutions was not supported by the regression results. Region demonstrated a substantial beta weight of .22 in the Sunday school model, yet it had a negligible effect on the number of years of day school and part-time training, indicating the region is a fairly unimportant variable in determining duration of the more intensive types of education. The large and statistically significant coefficient for Model [4] may reflect the propensity of Jews living outside of traditionally Jewish regions to obtain the least rigorous of the forms of Jewish education. Part of the problem would seem to lie in the variable itself. The NJPS asked respondents in what region they were born, but, taking into account patterns of mobility, respondents' answers might not have been reflective of the region in which they spent their school years. The region variable is also difficult to interpret because its status as an ordinal variable is uncertain. That is, it is not clear what it means to "increase" from Northeast (= 1) to Midwest (= 2) in terms of rank order.

The final model in Table 7.22 produces clear and predictable conclusions. Having converted to Judaism best explains how much time was spent with a private tutor. Being raised in any denomination has a consistent and strong negative effect on the likelihood of receiving this type of education.

Finally, it should be noted that once the type of education had been controlled for, the fit of the models improved. Model [1] had a total variance explained of .29. The R^2 jumped to .55 once Model [2] controlled for day school graduates and dropped to .40 and .34 for part-time and Sunday school graduates, respectively.

Consequences and Jewish Identity

Table 7.23 presents the five models used to analyze the consequences of formal Jewish education. Model [1] confirms that duration is one of the better predictors of Jewish identity. However, though the effect of Jewish education is strong and significant when controlling for other covariates,

TABLE 7.23

Regression Analysis of Formal Jewish Education Consequences
Dependent Variable: Jewish Identity Index

VARIABLES	MODEL 1	MODEL 2	MODEL 3	MODEL 4	MODEL 5
Orthodox	.08*	.00	.09*	.09*	.12*
Conservative	.06	.20**	.04	.05	.11
Reform	.02	.13*	.03	.00	.08
Secular	.04	.15*	.05	.03	.03
Gender	−.07***	−.17***	−.09***	−.06*	−.07
Generation	−.05*	.03	−.07*	−.06	−.07
Age	.02	.05	.02	.02	.01
Jewish Education of any Type	.10***	—	—		—
Day School	—	.52***	—		—
Part-Time	—	—	.13***		—
Sunday School	—	—	—	.09*	—
Private Tutor	—	—	—	—	.17***
Secular Education	.00	.05	−.01	.00	.00
Synagogue Attendance	.64***	.49***	.63***	.65***	.63***
Trips to Israel	.16***	−.05	.15***	.17***	.17***
Income	.10***	.11***	.10***	.10**	.08*
Region Born	−.03	.03	−.01	−.04	−.06
Constant	−.80	−2.6*	−.05	−.10	.17
Adjust R²	.63	.67	.63	.62	.64

The dependent variable remains the same for all four models: the Jewish identity index. Reported results are standardized coefficients. P < .0001***, P < .005***, P < .05*.

166

synagogue attendance and visits to the Jewish homeland are stronger correlates of Jewish identity.[11] The more frequently the respondent attends the
synagogue and visits the Jewish state, the higher the Jewish Identity score.

Controlling for type of schooling, Model [2] shows that respondents'
time spent in day school has the most significant effect on Jewish identity
of all the model's variables. This is confirmed by the magnitude of the
standardized score at .52. As reported in Models [3] and [4], duration of
part-time and Sunday school education have a smaller effect on Jewish
identity with betas of .13 and .09. In short, Jewish education programs
that require a greater time commitment have greater impact on Jewish
identity after controlling for other important covariates. The difference
between attending day school and enrolling in any other type of training is
considerable.[12]

Interpretation of the other independent variables is fairly straightforward, although a few interesting results appeared. Denominational differences, not unexpectedly, reveal themselves in different levels of Jewish
identity. In all of the models (with the exception of Model [2]), being
Orthodox has a greater positive effect on identity than being Conservative
or Reform. It is notable that a Secular background does not significantly
impact a respondent's identity in a negative fashion; this variable demonstrates a similar relationship with the dependent variable as did being
Conservative or Reform. Thus, denominational differences, though manifest, are not as important determinants of Jewishness as one might expect.

The factors and mechanisms that form women's Jewish identity vary
considerably from those for Jewish men. Despite women's lower Jewish
educational attainment, they are more likely to have higher Jewish identity
scores than men. Models [1] through [4] show statistically significant positive relationships between being female and Jewish identity.[13] As hypothesized, the mechanisms by which Jewish women consolidate their ethnic
and religious identities are clearly different from those for men. The results
correspond to what we know about religion in America, that generally,
women participate more than men.

Expectations regarding generational background, age, and region are
generally born out by the models—assimilation and living outside of the
"Jewish regions" of America contribute to lessened religious identity. On
the other hand, indicators of economic and educational success demonstrate interesting and unexpected patterns. When controlling for other
factors, increasing secular education levels have a negligible effect on identity. This is a consistent result common to every model, indicating that the
universalizing environment of academia neither positively nor negatively
impacts the Jewishness of respondents. The income variable, on the other
hand, was positively related to identity, contrary to the initial hypoth-

esis. According to these results, measures of socioeconomic success and assimilation—such as greater wealth and higher educational attainment—do not correlate with a weakening of individual identity. This indicates that assimilation is an important but complex process with multi-faceted (i.e., not wholly negative) ramifications for the community.

Conclusion

The determinants and consequences of Jewish education for adults are extremely consistent and logical. The duration of enrollment in Jewish educational programs and the type of education experienced is largely a function of intermarriage, denomination raised, including ethnic-secular, as well as gender. In the analysis of Jewish identity, religious training plays a significant role in determining levels of Jewishness, while behavior such as synagogue attendance and trips to the Jewish state are also positive correlates. Gender is also an important variable. With a few exceptions, the multivariate regressions support and clarify the basic conclusions of the contingency table analysis.

V. The Education of the Young

The 1990 National Jewish Population Survey, like the U.S. Census, inquired about children, thus permitting an analysis of the next generation's actual and planned exposure to Jewish learning. The survey included 1,241 children in 801 households. This sample comprises both school-age (ages six through 17) and younger offspring (ages zero through five). The question dealing with Jewish education for the under-18 population differs from those for adults reported in the previous sections in that the former inquired whether the children had received formal Jewish education in the *past year*, while adult respondents were asked whether they had *ever* received formal Jewish education. Similar categories were used for the type of education, i.e., day schools, Sunday schools, etc. Parents who did not report offspring enrollment were then queried as to whether they expected to register their children in the future. As Table 7.24 indicates, one-fifth of the children were enrolled in school, while almost another quarter—23 percent—largely those under six, were expected to go sometime in the future. Over two-fifths, 44 percent, of all youth in Jewish households were not attending Jewish classes and were not expected to do so in the future. The future status of the remaining 12 percent is unclear. The proportion of parents who anticipate enrolling their children (identified as less than six-years-old) is less than half—40 percent—a troubling statistic for the com-

TABLE 7.24
*Children's Enrollment Status in Formal Jewish
Education in the Past Year (Percent)*

Enrolled in past year	21
Not enrolled in past year, yet expect to enroll in future	23
Not enrolled in past year, and will not enroll in future	44
Do not know	12

TABLE 7.25
*Children's 6–18 Enrollment Status in
the Past Year by Type of Education (Percent)*

Day School	29
Part-Time	35
Sunday School	28
Private Tutoring	8

munity. Thirty-five percent said they would not send the children to Jewish schools, while the rest—24 percent—were uncertain (Table 7.26).

The children participating in Jewish training (one-fifth of the total) were fairly evenly divided as to the type of education they were receiving. Of those enrolled, 29 percent were in day school while 35 and 28 percent, respectively, attended part-time and Sunday school. Eight percent had a private tutor.

The age of the older children did not markedly differentiate attendance in the past year. Given the emphasis on being confirmed at age 13, the natural expectation is that enrollment peaks at ages 12–13. It does in fact do so, but not to the degree expected. Almost half, 47 percent, of the former are receiving some sort of Jewish education. This is five percent more than among both the 11-year-old group and the 13-year-old cohort. Overall, the variations among those between six and 13 years of age are not striking. They do not increase steadily among older cohorts. As expected, however, they do go down sharply for those 14 and older.

What is perhaps most striking is that at every age a majority of young people are not obtaining any form of Jewish training (Table 7.26). Two-thirds of all those school age—66 percent—were not enrolled in 1990. And among those past the Bar/Bat Mitzvah age, around three-quarters are outside the Jewish educational system. These totals represent a decline, since "approximately 40 percent . . . were enrolled . . . in 1978/79."[14]

Parents' expectation to register children who are under six years of age in Jewish education declines with increasing age of the children. Anticipation is highest for infants and lowest for those five through six years of age.

TABLE 7.26

Children's Ages by Formal Jewish Education Enrollment
in the Past Year for Those 6 through 17 Years Old (Row Percent)

	ATTENDED IN PAST YEAR	EXPECT TO ENROLL, YET DID NOT ATTEND	DID NOT AND WILL NOT ATTEND	DO NOT KNOW	ROW TOTAL
6 Years	35	26	32	7	10
7 Years	38	21	35	6	11
8 Years	45	10	37	7	10
9 Years	39	13	38	9	10
10 Years	37	14	48	2	9
11 Years	38	4	55	4	9
12 Years	47	9	39	5	7
13 Years	38	5	55	2	8
14 Years	25	6	68	1	7
15 Years	23	9	67	1	6
16 Years	15	4	81	—	7
17 Years	20	4	76	—	7
Column Total	34	11	50	4	100

This pattern is understandable since parents' plans for their children's education are relatively unrealistic when offspring are younger. The prospects for securing a Jewish education either solidify or weaken as children get closer to being enrolled in a particular type of education.

The major factors associated with children's actual or planned attendance are, as expected, the same as the correlates of parental education. Family educational background, denomination, Jewish identity, and intermarriage are strongly associated with whether children secure or will be receiving Jewish religious training.

Thus, when both parents have had some formal Jewish education, 58 percent have enrolled or expect to enroll at least one child. The percentage of actual or planned attendance for children from families in which only one parent is Jewishly educated drops off to 32 percent. The proportions for the two groups who actually were attending Jewish educational programs when the interview occurred were 23 and nine percent, respectively. And only four percent of the households in which neither parent has a Jewish education reported enrolling at least one child, while another 14 percent said they expect their children to attend. The differences are similar among single-parent households. Two-fifths—42 percent—of the households in which the parent is Jewishly trained had at least one child enrolled or expected to do so. This is in contrast to the 11 percent of households in which the single parent had not received a Jewish education.

As hypothesized, the depth of parental Jewish education has a strong effect on the probabilities that children will receive Jewish training also. The more years a respondent has spent in Jewish institutions, the more likely it is that s/he will enroll his/her children in school. A less powerful relationship exists between type of education a parent had and that which his/her children are securing. Thus, as noted in Table 7.29, of those

TABLE 7.27

Parent's Intentions for Formal Jewish Education
Enrollment Intentions for Children under 6 Years of Age (Percent)

CHILDREN'S AGES	EXPECT TO ENROLL	WILL NOT ENROLL	DO NOT KNOW	ROW TOTAL
Under 1 Year	50	30	20	17
1 Year	45	37	18	18
2 Years	46	40	14	17
3 Years	41	31	27	15
4 Years	35	32	32	17
5 Years	23	41	36	16
Column Total	40	35	24	100

TABLE 7.28

Parents' Jewish Education Background by Their Intention to Enroll Their Children in, and Actual Attendance by Their Children in Formal Jewish Education (Percent)

Parents' Education Status		Attended in Past Year	Expect to Enroll, Yet Did Not Attend	Did Not and Will Not Attend	Do Not Know	Row Subtotal
Households with both parents						
Yes-Yes	Row	23	35	24	19	29
	Column	57	41	14	33	
Yes-No	Row	9	23	50	17	46
	Column	33	42	46	46	
No-No	Row	4	14	70	12	27
	Column	10	15	40	21	
Column Subtotal		12	24	48	16	100
Single Parent Households						
Yes	Row	18	24	50	10	40
	Column	60	83	30	30	
No	Row	8	3	73	15	60
	Column	40	17	70	70	
Column Subtotal		12	12	63	13	100

172

TABLE 7.29

Respondent's Type of Formal Jewish Education
by Children's Type of Formal Jewish Education
in the Past Year (For Children 6 through 17)

RESPONDENT'S TYPE OF FORMAL JEWISH EDUCATION	CHILDREN'S TYPE OF JEWISH EDUCATION IN PAST YEAR (PERCENT)			
	DAY SCHOOL	PART-TIME	SUNDAY SCHOOL	PRIVATE TUTOR
Day School	43	11	4	50.5
Part-time	23	49	26	21
Sunday school	13.5	14	30	2
Private	21	10	8	8
None	—	15.5	32	18
Total	7	24	26	12

children in day school at the time of the NJPS, 43 percent had parents with a similar background. And of children enrolled in part-time/afternoon classes, 49 percent had a parent with a comparable experience. Thirty percent of the Sunday schoolers had a parent who went there as well. But of the children with a private tutor (an idiosyncratic form), eight percent had a parent with the same background.

The denominational background of the children's household is obviously a major determinant. As noted in Table 7.30, a large majority of the scions of the Orthodox—61 percent—had their children attend school during the past year, while another fifth—20 percent—expected to enroll their children. The proportions of young people among those of Conservative and Reform backgrounds who attended school were nearly identical, 31 to 32 percent. Reform supporters, however, were insignificantly less likely than Conservatives to say that their youth will not attend in the future. Around two-thirds of ethnic-secular Jewish families said that their children do not receive any Jewish education and are not foreseen to secure any in the future.

The effects of intermarriage and conversions out of Judaism may be seen in Table 7.31. Only four percent of the mixed households enrolled at least one child in Jewish schools in which the only Jewish parent is also identified denominationally. When the parent is ethnic-secular, only two percent did so. In fully Jewish households in which both parents are ethnic-seculars, no children were enrolled. Conversely, for those who did not and will not register their children, the figures are 24 percent for households with two religious Jews, 53 percent for the intermarried house-

TABLE 7.30
Denomination of Children's Households by Children's Enrollment in Formal Jewish Education in the Past Year (Percent)

	ATTENDED IN PAST YEAR	EXPECT TO ENROLL, YET DID NOT ATTEND	DID NOT AND WILL NOT ATTEND	DO NOT KNOW	ROW TOTAL
Orthodox	61	20	4	15	6
Conservative	31	31	29	9	20
Reform	32	34	27	11	27
Mixed Jewish	37	19	41	7	3
Ethnic-Secular Jew	11	20	62	6	12
Jewish & Other (mostly ethnic-secular)	3	13	68	16	31
Column Total	22	23	43	12	100

174

TABLE 7.31

Religious Background of Parents for Children under Age 18 by Children's Attendance in Formal Jewish Education in the Past Year (Percent)

		Attended in Past Year	Expect to Enroll, Yet Did Not Attend	Did Not and Will Not Attend	Do Not Know	Row Subtotal
Households with both parents						
Both Denominationally Jewish	Row	26	35	24	16	39
	Column	86	57	19	38	
Denominationally and Ethnic-secularly Jewish	Row	—	18	66	16	5
	Column	—	4	6	4	
Denominationally Jewish and Non-Jewish	Row	4	22	53	21	33
	Column	11	30	37	43	
Both Ethnic-secularly Jewish	Row	—	14	78	8	4
	Column	—	3	7	2	
Ethnic-secularly Jewish and Non-Jewish	Row	2	9	78	11	18
	Column	3	7	30	12	
Column Subtotal		12	24	48	16	100
Single Parent Households						
Denominationally Jewish	Row	22	15	50	14	65
	Column	100	91	50	80	
Ethnic-secularly Jewish	Row	—	3	91	6	65
	Column	—	9	50	20	
Column Subtotal		14	11	64	11	100

holds with one religiously identified member, 66 percent for the Jewishly "mixed" religious and ethnic-secular households, 78 percent for households where the Jew in a mixed marriage is ethnic-secular, and 78 percent for households where both are ethnic-seculars.

Similar results were obtained in a smaller, earlier study among American Jews conducted in 1989 by the Israel Gallup poll for the Mandel Commission. Since the questions and sampling procedures for the Gallup poll vary from the NJPS, the findings are not directly comparable. Still, it may be noted that this study reported that 80 percent of the children with two Jewish parents had, at some point, attended day or supplementary schools (the only two choices offered), as compared to 22 percent of offspring of religiously mixed marriages.

The NJPS findings are particularly striking. Attendance is, by far, the greatest when both parents are denominationally identified. Among children aged 6 through 13, the proportion who attend or are expected to do so rises to 62 percent as reported in Table 7.32. They are also relatively high—44 percent—for single parent households. For intermarried families in which the Jewish parent is religiously linked, the proportion falls to seven percent enrolled, and to 24 percent who expect to do so. The estimates decline much further for mixed marriages involving an ethnic-secular Jew. Four percent of those parents have their children enrolled and 11 percent expect to do so. The situation is not better when one parent's identity is religious and the other is ethnic-secular. None of them had their children enrolled and only 16 percent planned to do so. Having two ethnic-secular Jewish parents produces a worse outcome in terms of enrollments than does intermarriage between a denominational Jew and a non-Jew. None of the children of the former are enrolled in Jewish education. Single parent religiously-identified households are more likely to educate their offspring in the Jewish tradition than all other combinations of family backgrounds except when both parents are denominationally-linked.

Other indicators of Jewish commitment produce the same results. The more the parents feel the importance of being a Jew, the more likely the children are to be counted in the ranks of those studying Judaism at present, or are expected to be when they reach school age. Of those who enroll their children, 78 percent think it is "very important," 20 percent "somewhat important," and three percent "not very important." None of those who feel it is not important have registered a child. Conversely, as indicated in Table 7.34, 87 percent of those parents who do not and will not enroll a child feel that being Jewish is "not important," compared to less than a quarter—24 percent—of those who think it "very important."

The relationship between synagogue attendance by adults of a household and a child's enrollment in Jewish education is strong. Only 13 per-

TABLE 7.32

Religious Composition of Parents for Children between Age 6 through 13 Years by Children's Attendance in Formal Jewish Education in the Past Year (Percent)

		ATTENDED IN PAST YEAR	EXPECT TO ENROLL, YET DID NOT ATTEND	DID NOT AND WILL NOT ATTEND	DO NOT KNOW	ROW SUBTOTAL
Households with Both Parents						
Both Denominationally Jewish	Row	*37*	*25*	*22*	*16*	*44*
	Column	86	53	20	65	
Denominationally and Ethnic-secularly Jewish	Row	—	*16*	*81*	*4*	*6*
	Column	—	4	2		
Denominationally Jewish and Non-Jewish	Row	*7*	*24*	*60*	*9*	*28*
	Column	10	32	34	24	
Both are Ethnic-secularly Jewish	Row	—	*5*	*85*	*11*	*4*
	Column	—	1	7	4	
Ethnic-secularly Jewish and Non-Jewish	Row	*4*	*11*	*82*	*2*	*17*
	Column	3	9	29	4	
Column Subtotal		19	21	49	11	100
Single Parent Households						
Denominationally Jewish	Row	*37*	*7*	*45*	*11*	*71*
	Column	100	100	55	74	
Ethnic-secularly Jewish	Row	—	—	*91*	*9*	*29*
	Column	—	—	45	26	
Column Subtotal		26	5	59	10	100

177

TABLE 7.33

Religious Composition of Parents for Children between Age 14 through 17 Years by Children's Attendance in Formal Jewish Education in the Past Year (Percent)

		Attended in Past Year	Expect to Enroll, Yet Did Not Attend	Did Not and Will Not Attend	Do Not Know	Row Subtotal
Households with Both Parents						
Both Religious Jews	Row	40	9	48	2	54
	Column	94	75	38	74	
Jews and Ethnic-secular Jew	Row	—	4	89	7	7
	Column	—	4	9	26	
Jew and Non-Jew	Row	5	2	94	—	24
	Column	6	—	33	—	
Both Ethnic-secular Jews	Row	—	—	100	—	4
	Column	—	—	6	—	
Ethnic-secular Jew and Non-Jew	Row	—	12	87	—	11
	Column	—	21	15	—	
Column Subtotal		23	7	69	2	100
Single Parent Households						
Religious Jew	Row	18	5	66	12	56
	Column	100	65	49	82	
Ethnic-secular Jew	Row	—	4	93	3	42
	Column	—	35	51	18	
Column Subtotal		10	4	77	8	100

TABLE 7.34
The Importance of Being a Jew by Enrollment of Child in Jewish Education
(Percent)

	ATTENDED IN PAST YEAR	EXPECT TO ENROLL, YET DID NOT ATTEND	DID NOT AND WILL NOT ATTEND	DO NOT KNOW
Not Important	—	—	87	13
Not Very Important	2	6	82	10
Somewhat Important	6	29	48	17
Very Important	23	43	24	11
Column Total	11	28	48	13

cent of parents who never attend services have children enrolled or expect to send them later (Table 7.35). For those who participate from one to three times a year, the proportion rises to 31 percent (three percent enrolled and 28 expected to be), while among families who partake more than three times a year, the actual and expected enrollment jumps to 54 percent (23 percent enrolled).

The survey inquired of those parents whose children under 18 are not currently enrolled or are not expected to be enrolled in the future: "What is the major reason you do not expect to enroll [name of child] in a program of formal Jewish education?" Responses were grouped into 11 categories (Table 7.36). One-tenth—11 percent—reported a child now in non-Jewish religious education, while slightly fewer—eight percent—said they are planning to enroll their offspring in the future in non-Jewish schools. Another nine percent did not qualify as candidates because they were too young, too old, or had sufficient education. Over a fifth, 22 percent, of the respondent parents said they were not interested, while another 12 percent

TABLE 7.35
Parents' Frequencies of Synagogue Attendance by Enrollment of Child in Jewish Education
(Percent)

	NOT AT ALL	LESS THAN THREE TIMES	MORE THAN THREE TIMES	ROW TOTAL
Attended in Past Year	2	3	32	13
Expect to Enroll, Yet Did Not Attend	11	28	31	26
Did Not and Will Not Attend	73	50	30	45
Do Not Know	13	20	16	16
Column Total	29	15	56	100

TABLE 7.36

*Reasons Given for Children Not Being
Currently Enrolled (Percent)*

REASON CATEGORY	PERCENT
Too young	4
Too old	1
Has sufficient Jewish education	4
Parents uninterested	22
Child uninterested	12
Schools are too expensive	4
Schools are too far away	4
School are poor quality	1
Now in non-Jewish religious education	11
Will enroll in future in non-Jewish schools	8
Other	28
Total	100

thought their child was not interested. Only four percent reported that Jewish education was too expensive for them.

Relating the reasons given to indicators of family Jewish identity produces a clearer picture, although the amorphous category of "other," which includes over one-quarter of the responses, confuses the issue. However, the pattern is still fairly consistent with expectation (see Table 7.37). A tenth—11 percent—of parents reporting that their child(ren) has sufficient education or is too old to continue are religiously identified Jews married to religiously identified Jews (J-J). The proportion approaches zero for the various categories of ethnic-secular or intermarried families. Why do some children of school age of the religiously identified not attend? The most common response is, by far, lack of interest, either by the parent (26 percent) or by the child (26 percent). Relatively few complain that Jewish schools are too expensive (four percent), too far away (four percent), or of poor quality (one percent). It is interesting to note that ethnic-secular Jews are more likely than the religiously identified to account for non-enrollment by citing cost or distance. The negative import of intermarriage seems again obvious. Close to 30 percent of parents with non-enrolled children explained the failure to give their children a Jewish education by the fact that their offspring were receiving a non-Jewish education or that they expected to place them in a non-Jewish religious school. This group of parents were also the most disposed to give responses which have been coded as "other" under current religion.

A consistent pattern emerges when parents are differentiated by whether they have had formal Jewish education or not. The main reasons

TABLE 7.37

Socio-demographic Characteristics by Jewish Group Identity

PARENTS	TOO YOUNG	TOO OLD TO CONTINUE	HAVE HAD SUFFICIENT JEWISH EDUCATION	PARENTS NOT INTERESTED	CHILD NOT INTERESTED	SCHOOL TOO EXPENSIVE	SCHOOL TOO FAR	POOR QUALITY SCHOOL	NOW IN NON-JEWISH EDUCATION	FUTURE NON-JEWISH EDUCATION	OTHER	ROW TOTAL
Households with Both Parents												
J-J	3	5	6	26	26	4	3	1	0	0	27	21
J-ESJ	—	—	14	18	7	16	13	—	11	0	21	6
ESJ-ESJ	—	—	—	16	8	7	—	—	19	13	36	35
J-NJ	1	—	—	42	20	—	8	—	0	0	29	7
ESJ-NJ	7	—	—	24	3	—	6	3	14	13	30	30
Column Total	4	3	2	22	9	4	4	3	12	9	28	100
Single Parent Household												
J	—	—	—	2	35	19	2	9	0	—	31	44
ESJ	—	—	—	—	71	—	—	—	6	—	22	55
Column Total	—	—	—	40	17	9	1	—	6	—	26	100

Key:
J = Religiously Identified Jew
ESJ = Ethnic-secular Jew
NJ = Non-Jew

TABLE 7.38

Relationship of Parental Jewish Education by Reason Given for Children Not
Being Currently Enrolled (Percent)

| | PARENT EDUCATION | | | ROW |
REASON CATEGORY	YES-YES	YES-NO	NO-NO	TOTAL
Too Young	4	1	7	4
Too Old	4	1	0	1
Have Had Sufficient Jewish Education	13	2	4	4
Parents Not Interested	33	16	24	22
Child Not Interested	20	9	12	11
School Too Expensive	0	3	5	4
Schools Too Far	4	5	6	5
Poor Quality Schools	0	3	0	1
Now in Non-Jewish Education	0	18	7	11
Future Non-Jewish Education	2	8	7	7
Other	19	33	26	28
Column Total	14	45	41	100

given for the failure to enroll their children by parents who were themselves Jewishly educated are lack of interest by the child (20 percent) and
by the parents (33 percent). Over 90 percent of the non-attendees have one
or both parents who did not receive a religious education. Those parents
most commonly say that their child is not Jewish or that they (the parents)
are not interested in giving their child(ren) a Jewish education.

Asking respondents why they do or do not act in a certain way does not
necessarily reveal the "true" reasons for their actions.[15] It is more fruitful
to compare indicators of behavior or position which logically may affect the
propensity for Jewish education. The survey permits the examination of
some possible sources such as the region of the country people are living in,
geographic mobility, and family income. Recent relocations have negative
effects on enrollment in Jewish educational institutions. The children of
the respondents who have moved to another community since 1984 are less
likely to attend Jewish schools than those in non-mobile families. Similar
to the findings for the parental generation, children living in the West and
South are less prone to be enrolled in Jewish education, or, if under six,
less likely to be intended for enrollment than those in the Northeast and
Midwest. There appears to be a very positive relationship between the
Jewishness of the district a family lives in and the enrollment of children in
Jewish schools. As indicated in Table 7.39, 52 percent of the children
living in what the respondent described as a very Jewish neighborhood are
enrolled or are expected to be; conversely 58, a slightly larger percentage,

TABLE 7.39

Jewish Character of the Neighborhood and Child Enrollment in Jewish Education (Percent)

Neighborhood	Attended in Past Year	Expect to Enroll, Yet Did Not Attend	Did Not and Will Not Attend	Do Not Know	Row Total
Very Jewish	21	31	24	23	7
Somewhat Jewish	17	24	41	18	22
Little Jewish	13	26	46	14	30
Not Jewish	7	21	58	14	41
Column Total	12	24	48	16	100

of those residing in an entirely non-Jewish area are not so registered or are not expected to be in the future. The figure for a "somewhat Jewish" neighborhood is 41 percent and for "a little Jewish" neighborhood 39 percent. This relationship, however, may be an artifact of self-selection. The more Jewish Jews are, the more likely they are to seek to dwell among their fellows, while those with little or no commitments may prefer to reside among Gentiles or are indifferent as to the ethno-religious character of the neighborhood.

Finally, the evidence indicates that in spite of what the respondents say, economic factors appear to play a role in determining parental behavior with respect to their children's attendance at religious schools. The cost of such an education is rarely given as a reason for not sending children to a Jewish school, but of those who attend, more children come from the higher income levels. Although Jewish identity—conformity to rituals—is stronger among the less affluent than the well-to-do, the latter are more disposed to have their children receive some Jewish education. As indicated in Table 7.41, more than half—58 percent—of those with a family income of under $40,000 a year neither send or expect to send their offspring for Jewish education. Conversely, less than half, 45 percent, of those with annual incomes of $80,000 or more do. There is a linear relationship between income and propensity to send children for religious education.

The findings reported point out both the weakness and power of Jewish education. The power is reflected in the finding that those who have received Jewish training are disposed to transmit their heritage through formally educating their children. The weakness refers to the fact that most children in the sample between six and 13 years of age were not exposed to Jewish education during the past year (Table 7.32). These figures decline sharply for parents with children between 14 and 18 years of

TABLE 7.40
Relationship between Family Income and Attendance at Jewish Schools
(Percent)

FAMILY INCOME	ARE ATTENDING	EXPECT TO ATTEND	NEITHER ATTEND OR EXPECT TO	DO NOT KNOW
Under $40,000	7	21	58	14
$40–$50,000	15	13	52	21
$50–$60,000	12	24	48	16
$60–$80,000	15	27	43	14
$80,000 +	14	26	45	15

age, and, as noted earlier, only 40 percent of parents with children under six state that they have definite expectations to enroll them (Tables 7.31 and 7.33). Given the growing rates of intermarriage among young people and the extremely low proportion of the children of mixed marriages who are sent to Jewish schools, the proportions of children of some Jewish parentage who are exposed to such education should be much lower a decade from now.

VI. Multivariate Analysis of Youth Respondents

Like the earlier multivariate analyses, this section seeks to confirm and further specify the determinants of formal Jewish education, although, in this case, for youth respondents only. The methodology for these regression models is identical to that used in examining the data for adult respondents.[16]

Data and Variables

The regressions utilize five different measures of Jewish education as dependent variables: 1) years of formal Jewish training not controlling for the type of education, 2) years of day school, 3) of part-time school, 4) of Sunday school, and 5) of private tutoring. The independent variables for each of these models include denomination (if any) of the respondent's household (Orthodox, Conservative, Reform, or Secular), gender (male = 1, female = 0), synagogue attendance (never = 1 to weekly = 4), Jewish education of parents (yes = 1, no = 0), income of household, intermarriage of respondent's parents (both parents Jewish = 1, intermarried = 2), current region (Northeast = 1, Midwest = 2, West = 3, South = 4), Jewishness of respondent's neighborhood (very Jewish = 1 to not Jewish = 4), and length of residence (always lived at current residence = 1 to lived at residence 5 years or less = 5).

Hypotheses

In general, it is expected that the pattern of relationships will be similar to that found for adult respondents, with some exceptions. Denominational background should again demonstrate a strong relationship with propensity to seek religious training, with Orthodox being the most—and Secular the least—predisposed. Intermarriage, an indicator of assimilation, should be negatively related. Parents with a higher Jewish educational background and income are expected to be associated with a longer duration of religious training for their children. Both of these variables were unavailable in the case of adult respondents and are of particular interest because they provide evidence regarding the generational continuity of religious training and the importance of economic resources in securing training. Specifically, greater resources should be related to greater duration of religious education, and having parents who themselves have underwent some training should increase the likelihood of their children being so trained. Living outside of the traditional concentrations of Jewish communities (i.e., the Northeast and, to an extent, the Midwest) should show a negative effect on the duration and type of education. Two new demographic variables have been included in this analysis of the children's data. As suggested in the bivariate tables, increasing geographic mobility (i.e., shorter length of residence) is anticipated to be negatively related to education. This is because frequent moving tends to disrupt educational patterns. Also, respondents who live in neighborhoods which they categorize as very Jewish are likely to secure more religious training than those who live in neighborhoods that are not very Jewish. Finally, gender is expected to show a different relationship from the one exhibited in the adult models. In recent years, the gender gap in Jewish education has been narrowing, with girls increasingly participating in contrast to past patterns.

Results: Determinants

As with the adult respondents, denomination plays a significant role in explaining both duration and type of formal Jewish education received. Most important, however, is the educational history of the parents of the youth respondents. Children of Jews with formal religious training are much more likely to be enrolled in some type of training themselves. Surprisingly, intermarriage does not reveal a strong negative association with education, as it did in the case of the adults. The complete results from Models [1] through [5] are presented in Table 7.41.

In Model [1], where type of schooling has not been controlled for, being Orthodox explains considerable variation in the dependent variable, with a standardized coefficient of .16. Contrary to the adult respondents, being Conservative or Reform has virtually no effect on the likelihood of receiving training. Living in a Secular household has an expected negative impact. Controlling for the type of education, different denominations again relate differently to the various types, although the relationships are not as clear and predictable as in the models for the adults. For Model [2], being Conservative or Reform shows a negative relationship (both have betas of − .36) with years of day school, as is the case for adults. However, the effect of being raised in an Orthodox household for this most recent generation of Jewish youth is meager. The beta weight of .00 reveals that the strength of this denomination in shaping educational patterns is waning. With a beta weight of .06, being Conservative is a minor predictor of part-time school attendance, although, relative to the other denomination variables, it is the only one to at least have a positive relationship. In Model [4], years of Sunday school is most strongly influenced by being raised in a Reform household (.36), but interestingly, the difference between Conservative and Secular households is minor by this measure. Both have small but positive betas—.05 for Conservative and .02 for Secular. Orthodox, who remain disproportionately enrolled in day school, are negatively disposed to this type of education.

The most powerful factor affecting the dependent variable in virtually every model is the fact of the parents of respondents having underwent some form of religious training in their youth. In Models [1] through [4], the variable for the Jewish education of parents has betas of .56, .68, .66, and .79, respectively. Clearly, a history of formal training is important in increasing the probability that Jewish youth secure their own Jewish education.

As predicted by the bivariate tables, household income is shown to be an important determinant of duration of training, once the type of training has been controlled for. Economic resources are relatively more important in the propensity to secure day school education (.23), the most expensive form of religious training, than in the likelihood of attending part-time school (.11) and, in turn, Sunday school (.02). Also as expected, synagogue attendance reveals a small but consistently positive impact on the duration of education.

One of the most interesting results of this multivariate analysis is the relative insignificance of the intermarriage variable, a factor which played an important role in explaining variance in the education models for adult

TABLE 7.41

Regression Analysis of Formal Jewish Education Determinants for Youth Respondents
Dependent Variable: No. of Years of Formal Jewish Education

VARIABLES	MODEL 1 YEARS OF FORMAL JEWISH EDUCATION NOT CONTROLLING FOR TYPE OF EDUCATION	MODEL 2 NO. OF YEARS OF DAY SCHOOL AS FORMAL JEWISH EDUCATION	MODEL 3 NO. OF YEARS OF PART-TIME FORMAL EDUCATION	MODEL 4 NO. OF YEARS OF SUNDAY SCHOOL	MODEL 5 NO. OF YEARS OF PRIVATE TUTORING
Orthodox	.16***	.00	-.11*	-.09*	-.32***
Conservative	-.02	-.36***	.06	.05	.32***
Reform	.00	-.36***	-.10	.36***	-.40***
Secular	-.08	-.18***	-.18**	.02	.05
Gender	-.02	-.05*	-.02	.02	.08*
Synagogue Attendance					
Jewish Education of Parents	.16***	.09***	.16***	.05*	-.06*
Income of Parents	.56***	.68***	.66***	.79***	.89***
Intermarriage of Parents	.00	.23***	.11***	.02	.21***
Jewishness of Parents	-.04	-.37***	.00	-.04	.18***
Neighborhood	-.09*	.06*	.03	.02	-.19
Current Region	.09**	-.18***	.00	.23***	.33***
Geographic Mobility	-.04	-.06*	.07*	-.06**	.01
Constant	11.55***	26.74***	8.7***	13.14**	9.5***
Adjusted R²	.56	.86	.70	.86	.80

Reported results are standardized coefficients. $P < .0001$***, $P < .005$**, $P < .05$*.

respondents. In the day school model, intermarriage reveals the expected, substantively large negative relationship with the dependent variable. However, in Models [1], [3], and [4], being raised by religiously-mixed parents has either a small negative effect on years of education or no effect at all. This is in contrast to the strong and statistically significant negative relationship born out in virtually every model for the adult respondents. Relative to older Jews in the NJPS sample, this measure of assimilation appears to be of less significance in negatively affecting the educational enrollment of this recent generation of Jewish youth. One explanation for this finding concerns the stigma attached to marrying outside of the religion. For older generations, choosing to marry a non-Jew often meant a clear break with the faith and sometimes family as well. Intermarriage for more recent generations has become more accepted, more tolerated. Thus, intermarried couples are still less Jewish in terms of religious identity, but it is now easier for them to remain a part of the community, which includes enrolling their children in less rigorous forms of religious training. A non-Jewish intermarried parent is under less pressure to raise his/her children as Christian than in the past.

The role of gender also illuminates the changing relationship between Jews and education. Whereas in the adult regressions being male increased the likelihood of receiving more years of training, data for the youth respondents show the opposite gender effect. Being a Jewish girl lengthened the duration of training in the day school ($-.05$) and part-time school ($-.02$) models, while only the Sunday school model demonstrated a minor advantage for boys ($.02$).

The nature of the NJPS questions for the child respondents allows a detailed examination into the effect of certain geographic and demographic factors, including region, geographic mobility, and the Jewishness of a respondent's neighborhood. Of these three variables, only geographic mobility performed as hypothesized, but the role of all three in determining years of formal education is minor compared to other covariates. As in the adult analysis, the region variable has an ambiguous effect on the duration of different forms of Jewish training. The hypothesis regarding the importance of being born in regions of traditional concentrations of Jewish communities and institutions is not supported by the regression results, with the notable exception of the day school model. Positive betas in the models for part-time ($.00$) and Sunday school ($.23$) models closely resemble the unexpected pattern of the region variable in the adult analysis. As noted, region has the hypothesized negative effect only in the case of determining years of day school attendance, a result which makes sense since these institutions require a larger immediate Jewish community and greater resources to support them than the less intensive forms of education. These institutions are often Orthodox, since their members may not ride on Saturday and therefore are obligated to live within walking distance of a synagogue.

The region variable for the multivariate analysis of the youth respondents possesses the same flaws noted above in the multivariate section on the adults. A more precise indicator of the concentration of Jews and Jewish institutions in an area is a respondent's perception of the Jewishness of their particular neighborhood. However, the association revealed by the regression results again disagrees with the initial hypothesis. After controlling for the type of training, living in a less Jewish neighborhood reveals a small but positive association with more years of religious education. From the results of both the youth and adult multivariate analyses, it is clear that living in a particular region represents neither an encouragement or discouragement to secure education. Finally, bivariate analysis indicated the importance of putting down roots in a neighborhood for an extended period of time. And indeed increasing geographic mobility is negatively related to the different types of religious training (with the exception of part-time school), but the relative significance of this variable is marginal.

The final model in Table 7.42 examines the determinants of the duration of private tutoring for youth respondents. Being raised in any denomination has a consistent and strong negative effect on the likelihood of receiving this type of education, although a Secular orientation has a small positive relationship. The strongest relationship is revealed to be the positive impact of the parents of the children having secured some Jewish education, with a large beta of .89. Interestingly, intermarriage is a positive covariate, and indeed Model [5] is the only model in which being raised in a mixed household increases the propensity for formal religious education. Not surprisingly, greater income is associated with more tutoring. The three demographic variables demonstrate interesting relationships with the dependent variable. The less Jewish the neighborhood, the fewer years of private tutoring. This result might be explained by the relative scarcity of such tutors in non-Jewish areas. Living outside of the traditionally Jewish regions in America is strongly and positively related to more years of tutoring. Again, this could be because of the lack of institutions (i.e., synagogues and Jewish schools) in such areas relative to the Northeast, for instance.

Finally, it should be noted that, as in the adults' regressions, once the type of education had been controlled for, the fit of the models for youth respondents improved. Model [1] had a total variance explained of .56. The R^2 rose to .86 once Model [2] controlled for day school graduates and was .70 and .86 for the part-time and Sunday school models, respectively.

TABLE 7.42

Secular Education and Attendance at Jewish Education by Gender
(Percent)

	MEN	WOMEN	TOTAL
Some High School - High School Graduate	61	41	51
Some College	81	56	68
College Graduate	84	65	74
Graduate School	87	73	80

The Future: College Students and the Campus

A discussion of educational trends among the Jewish community and particularly its youth would be incomplete without mention of the importance of higher education. Secular education has complex consequences for Jewish identity and continuity. On the one hand, higher levels of education correlate positively with Jewish training. Yet, as I will argue, the two types of learning environments have opposite effects on one's Jewishness. However, even though higher education should logically weaken commitment to the community through its emphasis on universalistic values, the geographic concentration of young Jews in higher learning institutions presents an opportunity for them to meet, and for organizations such as Hillel to reach students, at the same time as the university environment weakens their particularistic religious norms.

The linkage of Jewish to secular education is linear. That is, the more Jewish learning a person has received, the more likely s/he is to have an extended higher education. The lowest level of Jewish attendance is among those who have not completed high school. Only 51 percent of them have had any Jewish education. Conversely, 74 percent of all college graduates without post-graduate work, and 80 percent of those who have some—or have completed—graduate education, have had some Jewish training. The relationship is more consistent for women than for men.

Not surprisingly, the relationship between Jewish and secular education is similar when attained degrees are considered. Four-fifths of those with graduate degrees have had some Jewish training as compared to 51 percent for those whose only diploma is from high school. Those with the least secular attainments (less than grade 12) report the highest population of day school attenders, 11 percent, probably reflecting the behavior of some Orthodox. But there is no relationship between the two forms of education for the rest of the respondents, differentiated by extent of secular education from high school onward. The proportions going to day school are roughly the same for all groups from those with a high school diploma to persons with post-graduate training. Attendance at afternoon classes, however, increases steadily with secular education, moving up from 21 percent among those with high school diplomas to 39 percent among those with a bachelor's degree, and 47 percent for persons who went on to postgraduate work. Sunday school peaks among college graduates at 24 percent, but drops off to 21 percent among those who attended graduate school.

Ironically, Jewish education achievements may be a major source of the long-term trends that are undermining Jewish continuity. As noted, attendance at higher educational institutions is commonplace among young people. According to the Population Survey, more than five-sixths—87 percent—of religiously identified Jews who are 18 to 24 years of age have been to college. College attendance rates for Jews have remained constant since the 1970 NJPS.[17] For all Jews, religious or secular, it is the same. But as is well known, higher education—particularly in the leading liberal arts colleges and research universities where Jews tend to be disproportionately represented—is the most universalistic institution in the country with respect to attitudes toward ethnic particularism and religious identification and practice. A basic belief in this environment is that students should not "discriminate" according to religious and/or ethnic criteria with respect to dating and mating. This norm is strongest among the more politically liberal segment of the population, one which disproportionally includes Jews. It may be hypothesized, and perhaps even assumed, therefore, that a major source of the extremely high rate of intermarriage is the pattern of attendance by Jews at colleges and universities. Education makes for higher income and status, more culture, and greater influence, but it is also associated ultimately with lesser involvement in the Jewish community, although low income may be an even greater barrier to participation.

The college students exhibit a low resistance to intermarriage. Less than a quarter—22 percent—indicate that they would oppose or strongly oppose a child of theirs marrying a non-Jew (seven percent strongly), while 62 percent would support or strongly support such an action (17 percent strongly). The remaining 15 percent say that they would "accept" intermarriage. Not surprisingly, the proportions accepting or supporting intermarriage increase when the question is posed in terms of a spouse who converts to Judaism. Although these figures are discouraging, they are similar to the 16 percent response pattern of all Jewish adults with regard to opposition to intermarriage. The whole sample, however, exhibits much less support—33 percent—than the students' 62 percent.

Yet, as indicated in the multivariate analysis, "increasing secular education levels have a negligible effect on identity" (p. 44). These findings

TABLE 7.43
Attitudes of College Students to Intermarriage (Percent)

	IF A CHILD CONSIDERS MARRYING A NON-JEW	IF THE POTENTIAL SPOUSE WILL CONVERT
Strongly Support	17	39
Support	45	12
Accept	15	38
Oppose	15	10
Strongly Oppose	7	—
Do Not Know	—	—

conflict with the frequently voiced impression and logical deduction that secularly educated Jewish youth are less attached to Jewishness or to Israel than their elders. The evidence and logic are clearly contradictory. Since the Population Survey only included 88 students in its sample, 73 undergraduates and 15 graduates, it is impossible to seek to resolve the contradictions through further analysis. Hopefully these questions will be dealt with by future researchers.

On the positive side, three-quarters of students interviewed in the Population Survey reported a denominational affiliation: 31 percent Conservative, 36 percent Reform, and eight percent Orthodox. The proportion identified, however, is 13 percent lower than that of their parental families, from 88 percent to 75. Or conversely, one-fourth of the students are secular compared to 11 percent of their parents. Slightly over half—53 percent—had no Jewish education, compared to 64 percent among those over 25 who had been to college. In terms of gender, this breaks down to 73 percent for males and 59 for females for all Jews who have been to college. Men were less likely to have had a confirmation ceremony—42 percent— than women—58 percent. The best indication of continued Jewish religiosity is that close to half of the students—42 percent—said they fast on Yom Kippur. Thirty-six percent said that they have personally belonged to a synagogue. None believe that the "Bible is the actual word of God," while four percent refrain from handling money on the Sabbath.

The campus is particularly important for the Jewish community. It is easier to reach Jews in the university environment to make them aware of the Jewish message, existence, and activities than to find the unaffiliated anywhere else. Campus organizations can do this more easily than other organizations dealing with the general population. Students can be written to, personally contacted, leafletted, and the like. Hence, even the completely secular who have never partaken of any formal activity—educational or other—will hear about Hillel or other Jewish groups. For the

TABLE 7.44
*Denomination of Students
and Parents*

	STUDENTS	PARENTS
Orthodox	8	10
Conservative	31	41
Reform	36	37
Secular	25	11

great majority, to take part in them or to attend services is physically easier than it has ever been before they came to college or ever will be after they leave.

Therefore, Hillel and other Jewish campus organizations are potentially one of the most important forces for Jewish continuity. Yet the findings of this study indicate that they have only been effective for a small minority, that most students are not deeply involved in Jewish activities, and that on average, they are less committed than their parents. Only 21 percent of the 88 students in the Population Survey reported that they had taken part in any Jewish educational program during the past year. A more limited survey conducted by Israel Gallup in 1989 sampled identified American Jews and found that 21 percent of college-aged children took part in Hillel programs, while an overlapping 15 percent belonged to other Jewish student groups. Twenty-two percent of those interviewed reported belonging to at least one Jewish organization. Less than one in ten—eight percent— volunteered during the past 12 months for a Jewish organization.

VII. Conclusion

Concern over the state of religious education and its relationship to the continuity of the community is not a new phenomenon. Jewish immigrants of the nineteenth century were unable to replicate the extensive system of religious schools that existed in Europe. Referring to the Northeast in particular, Glazer writes: "The established American Jewish community offered no model for Jewish education. Following the collapse of the synagogue schools of the 1850s under competition from the public schools, the established synagogues of New York had limited themselves to Sunday or Sabbath schools. . . ."[18] The weakness of Jewish education was a persistent worry for later generations of German Jews. And as Irving Howe points out, "The Yiddish press during the early years of the [twentieth] century constantly laments the condition of Jewish education."[19] Headlines such as "Jews Neglect Jewish Education and Blame America" were not uncommon in publications such as *Tageblatt*. Following up on similar findings by Mordecai Kaplan eight years earlier, a 1919 survey by Alexander Dushkin found that "only 65,000 out of an estimated 275,000 Jewish children of school age were receiving Jewish instruction at any given time. . . ."[20] In the early 1900s, much as today, the focus of criticism was on the quality of the Jewish training that the young were receiving, as well as the limited numbers receiving it. With many living in poverty and possessing limited community resources, Jews in America were still struggling to break through the barriers of anti-Semitism to enter the ranks of the middle class and beyond. In 1993, their affluent descendants are concerned about the numbers who are not involved in any form of Jewish education and are defecting from the community—particularly through intermarriage.

Ironically, contemporary Jews have to worry whether their community will survive, not because of its enemies, but because the larger environment is too friendly, not sufficiently hostile. The walls of anti-Semitism, which once held Jews within the fold, have largely crumbled.[21] There is nothing to stop them from walking out. The status barriers which identify marriage with a Jew as a step down for a non-Jew no longer exist. Many non-Jews, particularly the well-educated among them, often view Jews as part of a superior culture, defined in educational and intellectual terms. In Europe, when Jews married non-Jews, the Jew almost invariably converted to Christianity or, at any rate, dropped all his or her affiliations to Judaism. Here, the opposite is true. Intermarried Jews on the whole remain identified as Jews, although with less commitment to the religion and the community, while, as noted, a minority of non-Jews convert and another considerable portion of them identify their family as Jewish. These developments have led the so-called "optimists" within the Jewish community to argue that intermarriage results in an increase of the number of self-identified Jews in the country. There is some evidence that this may be true in the short run, but in the long run, it is not. The children of the intermarried are very loosely affiliated, if at all, uneducated Jewishly, and even more likely to marry non-Jews than birth-right Jews, so their children—while perhaps aware of their background—will have no communal commitment. As Sidney Goldstein notes, of the children of intermarried couples, only 25 percent were being raised as Jews, while the remaining cohort was either being raised in another faith or without any religion at all.[22] The membership and financial problems faced by the American Jewish Committee, the American Jewish Congress, B'nai Brith, and ADL attest to the effects of these developments.

Beyond the impact of anti-Semitism, the changing relationship of

American Jewry to Israel is important. Clearly, hundreds of thousands, if not more, have become deeply involved in communal activities because of their interest and commitment to the Jewish state. Much of the activity of the community has been related to Israel. This has been true for the so called "defense organizations," the American Jewish Committee, the ADL, and the American Jewish Congress, as well as the local Jewish communal federations. Hillel, the main organization on campus, devotes a great deal of its activity to Israel. Synagogue and temple-affiliated groups are Israel oriented. The link to Israel, however, has been declining, especially among younger Jews. As with anti-Semitism, what has kept many Jews involved in Israel-oriented activities is concern about security, about the fact that the state has remained for so long a pariah nation, facing a military threat. But as of now, there is some reason to believe that this situation will end. Israel's Arab neighbors and the Palestinians are revealing a willingness to accept the Jewish state, to end the conflict by trading land for peace. Clearly this chapter of history is not written yet, but possible reactions of the American Jewry to something resembling a real peace might entail lessened interest in the Jewish state, reduced financial contributions, lesser participation in communal activities designed to help Israel in welfare, economic, and political terms, and as a consequence less identification with Judaism. The discussion about a possible merger of the U.J.A. and the C.J.F. reflect a concern on the part of their leadership about decline.

The problems of Jewry in the former Soviet Union still offer a cause to rally around. A great deal of activity and money has been dedicated, collected to help Soviet Jews resettle in Israel or elsewhere. There is foreboding about the future of the Jews left in the former Soviet areas. But still, their prospects there are reasonably good. In any case, the evidence suggests that this cause is not at all comparable to those of anti-Semitism or Israeli security as motives to take part in Jewish activities.

Beyond the conditions which affect the commitment of Jews to their community, it is necessary to emphasize the consequences of demographic factors. Jews have a very low birth rate, even less than most other extremely educated and well-to-do urban groups. Jews simply are not reproducing themselves. The one major exception, which also does not adhere to the generalization about high intermarriage rates is, of course, the Orthodox. But they constitute somewhere around seven percent of the total American Jewish population, that is about 300,000 people. They have very large families, but those who rely on them to reproduce or expand Jewry forget that in America, as in days gone by in eastern Europe, a significant minority of Orthodox young people do not stay Orthodox. The estimates for drop-outs by youth from Orthodoxy, though not from Judaism, run as high as one-third. All the indicators suggest the economic and social integration of Jews will continue.

In the future, as in the past, the great majority of Jews will be born into the faith. The basic problem for the community is and will be to hold them, to keep them Jewish. The most important means to do this is education. The findings reported here indicate that the longer and more intensive the Jewish training, the more likely people are to be committed to and practice Judaism.[23] But many drop out. In any case, as documented here, the main factors which determine school exposure are linked to family background. We obviously should try to develop better educational techniques, recruit more sophisticated educators, and provide a more meaningful social and physical environment for Jewish youth. We should also recognize that such improvements will not stop the decline. For all except the Orthodox, improving the content of Jewish education—what is taught—is more important than the technical factors which can be improved with more money. And here most of the Jewish community is at a loss. They, themselves, are not religiously observant, much less so than most Christians. They do not believe in the Torah. Yet, the schools are expected to teach the children what their parents basically reject by their actions. Beyond religion, America's universalistic openness undermines the message of ethnic particularism. The intermarriage rate will grow. Hence, while we must do what we can to reach out to those weakly committed, we must concentrate on the dedicated "remnant." There is, of course, the alternative of formulating a new secularized curriculum which corresponds to the way of life of most Jewish parents. But that is another topic, a different agenda.

Notes

1. The background of the survey and a description of the sample is presented in Barry Kosmin, et al., *Highlights of the CJF 1990 National Jewish Population Survey* (New York: Council of Jewish Federations, 1991), pp. 1–6. See also Sidney Goldstein, "Profile of American Jewry: Insights from the 1990 National Jewish Population Survey," in David Singer and Ruth Seldin, eds., *American Jewish Yearbook*, (New York and Philadelphia: The American Jewish Committee; The Jewish Publication Society, 1992), pp. 77–173.

2. For a more comprehensive description of the current state and historical background of American Jewry, see Seymour Martin Lipset, "A Unique People in an Exceptional Country," in Lipset, ed., *American Pluralism in the Jewish Community* (New Brunswick, NJ: Transaction Publishers, 1990), pp. 3–29.

3. Regarding fertility rates, Goldstein points out that average completed fertility for Jewish women "was not only 20 percent below the . . . average for those

aged 45–49 20 years earlier, but also 19 percent below the average for all white women aged 45–49 in 1988, and 10 percent below the 2.1 level needed for replacement." Goldstein, "Profile of American Jewry," p. 122. See also Calvin Goldscheider and Alan S. Zuckerman, *The Transformation of the Jews* (Chicago: University of Chicago Press, 1984), pp. 177–78; Marshall Sklare, "Intermarriage and the Jewish Future," *Commentary*, 37 (April 1964), pp. 46–52. For a report on extensive intermarriage before the massive East European immigration, see Chaim I. Waxman, *America's Jews in Transition* (Philadelphia: Temple University Press, 1983), pp. 25–6.

4. Goldstein, "Profile of American Jewry," p. 126. For similar documentation, see Sylvia Barack Fishman and Alice Goldstein, "When They Are Grown They Will Not Depart: Jewish Education and the Jewish Behavior of American Adults," *Cohen Center for Modern Jewish Studies Research Report 8*, March 1993.

5. Kosmin et al., *Highlights*, p. 16. See also Goldstein, "Profile of American Jewry," pp. 124–28.

6. Kosmin et al., *Highlights*, p. 15.

7. For a fulsome account of the leftist Yiddish culture, see Irving Howe, *The World of Our Fathers: The Journey of the East European Jews to America and the Life They Found and Made* (New York: Harcourt, Brace, Jovanovich, 1976).

8. Egon Mayer, "American-Jewish Intermarriage in the 1990s and Beyond: The Coming Revolution in Jewish Demography and Communal Policy," in Mayer, ed., *The Imperatives of Jewish Outreach* (The Jewish Outreach Institute and The Center for Jewish Studies, City University of New York, 1991), p. 39.

9. Goldstein, "Profile of American Jewry," p. 125.

10. The last category (no parents Jewish) is very small, containing only respondents who have converted into the faith.

11. The findings regarding synagogue attendance and visits to Israel are unsurprising, but one should be wary of their role in this analysis. In modelling the determinants of Jewish identity, there are numerous variables which can be used as either independent variables or components of the dependent variable. That is, one could plausibly reason that attendance and visits to the homeland are indicators of the construct Jewish identity. This, in part, explains the magnitude and statistical significance of these two factors when they are defined as independent variables.

12. A statistical note is needed here. This paper examines the determinants of Jewish education and then utilizes education as an independent variable in a model of Jewish identity. A complication arises because a number of the same independent variables (such as denomination, gender, generation, age, and region) are included in both regressions. Since the first regression shows correlations between these variables and religious training, when using training as a variable in the second regression, it contains the explanatory power not only of itself but also of those variables (denomination, gender, etc.). In a sense, then, those variables are given additional weight in the second regression in the guise of the Jewish education variable. This is a problem, but it is one inherent in the slippery nature of the subject matter, i.e., ethnic or religious identity.

13. The coefficients are negative of course because male is numerically defined as 1, female as 0.

14. Waxman, *America's Jews in Transition*, p. 187.

15. Paul Lazarsfeld, "The Art of Asking Why," *National Marketing Review*, 1 (1935), pp. 32–43, reprinted in Lazarsfeld, *Qualitative Analysis: Historical and Political Essays* (Boston: Allyn and Bacon, 1972).

16. See pp. 160–161 for a detailed description.

17. Goldstein, "Profile of American Jewry," p. 111.

18. Nathan Glazer, *American Judaism* (Chicago: University of Chicago Press, 1957), p. 71.

19. Howe, *World of Our Fathers*, p. 202. See also, Waxman, *America's Jews in Transition*, pp. 52–3 and Charles E. Silberman, *A Certain People: American Jews and Their Lives Today* (New York: Summit Books, 1985). pp. 173–174.

20. Howe, *World of Our Fathers*, p. 202. For New York City, there was a modest rise in participation between the mid-1930s when 25 percent of Jewish children of elementary school age attended Jewish schools and 1955 when the figure had increased to 31 percent. According to Glazer, the increase was attributable to the increased activity of the Orthodox. Glazer, *American Judaism*, p. 111.

21. See Gregory Martire and Ruth Clark, *Anti-Semitism in the United States* (New York: Praeger, 1982), pp. 113–19 and Lipset, "A Unique People in an Exceptional Country," pp. 16–18.

22. Goldstein, "Profile of American Jewry," p. 127.

23. For earlier results, see Harold S. Himmelfarb, *The Impact of Religious Schooling: The Effects of Jewish Education upon Adult Religious Involvement* (Ph.D. dissertation, Department of Sociology, University of Chicago, 1975).

8

Denominations and Synagogue Membership: 1971 and 1990

Bernard Lazerwitz

There have been two broad scale surveys of the American Jewish population: one in 1971, the second, in 1990. In this study, the information from both surveys is used to ascertain the characteristics of Jewish adults, 20 years old or older. Particular attention is paid to the relationship of denominational preference and synagogue affiliation, to age, generation-in-the-US, socioeconomic status, involvement in the Jewish and general community, political orientation, and intermarriage. The use of the two surveys enables the exploration of trends over the two decades separating them.

Survey Similarity

Given the differences in design of the two surveys, considerable effort was necessary to make their data comparable. Fortunately, each survey obtained a probability sample of the American Jewish population. The sample design for the first one is detailed in Lazerwitz (1974a and b); the second is in Kosmin et al. (1991).

Considerable care needs to be exercised to insure the comparability of the two surveys. There are subtle but important differences between them. For example, the second survey used Random Digit Dialing, a technique not available to the first. Further, while each randomly selected a respondent from among the Jewish household residents, the first survey did so by use of the Kish (1949) selection table technique. The second used an equivalent approach called "The Next-Birthday Method of Respondent

Selection" (see Salmon and Nichols, 1983) which was applied to all Jewish household residents.

In addition, question wordings and time frame often differ between the two surveys. For example, with regards to frequency of synagogue attendance, the first survey asked: "How many times, if any, did (Person) attend Jewish religious services during the past 12 months?" However, the second survey asked: "About how often do you personally attend any type of synagogue, temple, or organized Jewish religious service?" Note the absence of any specific time frame in the second question as well as the obvious shift in wording.

Every question used in contrasting the two surveys must be carefully scrutinized for compatibility with respect to time and wording. Sometimes differently worded questions about the same topic can be accepted as adequately equivalent. Sometimes useful questions cannot be used because of considerably different wording. For example, with respect to the question on attendance at Jewish religious services, it will be assumed that the specific time frame of 12 months used in the first survey is sufficiently similar to the unknown time frame used in the second one.

The major difference between the two surveys stems from their response rates. The first survey enjoyed a 79 percent response rate and yielded 5,790 interviews. The second survey obtained a 48 percent response rate. Eventually 2,441 interviews were obtained. Much of the lower response rate was the result of an inadequate number of call-backs for "not-at-home" telephone numbers. When screened-in Jewish households were found, they were interviewed at a 76 percent response rate. (The screening response rate for sample households was 63 percent.)

One result of compatibility problems and the lower response rate for the second survey is the risk that data quality could be poor. Fortunately, as shown in Table 8.1, they are not. Statistics derived from similarly worded questions on these two surveys can be contrasted if one ignores or compensates for their differential response rates.

Who Is a Jew?

The two surveys used the same definition for their respondents, namely: a) anyone who declares she or he was born Jewish and still is Jewish; b) anyone who regards him or herself as Jewish even though they were not born Jewish (such respondents would need to have converted into one of the denominations of American Jewry or, failing an official conversion, say they are practicing the Jewish religion); c) anyone who was born Jewish but is no longer practicing any religion (often such respondents regard

TABLE 8.1
Contrasting Various 1971 and 1990 Survey Percentages on Equivalent Age Groups

QUESTIONS AND PERCENTAGES

	SEPARATE MEAT AND DAIRY DISHES		NUMB. JEWISH ORG. MEMBERSHIPS				J. DENOMINATION				LIT. HANUKKAH CANDLES		KOSHER HOME	
	YES	NO	0	1-2	3-4	5+	ORTH	CONS	REF	NONE	YES	NO	YES	NO
1971 Respondents Who Are 40 to 79 Year by 1990 (N = 3973)	18%	82%	58%	30%	9%	3%	8%	43%	34%	15%	82%	18%	25%	75%
1990 Respondents 40 Years and Over (N = 1104)	16%	83%	60%	28%	9%	3%	6%	42%	37%	15%	71%	29%	18%	82%

	FAST YOM KIPPUR		JEWISH FREINDS			SYN. ATTENDANCE				SYN. MEMBERSHIP	
	YES	NO	FEW TO NONE	SOME	MOST OF ALL	0	FEW	SOME	OFTEN	YES	NO
1971 Respondents	50%	50%	10%	27%	63%	28%	34%	27%	11%	50%	50%
1990 Respondents	59%	41%	13%	32%	55%	17%	34%	31%	18%	49%	51%

themselves as ethnically Jewish); d) anyone who was born Jewish but is practicing another religion—usually some branch of Christianity; or e) someone who may have never had any contact with the Jewish religion or the Jewish ethnic community but has a parent who was born Jewish. These are primarily the children of Jewish-Christian marriages.

Since this paper focuses upon the degree to which respondents are involved with Jewish denominations, it will exclude respondents who were never Jewish themselves although they had a Jewish parent, or who have converted from Judaism to another religion. Such respondents were rare in the first survey. Just 10 reported converting away from Judaism; just 48 reported themselves as never having been Jewish, but as having a Jewish parent. Clearly, the data of the first survey are not affected by these one percent (58 cases out of 5,790) of the interviews.

The situation is, however, very different for the respondents of the second survey which includes 454 respondents who report themselves to be Christians who were not born Jewish. Moreover, they constitute a considerable 19 percent of the 2,441 second survey respondents. Obviously, for the two surveys to be comparable, all "non Jewish" households must be dropped from the denominational analysis. Consequently, the second survey sample size, for this analysis effort, is reduced to 1,905 interviews.

Response Rate Bias

One way of detecting survey nonresponse bias, such as that feared from the 48 percent response rate of the 1990 survey, is to contrast its statistics with equivalent statistics from a survey with a higher response rate (see Kish, 1965: 528–532). Clearly, the 1971 survey has the higher response rate. With appropriate adjustments it can be used to detect biases in the 1990 survey.

Twenty years passed between these two surveys of American Jews. Thus, the 1971 data can be projected 20 years into the future and contrasted with 1990 materials. To do so, all respondents 60 years old and older from the 1971 survey sample were dropped. By 1990, most of them were no longer alive; the rest were over 80 and institutionalized or otherwise excluded from the survey sample. The remaining 1971 survey respondents reached the ages 40 to 79 by 1990. In addition, those under 40 years of age were eliminated from the 1990 sample since they were too young to participate in the first survey. This study begins therefore, with 1,905 Jewish respondents in the 1990 survey.[1]

Table 8.1 shows that the 1971 and 1990 surveys are surprisingly close.

There are nine comparisons. Among them, four distributions—those pertaining to maintaining separate meat and dairy dishes, Jewish organization memberships, denominational preferences, and synagogue membership—are quite close, varying only by a percentage point or two. As for the rates of the other distributions: lighting candles on Hanukkah differs by 11 percentage points; keeping a kosher home by seven percent; fasting on Yom Kippur by nine points; having most or all Jewish friends by eight; and attending synagogue often by seven points. The differences here are in both directions: lighting candles on Hanukkah, keeping a kosher home, and having Jewish friends show declines from 1970 to 1990, while fasting on Yom Kippur and synagogue attendance show increases. Thus, taken as a whole, these replies are close enough to warrant comparison of the 1971 and the 1990 surveys.[2]

Denominational Preferences

Survey respondents were asked the following question: "Referring to Jewish religious denominations, do you consider yourself to be Conservative, Orthodox, Reform, Reconstructionist, or something else?" Respondents were coded as such in the order "1" for Orthodox, "2" for Conservative, and "3" for Reform. As was done in 1971, the handful of Reconstructionists were coded as Conservative (their denominational root). Respondents who had no denominational choice, for example those replying they were "just Jewish" or "secular," were classified in a fourth "no preference" code category. Again, the same procedure was followed in 1971. For all respondents (see A of Table 8.2), in the nearly 20 years between these two surveys, the Conservatives have decreased by a mere two percentage points and the "no preference" category has increased by a mere one percent. The Orthodox have fallen by five percentage points, reducing them to half of their 1971 size. The Reform have gained six percentage points.

Interestingly, these changes (Table 8.2A) support Lazerwitz' (1979) predictions based on the 1971 survey, that: the Orthodox denomination of the future would be just a few percentage points of the United States adult Jewish population; U.S. Jewry would be more inclined toward Reform than Conservative Judaism; and that Jews with no denominational preferences would be the most fluid of the four basic Jewish religious groupings.

A slightly different picture emerges when adults who are synagogue members are analyzed separately from those who are not (Table 8.2B, C). For example, while the more traditional denominations, the Orthodox and Conservatives, are preferred by only 46 percent of all adult Jews, they constitute 61 percent of synagogue members. This difference reflects a

TABLE 8.2
Adult Jewish Denominational Preferences
1971 and 1990

A.	DENOMINATIONAL PREFERENCE FOR ALL RESPONDENTS	1971	1990
	Orthodox	11%	6%
	Conservative	42%	40%
	Reform	33%	39%
	No Preference	14%	15%
	Base	100%	100%
	n	5790	1905
B.	DENOMINATIONAL PREFERENCE FOR SYNAGOGUE MEMBERS	1971	1990
	Orthodox	14%	10%
	Conservative	49%	51%
	Reform	34%	35%
	No Preference	3%	4%
		100%	100%
C.	DENOMINATIONAL PREFERENCE AMONG NON SYN. MEMBERS	1971	1990
	Orthodox	7%	4%
	Conservative	35%	31%
	Reform	33%	41%
	No Preference	25%	24%
		100%	100%

four percent drop for Reform and an 11 percent drop for those who have no denominational preference among synagogue members in 1990, compared to the population as a whole. Obviously, the reverse occurs for adults who are not synagogue members, i.e., there are fewer Jews in the more traditional denominations and more Jews who are Reform or have no denominational preference.

As might be expected, the almost exclusive concentration of adults with no denominational preference among non-synagogue members is mainly responsible for the differences between sections B and C of Table 8.2. While the percentage of respondents who indicate a preference for Reform Judaism is essentially equal to those who prefer Conservatism, the Conservatives maintain a sizeable lead in synagogue membership over the Reform.

Furthermore, the percentage of Orthodox is nearly doubled when only synagogue members are considered.

Synagogue Membership

Analysis of the 1971 survey as reported in Lazerwitz (1979) and Lazerwitz and Harrison (1979) showed that denominational analysis is aided by differentiating synagogue members from non-members. Table 8.3 gives the denominational preferences among synagogue members. As might be expected, in each survey the rate of synagogue membership is greatest among the Orthodox and smallest among those with no denominational preference. Nevertheless, synagogue membership itself is stable, changing little from 48 percent in 1971 to 47 percent of the adult Jewish population in 1990.

Moreover, even though they are a declining portion of the total American Jewish population, the percentage of Orthodox has increased among synagogue members. The percentage of synagogue members among the expanding group who prefer Reform Judaism has decreased from 1971 to 1990. There are only minor changes in the percentage of synagogue members among Conservatives and those with no denominational preference.

As was true in 1971, so in 1990, the number of interviews with Orthodox Jews who are not synagogue members, and with people who have no denominational preference but are synagogue members, is too small for detailed statistical analysis. Hence, these two sub-categories will be dropped from additional consideration.

Lazerwitz and Harrison (1979), using the 1971 survey, found that women were disproportionately represented among members of Reform synagogues; that those who preferred the Reform denomination, but who were not synagogue members, were disproportionately young, while over half of the Orthodox synagogue members were foreign born. In 1971, there

TABLE 8.3
Percentage of Synagogue Members in the Various
Denominational Preferences
1971 and 1990

DENOMINATION	1971	1990
Orthodox	66%	72%
Reform	57%	59%
No Preference	11%	13%
Total	48%	47%

was a clear educational gradient: Orthodox Jews had the least formal education, followed by Conservative Jews who were not synagogue members, Conservative synagogue members, and Reform Jews who were not synagogue members. Reform Jews who were synagogue members were the most educated group.

Table 8.4 reveals how by 1990, little remains of the 1971 relationships. However, in 1990 the Orthodox still show a disproportionate number of foreign-born, and Reform synagogue members still have the highest socioeconomic status.

A more detailed comparison of the 1990 population with the 1971 predictions can now be presented. For example, Reform Jews who are not synagogue members remain the youngest of all, as they were in 1971. The Conservative and Orthodox groups tend to be older. However, the Orthodox also include a large proportion of young members. Thus, the age distribution among the Orthodox tends to be bipolar.

The Orthodox group still has the most foreign-born and the fewest U.S.-born parents. In addition, in 1971, those with no denominational preference were the most likely to have U.S.-born parents; in 1990, those who prefer Reform Judaism are the most likely to have U.S.-born parents. Finally, those who prefer the Conservative denomination, but who are not synagogue members, have the smallest percentage of university graduates in both 1971 and 1990. Members of Reform congregations are most likely to be college graduates and, as in 1971, are most likely to be earning $80,000 or more.

If education and income are considered jointly, there appears to be a denomination socioeconomic gradient in 1990 from a low point among the Orthodox to a high point among members of Reform synagogues. However, members of Conservative synagogues rank just behind members of Reform synagogues on both education and family income, unlike 1971 rankings. Further, Reform Jews who are not synagogue members and those with no denominational preferences are rather similar with respect to education and income, as they were in 1971. Members of Orthodox congregations and Conservative Jews who are not synagogue members are the two lowest groups with regards to education and income. Both ranked low in these regards in 1971. However, in 1990, the Orthodox group has pulled ahead on education.

Table 8.5 contrasts the 1971 and 1990 denominational preferences for Jewish adults with native-born parents (third U.S. generation or more). The two sets of percentages are remarkably similar. As Lazerwitz (1979) predicted, the Orthodox constitute three percent of third, or more, generation Jews. However, there is an increase in percentage of non-synagogue

TABLE 8.4
Bio-Social Characteristics By Adult Jewish Denominational Preferences, NJPS, 1990

CHARACTERISTICS	ORTHODOX	CONSERVATIVE		REFORM		NO PREFERENCES
	MEMBERS	MEMB.	NOT MEMB.	MEMB.	NOT MEMB.	NOT MEMBERS
a. % Women	48%	53%	53%	53%	50%	41%
b. Age						
20–30 yrs.	46%	32%	37%	42%	48%	44%
60 + yrs.	30%	32%	31%	16%	20%	26%
c. U.S. Generations						
Foreign Born	28%	11%	7%	5%	4%	10%
With U.S. Born Parents	23%	44%	46%	70%	67%	56%
c. Socioeconomic Status						
College graduate	64%	70%	52%	80%	63%	65%
$80,000 or more family income	7%	26%	11%	35%	20%	17%

TABLE 8.5
Jewish Adults with U.S. Born Parents
1971 and 1990

| | U.S. BORN PARENTS | |
DENOM. GROUP	1971	1990
Orthodox	3%	3%
Conservative Member	19%	19%
Not Member	11%	14%
Reform Member	21%	22%
Not Member	20%	27%
No Preference	26%	15%
Base	100%	100%

members among both Conservative and Reform groups. The percentage of those with no preference declined.

If one were to chance a prediction, it seems likely that the Orthodox denomination has reached the end of its historic decline. It now displays an interesting combination of a sizeable number of young people and considerable growth in education coupled with the still low income levels of a group with many highly educated young people just beginning their careers.

Religious and Jewish Community Involvement by Denominational Groupings

Analysis of the 1971 data showed a clear rank order among the denominational groups on matters of religion and primary group involvement within the Jewish community. The Orthodox were the most involved, followed by members of Conservative synagogues, Conservative Jews who are not members of synagogues, members of Reform synagogues, and Reform Jews who are not synagogue members. Adults who had no denominational preference ranked the lowest.

Table 8.6 shows that the earlier rank order holds in 1990 with minor exceptions. For example, Reform Jews who are not synagogue members and individuals with no denominational preference are found to be rather similar in both 1971 and 1990. Nevertheless, there are some departures from the 1971 ranking. For example, members of the Orthodox and Conservative synagogues reverse their 1971 positions with regard to having a high level of Jewish education (54 percent and 59 percent, respectively). In addition, the percentage of members of Reform synagogues who attend

TABLE 8.6

Percent Having High Levels of Jewish Involvement By Adult Jewish
Denominational References, NJPS, 1990

JEWISH INVOLVEMENT INDICES	ORTH. MEMBERS	CONSERVATIVE		REFORM		NO PREFERENCE
		MEMB.	NOT MEMB.	MEMB.	NOT MEMB.	NOT MEMBERS
Jewish Education	54%	59%	33%	39%	20%	19%
Syn. Attend	76%	30%	7%	18%	2%	2%
Home Relig. Practices	91%	57%	23%	21%	10%	5%
J. Primary Groups	92%	57%	35%	31%	16%	10%
J. Org. Memberships	74%	64%	26%	52%	21%	6%
Attitude on Israel	75%	51%	30%	28%	20%	19%

services now exceeds that of Conservative Jews who are not synagogue members.

General Community Activity and Liberalism

Overall, synagogue members, whether Reform or Conservative, are most likely to be active in both Jewish and general community voluntary associations. However, while in 1971 adults without a denominational preference ranked low in community volunteer work—fourth among the six groups under consideration—by 1990, they are close to the high ranking Reform and Conservative synagogue members.

In 1971, Jewish adults without any denominational preference were the most likely to be liberal, followed by Reform Jews, whether synagogue members or not. Conservative and Orthodox synagogue members were next most likely to be liberal, and Conservative Jews who are not synagogue members were least likely to be liberal.

In 1990, there are minor but interesting changes. The group with the largest percentage of respondents reporting themselves to be liberal still are those with no denominational preference. Next in ranking, and up one place from 1971, are Reform Jews who are not synagogue members. Third place is now held by members of either Conservative or Reform synagogues. Conservatives who are not synagogue members come next. The Orthodox rank last. The major change, then, is the increased percentage of liberals among members of Conservative synagogues.

In summary, adults with the least involvement in the Jewish community are the most likely to be liberal. However, synagogue members of either major denomination, Reform or Conservative, are not far behind. Interestingly, the two extremes in Jewish involvement, those with no denominational preference and the Orthodox, represent the high and the low range points of liberalism, respectively. The groups between these extremes are rather alike with respect to the percentage of liberals among them.

Denominational Preferences and Intermarriage

Among the major issues in today's Jewish world is the impact of marrying within or outside the Jewish group. The wide range of topics involving intermarriage cannot be covered here. Within the scope of this study, the focus is upon the extent to which possessing a particular denominational orientation is related to intermarriage.

Table 8.8 relates current denominational preference to intermarriage. Table 8.9 relates intermarriage to childhood denomination. It is readily

TABLE 8.7

Percent with High Levels of General Community
Involvement and Liberalism, NJPS, 1990

INDICES	ORTHODOX MEMBERS	CONSERVATIVE MEMB.	CONSERVATIVE NOT MEMB.	REFORM MEMB.	REFORM NOT MEMB.	NO PREF. NOT MEMBERS
General Community						
Organiz. Activity	17%	42%	27%	44%	31%	41%
Liberalism Scale	23%	40%	34%	39%	44%	56%

TABLE 8.8

Marriage Types by Current Denominational Preference, NJPS, 1990

	MARRIAGE TYPES				
DENOMINATION	BOTH SPOUSES BORN JEWISH	ONE SPOUSE CONVERT-IN	ONE SPOUSE-JEWISH ONE SPOUSE-CHRISTIAN	ONE SPOUSE-JEWISH ONE SPOUSE "OTHER" OR NONE	BASE
Orthodox	93%	3%	4%	—	100%
Conservative	82%	7%	7%	4%	100%
Reform	60%	15%	19%	6%	100%
None	41%	3%	38%	18%	100%

212

TABLE 8.9

Marriage Types by Childhood Denomination, NJPS, 1990

| | | | MARRIAGE TYPES | | |
DENOMINATION	BOTH SPOUSES BORN JEWISH	ONE SPOUSE CONVERT-IN	ONE SPOUSE-JEWISH ONE SPOUSE-CHRISTIAN	ONE SPOUSE-JEWISH ONE SPOUSE "OTHER" OR NONE	BASE
Orthodox	85%	6%	6%	3%	100%
Conservative	73%	7%	14%	6%	100%
Reform	59%	7%	26%	8%	100%
None	60%	5%	25%	10%	100%

apparent from either table that denominational preference is closely related to intermarriage. The less traditional the denomination, the more likely its adherent is married to someone who was not originally Jewish.

If one includes those marriages in which the originally non-Jewish spouse states that he or she is now Jewish, then (see Table 8.8) 96 percent of Orthodox Jews, 89 percent of Conservative Jews, and 75 percent of Reform Jews are currently married to Jews. However, only 44 percent of Jews with no denominational preference fit into this category.

Marriages in which one spouse is Jewish and the other is reported as "other than Christian" or as having no religion are an intriguing, albeit an ambiguously defined category of intermarriage. According to the 1971 survey, many of them were actually born Jewish. Some came from marginally Christian families. In the 1990 survey, this category amounts to 126 households, or 21 percent of the 613 intermarriages. Obviously, how this ambiguous category is defined has a noticeable impact on the number of reported intermarriages. Here, this category is reported separately from the other marriage types.

Table 8.9 indicates that the percentage of intermarriage is higher among those with a denominational preference when respondents are grouped by the denominations of their childhood homes rather than by their current preference. However, the percentage of intermarried is lower among those with no denominational preference in childhood, compared to those who currently have no denominational preference. Apparently, the "no preference" category is the choice of Jews married to Christians when the non-Jewish spouse does not convert to Judaism.

The 1990 survey includes 1,952 married Jewish respondents of whom 280 (14 percent) state they have no denominational preference. Interestingly, this group includes 166 of the total of 613 intermarriages, or 27 percent (counting the marriages with "others" and "nones"). Furthermore, this group of married respondents includes only six percent of the spouses who converted to Judaism.

The group of 27 respondents who report that although raised as Jews they are now Catholic or Protestant is too small to enable any meaningful statistical treatment. Apparently, the route to disappearance from the Jewish community is not through a personal religious conversion but through marriage to a non-Jew and raising one's children as non-Jews. Disappearance into the non-Jewish world, then, is through the children of the intermarried.

On the other hand, 63 percent of converts into Judaism are married to Reform Jews. Reform, then, is the most likely denominational destination for Jews who are married to converts to Judaism.

With some effort, it is possible to compare the intermarriage percentages found in the 1990 survey with equivalent data from the 1971 survey. Lazerwitz (1981) has reported intermarriage percentages for married Jewish men from the 1971 survey. His findings for 1971 are given in Table 8.10, as are the 1990 intermarriage percentages. Table 8.10 indicates there has been a considerable increase in the percentages of currently intermarried Jewish men in all the denominational groups. Overall, there has been at least a three-and-a-half fold increase. Intermarriage has more than doubled among Orthodox men and has increased nearly four-fold among Conservative and Reform Jewish men. Among men with no denominational preference, the increase is about three-fold. In 1971, the rate of intermarriage was about the same among Orthodox and Conservative men. Furthermore, the 1971 intermarriage rate for men of the more traditional denominations, Conservative and Orthodox, was about half of that of Reform men, and one-quarter of the rate found among men with no denominational preference.

In 1990, the intermarriage rate among Conservative men is about twice as large as among Orthodox men. In the Reform Movement, the intermarriage rate of men is about five times higher than among their Orthodox counterparts, and about double that of Conservative men. The intermarriage rate of men with no denominational preference is around six times higher than among Orthodox men, three times higher than Conservative men, and about 25 percent larger than that of Reform men.

Table 8.11 introduces synagogue membership into the investigation of intermarriage. With this additional factor, an interesting pattern emerges: synagogue members are disproportionately in marriages formed by two born Jews or a Jew married to a convert to Judaism. Conversely, it is among non-synagogue members that intermarriage tends to exist. Indeed, if we add together the marriages in which both spouses are Jews and those in which one spouse is a Jew-by-choice, then 98 percent of Orthodox synagogue members are married to other Jews, as well as 96 percent of

TABLE 8.10

Contrasting Male Intermarriages for the 1971 and 1990 NJPS Surveys

	PERCENT MEN INTERMARRIED				
SURVEY YEAR	OVERALL	ORTHODOX	CONSERVATIVE	REFORM	NO PREFER.
1990					
a) With "nones" and "others"	32%	10%	18%	43%	55%
b) Without "nones" and "others"	25%	7%	14%	36%	41%
1971	7%	3%	4%	9%	17%

TABLE 8.11

Marriage Types by Current Denomination and Synagogue Membership, NJPS, 1990

MARRIAGE TYPES

DENOM-SYN.	BOTH SPOUSES BORN JEWISH	ONE SPOUSE CONVERT-IN	ONE SPOUSE-JEWISH ONE SPOUSE-CHRISTIAN	ONE SPOUSE-JEWISH ONE SPOUSE "OTHER" OR NONE	BASE
Orthodox	98%	—	2%	—	100%
Conservative					
Member	88%	8%	3%	1%	100%
Not Member	72%	4%	15%	9%	100%
Reform					
Member	66%	24%	7%	3%	100%
Not Member	55%	8%	29%	8%	100%
None-Not Member	38%	1%	41%	20%	100%

Conservative synagogue members and 90 percent of Reform synagogue members. Among Conservative Jews who are not synagogue members, 24 percent of the marriages fall under the "still Jewish-not Jewish" category, as are 37 percent of Reform Jews who are not synagogue members and 61 percent of those with no denominational preference.

Couples whose marriages involve a born-Jew and someone not born Jewish, but who resolve this difference by conversions into Judaism, generally join synagogues. Consequently, they are much more involved in Judaism than those intermarried couples who are not synagogue members. Thirty-four percent of married Reform synagogue members are intermarried. They represent 19 percent of all intermarried Jews in the 1990 survey. Finally, 45 percent of all conversions into Judaism are found among Reform synagogue members, 22 percent among Conservative synagogue members, and 18 percent among Reform Jews who are not members of a synagogue.

Summary

Survey respondents have been divided into eight denominational-synagogue membership groups, six of which have enough respondents for detailed study. For the most part, these groups have become more alike. Those characteristics which distinguished the six denominational-synagogue groups in 1971 no longer do so in 1990. Similarity is found especially when Conservative and Reform Jews are compared. Nevertheless, Reform synagogue members and non-members are younger than Conservative synagogue members and non-members. Orthodox Jews are no longer overwhelmingly composed of older people; they now include a solid percentage of young adults. Yet, the Orthodox still include the most foreign-born adherents and the fewest respondents of American-born parents. Reform Jews have the largest percentages of respondents with American-born parents. In addition, Reform synagogue members have the highest socioeconomic status in 1990 as they did in 1971. Conservative synagogue members have the next highest socioeconomic status. Orthodox synagogue members have considerably increased their educational achievements over 1971 but still have the smallest percentage with incomes of $80,000 or over.

In 1971, measures of Jewish community involvement showed a rank order in which Orthodox Jews led, followed by Conservatives, then Reform, and finally by those with no denominational preference. Overall, that order still pertains in 1990. However, there are now significant exceptions to the general rule. The level of involvement in the Jewish community of

Reform synagogue members now either exceeds or equals Conservatives who are not synagogue members. In general, it appears that today the Orthodox are the most religiously and communally involved, followed by members of Conservative synagogues. Conservative Jews who are not synagogue members, and Reform Jews, whether synagogue members or not, are the next most involved. Respondents with no denominational preference are clearly the least involved Jewishly.

Members of Conservative and Reform synagogues and respondents with no denominational preference are most active in voluntary associations in the general community. Furthermore, those with no denominational preference score highest on the survey's liberalism scale, followed by Reform Jews who are not synagogue members. Members of Reform and Conservative synagogues are next highest in liberalism, followed by Conservatives who are not synagogue members. The Orthodox are the least liberal. In short, the two least Jewishly involved categories, those with no denominational preference and Reform Jews who are not synagogue members, are the most liberal; however they are followed by the quite Jewishly involved Conservative and Reform synagogue members. In 1971 and in 1990, the Orthodox are the least liberal.

As might be expected, denominational preference and synagogue membership are closely related to whether one marries within or outside the American Jewish community. The less traditional the denominational preference, the more likely one is to marry a non-Jew.

Those survey respondents who were raised in Orthodox or Conservative homes, but who marry outside the Jewish community, tend to shift to the less traditional denominational groups. The absence of a denominational preference is the most likely outcome for marriages between a Jew and a Christian when the latter does not convert to Judaism.

The route to disappearance of those of Jewish parentage into the non-Jewish world does not appear to be through their own religious conversion. Rather, it results when a Jewish parent who has married outside the community raises his/her children as non-Jews.

From 1971 to 1990, there has almost been a four-fold increase in the percentage of Jews marrying non-Jews. This large increase is found among all the denominations as well as among those with no denominational preference.

Those intermarried couples who resolve their religious differences by conversions into Judaism customarily are synagogue members. They are, then, more Jewishly involved than those intermarried couples who are not synagogue members.

Thirty-four percent of Reform synagogue members are intermarried. Forty-five percent of all conversions into Judaism are found among Reform synagogue members; 22 percent of such conversions are among Conservative synagogue members, and 18 percent are among Reform non-synagogue members.

In contrasting denominational preference with synagogue membership in both the 1971 and the 1990 surveys, it is found that denominational preference is indicative of a broader, more communal orientation toward the Jewish religion and the Jewish community. Apparently, synagogue membership involves people in a web of institutional influences. Hence, it is likely that denominational preference per se is closely associated with home religious practices and involvement with Jewish primary groups; actual synagogue membership is more closely associated with attendance at religious services and activity in Jewish voluntary associations. Further analysis into such relationships is clearly called for. Fortunately, it should be possible to conduct such analysis by comparing the 1971 and 1990 National Jewish Population Surveys.

Notes

1. Of course, our procedure would be improved if life table survivor rates were applied to the 1971 data. Such an improvement would reduce the proportion of old to young. However, for the work given in Table 8.1, we can ignore this problem.

2. The possibility of bias is less important than the fact that most variables of concern to the issue of denominationalism are slowly changing ones. That is, they require an appreciable amount of time to show considerable changes. Jewish respondents and Jewish nonrespondents would conceivably differ by little in 20 years on such a slowly changing variable. If so, the potential for bias is considerably reduced.

To summarize then, it appears likely that for most of the analyses of concern here, the bias in the 1990 survey is not serious enough to preclude meaningful conclusions. It should be noted, however, that bias considerations may be more significant when analyzing more rapidly changing issues such as those dealing with opinions or attitudes deriving from matters less basic than religiosity and ethnicity, or when using more sophisticated power statistical analysis.

References

Kish, Leslie, "A Procedure for Objective Respondent Selection Within the Household," *Journal of the American Statistical Association*, Volume 44, (1949), pp. 380–387.

———, *Survey Sampling*, New York, John Wiley, 1965.

Kosmin, Barry A., et al., *Highlights of the CJF National Jewish Population Survey*, New York, Council of Jewish Federations, 1991.

Lazerwitz, Bernard, "The Sample Design of the National Jewish Population Survey," *National Jewish Population Study: Methodology*, New York, Council of Jewish Federations, 1974a.

―――, *Sampling Errors and Statistical Inference for the National Jewish Population Survey*, New York, Council of Jewish Federations, 1974b.

―――, "Past and Future Trends in the Size of American Jewish Denominations," *Journal of Reform Judaism* (Summer, 1979), pp. 77–82.

―――, "Jewish-Christian Marriages and Conversions," *Jewish Social Studies*, Volume 43, (Winter, 1981), pp. 31–46.

Lazerwitz, Bernard and Michael Harrison, "American Jewish Denominations: A Social and Religious Profile," *American Sociological Review*, Volume 44 (August, 1979), pp. 656–666.

Salmon, Charles and John Nichols, "The Next-Birthday Method of Respondent Selection," *Public Opinion Quarterly*, Volume 47, (1983), pp. 270–276.

9

Apostasy Among American Jews: The Individual Analysis

Samuel Z. Klausner

Apostasy and Social Authority

Consider the conversion of a people. Religious change is a societal event: from a Zoroastrian to Muslim society, from a Roman pagan to Christian society, or from a Jewish to a Christian society. The sweep of Christianity through the Roman empire following the conversion of Constantine in the fourth century is a historical example of societal conversion, as is the militarily established Islamic hegemony from North Africa, through the Arab East to India in the seventh century.

Societal conversion corresponds to a change in the authoritativeness of political, economic, religious, and other institutions. Zoroastrian or Roman pagan institutions, in the case of the above examples, were replaced by Muslim or Christian ones. Social order depends on the wide acceptance of the authoritativeness of these institutions.

With the decline in the legitimacy of the authority of a group's religious elite, an alternate source of legitimate authority is sought to sustain social order. A converted society is one that has found new legitimately authorized leaders. Adoption of a new faith by individual members of a society is their adaption to this new societal circumstance.

Societal conversion assimilates one society to another. It has both a structural and a cultural aspect. Structural assimilation refers to the merging of the social relationships, the institutions and organizations of the respective groups. An example is the acceptance of a common body of state law governing economic relations. Cultural assimilation involves accepting common symbols of group identity, a common semiosis or language, for mediating social relations. The acceptance, in Catalonia, of the language of Castile for daily commerce is an example of a common language amidst resistance to other common symbols of identity.

Contemporary scholars of religious conversion, likely influenced by modern Western individualism and voluntarism and the mystique of sudden personality change, have concentrated on shifts in individuals' religious commitment, their being "born again." In most societies in which several religions meet, people trickle continuously across the boundary between the faiths. Some of these passages are idiosyncratic events in the lives of people, not unusually, marginal to their own community. A societal conversion, on the other hand, is led by the group's elite and involves a massive shift in religious allegiance.

Students of individual conversion have tended to argue that: (1) societal conversion is a gradual process, a sum of individual conversions; (2) the societal assimilation of foreign cultural elements, through the education of individuals, is the leading edge of that process; and (3) that conversion of a society is the cumulative result of individual decisions to accept a new faith.

In fact, contrary to the above claims: (1) societal conversion is revolutionary, associated with the moment that a new authority is established. Individual withdrawals of fealty may be evolutionary, successive adaptations to the already legitimate societal authority. (2) Cultural change may be anticipatory, but mainly it follows after structural changes. Structural changes are changes in group boundaries, as well as changes in the norms governing social relations, and may include a syncretism of religions, subordination of a previously self-determining polity to the rule of another and the meshing of previously exogamous kinship groups. (3) The initial change is institutional rather than individual. Individuals are reborn in their identities as they adapt to a caesura in their society.

The structural assimilation of American Jewry has largely already taken place in several institutional spheres. American Jewry has, by and large, already been incorporated into the general economic, political, stratificational, educational, physical and mental health, and recreational and aesthetic systems and is, presently, being absorbed in the general kinship system. In practice, the term "general" means Christian. At this historical moment, the substitution of American civil law for Jewish law in the area of personal status coincides with the structural assimilation of Jewish to Christian kin groups. Formal religious conversion of the society is an easy sequel to the assimilation of families.

Much of this change is characterized as secularization, an expanding role of civil society. However, in fact, no societal activity is external to the religious system just as no societal activity is disengaged from economic and political institutions. The religious integration of a social system is as much a functional requirement as is an operating economy or polity. An apparent secular sphere, which Jacob Katz has termed the "semi-neutral society," is a transient bridge between religions of a society. The shift in religious identity follows relatively smoothly the meshing of the other institutional spheres.[1]

The National Jewish Population Survey

This study analyzes the correlates of conversions to Christianity of individual Jews that are currently in process amidst the already assimilating American Jewish society. The data for this analysis are drawn from the Council of Jewish Federation's 1990 National Jewish Population Survey. The survey units were both households and their members. The sample consists of 2,441 households identified as having at least one Jewish member and which were discovered through a random digit dialing sampling procedure. The respondents or informants were persons 18 or older interviewed by telephone. The present analysis is limited to those aged 22 or older, born or raised Jewish. Some of them remain Jewish by religion, while others reject religious identification with Judaism, and still others have adopted a religion other than Judaism.

The NJPS was not designed specifically for analyses of apostasy. Hence, it does not cover a number of specific measures needed for such research. This study, then, is a secondary analysis of data for a purpose not necessarily envisioned by those who designed the data collection. The aim here is to specify some correlates of individual apostasy insofar as these are discoverable within the limits of the survey data.

The survey estimated that 6,840,000 Americans are Jewish by religious or ethnic preference.[2] These include 210,000 classified as converts out, adults born or raised Jewish who have "rejected Judaism and currently follow a religion other than Judaism (JCO)." Another 415,000 adults are classified as having "Jewish parentage or descent who were raised from birth in a religion other than Judaism (JOR)." Some 1,120,000 individuals are of Jewish background but avow no current religion. Some of these consider themselves Jews by ethnicity or background. In addition, some 700,000 children under 18 are being raised in a religion other than Judaism.

Types of Structural Assimilation

An "apostasy" or assimilation variable was constructed by comparing the religion into which an individual claims to have been born (Q19A: i.e., Question 19A on the schedule) or raised (Q20A), if any, with the one with which he or she now identifies (Q17A). (Actually, relaxing the definition to include those raised Jewish but not born Jewish added only 18 persons. Thus, practically speaking, the criterion is born-Jewish.) Seventy-six percent of the respondents claimed to have been born Jewish, the others claiming Catholicism, Protestantism, some other religion, or none as the religion of the household into which they were born. Those not born Jewish (other than the 18 raised Jewish) were eliminated from this analysis. Those reported not having been born into any religion but who may consider themselves Jewish solely by an ethnic or national criterion are also set aside. In this sense, the strict understanding of apostasy as a change in religion rather than, say, ethnic or national identity, is adhered to. Two generations ago, ways of expressing Jewish communal identification included numbers of Jews who identified as Yiddish socialist secularists, secular Zionists, among other groups. These alternatives, in their formal organizational sense, are rare today. As a consequence, limiting the definition to religion in the American setting should not be terribly distorting of the wider picture of the Jewish-American population.

Some of those with no religion at birth may have been the children of parents who were born Jewish, cases in which the shift took place more than one generation ago. While this departure from Judaism over two or three generations is a numerically significant event, the current analysis is limited to cases in which the change is observable within a single generation.

The "apostasy" or assimilation variable has five categories into which respondents are classified, four of which involve types of structural assimilation. The first consists of those born into Judaism or raised as Jews and who currently claim Judaism as their faith. They are 87.8 percent of the respondents. These consistently Jewish individuals are subdivided into three categories. The first will be termed Jewish/Jewish or steadfastly Jewish. They constitute a baseline group and include about two-thirds of the respondents. If these individuals contribute to charities they give to Jewish or to both Jewish and non-Jewish causes. If married, they have a Jewish spouse. The significance of these last two characteristics for our categorizing will be apparent from the following two paragraphs. About two-thirds of the respondents are in this baseline category.

Individuals who were born as and are still Jewish may cross one or another social structural line between the Jewish and non-Jewish communities, that is, assimilate structurally in some respect. Some cross over social interactionally, not living in neighborhoods with a significant proportion of Jews, nor having many close Jewish friends. Some contribute only to non-Jewish causes, giving nothing to Jewish charities. Some belong to non-Jewish organizations exclusively, having no membership in Jewish organizations such as a synagogue or a Jewish civil rights group. Some people fall in more than one of these categories. These characteristics are highly intercorrelated. One who gives to no Jewish charities is likely not to belong to Jewish formal organizations. We will use the evidence of crossing the communal charities boundary as an economic measure of ideological commitment in the area of voluntary associations. This simple economic measure seems to act as a proxy for a wide spectrum of communal associations or non-associations. Persons who identify as Jews and who contribute to non-Jewish causes but not to Jewish causes will be termed Economic Emigrants (abbreviated EC to signify the crossing of the Economic boundary). They constitute a second category or status, accounting for 16.6 percent of the study sample. (They are 19 percent of those in the three categories currently identifying as Jewish by religion.)

Those born Jewish and still identifying as Jewish but who have a gentile (nonconverted) spouse have crossed the family boundary in establishing a mixed religious household. These are a third status and will be designated Jewish/Jewish GS (abbreviated GS for Gentile Spouse). They constitute 3.4 percent of the sample as a whole.

Then we have two categories for those born Jewish but no longer identifying as such. The first consists of those born Jewish but claiming no current religion. They will be termed Jewish/None and constitute 6.7 percent of the sample. Those born Jewish but now considering themselves of another religion, mostly Christian, will be termed Jewish/Christian, 5.5 percent of our sample of respondents. Only these last have apostatized literally. We do not know how many of these did so canonically by visiting the Baptismal font, and how many have taken advantage of the flexible practice of certain Protestant churches and have merely self-identified as Christians. The frequencies in the sample of those meetings each of these criteria are summarized in the following tabulation:

TABLE 9.1[3]

Proportion of Cases in Each Assimilatory Category

Jewish/Jewish	67.8%
Jewish/Jewish EC	16.8%
Jewish/Jewish GS	3.4%
Jewish/None	6.7%
Jewish/Christian	5.5%
	(1713)

These categories may be thought of as defining a sequence of social positions, each successive form of structural assimilation being closer to conversion. It is a sequence in the sense that each successive status is increasingly similar (in the associated values of its correlate variables) to the converts. The last position consists of converts from Judaism during their lifetimes. This report will demonstrate the sequence empirically by correlating each status measure with relevant variables. We do not argue that there is an apostatizing career, that individuals assume each of these successive statuses in turn. Individuals may take the step to apostasy from any one of the other four statuses, including the steadfastly Jewish.

The analytic tactic will be to show that each of these statuses, more or less in the order given, corresponds to a decrease in measures of Jewish identity, or factors associated with Jewish identity, and an increase in the values of measures of Christian identity. The criterion for apostasy is not simply the decline in Jewish observance and identification but such decline in association with a rise in Christian observances and identifications. There is little difference between those who claim to be Christians and those who claim to adhere to no religion. The overwhelming Christian ethos of the society defines those who claim no religion as marginal Christians, just as a number of them may be marginal Jews.[4]

Some Irrelevant Variables

Discussions as to whether Jews constitute a religious, ethnic, or national community are frequent among sociologists. Implicit in such discussions is the notion that one or another of these social forms may contribute in its own way to Jewish survival. The Jewries of the world tend to be designated as national, ethnic, or religious groupings more in response to reigning ideologies, Jewish or gentile, than in response to the objective characteristics of the communities.

Respondents were asked whether they considered Jews in America as a religious, ethnic, or national community. We find no difference in the distribution of these popular attributions among our five categories. A Jew who became a Christian is just as likely to see Jews as a religion or as an ethnic group as are those who are holding steadfast to their faith. Apparently, the average person sees little relation between these as academic labels and the depth of his or her own identity.

It does not follow that were members of the community to behave as an ethnic, religious, or national community, objectively defined, it would bear no relation to apostasy. Indeed, were Jews simply an ethnic group, in the American sense, not members of a religious civilization, apostasy could well be facilitated. Ethnic groups in the United States are ideologically readied for the "melting pot." Ethnic Jewishness is reduced to some expressive symbols ready to be cast into the great crucible to blend with other ethnic symbols in the new American type.[5]

Class is another major variable which seems irrelevant to individual apostatizing. Conversion is sometimes viewed as economically opportunistic. Yet, there is no income difference between converts and steadfast Jews. Further, the distribution among the usual occupational categories (managers, white collar, blue collar, service workers, etc.) bears no relation to the several types of structural assimilation. Again, I do not argue that broad economic factors, such as economic deprivation based on political discrimination, would not affect the rate of apostasy. The finding simply shows that in the United States the factors promoting apostasy at this time, at this particular advanced stage of the process, act across the economic spectrum. Finally, there is no gender difference between the categories, all of the groups consisting of about half men and half women. (The gentile spouses of Jews in the second category are just as likely to be women (51 percent) as men (49 percent).)[6]

Socialization for Apostasy

While the ultimate "causes" of apostasy are to be sought on the collective level, some early individual experiences contribute to selecting candidates for conversion. The fact that such socialization is available attests, in itself, to an already accomplished collective conversion. The assimilatory types were defined with reference to a single generation. The influences, though, include transgenerational ones. Socialization effects may accumulate across generations—or, in fewer instances, a generation may reject its parents, canceling some aspects of their influence. Factors affecting conversion that are explored in this section include the religious ambience of the parental home, Jewish education or the lack of it, the scope and salience of Judaism for individuals, and their social location with respect to the currents of political liberalism and conservatism. The socializing implications of each of these will be commented upon in turn.

Respondents were asked about the religion in which they were raised. In the sample as a whole, 75 percent of the respondents were raised as Jews with six percent raised as Catholics, six percent Protestants, seven percent in another religion, and seven percent in no religion (Q85). Recall that those born into a religion other than Judaism are excluded in this analysis. Most of those raised in a non-Jewish religion are the spouses of Jews, of whom somewhat less than half now identify as Jews. (Of those who say they have converted to Judaism, 65 percent, 88 respondents, claim a formal conversion.)

The following tables show the distribution of childhood religious upbringing among the five types. Table 9.3 treats the religion in which the persons were raised as an independent variable. (Tables 9.2 and 9.3 display the same data percentaged in two directions.)

All of the 1,376 persons in Tables 9.2 and 9.3 were born to at least one

TABLE 9.2

Assimilatory Types By Religion in Which Raised
(in percents)

	JEW/JEW	JEW/JEC	JEW/JGS	JEW/NONE	JEW/CHR
Judaism	99	96	97	75	65
Christian	0	2	2	7	24
None	1	2	2	19	11
	(932)	(207)	(58)	(91)	(88)

TABLE 9.3

Influence of Religion in Which Person Was Raised
on Assimilatory Type
(in percents)

TYPE	RELIGION IN WHICH RAISED		
	JUDAISM	CHRISTIANITY	NONE
Jewish/Jewish	71	3	20
Jew/JewEC	16	12	12
Jew/JewGS	4	3	2
Jewish/None	5	12	42
Jewish/Christian	4	64	24
	(1302)	(33)	(41)

Jewish parent. A few were defined at birth as having no religion or as belonging to another religion, usually Christianity, but were raised as Jews. The tables indicate how the first three types differ from the last two. There is a much greater likelihood that those with no religion and the converts were raised in homes with either no religious commitment or with a Christian one. Almost all of those raised as Jews consider themselves Jews, including those who have crossed the kinship or economic boundary. Looking at Table 9.3, we see that of those born to at least one Jewish parent but with a Christian upbringing, 83 percent have no religious identification as a Jew. Of those not raised in any faith, 66 percent do not currently identify as Jewish. The culture of the childhood home is the overwhelming determinant. More precisely, the religion of the home determines a number of social relational and institutional involvements. Many conversions occur over two generations. A home may become Jewishly vacuous and then bear children who have a higher probability of converting than those from affirmatively Jewish homes.

A Jewish education, or lack of it (part of what is implied by being raised Jewish), is also associated with the likelihood of structurally assimilating or converting. A Guttman scale combining items of formal Jewish schooling as a child, the reading of Jewish literature, and attending Jewish adult education courses provides an index of Jewish education.[7] About 42 percent neither read Jewish periodicals, attend adult courses, nor claim formal Jewish education. Most of the remaining 58 percent report several years of an afternoon Hebrew school or a Sunday school. A small number attended a Jewish parochial school. These individuals have, at least, the technical ability to participate in Jewish religious worship and to share something of Jewish cognitive culture. Insofar as they read Jewish periodicals, they evidence an interest in the Jewish community. Of course, childhood Jewish education says more about the climate provided by the parents than about childhood motivation. Substance aside, it indicates some early involvement with Jewish communal institutions, the providers of Jewish schooling.

Sixty-four percent of the steadfast Jews have at least some minimal Jewish education, as do 54 percent of the Jews who donate solely to non-Jewish causes, 51 percent of the intermarried, 38 percent of those with no religion, and 40 percent of the converts. As low as the proportion with any Jewish education is among the steadfast Jews, it is lower among all the other types. Those who have no religion do not differ at all (38 percent vs. 40 percent) from the converts with respect to the proportion who have a minimal level of Jewish education. (Some functional level of Jewish education, say four or more years of Hebrew School and reading a periodical, characterizes 32 percent, 10 percent, 15 percent, two percent, and six percent of each of the types in the order given previously.)

While education need not make for a Jewish commitment, early alienation from the educational institution is followed by adult alienation from the community. Those holding Judaism more closely may seek more Jewish education for their children and for themselves as adults. Those moving toward apostasy abandon it in both instances. The climate of abandonment is set by the parental generation as a gatekeeper to Jewish institutional participation. The lack of Jewish knowledge would not, of course, make the respondents apostates. They must accept another faith and would probably acquire knowledge of that faith. What is clear here, though, is that those with no religion and the converts tend, more than the others, to grow up in an environment outside of the Jewish cognitive system.

In a sense, persons moving toward apostasy should be vitally concerned with the faith they are abandoning. Apostates might be notoriously concerned about being misidentified as Jews. Respondents were asked about the importance of Judaism in their lives. There is some ambiguity about the respondents' interpretation of the terms "importance." The question in its major meaning is intended to be more than an attitudinal measure. It should reflect something of the objective scope and salience of Jewish involvements. The larger the number of life domains in which Judaism, Jewish culture, or Jewish institutions are relevant, the more the importance of Judaism in the respondent's life.

Their responses vary directly with type of structural assimilation and apostasy. Some 48 percent of all respondents said Judaism was "very important" in their lives. They included 63 percent of the steadfast Jews, 28 percent of Jews who donate solely to non-Jewish causes, 67 percent of those with gentile spouses, three percent of those with no religion, and 21 percent of those who had converted. The apostate consciously distances himself or herself from the old faith and, in attitude, reduces it to irrelevance as a determinant of his or her action. Those with no current religion seem less concerned with Judaism or Jewishness than those who have converted to Christianity.[8] The expressed lack of importance of Judaism for those with no religion is evidence of their social separation from the Jewish community. Judaism is not something they think about, even in a negative sense. We do not know how much the distribution would have differed had the respondents been asked about the importance for them of Jewish peoplehood.

Apostasy is associated with political attitude, more an adult adaptation than an early socialization factor. Part of the broader theory of societal conversion is that an anti-establishment, liberal, or revolutionary sector of the host society recruits members of the minority to the majority. As participants in this sector, the candidates for assimilation adopt liberal attitudes.[9] Further, liberalism in American society is also associated with more permeable boundaries between ethnic and religious groups, if not with a distancing from the more fundamentalist forms of Judaism and Christianity. With actual conversion, the person is drawn toward the conservative majority, no longer being marginal. American Jewry, as a whole, has tended to be relatively politically liberal.

Respondents were self-classified as liberal or conservative. On the whole, 45 percent of the respondents self-define as relatively liberal. This category includes 42 percent of the steadfast Jews, 56 percent of the Jews who donate solely to non-Jewish causes, 40 percent of the intermarried, 70 percent of those with no religion, and 29 percent of the converted. Those with gentile spouses seem more conservative than the Jews who donate solely to non-Jewish causes and those with no religion, but the number of cases in this category is too small for reliable assessment. Liberalism sharply increases among those with no religion. The liberal here may well be critical of both the Jewish and the non-Jewish societies. In this sense, liberalism, particularly that of the people with no religion, becomes a preparation for disengagement and boundary-crossing, structural assimilation. The converts, now part of the larger society, are the most conservative. Notably, the two most conservative types are those with direct social and familial involvement with Christian society, those with a gentile spouse, and the converts.

Permeable Institutional Boundaries

Structural assimilation involves the merging of statuses and institutions of formerly distinct societies. In this section, several indicators of individuals crossing the kinship, formal organizational, communal, social interactional, and religious organizational boundaries will be observed. While progressing from steadfast Jews to Jewish converts to Christianity, one can observe a person's declining probability of occupying a Jewish status and participating in Jewish social sectors.

If Jewish and Christian kinship groups are joined under one general "civil" kinship system, we may speak of structural assimilation of families. Christianity is hegemonic in the United States. The "civil" system is a dilute Christian or liberal Protestant system. If family status is authorized by the "civil," or Christian, system, Jewish persons, as members of families, become incumbents of a Christian status. One of our assimilatory types presents a person who was born Jewish and currently identifies as Jewish but has a gentile spouse, has a household and an extended kinship group of mixed religions. The Jewish partner participates in a non-Jewish kinship system insofar as he or she has gentile in-laws, and other relatives. A Jew marrying a convert to Judaism would not be contracting an intermarriage but would be establishing a household amidst relatives of different faiths. The children may have both Jewish and non-Jewish aunts, uncles, cousins, and grandparents.

The attitude toward intermarriage expresses the readiness to cross the family boundary between Jewish and Christian societies. In general, the proportion of American Jews accepting intermarriage has increased significantly over the past three decades as shown in Jewish community studies. The 1,707 respondents for whom we have data were classified according to whether they opposed (19 percent), accepted (49 percent), or supported (32 percent) the notion of intermarriage for their child. Some in the last category would "strongly support" their child's decision to intermarry. It is not clear whether the respondents are reflecting their approval or disapproval of intermarriage for their child or whether they would be supportive of the child's decisions, whatever that might be. The distinction between the attitude toward crossing the group boundary and the attitude toward parent-child relations may not even be clear to the respondents. Support ing an intermarriage of their child are 24 percent of the steadfast Jews, 45 percent of the Jews who donate solely to non-Jewish causes, 36 percent of the intermarried, 48 percent of those with no religion, and 46 percent of the converts to Christianity. Only the steadfast Jews differ here. That one-fourth of them support intermarriage may seem surprising but, recollect, this is a category which includes some who are currently only nominally or marginally Jewish.

In this climate, intermarriage, far from having to overcome opposition from the community, becomes consistent with communal norms. The overall study estimates the current intermarriage rate at 52 percent nationally. That the proportion of Jews with a gentile spouse constitutes so small a proportion of our sample (3.4 percent) reflects the recency of so high a rate and the earlier tendency for the non-Jew to convert to Judaism. The NJPS sample includes a good number of older people who married at a time when the rate of intermarriage was considerably lower. Also, additional born-Jews with nonconverted gentile spouses are included among those with no current religion and those who, themselves, have converted.

Formal organizational affiliation offers an important setting for structural assimilation. Respondents were asked, in two separate questions (Q109, Q110) about their memberships in Jewish and non-Jewish organizations, presumably voluntary service groups. Combining the responses to the two items, respondents were classified into those who belong only to Jewish (10 percent), to Jewish as well as to non-Jewish (11 percent), and solely to non-Jewish organizations (32 percent). Forty-seven percent belong to no organizations at all. These latter are not publicly expressing themselves on the choice between Jewish and non-Jewish organizations. The 32 percent belonging only to non-Jewish organizations are "organizational emigrants," and they are differentially distributed among our categories. Belonging only to non-Jewish organizations are 22 percent of the steadfast Jews, 47 percent of the Jews who donate to non-Jewish causes only, 40 percent of the intermarried, 59 percent of those with no religion, and 58 percent of those Jews who converted to Christianity. This is a rather regular progression. Jews who donate exclusively to non-Jewish causes differ little in this respect from those who have gentile spouses. Similarly, those who currently have no religion are nearly indistinguishable from those who have converted to Christianity with respect to this variable. Some three-fifths of these latter two types choose to participate solely in non-Jewish voluntary activities with most of the others not joining voluntary organizations of either type. This pattern fits our own basic imagery of apostasy as involving a new set of activities in place of the Jewish ones, not simply a decline in Jewish participation.

A similar picture emerges from a comparison of philanthropic contributions, the measure used to create the category of "Economic Emigrants." Implicitly, the steadfast Jews and the intermarried all contributed to some Jewish, and many to non-Jewish, charities as well. The Economic Emigrants, by their defining characteristic, contributed solely to non-Jewish causes. Charitable contributions reflect the person's ideological placement and social identification at the community level. Almost any sort of involvement in the organized Jewish community, or public identification of oneself as a Jew in a workplace, exposes one to appeals from Jewish charities. Not giving implies either a detachment from these organizational settings, non-identification as a Jew in public, or a refusal to contribute. Those who do not contribute to any charities are not considered here.

Responses to Jewish (Q122) and secular donating (Q126) were combined. Respondents were classified according to whether they gave only to Jewish philanthropies, to non-Jewish only, to both, or to neither. On the whole, 11 percent of the sample give only to Jewish organizations. At the other extreme, 23 percent give only to non-Jewish charities and nothing to Jewish ones. None of the steadfast Jews and none of the Jews with gentile spouses fall in this last category. By definition, Jews who donate exclusively to non-Jewish causes are in this category. We find that 52 percent of those with no religion and 51 percent of the converts give to non-Jewish charities alone, strikingly different from the 23 percent of the entire sample in this category. A reduction in Jewish philanthropy meets the criterion of structural assimilation when it is paralleled by a rise in non-Jewish philanthropy. Those with no religion are as alienated from Jewish causes as are the converts.

Social or communal structural assimilation is reflected in personal associations. A Guttman scale was formed of two items: one referring to the proportion of close friends who are Jewish, a second to the extent to which one's neighborhood is Jewish. In the sample as a whole, 26 percent report that they live in a gentile neighborhood and have almost no Jewish friends. A gentile social ambience, defined in this way, characterizes 16 percent of the steadfast Jews, 35 percent of Jews who donate exclusively to non-Jewish causes, 50 percent of the intermarried, 49 percent of those with no religion, and 63 percent of those converted to Christianity. The sequence of assimilatory statuses is positively associated with moving from a Jewish to a non-Jewish social circle. The intermarried, those with no religion, and the converts are the most socially distant from the Jewish community. Nearly two-thirds of the converts have few Jewish friends and live in non-Jewish neighborhoods. Traditionally, the Jewish milieu has been integral to being Jewish, involving access to Jewish facilities such as a synagogue, a kosher meat market, a *mikvah*, and an educational facility. Dispersed suburban living styles break these territorial ties but Jewish residential clusters, albeit less compact, have emerged in suburbia. The willingness to break away from the Jewish ambience shows the insignificance of these Jewish facilities for the intermarried, those with no religion, and the converts. At the same time, it proves their readiness to settle in an environment where there are few Jews. In addition, in the age of the automobile, not having Jewish friends is as much a matter of social interests as it is of residential ecology.

Withdrawal from religious social interaction, especially around the synagogue, should certainly follow the sequence of assimilatory statuses. About 55 percent of the members of the sample never attend synagogue or do so only a few times a year. This includes 33 percent of the steadfast Jews. A third of those in the baseline category are no longer treating the synagogue as a site for expressing their Jewishness. At the same time, 73 percent of those who donate exclusively to non-Jewish causes, 66 percent of the intermarried, 99 percent of those with no faith, and 88 percent of the converts tend not to go to synagogue. The 12 percent—or five converts—who attend synagogue may do so with their Jewish spouses, friends, or Jewish parents.

Disengagement from the synagogue, part of the reorganization of social relations, is not, by itself, evidence of conversion. It could simply express alienation from the organized religious community. Unlike the traditional synagogues, American synagogues have become centers for activity which is not specifically culturally Jewish—lectures on foreign affairs, blood drive collection centers, and New Year's balls. For those who do not enter the synagogue, it serves none of these functions. For converts, the synagogue is replaced by the church, probably for communal as well as for specifically religious activities. The NJPS allows a comparative measure of synagogue (Q92) and church attendance (Q93). Respondents were classified on the basis of these two items into people who attend synagogue only, those who attend neither, and those who attend church as well as synagogue.

That a good number (21 percent) of the steadfast Jews go to church at all suggests open social and religious relations with their Christian neighbors. It might also suggest an openness in maintaining relations with the other structural assimilation types. A high proportion of those with a gentile spouse neglect both institutions. True to form, those affirming no religion are the most likely to stay away from both synagogues and churches. It does, in fact, seem surprising that a third of them do enter one or another of these institutions. Again, they are not alone in the world and are probably drawn by family and friends to various rites of passage. That 60 percent of the converts attend church is not surprising. That 26 percent of them may still enter a synagogue on occasion may, again, suggest a continuing

TABLE 9.4
Synagogue and/or Church Attendance Among Assimilatory Types
(in percents)

	Jew/Jew	Jew/JewGS	Jew/JewEC	Jew/None	Jew/Chrs
Syn. Only	40	33	28	11	4
Neither	38	48	51	67	36
Both	20	11	15	8	22
Chr. Only	1	7	6	14	38
	(214)	(27)	(118)	(101)	(45)

relationship with Jews who have not converted. In Eastern Europe of the nineteenth century, the Jewish convert to Christianity was clearly outside the pale. However, in periods of mass assimilation and apostasy, relations between Jews and the New Christians have been fluid. Marranos mixed with traditional Jews in the Spanish diaspora and converts were found in the salons of nineteenth century German-Jewish society. The return of this very fluidity is a sign of our times.

Religio-Cultural Assimilation

At the collective level, structural assimilation precedes cultural assimilation. Individual cultural assimilation is an adaptation to collective structural assimilation; the individual adapts his or her position to that of the new group. It may be "anticipatory socialization" preceding in time the actual shift in commitment. We turn to measures of Jewish cultural attachment. The sequence of assimilatory statuses is associated with a decline in commitment to Jewish ritual and culture.

Jewish religious-cultural practices, on which the survey collected data, are divided into three types established from an intuitive sense of the social meaning of the practices and validated empirically by a factor analysis. The items that entered the analysis referred to common religious practices such as attending a Seder, observing the Sabbath, and eating kosher food, among others. The items form three Guttman scales, each representing a single dimension of meaning.

The first scale reflects the Holiness tradition, the attitude of Judaism to the sanctification of nature and time. The scale is built of three items. The first and second refer to dietary laws, the use of kosher meat and separating milk and meat utensils. These are indicators of a religious attitude toward the world of living organisms and of some intrinsic order in this world. The third item refers to carrying money on the Sabbath, essentially a time-bound withdrawal from the world of secular commerce.

Fifty-nine percent of the respondents do none of these.[10] About a quarter of them buy kosher meat, while 11 percent follow through with a traditionally kosher home; six percent attend to the holiness of the Sabbath and observe the first two items. The Holiness tradition has been abandoned by most of the community, and to a greater extent as we move through the assimilatory statuses.

Those who observe two or three of these laws—17 percent of the sample—may be thought of as the relatively more committed Jews. With this level of commitment we have 23 percent of the steadfast Jews, five percent of the Jews who donate solely to non-Jewish causes, seven percent of the intermarried, none of those with no religion, and eight percent of those identifying as Christians. Clearly, only the steadfast Jews, and a minority of them, are committed to this core position. Had more commonly observed practices been used to establish the scales, such as avoidance of pork or having a special Sabbath meal, the distributions might have been less blunted at the lower end, though the relative order of the respondents on the scale would remain the same. Any needs this population may have for defining their relation to organic nature, food, and to sacred time are increasingly met with practices drawn from the wider culture.

The second scale, home observances, is composed of four items: attending a Seder (the most frequent practice), lighting Hanukkah candles, fasting on Yom Kippur, and lighting Sabbath candles (the least frequent practice). Thirty-three percent of those questioned do none of the home observances; 32 percent do one, two, or three of them; and 36 percent do all four.[11] The relatively home observant can be defined as those who report three or four observances, 51 percent of the sample. This category includes 69 percent of the steadfast Jews, 28 percent of the Jews who donate solely to non-Jewish causes, 38 percent of the intermarried, two percent of those with no religion, and five percent of those who have become Christians. The decline in home observance parallels the sequence of assimilatory statuses. The precipitous decline between the steadfast Jews and Jews who donate solely to non-Jewish causes suggests that the break from communal attachment is paralleled by alienation from household Jewish practices. Again, there is a similarity between the people who have no religion and the converts.

The third scale consists of four items more directly measuring communally-oriented or public Jewish expressions. The items refer to reading Jewish literature, most often the Jewish communal newspaper, and observing Purim, generally going to a festive reading of the Megillah. The third item refers to observance of Israeli Independence Day (also a public ceremony, perhaps accompanied by a parade), and the last refers to adult Jewish education. An overwhelming 74 percent do not participate in any of these public Jewish expressions. Those who participate in one or more of them include 37 percent of the steadfast Jews, 11 percent of Jews who donate solely to non-Jewish causes, 28 percent of the intermarried, five percent of those without a faith, and three percent of those who have converted. The break with Jewishness comes when Jews begin donating to non-Jewish causes only; their public Jewish expression drops from 37 to 11 percent and points to a change in their communal identification.

The decline in public expression of Judaism is tied to the acceptance of public expression of Christianity. Respondents were asked whether anyone in their household never, sometimes, usually, or always displays a Christmas tree on the holiday. Sixty-eight percent of the sample report never displaying a tree while 21 percent usually or always do. Ten percent of the steadfast Jews usually have a Christmas tree. Some of them may have had Christian spouses by a second or later marriage or simply accept a communal custom rationalized as nonreligious. In addition, 36 percent of Jews who donate solely to non-Jewish causes, 38 percent of the intermarried, 43 percent of those with no religion, and 64 percent of the converts usually or always have a Christmas tree. That nearly half of those with no religion have a tree suggests the influence of Christianity in these non-religious households. Fourteen percent of the Christian converts never have a Christmas tree. Some may be without regular homes and some may avoid displaying a tree out of deference to Jewish relatives. We do not know what proportion of the general Christian population never displays a Christmas tree, but it may not be far from the 14 percent of Christian converts.

A Matter of Morale?

A fertility rate below that of other Americans has characterized the Jewish population. Low fertility is associated with a variety of factors such as late marriage, women in the labor force, desire to provide better for fewer children, and low morale. Respondents to the NJPS were asked to state the number of children they anticipated having. On the whole, 27 percent anticipated three or more children. Such is the case for 28 percent of the steadfast Jews, 19 percent of Jews who donate exclusively to non-Jewish causes, 16 percent of the intermarried, 27 percent of those with no religion, and 49 percent of the converts. That actual fertility, and, presumably, expected fertility, is lower in intermarried households is well-known. Its comparably lower levels among Jews who donate solely to non-Jewish causes suggests a depressive effect of isolation from the community. The relatively higher fertility among converts is impressive. Since converts do not differ occupationally in income and in marital status from the others, we may be witnessing a morale effect. Having arrived in a new social system, regulated by authority they now accept as legitimate, a greater feeling of social stability may contribute to a more positive outlook on the future. Historically, voluntary acceptance of a new faith has been associated with certitude and enthusiasm. Further, simple conformity to the child-bearing norms of the wider, rather than the Jewish, society may account for some of the increase in expected fertility.

Summarizing the Findings

The idea of a sequence of assimilatory statuses that are social positions in society, and sustain a certain social order, seems to be a viable one. This study specifies some correlates of apostatizing in the biography of the individual. By this classification, 5.5 percent of those born or raised as Jews have apostatized during their lifetimes (defined as from birth to the average age of a respondent). This underestimates the whole picture of apostasy since it does not deal with intergenerational conversions nor with the children (700,000 according to the overall NJPS report) who are being raised in a religion other than Judaism.

   Not having information on the age at conversion, it is difficult to specify factors particularly relevant to one rather than another stage. Further, since this is a secondary analysis, many of the variables that a student of apostasy might want to measure do not appear in the data set. Be that as it may, however, we can identify factors which establish a predisposition for apostasy. These include the socialization factors, the matter of permeable boundaries, and the associated cultural expressions. These are associated with being in the assimilatory statuses defined by economic emigration, having a gentile spouse, and having no current religion as well as with apostasy. The lack of differences between those with no religion and the converts in 10 of the 15 measures suggests that having no religion in an overwhelmingly Christian environment is tantamount to tacit participation in Christian institutions, excepting for the specifically religious institution. That those with no religion are less likely than the apostates to display a Christmas tree, are more liberal, and less likely to seek a large family than do the converts shows where some of the differences between the two statuses lie.

   While those who have no religion are more likely to display a Christmas tree than other born-Jews, a segment of them still resists this open statement. Their children are more likely to become Christians than the children of other Jews and they will, doubtless, match the level of the converts in displaying the tree. The liberalism of those with no religion indicates their status within the anti-establishment sector of the host society, the gateway through which they enter. Following their full entry, they become more supportive of traditional ways. That they have low fertility reflects the instability of their transient status. While apostasy may take place intergenerationally, some proportion of born-Jews and their children develop stronger Jewish ties and, as the larger study shows, a small number of Jews by choice, 185,000 according to study estimates, joins the community. The rate of flow in and out of Judaism remains to be determined but it is clear that the preponderant flow is outward.

The following table summarizes the findings presented in this study.

A Policy to Reaffirm Jewish Social Authority

Though these initial analyses are sketchy, the results are consistent with the underlying hypothesis of a crisis in the legitimacy of Jewish social

TABLE 9.5[12]
Summary Description of Assimilatory Types
(in percents)

	Jew/Jew	Jew/JEC	Jew/JGS	Jew/None	Jew/Chr
Predisposing Factors					
Raised Jew	99	96	97	75	65
Jew Educ.	64	54	51	38	40
Importance	63	28	67	3	21
Liberal	42	56	40	70	29
Social Structure Boundary Factors					
Intermarry	24	45	36	48	46
NJOrganiz's	22	47	40	59	58
NJCharities	0	100	0	52	51
NJFriends	16	35	50	51	63
No Synagogue	33	73	66	99	88
Church Only	1	7	6	14	38
Cultural Outcomes					
Holiness Obs	23	5	7	0	8
Home Observ	69	28	39	2	5
Public Obs	37	11	28	5	3
Xmas Tree	11	34	43	40	64
3+ Children	28	19	16	27	49

authority. In the light of this, we may consider Jewish communal policies that could confront the trend. A social policy involves actions inserted into an ongoing social system in such a way as to increase the probability of that system changing in some desired direction.

The analysis deals with correlates of assimilatory statuses and, ultimately, with apostasy. The apostasy status is a function of a system of factors: group identifications, socialization practices, political attitudes, intermarriage, social organizational memberships, religious behavior, and fertility. These tend not to be available as levers of change. For the Christian evangelist who would increase the rate of Jewish conversion to Christianity, or the Jewish preservationist who would seek to reduce that rate, knowing that being raised Jewish or having a Jewish education extends understanding but does not point directly to policies. The character of socialization depends on a prior commitment to the group. Socialization activities serve to buttress the already present commitment with substance.

These correlates need to be viewed in a context of a broader theory of group viability. Viability turns on the issue of the firmness and permeability of group boundaries. A group dissolves, definitionally and practically, when the boundaries between its institutions and those of another society disappear. On the individual level, we observe the person crossing a boundary from one to the other group, shifting allegiance from one way of life to another. When an institution does not enjoy legitimate authority in the eyes of those oriented to the institution or its leadership is not considered authoritative, it fails to perform its ordering function for the behavior of its members. The members then seek social order through a comparable institution associated with another group. Essentially, we have a dissolution of the institutional and social boundaries of the no longer authoritative group. Disappearance of a boundary is commonly given as the definition of the death of a group, paralleling the definition of the death of an individual as the dissolution of the boundary between the physical person and the environment. Group survival is a matter of controlling the structural assimilation of that group with some broader social system.

Conceivably, one might have a policy promoting such full integration, including religious integration of Jewry to its host society. History has tended to do that for American Jewry to a rather large extent. A "do nothing" option (that is, nothing different from what is currently occurring) may well eventuate in producing Jews as members of a denomination of the American civil religion, such as that to which Rabbi Samuel Holdheim, the nineteenth century Reform leader, might have aspired. A small community of highly religio-national Jews might exist as well. Alongside these two communities, which may well not recognize one another, we would have a large number of Christians who count Jews among their ancestors. The numbers or proportions of individuals in each of these categories is open to debate.

Consider, though, that a policy might be affirmed for American Jewry with the aim of enhancing Jewry as a religious civilization, a nation. It could be pursued within the framework of any of the current major Jewish denominations. Each of the denominations would advocate its own vision of substantive norms, the beliefs and behaviors that define a Jewish community. Whatever the substance of the norms, legitimacy is characterized by a rather clear and effective sanction system in support of the norms and clear and effective sanctions for behavior deemed to deviate from these norms. Such a policy would also entail meaningful and enforced criteria for membership—an assertion of who is and who is not a Jew. It becomes necessary to reassert the legitimate authority of the Jewish community in its commitment to these norms.

One way of approaching such legitimacy is through a reassertion of rabbinic authority, especially in the area of personal status. Whether the authority is Orthodox halakhic, Conservative, or Reform, the notion of individual voluntarism in conforming to the group norms, particularly its legal norms, is incompatible with the survival of the system. Voluntarism is a basis of belonging, but some code must govern the behavior of those who choose to belong. In a sense, this involves drawing the wagons around in a circle and, for example, offering neither solace nor sanction to non-conversionary intermarriages invalid under the code. Another possible element might relate to national existence. It could revolve around the centrality of Israel as a serious element in the Jewish national renaissance, supporting the ideal of *aliyah*. Economic and political structural assimilation would proceed, but the assimilation of kinship systems would be resisted. One could go on, but such would be the spirit of the adaptation.

An alternative policy could promote the role of Jews as a religious denomination within American civil religion, taking on some of the general liberal Protestant forms but striving to give them a distinctly Jewish cast. Jews then become very much an American religio-ethnic group. The personal status law of the civil society would be regnant, and religious intermarriage acceptable. The system would still need a legitimate authority and, moreover, the content of the norms supported by that authority might be quite different from those associated with Jewish nationhood. No social group persists without an authoritative social order. The offering of a social philosophy with belief and behavioral options open to choice characterizes an intellectual more than a religious movement.

Notes

1. A more extended historical and theoretical sketch of this argument may be found in the author's "Assimilation as Social Death" in Mor, Menachem, ed., *Jewish Assimilation, Acculturation and Accommodation*, University Press of America, 1992, pp. 262–303.

2. The base figure includes 4,395,000 individuals who claim Judaism as their religion. Kosmin, Barry A.; Goldstein, Sidney; Waksberg, Joseph; Lerer, Nava; Keysar, Ariella; and Scheckner, Jeffrey. *Highlights of the CJF National Jewish Population Survey*, New York, Council of Jewish Federations, 1991.

3. These proportions are based on the entire sample of 2,441 cases. About a quarter of the cases lack data either on religion at birth or on current religion. Allowing for the exclusion of 100 cases under 22 as well as for missing data on the correlated variables, the number of cases in subsequent tables will be lower. Also, as mentioned in the text, converts to Judaism are not included here.

4. A technical note—the initial presentation will simply describe the five types in terms of their correlates. Though the percentaging will be by the columns represented by the types, these types are not, in the way they are presented, to be considered independent causal variables. These are not analytic tables. We are partitioning the population into five categories and comparing the distributions of characteristics in each of these types. Nevertheless, in order to have a "rule of thumb" for judging the descriptive differences, Chi-square tests of significance of differences for the tables taken as a whole are used but not presented here. The differences between the distributions observed and those that might be expected by chance are, in all of the cross-tabulations offered, statistically significant at the .05 level or better.

5. This issue is discussed in the author's "Ethnicity as Ideology," a paper delivered at the meetings of the American Sociological Association in Cincinnati, August 26, 1991.

6. Some gender differences appear in the correlates of apostasy and the types of structural assimilation. They will be presented in a later study.

7. A Guttman scale is a mathematical method for assessing the common underlying theme of a series of measures. Such a scale is more valid and more reliable than any of the component measures taken alone.

8. The difference between the two percentages is statistically significant by the Chi-Square test, $P<.05$.

9. Refer to endnote 1.

10. They score zero in commitment to the Holiness dimension as here defined. The achievement of a Guttman scale implies that the selected items are a sample of a universe of items that might have been selected to measure the same underlying dimension. Thus, the resulting distribution is not simply reflective of the three indicator items alone. By implication, those who score zero in the scale also do not engage in other observances not asked about but which are associated with the Holiness tradition. These might include observance of the menstrual taboo, male avoidance of shaving, or avoiding clothing made of linen and wool mixtures.

11. Following upon the parenthetical remark on Guttman scaling in footnote 9, the meaning of these practices taken one at a time is indeterminate. The respondent who fasts on Yom Kippur may have a different type of Seder from that of the one who attends a Seder and does nothing more. As a set, they are indicators of positions on an underlying conceptual dimension reflecting religious expression in the household.

12. The full definitions of terms and categories are found in the text. Following are brief definitions:

ASSIMILATORY TYPES:

Jew/Jew: Born and/or raised Jewish and currently Jewish and, if married, has a Jewish spouse.

Jew/JEC: As above but contributes exclusively to non-Jewish charities.

Jew/JGS: Same as Jew/Jew but is married and has a gentile spouse.

Jew/None: Born and/or raised Jewish but now identifies with no religion.

Jew/Christian: Born and/or raised Jewish or born Christian and raised Jewish and now identifies as a Christian.

DESCRIPTIVE VARIABLES:

Raised Jew: Whatever the religion at birth, the individual was raised as a Jew.

Jewish Education: Has some Jewish education, either from formal schooling or from reading Jewish periodicals.

Importance: Considers Judaism very important in his or her life.

Liberal: Identifies as relatively liberal, rather than conservative.

Intermarry: Respondent would be supportive or strongly supportive of child's marriage to a non-Jew.

NJOrganiz's: Respondent belongs to non-Jewish community organizations but not to any Jewish organizations.

NJCharities: Respondent gives to non-Jewish charities but does not give to Jewish charities.

NJFriends: Respondent counts no Jews among her or his close friends and does not live in a Jewish neighborhood.

No Synagog: Respondent rarely or never attends synagogue.

Some Church: Respondent sometimes attends church as well as synagogue.

Holiness observance: Respondent observes some of abstinence of the Holiness Scale.

Home Observ: Respondent observes some of the home celebrations of the Religious Celebration scale.

Public Obs: Respondent observes one or more public acts such as Purim, Israel Independence Day, attending a Jewish school, or reading Jewish literature.

Xmas Tree: Respondent usually or always has a Christmas tree in his or her home.

3+ Children: Respondent anticipates having a completed family with three or more children.

PART THREE

Political and Economic Issues

10

The Economic Status of American Jews

Barry R. Chiswick

Introduction

There are growing concerns that the favorable economic status of American Jews in the post-war period is eroding; that assimilated American Jews, third- and fourth-generation descendants of immigrants who arrived in the United States between 1880 and 1924 may not be as hard working, motivated, entrepreneurial, or successful as their immigrant ancestors.[1] Expressed differently, Jews may be behaving more like non-Jews in educational attainment and in the labor market. Alternatively, non-Jews may be behaving more like Jews in acquiring high levels of schooling and professional skills, thereby also narrowing the differences.

The economic status of American Jews in the twentieth century is important for understanding the historical experiences of the Jewish community, as well as for a deeper understanding of the mosaic of racial, religious, and ethnic groups that comprise the American population. Yet this topic reflects some more immediate concerns within the Jewish community. The level and distribution of skills, labor supply, and earnings or income reflect the extent of economic distress among Jews who require assistance, whether in the form of job training, supplemental income support, or subsidies from Jewish communal institutions, such as synagogues, community centers, and day schools. The central role that these institutions play in preserving and passing down Jewish identity and values should spur action to ease the cost of participation in these institutions by middle and lower income Jews.

The community's well-being depends on the success of fund-raising efforts to support its institutions, aid needy Jews in America and in other diaspora countries, provide assistance to Israel, and more recently, to facilitate resettlement in Israel and elsewhere of Jews who have left the former USSR, other Eastern Bloc countries, and Ethiopia. The community's well-being also depends on its political influence, a matter of grave concern to all minority groups. Political influence is determined not only by the extent to which members of the group vote but also by their ability to marshal economic resources in support of their perceived interests.

Long-term changes in Jewish identity can influence the economic position of American Jews. Those who abandon Judaism (the "exits") may differ from non-Jews who become Jewish (the "entries") if, for example, the exits are more skilled and have higher incomes than those who remain Jewish and if the latter are more successful than the entries into Judaism.

Research on the skills and economic status of American Jews is more difficult to conduct than comparable research on blacks, Hispanics, or Asian-Americans. The major sources of data for racial and ethnic groups and the population as a whole are from surveys conducted by the U.S. Bureau of the Census. While their questionnaires routinely ask about race and ethnicity, there are no questions on religion. As a matter of policy, the Bureau masks any ethnic ancestry response that might explicitly reveal religious identification or heritage.[2] Furthermore, private or other governmental surveys that include questions on religion generally have too few observations on Jews for reliable statistical analyses because of their relatively small proportion, about two percent of the population. Thus, studies of the economic status of American Jews must rely on those rare opportunities in which they are identified in the data and there are a sufficiently large number of Jews in the sample and on indirect procedures for identifying Jews in general data.

The 1990 National Jewish Population Survey (NJPS) provides an excellent opportunity for exploring the economic status of American Jews. By comparing the data on Jews in the NJPS with data on the general population, Jewish/non-Jewish differences can be discerned for 1990.

To analyze long-term trends, these data can be compared with differences between Jews and non-Jews computed for earlier time periods.[3] The NJPS provides for the first time sufficient data to analyze in a systematic manner the characteristics of those who remain Jewish and the "exits" and "entries" to Jewish religious self-identification.

The 1990 NJPS contains important information for the study of the economic status of American Jews. This includes data on school attainment, occupational status, and labor market participation.[4] It also gives information on household income but unfortunately does not ask a question crucial for many analytical purposes—the weekly or annual earnings of the respondent.

The second section of this study presents an analysis of Jewish/non-Jewish differences in economic status for five time periods over the past half-century, with the 1990 NJPS providing the most recent data.

Analysis Over Time

Using four different data sets, it is possible to compare differences in the skills and economic status of Jews and non-Jews during five time periods since World War II: the early post-war period, 1957, 1970, around 1980, and 1990. Table 10.1 summarizes the characteristics of the data sources. Although there are some variations in survey methodology, sample sizes, and definitions across the data sources, which necessitate cautious interpretations of small changes, the data are valid for interpretations of larger and continuous developments over the half century. Table 10.2 presents the data available on education, occupation, self-employment status, labor supply, and earnings for Jews and non-Jews in the five time periods.

Educational Attainment

Among adult Jewish men, the proportion of college graduates increased from 24 percent in the early post-war period to 71 percent in 1990, while the proportion among non-Jews increased from 11 to 25 percent. The difference in college graduates increased from a 13 to a 46 percentage point differential by 1990. Similar findings emerge in an examination of the average (mean) schooling of adult men.

Jewish and non-Jewish women experienced increases in the proportion of college graduates and mean schooling over the post-war period. Yet Jewish women achieved higher levels of schooling than non-Jewish women, and the differences only increased. For example, consider the proportion of women college graduates. In the early post-war period 13 percent of the Jewish women and seven percent of non-Jewish women were college graduates. By 1990 the proportions were 57 percent and 19 percent, respectively. The difference in percentage points increased monotonically over the period.

Thus, while the level of education has overall increased for both Jews and non-Jews, Jews have higher educational attainments, and the differential has increased over time, whether measured by percent college graduates or mean schooling, and irrespective of gender.

Yet, among women, both Jews and non-Jews have a lower educational

TABLE 10.1

*Summary of Characteristics of Data Used for
Time Series Analysis, Adult Jews and White Non-Jews*

TIME PERIOD	DATA SET	IDENTIFICATION OF JEWS	COMMENTS
Early Post WWII	Parents of Respondents in the General Social Surveys (1972–87)	Religion of Respondent at age 16.	Characteristics of parents when respondent was age 16.
1957	Current Population Survey, March 1957	Current Religion.	Only a limited set of cross-tabulations were released by the Census Bureau. Some data include non-whites.
1970	1970 Census of Population, Second-Generation Americans, One-in-a-hundred public use sample.	"Mother tongue" (language other than or in addition to English spoken in the home when the person was a child) Yiddish, Hebrew, or Ladino.	Underestimates number of Jews and may bias downward Jewish/non-Jewish differences.
Around 1980	Respondents in the General Social Surveys (1972–87)	Respondent's Religion at age 16.	Samples taken over 15 years centered on 1980.
1990	For Jews, 1990 NJPS. For non-Jews, data from the Current Population Survey, for 1989.	Religion at birth.	Published data from CPS for the population used for non-Jews. Some data include non-whites.

Note: For further detail on the sources and definitions of the data used for the time periods, see Barry R. Chiswick, "Tables for Time Series on Jewish and Non-Jewish Differences in Skills and Economic Status," Department of Economics, University of Illinois at Chicago, xerox, August 1991, and the references therein.

level than men. The gender gap in educational attainment in absolute terms is greater for Jews than for others. For example, in 1990 Jewish men had a 14 percentage point advantage over women in the proportion of college graduates, while non-Jewish men had only a six percentage point advantage (Table 10.2). Similar patterns appear for the mean level of educational attainment. According to the 1980 data, Jewish men had a 1.3 year schooling advantage over Jewish women while non-Jewish men had only a 0.5 year advantage. In general, there appear to be smaller differences in the educational attainment of women across racial and ethnic groups than of men. The gender difference in schooling tends to be larger the greater the

TABLE 10.2
Characteristics Over Time of Adult Jews and White Non-Jews[a]

ITEM	EARLY POST WWII	1957	1970	AROUND 1980	1990
A. *Education: Men*					
Percent College Grad:					
Jews	24	29	36	65	71
Non-Jews	11	10	14	25	25
Difference	13	19	22	40	46
Mean Schooling					
Jews	11.6	NA	13.7	15.7	16.5
Non-Jews	9.7	NA	11.5	12.8	NA
Difference	1.9	—	2.2	2.9	—
B. *Education: Women*					
Percent College Grad:					
Jews	13	16	16	40	57
Non-Jews	7	9	7	16	19
Difference	6	7	7	24	38
Mean Schooling					
Jews	11.4	NA	12.5	14.4	15.4
Non-Jews	10.2	NA	11.1	12.3	NA
Difference	1.2	—	1.4	2.1	—
C. *Occupation: Men* (Percent)					
Professional and Technical					
Jews	14	20	27	43	46
Non-Jews	9	10	15	18	15
Difference	5	10	12	25	31
Managers (Non-farm)					
Jews	45	35	27	26	16
Non-Jews	15	13	13	17	12
Difference	30	22	14	9	4
"Blue Collar"[b]					
Jews	24	20	16	6	9
Non-Jews	49	51	47	45	40
Difference	−25	−31	−31	−39	−31
D. *Self-Employed Males* (Percent)					
Jews	55.6	31.8	31.9	35.1	31.0
Non-Jews	36.2	NA	14.1	16.3	NA
Differences	19.4	—	17.8	18.8	—
E. *Labor Force Participation: Women* (percent)					
Age 25–34					
Jews	NA	26	40	66	76
Non-Jews	NA	35	42	61	74
Difference	—	−9	−2	+5	+2

(continued)

TABLE 10.2 (continued)
Characteristics Over Time of Adult Jews and White Non-Jews[a]

ITEM	EARLY POST WWII	1957	1970	AROUND 1980	1990
Age 35–44					
Jews	NA	34	49	69	75
Non-Jews	NA	43	47	64	76
Difference	—	−9	+2	+5	−1
F. Earnings: Males (Annual $, Means, Medians for 1957)					
Jews	NA	4,900	16,176	27,322	NA
Non-Jews	NA	3,608	10,431	19,750	NA
Ratio Jews to Non-Jews:					
(a) Simple	—	1.36	1.55	1.38	—
(b) Other Variables held constant	—	1.07	1.16	1.15	—

Note: Because of differences in definitions and survey methodologies small differences need to be interpreted with caution.

[a] Data on non-Jews are limited to whites, except for certain data for 1957 and 1990.

[b] "Blue Collar" includes craft, operative, and transport workers and laborers. Farmers, and where possible farm laborers, are not included.

NA: Not available in source.

Source: Barry R. Chiswick, "Tables for Time Series on Jewish and Non-Jewish Differences in Skills and Economic Status," Department of Economics, University of Illinois at Chicago, xerox, August 1991.

education accomplishment of the group. There is evidence in the data that male educational attainment has increased over time more rapidly than that of females for both Jews and non-Jews (Table 10.2).

Occupational Status

Partially reflecting their educational attainment, American Jews are highly concentrated in professional occupations (Table 10.2). In the early post-war period, 14 percent of Jewish and nine percent of the non-Jewish men were in professional occupations ("professional, technical and kindred"). Occupational attainment for both groups increased over time but for Jews the increase was much larger than for non-Jews. By 1990, the different participation rates in professional occupations increased sharply—to include nearly half of American Jews (46 percent) as compared to only one in seven non-Jews (15 percent).

On the other hand, Jewish participation in non-farm managerial jobs decreased sharply from nearly half of the men (45 percent) in the early post-war period, to 26 percent in 1980 and further to 16 percent in 1990. Among non-Jews the proportion of men in managerial positions showed little change over the same period. From being three times more likely to hold managerial jobs in the early post-war period, there is now little difference in the proportion of Jews and non-Jews in those positions.

Another area of dramatic decline in Jewish participation is the blue collar occupations. Male Jewish employment in craft, operative, transportation, and laborer jobs decreased from 24 percent in the early post-war period to nine percent in 1990. In comparison, the data show less change for non-Jews—from 49 percent to 40 percent—in the same time periods (with an additional 16 percent and four percent, respectively, for non-Jewish farm managers and farmers).

Occupational prestige scores can be computed for some of the time periods, most effectively for the early post-war period and the period around 1980. The adult male occupational prestige score increased from 46.6 to 53.2 for Jews and from 40.5 to 41.9 for non-Jews. Thus, Jews had a higher occupational attainment at the start of the period under study. Although both groups experienced improvements over the post-war period, these were greater among the Jews, and resulted in a widening of the occupation differences.

Self-Employment Status

The decline of Jews in non-farm, managerial occupations affected the proportion of Jews reporting they are self-employed. In the early post-war period more than half (56 percent) reported they were self-employed but only one-third (31 percent) did so in 1990 (Table 10.2). In part, the large proportion still reporting themselves as self-employed reflects the predominance of self-employed professional activities among Jews. Self-employment also declined among non-Jews, but this was primarily a result of a decline in the agricultural sector. Agriculture remains an important source for self-employment among non-Jews but it has never been a significant sector for American Jews.

Labor Force Participation

Labor force participation rates are an index of the supply of labor to the marketplace. This measure is particularly interesting when studying women because of the high incidence of intermittent participation and total absence from the labor force. Among Jewish women age 25 to 34, the prime child bearing years, the participation rate increased from 26 percent in 1957 to 76 percent in 1990 (Table 10.2). It far exceeded the increase for non-Jewish women, which rose from 35 to 74 percent. Jewish women between the ages 35 and 44 increased their participation rate by nine percentage points from 1957 to 1990, and by 1990 they did not differ from non-Jewish women of the same age—their participation was only one percentage point lower.[5]

The NJPS data also indicate that married Jewish women (husband present) are less likely to work than other married women when they have young children: when children are under age six the labor participation rate is 49 percent for Jewish and 58 percent for non-Jewish women. When children are between the ages of six and 17, Jewish women have only a slightly higher participation rate—76 as compared to 73 percent for non-Jewish women—in spite of their much higher level of schooling and fewer children, both of which would imply a greater labor supply.

More detailed statistical analyses using 1970 Census data and holding other variables constant indicate that Jewish women with children under age 18 living at home were less likely to work, especially if the children were under age six (Chiswick, 1988). Furthermore, employed Jewish women with school-age children were more likely to work part-time or part-year. The study found a higher labor-force participation rate for Jewish women only when no children under age 18 were living at home. Additional years of schooling were found to have a larger positive effect on working among Jewish, rather than among non-Jewish, women. Thus, the Jewish female labor supply was found to be more responsive to the effects of incentives and disincentives for working.

The relative long-term growth of the Jewish female labor supply may therefore be due to a combination of factors, including an increased level of education and the sharp decline in the birth rate among Jews.[6]

Income

Data on the income of adult Jewish men were not available for the earliest and latest time periods under study. Although definitions differ somewhat, the three remaining time periods indicate that the annual earnings of Jewish men substantially exceeded that of non-Jews by about 40 to 50 percent (Table 10.2). Statistical control for skill level (occupation in the 1957 data; age, schooling, and weeks worked in the General Social Survey and 1970 Census data) and place of residence substantially narrow the earnings differences. Yet, a statistically significant differential remains—seven percent in 1957 and about 15 percent in the other two time periods. Because of the difference in definitions (medians in 1957, means elsewhere) and statistical control methodology used in the 1957 data, one should not infer that there has been an increase in the Jewish/non-Jewish earnings differential if other measured variables are held constant.

The only data on income in the NJPS are total household income in 1989 which include the labor market earnings of all household members and non-labor sources of income such as interest, dividends, and pensions. The non-reporting rate is particularly high—12 percent—for this variable in the NJPS. Fifty-six percent of the Jewish respondents lived in households with incomes of $50,000 or more in contrast to 26 percent of white households in the general population.[7]

In spite of the high average income in the community, there are Jewish households in economic distress. In the 1990 NJPS, three percent of the households reported annual incomes of less than $12,500, another three percent had over $12,500 but less than $20,000, and nine percent reported between $20,500 and $30,000. The cost of participation in Jewish religious and communal activities—synagogues, community centers, day schools—increases the economic pressure on those in lower- and middle-income brackets.

Skills and Economic Status by Jewish Identification

This section is concerned with whether the economic status of Jews varies according to their religious identification. By asking for a person's religion at birth and their current religion it is possible to divide respondents into those who were born Jewish, were born Jewish but are not now Jewish (exits), were not born Jewish but are Jewish now (entries), and those who reported they were Jewish at the time of the interview.[8]

Table 10.3 includes data on the education level, labor market characteristics, and household income of Jews in each of the four categories.[9] The sample sizes indicate that changes in Jewish status are rare—less than 10 percent exit and a smaller ratio enter Judaism. Moreover, the exits are more concentrated among men, whereas the entries are more frequently women.

There is evidence that among men the exits are somewhat more highly skilled than those born Jewish, with the entry group being the least skilled (Table 10.3). The exits have 16.9 years of schooling, 51 percent are professionals and their mean prestige score is 51, in contrast to 15.7 years of schooling, 32 percent professionals and a prestige score of 45 for the entry group. As a result, those born Jewish have higher values for these characteristics than those Jewish now, but the differences are small.

Note, however, that the entries into Jewish religious identity are slightly

TABLE 10.3
Characteristics of Jews Defined by Religion
By Jewish Status at Birth and in 1990

ITEM	BORN JEWISH	EXITS	ENTRY	NOW JEWISH
A. *Education (Mean Schooling)*				
Men	16.5	16.9	15.7	16.4
Women	15.4	15.2	15.7	15.4
B. *Occupations: Men*				
Professional, Technical and Kindred (percent)	45.8	50.6	32.0	44.3
College and University Teachers (percent)	3.1	7.4	2.2	2.5
"Blue Collar"[a] (percent)	9.4	9.5	13.1	9.4
Occupational Prestige Score	51.4	51.3	45.4	51.3
C. *Labor Force Participation: Women* (percent)				
Age 25–34	76	75	69*	75
Age 35–44	75	68*	75	75
All Ages (Age 18 and over)	53	54	71	55
D. *Household Income*	56.7	61.1	52.2	56.0
(Percent with reported household income of $50,000 or more in 1989)				
E. *Sample Sizes (Education, Age 25–64)*				
Men	1,016	103	39	952
Women	935	77	71	940

Note: Data are weighted by person or household weights. *Labor force participation rate based on 20 or fewer observations.

[a] "Blue Collar" includes craft, operative, and transport workers and laborers.

Source: *1990 National Jewish Population Survey*, North American Jewish Data Bank, New York, 1991.

lower-skilled only in comparison with other Jews. Compared with non-Jews, they have a high level of schooling, a high proportion of professionals, and a high occupational prestige score (Tables 10.2 and 10.3).

Changes in Jewish religious identity are noticeable among college and university teachers: they constitute 3.1 percent of those born Jewish, but as much as 7.4 percent of exits and only 2.2 percent of entries into Jewish religious identity. The extent to which a cause-and-effect relationship exists between occupation and Jewish identity is beyond the scope of this study. Nevertheless, this segment of the adult Jewish population may have the greatest influence on college-age Jewish youth, aside from parents and other immediate relatives.

As indicated in Table 10.3, there is a smaller difference in the educational attainment of women categorized according to their Jewish identity. Women who abandoned their Jewish religious identity and non-Jewish women who entered Judaism have a similar education level to those who were born and remain Jewish. However, women who became Jewish are much more highly educated than other non-Jewish women.

The analysis of the labor force participation of women is hindered by the small sample size when the data are stratified by age. Yet this is important as participation rates vary by age and the exit/entry groups are younger than those who were born and remain Jewish. Little difference appears in the labor force participation rate across the Jewish identity groups when examined within age groups (Table 10.3).[10] And these rates differ only slightly from those of non-Jewish women.

The data in the NJPS on the household income of the respondents reflects the combined effects of the skills of household members, the degree of participation in the labor market, the size of the household, and non-labor sources of income. Household income varied across the Jewish identity categories. Income was $50,000 or more in 61 percent of the households in which the respondent was born Jewish but was not now Jewish by religion, 57 percent among those born Jewish, 56 percent among those now Jewish by religion, and 52 percent among those who were not born Jewish but became Jewish.

Summary and Conclusions

This study has used the 1990 National Jewish Population Survey to examine two aspects of the skills and economic status of contemporary American Jewry.

By combining the NJPS with data on Jews and the non-Jewish general population from other sources, it is possible to create a time series on Jewish and non-Jewish schooling, occupational status, labor supply, and earnings over the course of the post-war period. These data indicate that both male and female adult Jews have higher levels of schooling than adult non-Jews, and that these differences appear to have increased over the past half-century.

Compared with non-Jewish men, Jewish men are far more likely to be in professional occupations, with the disparity increasing over time. By 1990 about half of Jewish men were in professional and technical jobs. The proportion of Jewish men in managerial occupations diminished sharply, from nearly half to one-in-eight, and now differs only slightly from the proportion of non-Jews in these occupations. Jewish blue-collar employment also declined sharply. Jews now constitute a smaller proportion of the blue collar labor force than in the past.

Self-employment among Jewish men remains about double that of non-Jewish men, although it has declined for both groups. There is, however, a fundamental difference in the nature of this self-employment: professional activities are relatively more important among Jews, while among non-Jews farming is much more important.

Among men, Jews earn substantially more than non-Jews, by 40 to 50 percent, but about two-thirds of this differential is explained by their higher level of schooling, place of residence, and other variables, leaving about one-third of the gross differential unexplained. Overall, other things being equal, Jewish men earn about 15 percent more than non-Jewish men.

The labor force participation of Jewish women has increased sharply over the post-war years, from a level below that of non-Jewish women to a level about equal to that of other women. The increasing Jewish/non-Jewish disparity in schooling and low rates of Jewish fertility are partially responsible for this development.

The high skill level of American Jews, together with a high rate of labor market participation among Jewish women, is largely responsible for the very high household income of Jews. Among Jews 56 percent of the households had incomes of $50,000 or more in contrast to 26 percent in the general white population. Yet there are many Jewish households with low incomes—15 percent had less than $30,000 in 1989.

The survey also gives an insight on respondents who left Judaism (born but not presently Jewish by religion) and those who entered Judaism. Among men, those who left have more schooling, a higher occupational status, and higher income than those who were born and remain Jewish. The differences are small, however. Those who became Jewish have more schooling and a higher occupational status than non-Jews but slightly lower levels than those who were born and remain Jewish. Among women, there were only small differences in educational attainment and labor force participation by type of identity, although converts to Judaism have a somewhat higher level of schooling.

Thus, since the exits from and entries into Judaism are relatively few— about 10 percent in each instance—and since their skills do not differ much from those of other Jews, such demographic changes have little impact on the average skill level, labor supply, and income of American Jews.

In conclusion, concerns that the relative levels of achievement of American Jews are eroding appear to be without foundation. Although the rate of improvement in relative skill and economic achievement may not be as great in the second half of the twentieth century as in the first half, there is no evidence of a deterioration in relative status.

Whether these achievements will persist in the twenty-first century remains to be seen. For young adults completing school and entering the labor market, the experiences of their immigrant ancestors are in the distant past. The American Jewish culture has evolved as a consequence of assimilation, Americanization, and intermarriage. Increasingly, it will be a population whose American-born grandparents achieved impressive successes. One cannot rule out a withering of whatever characteristics were responsible for the high level of achievement in the twentieth century. Nor can one rule out the continued persistence of these characteristics across generations.

Notes

1. This is to acknowledge my appreciation of the North American Jewish Data Bank, Center for Jewish Studies, Graduate Center, CUNY for making available the 1990 National Jewish Population Survey and of Xiao-Bo Li for his research assistance. Partial financial support for this project from the Council of Jewish Federations is also appreciated.

2. A response "Polish Jewish" would be coded as "Polish" and a response "Jewish" would be coded as "other."

3. To as great an extent as possible, every effort has been made to maximize the comparability of definitions and concepts in the Jewish/non-Jewish comparison in each time period and across time periods (see Chiswick, 1992 and Chiswick, 1991). Since the non-Jews in the NJPS are not a random sample of non-Jews in the population, their characteristics are not relevant for this analysis. Some of the data labeled as being for non-Jews are for the total population or for the white population, including Jews. Since Jews are only about two percent of the population, this does not introduce a significant statistical bias. Furthermore, to the extent that a statistical bias exists, the Jewish/non-Jewish differences are diminished.

4. An "occupational prestige score" was added by the author to the NJPS data file using the same scores for each occupation as in the General Social Survey (see *General Social Survey*, 1987).

5. Ritterband (1990) also reports a narrowing in the married female labor force participation rate and a disappearance of the differential in recent years. See Ritterband (1990) and Condran and Kramarow (1991), and the references therein, for commentary on the particularly low married Jewish female labor force participation rate at the turn of the century.

6. The growing availability of child-care facilities for pre-school children and after-school programs for school-age children may also play a role. However, while it is not obvious that this has been more important among Jews than non-Jews, it is an area where Jewish communal resources can enhance quality Jewish educa-

tion among children, attract Jewish families into communal institutions, facilitate labor market employment among Jewish women, and enhance Jewish family income.

7. Among the General Social Survey respondents (period around 1980) Jewish mean family income was higher by 52 percent. In the 1957 CPS data Jewish median family income exceeded that of white Protestants (by 34 percent) and Roman Catholics (by 23 percent), but the advantage diminished when the data were limited to urban families (19 percent higher incomes than White Protestants and Roman Catholics). When GSS respondents were asked how their family income at age 16 compared to that of the average American family, 30.8 percent of the Jews and 16.8 percent of the white non-Jews reported it was above average or far above average. Studies of non-labor income may be needed to more effectively evaluate family and household income patterns over time (Chiswick, 1991).

8. This procedure relies solely on self-identified religion. It does not address whether "entries" were formally converted nor does it include among Jews those who identify with another religion, no religion, or refused to answer but who considered themselves Jewish on the ethnic identity question.

9. Caution is required in interpreting some of the results, however, because sample sizes can become small (e.g., female labor force participation by age for those with a change in Jewish identity).

10. Although participation rates are lower among the exits age 35 to 44 and the entry group age 25–34, the sample sizes are very small.

References

Chiswick, Barry R., "The Post-War Economy of American Jews," *Studies in Contemporary Jewry*, Vol 8, (1992), Oxford University Press, pp. 85–101.

———, "Labor Supply and Investment in Child Quality: A Study of Jewish and Non-Jewish Women," *Contemporary Jewry*, (Fall 1988), pp. 35–61.

———, "Tables for Time Series on Jewish and Non-Jewish Differences in Skills and Economic Status," Department of Economics, University of Illinois at Chicago, xerox, August 1991.

Condran, Gretchen A. and Kramarow, Ellen A., "Child Mortality Among Jewish Immigrants to the United States," *Journal of Interdisciplinary History*, Vol. 22, No. 2, (Autumn 1991), pp. 223–254.

General Social Surveys, 1972–1987: Cumulative Codebook, National Opinion Research Center, University of Chicago, 1987.

1990 National Jewish Population Survey, Data Tape and Codebook, North American Jewish Data Bank, CUNY, New York, 1991.

Ritterband, Paul, "Jewish Women in the Labor Force," Report prepared for the American Jewish Committee, mimeo., March 1990.

11

Political Liberalism and Involvement in Jewish Life

Alan M. Fisher

I. Overview

Although everyone seems to acknowledge the tenacity of liberalism among American Jews, no consensus exists about either its cause or what maintains it. This liberal approach to the political world persists long after the conditions which typically foster liberalism—poverty and oppression—have weakened or largely disappeared. The ideological persistence leads many observers to see liberalism as endemic to American Jewish culture. It seems plausible, therefore, that those most deeply immersed in this culture would be the most liberal whereas those least involved should be the most different, that is, most conservative.

Here, we observe a variety of measures of involvement in Jewish life in order to examine the traits of the most and the least liberal Jews and thus, perhaps, provide insight into the dynamics of that liberal culture. The data from the 1990 National Jewish Population Survey allow us to study Jewish life more extensively than has been possible heretofore. The data suggest that for most Jews there is no simple patterned relationship between involvement in Jewish life and political liberalism. For two opposite subgroups, a parallel relationship unfolds. For the Orthodox, closeness to their own community and life-style is related to political conservatism. On the other end, for the secular Jews, attachment to Jewish ritual and institutions is also related to conservatism whereas for the mainstream Conservatives and Reform there is no clear pattern.

II. Background

Public opinion surveys, voting records, and some earlier anecdotal evidence suggest that the overwhelming number of American Jews have been solidly liberal since at least 1912, when the East European immigrants started to cast their ballots in large numbers. Ever since the development of systematic polling in the 1940s, the findings have shown consistently that Jews are among the most liberal and Democratic citizens.[1]

What is the source of Jewish liberalism? For almost half a century, scholars have bandied about three main ideas, depending on how aware they are of the literature and of the Jewish community. The most frequently cited by academic political scientists is Lawrence Fuchs' standard cultural argument.[2] Fuchs claims that the orientation of Jews reflects a traditional body of beliefs and norms that support a liberal approach to the political-social world, specifically, a this-world orientation, intellectualism, and the primacy of charity (*tsedakah*).

Fuchs' ideas are still powerful and not without merit and insight but they are problematic for several reasons. First, there are many Jewish textual sources which support conservative postures on a wide variety of issues: abortion, homosexuality, gender equality, capital punishment, property rights, etc. In addition, the growing conservatism of the Orthodox, for whom traditional culture and Jewish texts are most important, also contradicts Fuchs' theory.[3]

The second argument for Jewish liberalism posits that the current political orientation reflects the realities of modern Jewish history.[4] Economically, until the 20th century, the Jewish masses, especially in Eastern Europe, were mostly very poor; politically, they were disenfranchised and oppressed. Support for the rights of Jews came from the egalitarian left, while the traditionally aristocratic Christian right continued across several centuries to oppose equality for Jews.

Thus, politically, economically, and socially, it was perfectly natural that Jews would be openly accepting of liberalism, a philosophy that protects the rights of the minority against a despotic government; that limits the political influence of religion (Christianity in the West); and that protects the rights of the workers and deploys state resources to maintain the subsistence of those who are economically underprivileged.

A derivative of the historical argument borrows directly from political socialization. The strongest correlate of party identification and level of political participation is parents' political partisanship and interest. We tend to reflect the primary political values of our parents. For the descendants of Eastern European Jews, that tradition has been strongly liberal and Democratic.

Both theories are entirely plausible yet limited because they deal with the world that was. Admittedly, we are all, to some extent, a product of our tribal history. Nevertheless, the world of American Jews at the end of the 20th century is very much different from that of their immigrant grandparents and great grandparents. Anti-Semitism has declined considerably. As a group, Jews are socioeconomically and politically decidedly advantaged. In terms of narrow self-interest, most American Jews are better served by the conservative than the liberal position on taxes, welfare spending, affirmative action, private school vouchers; and increasingly, support for Israel is being voiced by the Christian right.

Two other related though lesser-known theories also attempt to explain liberalism. Arthur Liebman, Seymour Martin Lipset, and Earl Raab have argued that Jews are institutionally tied to liberal organizations and their presence serves to maintain the liberal-Democratic link.[5] Thus, Jewish presence in the leadership of labor unions, liberal universities, and think tanks—especially in the professions of law and economics—and within the Democratic party, helps to give other Jews a sense of belonging there. And their presence influences those organizations to maintain policies which are sympathetic to positions taken by the largely educated Jewish citizenry.

The problem with this theory is that groups like labor unions—even at the management level—contain far fewer Jews today than they used to. Moreover, even where moderate numbers of Jews are involved—such as in contemporary left-wing groups—they are not likely to have strong ethnic or religious ties, especially if they are young. In addition, a very large number of American Jews are intermarried and have only a limited interest in other Jews.

The last theory of liberalism builds upon the unusually high educational level of Jews, particularly their success in the fields of law, communications, and entertainment, and in the more prestigious universities where left-wing politics still flourishes.[6] In its pejorative moniker, this political style has often been labelled radical chic.

No longer are poverty and unemployment the immediate sources of Jewish liberalism. Quite the opposite, it is economic security that enables this highly insulated group to pursue a politically correct radicalism which—except for issues of life-style (often dealing with sex) and affirmative action—is still fundamentally 20th-century American liberalism. The social composition of these radical chic groups, typically found in large coastal cities, particularly New York, Boston, and Los Angeles, is heavily Jewish though without any formal religious or even ethnic identity.

However interesting and historically unique (for Jews) the radical chic theory appears, it is by definition limited. Even given their academic and financial success, the number of Jews who find themselves in this elite environment is likely to be very small. Jewish subscribers to *Tikkun* and the *Nation* are undoubtedly far fewer than those who subscribe to *Commentary* and the *Jewish Press*.

Each of the four theories presented here tries to identify some experience or condition of the Jewish people that would support a liberal bent. For explanations that build on historical oppression of the Jews and the greater acceptance proffered by forces on the left, it should be the case that those most aware of the tradition, that is, Jews involved in some aspect of community life, also ought to be the most liberal.

By extension, people with the strongest sense of Jewish identification also ought to be the most liberal. Especially for people who are older, the explanation of parental inheritance assumes some closeness to the immigrant world in which Jewish identity and memory of oppression were stronger than they are for young, American-born Jews. The latter two theories argue that the presence of Jews in liberal political and other voluntary organizations acts as a pull to other Jews and reinforces the importance of Jewish communal ties.

With the partial exception of the radical chic hypothesis, all the explanations above assume that the more one is drawn into Jewish life, the greater the likelihood of political liberalism. The most obvious ideological linkage is for that theory which argues that liberalism reflects inherent Jewish values; those who are closer to that tradition ought to be more liberal.

It would then seem only logical that the weaker the involvement in the Jewish world, the weaker the commitment to liberalism. In an open society, most minority group members assimilate, that is, they move toward the dominant group in areas of residence, education, organizational membership, cultural and political values, etc. Those most outside the sphere of the Jewish world ought to be the most involved in the dominant white Anglo-Saxon Christian world. Hence, they ought to be the least liberal and the least Democratic.

Theoretical underpinning for this explanation comes from the study of assimilation. We know from research on many ethnic groups that in an open society change occurs in the direction of the dominant group. That is part of what it means to be dominant. As an obvious example, over time, almost all foreign-speaking groups in the United States lose their native tongue.

Minorities take on the values and characteristics of the dominant group as part of the assimilation process. For Jews, that ought to mean moving from a political culture of hard-core liberalism to one which at least conceptually is largely conservative, especially on economics.

One of the few systematic presentations of this idea is found in Steven M. Cohen's seminal book, *American Modernity and Jewish Identity*.[7] Cohen used very elementary measures of Jewish involvement on a geographically limited population. Here, we have the opportunity to expand significantly the number of different measures in order to amend the theory on a sample that is unmatched in any previous survey of Jews.

Before proceeding to test the theory, it is clear that there already exists a difficulty. If Jewish values are fundamentally liberal, then the most zealous guardians of those values ought to be the most liberal. If we assume that the Orthodox are the group most attracted to the tradition, then it would seem logical that they would be the most liberal.

As Charles Liebman suggested 20 years ago, as Cohen demonstrated empirically and as almost all observers know, the Orthodox are one of very few Jewish groups that are politically conservative and, in national elections, give a sizeable proportion of their vote to the Republicans.[8] The easy example of Orthodoxy and right-wing mentality is Meier Kahane. Although Kahane's extremism put him outside the pale, many of his fundamental assumptions are shared by the mainstream yeshiva world.[9] They do not accept the secular Jewish emphasis on universalism; nor have they much sympathy for the secular expression of Jews as primarily—if not solely—an ethnic group; they place great weight on rabbinic law and less stress on the prophetic tradition; and, like their fundamentalist Christian cousins, they actively reject cultural and social norms, particularly alternative sexual relationships, which threaten traditional family values.

Cohen was one of the first researchers to document the relative political conservatism of the Orthodox. He noted an unusual relationship: among the non-Orthodox, those with the weakest links to tradition were the least liberal, whereas those with the strongest links, the Orthodox, were also relatively less liberal.[10] I refer to this phenomenon by the parabolic shape of the liberalism curve which it forms—low among the Orthodox, increasing among the Conservatives-Reconstructionists and Reform, and then decreasing among those with no formal religious ties. This parabola is in contrast to most social science theories, since they usually assume a monotonic relationship in which increasing Jewish involvement would lead to increased liberalism at every point.

In his original work, Cohen looked at a combination of ritual observance and synagogue affiliation. Later studies examine a slightly wider set of measures. Two of them rely on denominational self-identification, not a perfect measure of ritual practice, although it does provide an indication of religious preference.[11] The Jewish experience, however, extends far beyond ritual practice. The NJPS allows us to differentiate Jewish identity, family, religious affiliation, membership and ritual practices, communal involvement and ethnic attitudes, American experience, and orientation to Israel.

III. Previous Research

How has the Jewish immersion (versus assimilation) hypothesis fared in research published after Cohen's book? Unfortunately, our sources are limited by the dearth of survey research that asks questions about Jewish identification and religious practices. The best sources of that information are Cohen's later surveys for the American Jewish Committee, particularly the detailed study done in 1988 that asked a number of political questions. In addition, one question of political self-identification was asked on a 1988 Los Angeles Times Poll that was otherwise almost entirely devoted to Israel. To bring the study up to date, we look at the findings of a 1992 Election Day exit poll (Fisher) distributed to Los Angeles voters.[12]

The findings on the Orthodox being more politically and socially conservative are borne out across a variety of measures in all the studies. The Orthodox consistently vote more Republican than do other Jews across a large number of elections.

On substantive issues, the Orthodox are programmatically comparatively conservative. Differences between them and other Jews are strongest for two kinds of issues. First, the Orthodox are the most ethnocentric on Israel. They tend to take a hawkish position on Israeli defense, they are relatively strong supporters of the right-wing Likud, and they are more anti-Arab, especially against political groups like the PLO.

Domestically, the Orthodox differ most on religious issues like aid to private (religious) schools, prayer in school, abortion, and probably a variety of measures about sexuality. Both the Cohen and Fisher studies show that the Orthodox see themselves as more conservative than do the other Jews, although the magnitude of the differences varies by study and by question.[13]

What about the other end of the continuum, the position of the most secular Jews, those without any denominational sense of belonging? Cohen's original data suggest that their religious assimilation is matched by their assimilation to a more politically conservative orientation.[14]

In fact, across a large number of issues, Cohen's later studies (1984, 1988) found that those Jews who see themselves as "just Jews" are not politically different from the affiliated Jews who are not Orthodox. Even on the question of abortion and government aid to private schools, the non-affiliated Jews were strikingly similar to the affiliated non-Orthodox Jews.

According to Fisher's (1992) data, differences on party affiliation were small and not significant, although on one measure slightly fewer non-affiliated identified as strong Democrats. On ideological self-definition, slightly more of the non-affiliated were in both the strong liberal and strong conservative categories, a pattern which will be found in the NJPS data.

Results from the later (1992) Fisher study differ in some specifics from the other two but, like the 1988 Cohen study, they also challenge the earlier findings that secular Jews are significantly more conservative than affiliated Jews. Rather, the Fisher study finds that the secular differ in direction: they are (slightly) more Democratic, more liberal, and less conservative than are the denominationally more identified Jews. These recent studies consistently challenge the idea that denominational involvement in the (non-Orthodox) Jewish world leads to greater liberalism.

IV. Data, Methods, and Statistical Issues

The data to test the theory that involvement in Jewish life leads to liberalism come from the 1990 National Jewish Population Survey.[15] The sampling for the NJPS is better than for any other large-size Jewish study, since most have been characterized by an overrepresentation of identified, committed, and involved Jews. The NJPS provides a much better cross-section of American Jews than available heretofore.

In contrast to other studies of Jews in the U.S., the NJPS has an extensive array of measures of Jewish identification and involvement, allowing a fine-tuned set of measures of attachment to Jewish life. We can look at certain personal qualities almost never available, e.g., people who have converted in or out of the religion, membership in Jewish associations outside of synagogues, etc. Thus, the theory can be tested and elaborated with greater detail and greater precision than has been possible previously.

The major drawback of the NJPS is the inclusion of only one political question of immediate relevance. However, the one measure we examine—self-revelation of political ideology—provides a surprisingly insightful, comprehensive, and often clear picture of Jewish attitudes and voting behavior.

A second problem is sample size. Although the total NJPS includes a very healthy sample of 2,441 heads of households with at least one Jew—one of the largest Jewish samples publicly available—only 803 respondents were asked the important question of political ideology. In looking at the kinds of Jews who are likely to be liberal, that sample size allows for a good deal of confidence in the results (plus/minus 4 percentage points). For items which have a two- or three-way breakdown like gender, the resultant sub-sample groups, e.g., men and women, have relatively large sizes. But for groups which are only a small proportion of the population, e.g., the low educated, or people under 30, the error margin becomes wider because of the limited number of people. This is especially a problem for the small number of Orthodox interviewed—only 38 people—a category of great importance in this paper.

As Table 11.1B shows, the distribution of the answers on political

TABLE 11.1A

Political Ideology of Jews and Non-Jews (*in percent*)

| | 1988[a] | | 1990[b] | 1992[c] | |
	JEWS	NON-JEWS	JEWS	JEWS	NON-JEWS
Liberal	47	25	49	40	21
Middle of the road	29	31	32	50	49
Conservative	24	44	19	10	31
Total	100	100	100	100	100[d]

[a] 1988 ABC National Exit Poll (Jewish N = 1152)
[b] 1990 NJPS (N = 803)
[c] 1992 Voters Survey Research National Exit Poll (Jewish N = 282)
[d] Error due to rounding

TABLE 11.1B

Political Ideology of Jews 1990[b]

Very Liberal	12
Liberal	37
Middle of the road	32
Conservative	17
Very Conservative	1
Total	100[d]

ideology presents statistical problems. Very few Jews of any kind (one percent) consider themselves to be very conservative, and only a relatively small number (12 percent) say they are very liberal. The overwhelming majority locate themselves in the liberal (37 percent) and middle-of-the-road (32 percent) categories. Unfortunately, the heavy concentration of Jews in two contiguous categories and the lack of Jews at the extremes— especially conservatism—places limits on the standard statistical tools of social science survey research.

In addition, as Cohen had suggested, in a number of cases the relationship between two variables is not a straight line. That is, levels of liberalism first increase with importance of being Jewish but then they start to decrease (see Figure 1). Moreover, for several variables the impact is not politically symmetrical but is seen in only one direction. For example, respondents who strongly agree that anti-Semitism is a serious problem are less likely to call themselves liberal than are other Jews but they do not see themselves as noticeably more conservative.

Unfortunately, in order to make sense out of some of these statistical obstacles, one cannot simply display a standard correlation matrix of how each variable scores with liberalism. Instead, it has been necessary to look at each table individually for the exact dynamic, and then compare across other variables that measure the same general trait. This is cumbersome and difficult to read but it is methodologically prudent. Where appropriate, numbers and tables are introduced. General summary statements follow in order to simplify the detailed results.

Because of a number of methodological caveats, most of the findings need to be tested on larger samples, with more political measures. Nevertheless, certain patterns do appear regularly, they follow some logical order, and are explainable by certain social science theories. Until we obtain some contravening data, the findings here are the best that are available. Where appropriate, specific points have been augmented by data drawn from the previously cited surveys of Jews as well as from the national media exit polls.

V. Findings

Respondents were asked how they considered themselves politically: the five choices ranged from very liberal to very conservative, with an intermediate middle-of-the road position. Since that is our sole political question, it is essential to demonstrate that it correlates with, or predicts, other political attitudes and behavior.

Social scientists have argued about the validity of self-rating and self-definition. Given the generally low level of political sophistication of Americans, it might be thought that simple self-labeling, e.g., conservative or liberal, might not be a very useful measure.

However, as other studies demonstrate, for Jews especially, political self-identification is indeed a most meaningful indicator. It is a very powerful predictor of party affiliation, voting, and political attitudes. Cohen reported strong correlations from his 1981 data.[16] Responses a decade later replicate those findings in spades.

In the 1992 study of Los Angeles Jews, among the very few conservative Jews, 80 percent report a Republican party affiliation compared with exactly none of those who defined themselves as very liberal. The correlation for the California Senate vote between Republican Bruce Herschensohn and Democrat Barbara Boxer is even stronger.

Although correlations are slightly weaker with several political attitudes, they are still consistently very strong, the strongest predictor of particular attitudes. For example, more than twice the percentage of self-defined very liberal Jews as compared with conservative Jews (85:42 percent) support an increase in the tax on families who make more than $100,000.[17] For the Jews, self-rating on ideology is an unusually good indicator of political orientation.

Another major concern about the NJPS is its comparability with other national data generated from the larger American population. In order to compare, we looked at a very large ABC Election Day exit poll in 1988 and the major media Voter Survey Research exit poll in 1992.

First, the proportion of Jews who define themselves as liberal is generally comparable in all three studies: 49 percent of the NJPS as compared with 47 percent of the 1988 sample and 40 percent of the 1992 survey. (See Table 11.1 for a breakdown.) Note also that Jews continue to be much more liberal than other Americans. (For non-Jews in the NJPS, see Table 11.2.)

Second, although the correlates of both gender and age on ideological self-identification differ across the three studies, the NJPS is close to the average. For example, in the NJPS data, women are six percentage points more liberal than the men. The comparable (gender differential) figures for Jews in the 1988 and 1992 elections studies are 12 and four percentage points, respectively. (Most other studies confirm a slightly declining gender gap during this period.) Comparable similarities are found for age differences. In short, although the absolute figures do not match exactly—to be expected of surveys given over a four-year period—the data are not dissimilar, the underlying relationships are closely parallel, and the NJPS data are in between the other two studies. We can use these data with full confidence.

Before looking at the mass of the findings, the various forms of attachment to Jewish life are noted, after which each series of measures is examined. Readers interested in the particular questions are referred to the original survey questionnaire.

1. Jewish Identity

At the base of the structure of involvement in Jewish life stands identity. Not everyone, however, defines a Jew by the same criteria. Rather than trying to impose a definition, the most obvious measures are utilized in this study—identification of parents as Jewish and, equally important (though not *halakhic*), the individual's subjective identification of himself or herself as Jewish, as well as an attitudinal item about the importance of being Jewish. In addition, there are questions about one's non-Jewish (religious) involvement and conversion.

Denominationally, people of Jewish birth might be divided into three groups: those who define themselves as a) not Jewish; b) secular Jews—Jewish but with no religious affiliation; and c) Jewish with some denominational identity. (Differences among the denominations and levels of involvement are measured separately.)

On the most primal measures of Jewish identity, the findings of this study clearly are at odds with the theory of Jewish immersion. According to this hypothesis, the level of liberalism should increase from a to c: Jews who see themselves as completely assimilated, viz., not Jewish, should be less liberal than those who see themselves as Jewish with denominational identification. Based on responses to a number of the questions, the immersion theory is, at best, only partly true for those who are no longer Jewish, but it is clearly not true for those who see themselves as Jews.

Table 11.2 sets out five categories of Jews, from those born Jewish who still consider themselves Jews, to the smallest group, born-Jews who have become and define themselves as Christians. (The minute sample size of seven makes this category virtually unusable although the decidedly higher figure on conservatism makes this suggestive. In general, this table must be read with caution because of the very small sample sizes of several categories.)

In addition, there are three categories of non-Jews who were found in households containing Jews. However, these are a select group of non-Jews, much more liberal than the larger population, as the Fisher (1992) data clearly demonstrate. Thus, the overall differences between American Jews and non-Jews are much greater than those reported in the NJPS (see Table 11.1).

Indeed, the two most conservative groups are born non-Jews who have remained either Protestant or Catholic or some other religion. (Many Americans now define themselves as Christian rather than as Protestant or Catholic so there may be some overlap.) Those who have joined "other" religions are the most conservative among born-Jews. These findings clearly support the theory of Jewish involvement and liberalism: as Jews become more like the larger world religiously, they also begin to assimilate politically. That would lead us to guess that the Jews who have become Christian would be relatively conservative, somewhere between the position of born-Jews who have remained in the fold and Christians who were born into that religion.

Among those who currently define themselves as Jews, however, the theory breaks down in ways we have already seen. Those who were born Jewish but currently have no religious attachment (or who took the positive commitment to "secular") are by far the most liberal. About two-thirds are politically liberal. However, the same liberal pattern is found among secular non-Jews who have no formal religion—people outside of Christian-American conservatism.

Clearly, the most liberal and least conservative of the Jewish groups is that of secular Jews. The same basic findings occur when the religion in which they were raised is examined: Jews raised without formal religion are more liberal than Jews raised within some denomination. Similarly, on

TABLE 11.2

Jewish Identity and Political Ideology (in percent)
Religion Raised/Religion Now Identified with

	JEW/JEW	NON-JEW/JEW	JEW/NO RELIGION	JEW/OTHER	CHRISTIAN/CHRISTIAN	JEW/CHRISTIAN	OTHER/OTHER	NONE/NONE
Very Liberal	9	12	26	18	15	x	8	24
Liberal	37	33	42	20	26	x	20	45
Middle of the road	35	24	24	33	28	x	34	23
Conservative	18	25	8	24	26	x	32	8
Very Conservative	1	6	0	5	4	x	6	0
Total	100	100	100[a]	100	100[a]	x	100	100
(Sample size)	(512)	(49)	(407)	(20)	(75)	(7)	(27)	(26)

[a]Error in rounding

x Sample size (N=7) too small

Eta. = .19   p (chi sq.) < .01

Source: NJPS (1990)

an attitudinal question about the importance of being Jewish, those who said that it was relatively unimportant tended to be more liberal than those saying that it was very important.

It is on this attitudinal measure of Jewish identification that the parabolic pattern appears. Overall, there is a slight negative relation between increased importance of Jewish identity and level of liberalism. However, a closer look at the data reveals that not only is there a significant drop-off in liberalism among the *most involved* but those for whom being Jewish is *not important* are also less liberal (Figure 1). Based on the score of the very liberal and liberal, those who have the weakest Jewish identification are the least liberal, followed in second place by those with the strongest Jewish identification.

What about those people who were born non-Jews but have come to see themselves as Jews (with or without formal conversion)? One hypothesis suggests that they would be a select group of liberals, attracted to Jews because of their liberalism. A second hypothesis argues that since they come primarily from the dominant world, they would be more like other Americans, e.g., more conservative. The data provide support for both hypotheses in part, but more for the latter, namely, that Jews by choice bring part of their political world with them in that they are more conservative (31 and 19 percent, respectively) than born-Jews. However, the total number of liberals is almost exactly the same for both groups (45 and 46 percent, respectively). In general, Jews by choice are considerably more liberal than the non-Jewish world from which they come.

Controlling for denomination does not change many of the findings. Data for the Orthodox are unusable because of the small number of converts to and from Orthodoxy, although the few non-Jews who convert and become Orthodox tend—like the Jewish-born Orthodox—to be relatively conservative. Parallel to born-Jews, those few Jews by choice who come from no religious background tend to be more liberal—within each Jewish denomination—than those who were once Christian, although the very small numbers make this hard to confirm.

The most interesting findings when controlling for denomination deal with the importance of being Jewish. Those few self-identified Orthodox (all non-observant) who said that being Jewish was not very important to them are much more liberal than the large Orthodox majority, for all of whom it is very important.

For Conservative and Reform Jews, there are no clear associations between liberalism and the importance of being Jewish. Yet among secular Jews, the association follows the Orthodox pattern: Those for whom being Jewish is most important are more conservative than most other Jews. This indeed contradicts the immersion theory.

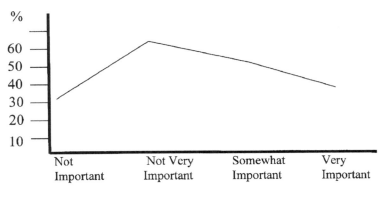

Figure 1A: The Importance of Being a Jew and Liberal
Political Ideology [in percent]

Source: NJPS [1990]

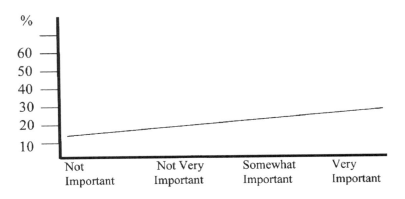

Figure 1B: The Importance of Being a Jew and
Conservative Political Ideology [in percent]

Source: NJPS [1990]

Non-Jewish Religious Involvement

Clear support for the assimilationist model comes from answers to three questions which tap involvement in non-Jewish religious life. Among the few Jews who participate in some non-Jewish religious activity, the proportion of political liberals is only about half that of those who do not participate in non-Jewish religious activities.

As expected, the practicing Orthodox do not live in a household with non-Jews, and hence they are not immediately exposed to non-Jewish religions. Looking only at the other denominations: Jews who live in a household where someone (themselves included) belongs to a non-Jewish religious group tend to be politically more conservative than those who live in households where no one participates in non-Jewish religious groups (see Table 11.3).

The theory of involvement in Jewish life comes across most strongly in the case of Jews without denomination. The secular Jews who do *not* participate in non-Jewish—particularly Christian—religious activities, are much more liberal than those who do. For example, among secular Jews who live in a household with a Christmas tree, 60 percent are politically liberal compared with 83 percent who live in a household without a tree. The sub-sample size is small but the findings are consistent over three separate measures.

2. Family

Closely related to self-identification is the Jewish identification of family members. Are people who intermarry more liberal than other Jews? And

TABLE 11.3

*Affiliation in Non-Jewish Religious Group
(By Any Householder) and Political Ideology
(in percent)*

	YES	NO
Very Liberal	6	23
Liberal	25	35
Middle of the road	52	29
Conservative	18	14
Total	100[a]	100[a]
(Sample Size)	(31)	(145)

[a] Error due to rounding

Gamma = −.41   Pearson's R = −.19   p (chi sq.) < .01

Source: NJPS (1990)

what happens to their children? If Jewish involvement is important for nourishing liberalism, then the intermarried should be less liberal.

The findings are neither consistent nor of great magnitude. Nevertheless, there is a general trend complementing the results of the previous set tapping involvement in the non-Jewish religious world. People whose parents are both Jewish are less conservative than those who have only one or no Jewish parent. Jews who have married a Jew or one non-Jew are less conservative than those who have married more than one non-Jew. In a parallel relationship, Jews whose children consider themselves Jewish are less conservative than those with non-Jewish children.

On the other hand, those who had intermarried someone without any religious background or someone who was not Christian are more liberal than those who married Christians or Jews. In all these cases, except one, immersion holds: those more Jewish are less conservative, though not always more liberal. The qualification is that those who are married to people without a formal religious identification are more liberal than those with a denominational attachment.

There are also some *attitudinal* questions which suggest the opposite, namely, that disapproval of intermarriage is related to conservatism. Those most supportive of a non-Jewish spouse converting and those most opposed to children marrying non-Jews are politically more conservative.

The remaining two measures do not involve intermarriage but are important in projecting to the future. Jews who have never married or who are divorced are more liberal than those married or widowed. If the norm of Jewish tradition is to be married with children, these unmarried and/or non-parents are the ones most like the larger society, that is, they are culturally more assimilated. But here, it is the larger society's norms which are more liberal than Jewish norms. In this case, a more liberal approach to family life is tied to a more liberal approach to politics. A parallel finding is that younger Jews who plan not to have children are more liberal than those who express the more traditional family norms.

Most of the patterns are the same across denomination. Because intermarriage is so infrequent among the Orthodox, their sub-sample size is minute and any findings are highly tentative, though an interesting pattern seems to take shape. For the Orthodox—who are relatively conservative— having a non-Jewish parent or ex-spouse is related to being more liberal. For the secular Jews—who are fundamentally liberal—having non-Jews in the family is related to being slightly more conservative. Again, however, at least for the secular Jews, this does not carry over to attitudes. Those more accepting of a non-Jewish son- or daughter-in-law are strongly liberal.

3. Religion

The simplest and most frequently used measure of religious attachment is self-identification of denomination (see Table 11.4).

Among the practicing Orthodox (those who keep kosher all the time), only 23 percent see themselves as liberal (none very liberal) and fully 36 percent see themselves as conservative. Although their numbers are very small, there is a definite increase in liberalism among the non-practicing Orthodox, who are very close to the Conservative/Reconstructionist Jews. The Reform are noticeably more liberal and less conservative than the other denominations.

Most dramatically different and most overwhelmingly committed to liberalism are the non-denominational self-identified Jews. More than two out of three are liberal and less than one in 10 is conservative. Within this combined category (as opposed to the "just Jewish"), the self-defined "secular Jews" are almost completely liberal; politically, they are almost a different species from other Americans. Of the 16 "secular Jews," not a single one defines himself or herself as politically conservative; 68 percent say they are very liberal and an additional 22 percent say they are generally liberal.

The relationships are parallel, though a little weaker, on questions concerning parents' denomination and the denomination that respondents were raised in. Those raised Orthodox but who no longer see themselves that way are more liberal than those who remained Orthodox. The most liberal among those raised Orthodox may have felt a push to leave Orthodoxy for a more liberal home, while the most conservative among those raised Reform may have drifted toward Conservative Judaism. At the same time, some of the most liberal among the Reform may have become secular. People who change tend to be drawn to that which feels most comfortable and congruous. As a result, the children and grandchildren of immigrants selected denominations which are more fitting to their values, thus sharpening the differences among the denominations.

The political differences between the Orthodox and other Jews become even more prominent in the findings on specific ritual observances, especially those which screen out Jews who claim Orthodox affiliation but are not observant. For the more commonly observed rituals, e.g., going to a Passover seder or lighting Hanukkah candles, individuals in households where it is done all the time—including virtually all the Orthodox—tend to be slightly more conservative; those who live in households where rituals are never observed are more likely to be very liberal. The other ritual practices evoke fewer political differences. These practices are sufficiently widespread that they do not have the ability to differentiate sharply.

TABLE 11.4
Denomination (Self-Identification) and Political Ideology (in percent)

	Observant Orthodox	Non-Observant Orthodox	Conservative Reconstructionist	Reform	Secular/Just Jewish	All Jews
Very Liberal	0		7	8	43	12
Liberal	23	37	35	44	27	37
Middle of the road	41	29	34	31	22	32
Conservative	32	21	24	15	6	17
Very Conservative	4	6	1	2	2	1
Total	100	100[b]	100[b]	100	100	100[b]
(Sample size)	(22)	(13)	(225)	(261)	(48)	(569)

[a] Defined as not keeping kosher all the time
[b] Error in rounding

Gamma = −.29   Pearson's R = −.25   p (chi sq.) < .01

Source: NJPS (1990)

For fasting on Yom Kippur, the total differences are small but they show up at the levels of conservative (high for those who fast) and of very liberal—twice as many among the non-fasters. For practices which today are not widely observed, such as lighting candles Friday night and buying kosher meat, the differences increase, as Table 11.5 shows.

For the most restricted practices, differences are stark. Among those who do not handle money on the Sabbath—overwhelmingly the observant Orthodox—41 percent say that they are politically conservative or very conservative—just over double the percentage of the other Jews. The difference between the Orthodox and other Jews parallels differences among the Orthodox themselves on the least observed ritual in the list, refraining from eating on the Fast of Esther. Among the Orthodox who fast, fully 46 percent say that they are politically conservative (or very conservative), compared with 33 percent of the Orthodox who do not fast and 18 percent of all the non-Orthodox (almost none of whom fast). In short, the more strict the level of Orthodoxy, the greater the political conservatism.

Among Jews, the single most conservative sub-group is the practicing Orthodox. It deserves notice, however (in comparing these numbers with Table 11.1), that even the most solidly conservative group of Jews is not different from the larger population of American non-Jews. If a very small difference exists, it is that the Orthodox see themselves as more liberal.

In the Western world, the most common measure of religious involvement is church, including membership and attendance. The NJPS allows us to look at both factors. The results for the two separate measures are generally but not completely similar. The findings challenge the idea of religious immersion leading to liberalism but rather reinforce the popular belief that church/synagogue ties are related to conservatism.

TABLE 11.5
Buying Kosher Meat for Home and Political Ideology
(in percent)

	NEVER	SOMETIMES/ USUALLY	ALL THE TIME
Very Liberal	16	5	4
Liberal	37	38	40
Middle of the road	32	33	35
Conservative	16	25	22
Total	100[a]	100[a]	100[a]
(Sample size)	(360)	(185)	(90)

[a] Error in rounding

Gamma = .20   Pearson's R = .12   p (chi sq.) < .01

Source: NJPS (1990)

Those Jews who do not belong to a synagogue and do not attend services are consistently the most strongly liberal. More than twice as many Jews who have never belonged to a synagogue are very liberal (18:8 percent) compared with those who have belonged. And respondents who live in a household without a synagogue member (themselves included) are three times more likely to be very liberal than those who live in households with synagogue members (see Table 11.6). Jews who never, or rarely attend services are more liberal than those who go more frequently. This matches the general finding of very strong liberalism among people who still define themselves as Jews but who have very low ritual involvement—the archetype secular Jew.

Jewish education is the last major behavioral indicator of religious attachment, since such education normally occurs within the context of a Jewish religious organization. (The establishment of formal secular Jewish education has dramatically declined over time.) The findings here are not consistent. On the most general measures—whether respondents ever received any formal Jewish education and/or participated in adult Jewish education in the past year—there are no patterned differences. Beyond that, the findings are mixed.

The last religious measure is attitudinal but abstract—how individuals think of Jews as a group. Respondents were asked to agree or disagree with four statements about the nature of being a Jew. Those who think that the group should *not* be focused around religion are slightly more liberal than those who see Jewishness as being focused on religion. In a parallel finding, Jews who define themselves as an ethnic or cultural group are very slightly more liberal than those who see Judaism as a religious grouping. The least liberal response was for the Jews who see themselves as a nationality. (The choices were not exclusive; one could say yes to all the concepts.)

Controlling for denomination reinforces some relationships noted previ-

TABLE 11.6

Synagogue Member in Household and
Political Ideology (in percent)

	YES	NO
Very Liberal	5	15
Liberal	39	37
Middle of the road	33	31
Conservative	23	17
Total	100	100
(Sample Size)	(246)	(398)

Gamma = .20   Pearson's R = − .13   p (chi sq.) < .01
Source: NJPS (1990)

ously. Political differences between those who observe and do not observe ritual practices are greatest among the Orthodox; those who do not practice most rituals are noticeably more liberal than the Orthodox who do. A parallel set of somewhat weaker findings on the other side is the tendency for the non-affiliated who practice certain rituals to be less liberal and more conservative than their completely non-observant friends. This relationship does not hold among the Conservatives-Reconstructionists or the Reform.

Systematic denominational political differences concerning synagogue involvement are found primarily among the Orthodox (as they are found for other measures): Those least involved in the synagogue and in ritual are the least conservative. Beyond the Orthodox, differences are neither significant nor systematic, especially in the other denominations. For the secular, however, some of the associations tend to parallel those among the Orthodox, viz., those who practice rituals and go to synagogue tend to be less liberal and/or more conservative than the Jewishly-involved secular.

4. Communal

Communal involvement, the most broadly denoted area, includes several disparate measures: paid membership in a Jewish community center (for anyone in the household); participation in Jewish voluntary organizations; paid subscription to a Jewish periodical; donation to Jewish charities; number of close friends who are Jewish; proportion of the neighborhood which is Jewish; geographical section of the country; two sets of attitudes, one on the definition of the group (ethnic, cultural, and nationality), and the other on the experience and the perceptions of anti-Semitism.

Several questions deal with associational involvement or membership in Jewish organizations. Overall, the findings are mixed and although there is a tendency for the less involved to be more liberal, it is not a consistent relationship. The most striking finding is that in homes where no one pays dues to a Jewish community center, the household heads are significantly more liberal than where there are center members. Most of the other findings are skewed in that direction although the results are not uniform.

One of the advantages of the NJPS is a pair of questions about charity, especially meaningful in light of Fuchs' explanation that *tsedakah* is one of the foundations of Jewish liberalism. This measure is limited to Jewish charities. (The findings for non-Jewish charities are parallel though very weak.) The evidence concerning Jewish philanthropies refutes the hypothesis that individuals who donate to charity are more liberal. Rather, those who do *not* contribute to Jewish charities are more liberal than those who do. And among the contributors, those who give the largest sums are the most conservative. This would be just natural if conservatism is defined according to economic criteria, since only very wealthy individuals would have the wherewithal to donate very large sums of money.

One of the most important indicators of communal involvement, and one which has not been sufficiently utilized in previous research, is friendship ties. Jews whose closest friends are all Jewish tend to be the most conservative; those with some or a few Jewish friends are the most liberal, although not less conservative. However, the pattern does not continue to those with no Jewish friends. They are noticeably less liberal than those with just a few or some Jewish friends. This is one of few cases, but a very important one, where the findings fall along a parabolic curve. In shape, it looks much like Figure 1A (see Table 11.7).

The most politically conservative Jews are those surrounded only by other (relatively highly ethnic) Jews; those next highest in conservatism are Jews with no Jewish social ties, those most assimilated and hence most like the larger non-Jewish world.

An extension of both friends and family is neighborhood. Most people choose a specific neighborhood for sundry reasons, one set of which may be for the quantity and quality of ethnic life. It is clear that the residential distribution of Jews is not random. Like other groups, Jews who live in ghettoized communities generally feel closer to the group than those who alienate themselves to largely white areas, typically on the distant periphery of the metropolis or in medium-sized cities, with little Jewish presence.

The Jewish immersion theory receives only marginal support when neighborhoods are considered. Those few respondents who had no idea about the Jewish makeup of their neighborhoods—probably the most assimilated who do not care enough to find out—were politically the most conservative. Much more challenging to the theory is the finding that those

TABLE 11.7
Closest Friends Who Are Jewish and Political Ideology
(in percent)

	NONE	SOME	MOST	ALL
Very Liberal	12	16	7	5
Liberal	33	40	33	35
Middle of the road	37	27	43	26
Conservative	19	17	17	34
Total	100[a]	100	100	100
(Sample Size)	(37)	(357)	(186)	(64)

[a] Error in rounding

Gamma = .17   Pearson's R = .11   p (chi sq.) < .01

Source: NJPS (1990)

who live in the most Jewish neighborhoods score the highest on conservatism; those who live in the least Jewish neighborhoods score highest on strongly liberal and slightly higher in total liberalism. Although differences are small, if the formal and informal Jewish community acts as a liberalizing agent, the findings should be exactly the opposite.

The relationship between political and ethnic orientations to residential community is slightly stronger and more linear when respondents are asked how important it is to live in a Jewish neighborhood. Again, it is in the direction opposite to that suggested by immersion. Those for whom a Jewish neighborhood is most important are by far the most conservative; those who think that it is not important are only half as likely to be conservative as those who think that it is very important to live in a Jewish neighborhood (16 and 30 percent, respectively).

A much more indirect measure of the residential Jewish concentration is the larger geographical region. Jews are still highly overrepresented in the generally liberal Northeast and they are greatly underrepresented in the conservative South; they are proportionately represented in the most liberal parts of the West but a little underrepresented in the more moderate cosmopolitan sectors of the Midwest.

The political ideologies distribution of Jews nationally reflects the regional cultures and the degree to which Jews are integrated into them. Jews in the South (except the elderly Northern transplants in south Florida), tend to be by far the most conservative (see Table 11.8). Because they are less residentially segregated, less insulated against the non-Jewish world, Southern Jews are most like their environment, that is, the most conservative. In the Jewishly overrepresented Northeastern areas, Jews reflect the concerns of more ghettoized Jews, and thus are slightly less liberal than their counterparts either in the Midwest or in the West (primarily liberal California).

Definitions of Jews and Anti-Semitism

Those who see Jews as a religious group tend to be slightly less liberal than those who do not. What about Jews as an ethnic or cultural group? The correlations are minuscule but in the opposite direction: Jews who see themselves as an ethnic or cultural group tend to be very slightly more liberal. These attitudes are not always matched by behavior, however, since most other measures of Jewish communal life show that the people most involved in the ethnic community are not the most liberal; they probably just feel much more comfortable defining themselves and their Jewish attachment as ethnic rather than as religious.

On the more personal psychological level, those who feel that being a

TABLE 11.8
Region and Political Ideology (in percent)

	NORTHEAST	MIDWEST	SOUTH	WEST
Very Liberal	8	20	6	21
Liberal	42	39	31	34
Middle of the road	32	31	33	31
Conservative	18	10	30	15
Total	100	100	100	100[a]
(Sample Size)	(319)	(73)	(121)	(132)

[a] Error in rounding

Eta = .20   p (chi sq.) < .01

Source: NJPS (1990)

Jew is very important tend to be the most conservative. This evidence is much more directly challenging to the idea of immersion than any of the other measures in this area. The response pattern to this emotional question follows the parabola rather than a straight line. The lowest levels of liberalism are expressed by those who think that being Jewish is not important, followed by those for whom it is very important. The highest levels of liberalism are from those in the middle (see Figure 1A).

The other major questions that deal with attitude cover anti-Semitism. The first, a measure of behavior, finds that few Jews have personally experienced anti-Semitism and that experience does not seem related to any particular political preference. But differences in attitude were apparent when interviewees were asked whether anti-Semitism is a serious problem. Those who replied that it is are less liberal, though not more conservative, than those more disposed to dismiss anti-Semitism. Jews who feel strongly that anti-Semitism is *not* a problem are the least conservative.

This relationship between political predisposition and wariness about the larger non-Jewish world is stronger in the response to a question concerning whether in a time of crisis one can depend only on other Jews. Those who agree most strongly, those most distrustful of the outside world, are the most conservative. Those who are most convinced that non-Jews can be trusted are the most liberal. Those who strongly disagree that non-Jews cannot be trusted are five times more likely to be very liberal than those who ultimately do not trust non-Jews (25 and four percent, respectively).

The correlations between all the communal measures and political orientation appear to be weak. Embedded in those tables, however, are important relationships, but they are hidden by the fact that the correlations differ by denomination.

Since the Orthodox are strongly communal people who elect to live within Orthodox Jewish enclaves and pick other Orthodox as their closest friends, it is essential to examine all of the communal associations controlling for Orthodoxy. Indeed, the data reveal that 58 percent of the practicing Orthodox cite that all or almost all of their closest friends are Jews compared with only 19 percent of all the other Jews.

Among the Orthodox, those who have mostly Jewish friends in tightly-knit Orthodox sub-communities tend to be more conservative; those who are very involved in non-religious Jewish institutions in the larger community are more liberal. That probably reflects greater exposure to the mainstream liberal American-Jewish political and social ethos.

For secular Jews, this subtle distinction does not exist. Rather, those who are more tied to Jewish life are—though strongly liberal—less liberal than the less involved secular Jews. The sample size is small and the associations occasionally irregular, but the general pattern is there. For the mainstream denominational Jews, differences are much weaker and irregular.

Differences in Jewish charitable contributions are based on small sample sizes and are barely notable except that they parallel earlier findings. Among the Orthodox, the few who do not donate are more liberal than the Orthodox givers. No hard evidence is available, but it seems reasonable that the more politically conservative among the Orthodox are more likely to give to Orthodox, rather than to general, Jewish causes. Among the secular, those who give to Jewish causes are also relatively less liberal, but the absolute level of liberalism is still very high. For the Conservatives and Reform, the correlation between Jewish charity and political ideology is barely observable, although it is in the same direction of the others.

On the important question of close friends, the basic pattern reappears. Among the Orthodox, those with the largest number of close Jewish friends are the most conservative. (The only Orthodox Jews who do not have almost all Jewish friends are the non-practicing.) For the other denominations, the association is not clear. But among secular Jews, those with only a few close Jewish friends tend to be the most liberal.

A slightly parallel, although weaker, finding emerges when the concentration of Jews in the neighborhood is examined. Again, the Orthodox who live in ghettoized communities—typically with large numbers of other Orthodox—tend to be more conservative, while the Orthodox outside those confines (largely the non-observant) are less conservative. The same strong association occurs among the secular, whereas among mainstream Jews the associations are much weaker, though they are still in the same direction.

Findings for the attitudinal question that deals with the importance of living in a Jewish neighborhood very closely follow those concerning how

Jewish the neighborhood actually is. The only slight difference is that among Conservative Jews, those who feel it is very important to live in a Jewish neighborhood tend to be politically more conservative than those less concerned about the area's religio-ethnic composition. For the secular Jews, like the Orthodox, a heightened concern with living in a Jewish neighborhood is related to a less liberal orientation.

The impact of region on political orientation is strong among all denominations and those without affiliation. For each group, the most conservative members are in the South. There is an interesting divergence in the West between the Orthodox and the secular. The Orthodox, most of whom have left relatively tightly-knit Orthodox communities in the East, tend to take on a little of the liberalism of the West, where they have more contact with the non-Orthodox world. (For the Orthodox, that almost invariably means southern California, more specifically, Los Angeles.) Undoubtedly, those who could uproot themselves were less tightly drawn to the conservative community of origin. For the secular, the opposite is true: They probably left strongly liberal pockets, typically with a significant presence of Jews, for the more loose style of the West and so they are somewhat *less* liberal than their Northeastern cousins.

How one defines Jews has different political ramifications for the Orthodox and the secular. Among the Orthodox, the few who do not define Jews as a religious group are the most liberal since they are more open to the larger secular Jewish-American liberalism. Those Orthodox who see the Jews as an ethnic or cultural group in addition to being a religious entity tend to be more conservative than other Orthodox Jews, probably because of the influence of their conservative Orthodox peer group. The secular, however, focus instead on the cultural as a replacement for the religious. Their own Jewish peer group influence is likely to be liberal. And so those who think of Jews as an ethnic or cultural group or even national group tend to be slightly *more* liberal, whereas the few secular who think of Jews as a religious group are decidedly *less* liberal.

The last set of questions deals with anti-Semitism. Since so few report having personally experienced anti-Semitism, no breakdown is possible. The Orthodox who think that anti-Semitism is a serious problem in the United States tend to be more liberal, probably a reflection of their greater involvement in the larger American world. Among the secular, however, the more liberal are those who think that anti-Semitism is *not* a serious problem.

The very last question is one that evokes a similar response from Orthodox and secular. In both groups, people who think that in a crisis Jews can depend only on other Jews tend to be more politically conservative. That makes sense since some members of both groups assume a hostile non-

Jewish world which cannot be trusted. The difference between them is in degree: a much higher proportion of the Orthodox strongly agree that non-Jews cannot be trusted in a crisis (54 percent of the Orthodox and 10 percent of the secular). Secular liberals, who tend to be egalitarian and humanist, see the non-Jewish world as much less alien and less threatening.

5. Americanism

Since the American experience has been liberalizing, it seems logical that the Jews born into this society would be more liberal than those born abroad who are, therefore, more marginal to both the American and the American Jewish political culture. According to the data, however, that is not so clear. Neither first-generation (foreign-born) nor second-generation (parent born abroad) Jews are statistically politically different from all other Jews. There are, however, some signs of differences when the two categories are combined. Jews whose grandparents were born in the United States are slightly but irregularly more liberal than those born abroad or children of the foreign-born.

A more significant political difference occurs between Ashkenazi and Sephardi Jews. American Jewish liberal politics has been an Eastern European tradition, a continuation of the Russian radical tradition. The Sephardim have justifiably complained about being pushed to the margins or even excluded from the American Jewish culture. Many of the Sephardim came from lands where liberal democracy was foreign, and so they ought to have a weaker attachment to liberalism. Indeed, that is the case, although the difference between the two groups is not great: 25 percent of the Sephardim see themselves as conservative, compared with 17 percent of the more Americanized Ashkenazim (see Table 11.9).

Controlling for denomination does not alter the relationships. Although the differences are not statistically significant, country of origin makes more of a difference in the views of the Orthodox than for the other groups. The Orthodox born in the United States are better educated and play a more active role in the larger society than do their counterparts in Europe, thus giving them a greater personal exposure to liberalism.

6. Israel

The last area, Israel, reveals some interesting and unexpected results. The questions all deal with how attached respondents are to the Jewish state. Unfortunately, the in-depth questions were asked only of people who have visited Israel at least once. They include: the number of friends, relatives

TABLE 11.9
Jewish (Cultural) Ethnicity and Political Ideology
(in percent)

	SEPHARDI	ASHKENAZI
Very Liberal	3	13
Liberal	35	38
Middle of the road	37	33
Conservative	25	17
Total	100	100[a]
(Sample Size)	(38)	(283)

[a] Error in rounding
Gamma = −.25   Pearson's R = .11   p (chi sq.) < .01
Source: NJPS (1990)

and visits there; intention to visit; how frequently they talk about Israel; and how emotionally involved they are.

Recent popular perception has it that strong pro-Israel sentiment is tied to a strong hawkish position and a general political conservatism. That certainly seems to be the stereotyped Orthodox position. In fact, stronger ties with Israel are irregularly related to only a slightly conservative position. However, how emotionally involved one is—the one measure where the association is clear, though moderate—is likely the most important indicator. One-quarter of those who are very or extremely attached to Israel are politically conservative, compared with only one-tenth of those who feel no such attachment.

As several public opinion surveys in the last two decades demonstrate, with the exception of the Satmar Hasidim, no religious segment of American Jewry has voiced more support for Israel than the Orthodox. For example, slightly more than half of the Orthodox feel extremely attached to the Jewish state, compared with only one-tenth of other Jews.

When the denominations are controlled for, an interesting previously noted parallelism recurs. For Conservative and Reform Jews there is almost no association between attachment to Israel and political ideology. However, among Orthodox and secular Jews, those who visit and have close friends in Israel and are emotionally attached to the Jewish state are noticeably more politically conservative than those with weak attachments.

VI. Summary and Discussion

Evidence for the domination of liberalism among American Jews is overwhelming. Its modern roots go back to the French Revolution, where it evolved later into socialism and spread from Germany to Poland and Russia, from where it was transported to America by working-class immigrant intellectuals. It found a sympathetic audience among the Jewish toilers who transmitted that worldview to their American-born children. Their grandchildren stand out from other white ethnic and religious groups in the United States by continuing to vote for liberals at least one full generation after they pulled themselves out of the conditions which normally foster liberalism—poverty, low socioeconomic status, and high levels of group oppression and exclusion.

The simple but important relationship which has been tested here is based upon an assumption that to be Jewish in the United States today is to be liberal. All the major theories of Jewish political behavior assume that the American Jewish experience is liberalizing and that the community is solidly liberal. They imply that participation in Jewish life ought to reinforce that liberal-Democratic attachment. On the other end, the greater the separation, the more complete the assimilation into the non-Jewish world, the less liberal the Jew.

What light is shed on this relationship by the NJPS? We have been limited by the availability of only one political question, but that one measure of ideological self-identification proves to be a very powerful predictor of party affiliation, vote, and support for specific issues. More troubling is the small sub-sample of some groups which deserve close attention. Thus, many of our significant findings require additional verification.

What is clear from the data is that for American Jews, liberalism is pervasive among almost all sub-groups. Within the community, denomination is very significant, far more so than the standard social science demographic variables like education, gender, age, or even economics. As might be expected from their theology, among the denominationally affiliated, the Reform are the most politically liberal. Confirming another recent study, among all Jews, the secular are the most strongly liberal. Even more clear, the Orthodox are the most conservative.

It is this stark contrast between the politically conservative Orthodox and liberal secular Jews that presents the first major challenge to the immersion theory that involvement in Jewish life deepens attachment to liberalism. If mainstream religious tradition were the essential source of liberalism, it should follow that the Orthodox would be the most liberal. The second challenge is the fact that among Conservative-Reconstructionist and Reform Jews, there is no pattern of a relationship between involvement in Jewish life and political ideology.

The third challenge is the ironic similarity between the Orthodox and the secular in those factors which correlate with political attitudes. In both groups, involvement in Jewish life is related to a relatively greater conservative response. For example, both the Orthodox and the secular who engage in relatively more ritual practice, who have more close Jewish friends, and who have more emotional ties to Israel are less liberal than their respective compatriots with weaker ties. Of course, in absolute terms, the secular are always more liberal. But for both, involvement in Jewish life tends to make for a weaker liberal predisposition.

That the secular are more liberal seems perfectly natural. It is certainly true for non-Jews: Americans who profess no religion have been consistently more liberal than self-defined Christians. Why should it not also be true for Jews? Indeed, American Jews have had a disproportionate place among the leaders and outspoken supporters of secular humanism, from Ethical Culture to Unitarianism. And the values and agenda of secular humanism match those of the traditional Jewish left: equality, justice, and peace. The text could easily come from a Reform Jewish social bulletin.

This religious split is not new. Throughout most of Jewish history, it was the folk, *amcha*, much more than the established religious leadership, who were open to the outside world and to the democratic spirit. Especially since the 18th century, the larger world which had special appeal to Jews was the world of liberal values, where Jews hoped to be accepted and provided with equal opportunities.

The religious leadership—among both Ashkenazim and Sephardim— has almost always been more conservative than the secular leadership. Indeed, Orthodoxy in America was very slow in developing because early in the immigration the Orthodox leadership refused to come to this *trayfeh medina* (nonkosher state).

That the Orthodox who are immersed in their own community tend to be the most conservative seems eminently plausible. It is their values which are most threatened by the secular norms, particularly those demanding separation of church and state, and specific traditional norms like gender equality and tolerance of different life-styles, especially homosexuality.

The more interesting question for our general hypothesis is why the secular with deeper Jewish roots are not as liberal as those secular Jews with weaker ties. Part of the answer is that the organized Jewish community, although strongly liberal, also maintains some of the conservatism inherent in any mainstream religious (or ethnic) enclave, particularly that of a higher socioeconomic group.

In foreign affairs, although their anti-war sentiments are clear, the organized Jewish community supports American military aid to Israel. Domestically, they are against a quota system, which would invariably discriminate against Jews; increasingly, they want some public acknowledgement of their own religious tradition; as educated people, American Jews are growing frustrated with the failure of public education in large cities and are open to solutions once thought of as conservative; and as members of a highly urban group, with many elderly people, they are increasingly worried about crime in the streets.

Given the broad findings, it is tempting to reject the immersion hypothesis completely. Nevertheless, at least part of it does seem viable: Those Jews who are most completely assimilated into the larger American culture are most like that culture politically, namely, considerably less liberal than are the rest of the Jews. That level of profound acculturation is seen most clearly among Jews who participate in Christian practices (or who live in such a household) and among those who live in the South, where Jews are very poorly insulated against the largely conservative culture.

The fact that liberalism and involvement in Jewish life are not correlated does not automatically rule out the Jewish experience as a source of liberal values. The fact that Jews remain consistently more liberal and Democratic than all other white ethnic and religious groups is itself strong evidence that they come from a liberal culture. Moreover, the data suggest that a majority of the Jews have kept those liberal universalist values as part of their cultural norms, while first discarding many of the rituals and later, some of the communal attachments. Indeed, as the 1988 Los Angeles Times Poll revealed, far more American Jews personally define Judaism in terms of its (liberal) social values rather than its ritual practice. Jews are still sensitive to ethnic-religious persecution and still tend to identify with the underdog, in spite of their relative economic and political success.

How can we explain the slightly greater liberal predisposition of secular Jews, particularly those with relatively little involvement in Jewish life, and still maintain that the Jewish experience is essentially liberalizing? One possibility is that of a culture lag, a period during which old attitudes prevail even as circumstances change; Jews still carry the effects of the Jewish experience although they have drifted away in some areas. It may be that in the next generation, as younger people become more distant from the immigrant experience, levels of economic liberalism will decline. The increased level of support for Reagan by young Jews in the 1980s partially corroborates this anticipation. There is change but it takes time. Nevertheless, even when considering only young people, where differences are smaller than they are among the elderly, American Jews are still significantly more liberal than non-Jews.

A second explanation of Jewish liberalism is that many secular Jews who have dropped out of much of Jewish life have not left the liberal environment. Instead, they live in neighborhoods with high concentrations of liberal Democrats; they work in sectors where liberals are still prominent—the university and schools in general, human services, media, law, and even in (research) medicine. Very few Jews face the social and economic forces of small-town Christian parochialism. Rather, the immediate worlds in which the secular Jews live are filled with other secular liberal people, reinforcing political positions which may have once come from the immigrant Jewish experience.

The Future

Can Jews maintain their liberalism in a non-Jewish environment, and has the Jewish community become more conservative than in the past? The latter question is easier to answer. Outside of Orthodoxy (the more strict communities in particular), mainstream denominational Jewry is strongly liberal, especially when compared with the rest of America. There is little indication that these Jews have changed their voting behavior, ideological self-identification, or position on most political issues.

Whether secular Jews, in particular, can maintain their liberalism depends in part on the viability of the islands of liberalism, usually in cosmopolitan coastal communities. Indeed, one of the reasons these areas are liberal is because of the Jewish presence. Patterns of selective migration suggest that liberals will continue to move to these communities, thus maintaining their ideological character.

So long as Jews gravitate toward—or remain in—these communities, their liberalism will persist. Marriage with secular liberal mates, and the ongoing patterns of high education and preference for vocations in the social services and intellectual professions, will support both residential as well as ideological patterns.

Nevertheless, as the NJPS shows, there are also findings which suggest a future decline in liberalism. Jews are leaving some of the traditional liberal enclaves in the Northeast and Midwest and rates of intermarriage are increasing precipitously. In the short run, some of the conservatizing effects of intermarriage are likely to be mitigated by the fact that a significant number of the non-Jewish spouses are from liberal backgrounds, thus reinforcing liberalism.

However, as intermarriage increases, a greater number of spouses will be representative of the larger American community, where the proportion of conservatives is higher than among Jews. As these families move into a more typical American environment, the number of liberals is bound to decline. On the other hand, unless some change occurs, the majority of the children of these marriages will not consider themselves Jews, so the community will lose this bloc of relatively conservative people.

In addition to the growth of the conservative Orthodox through larger families, another source of conservatism is Jewish Russian, Iranian, and

Israeli immigrants. Although few show up in the NJPS, their numbers are increasing and their political history is much less liberal than that of the earlier Russian and Polish immigrants to America.

When they first migrated to the United States, the hordes of East European Jews carried a common religious and social culture. Their initial political development in this country was relatively homogenous. Over time, they have experienced different levels of assimilation and their numbers have been supplemented by Jews from different political cultures and by the growth of an Orthodox sub-group which is politically different. If this picture is fundamentally correct, we should expect to see in one generation a group of American Jews who will be significantly less united in their liberalism and for whom politics will be increasingly divisive rather than unifying. This marks another arena in which American Jewish life will become more polarized than it was at mid-century.

Notes

1. For earlier material, see Fisher, Alan, "Continuity and Erosion of Jewish Liberalism," *American Jewish Historical Quarterly*, v. 66 (1976) pp. 322–347; for later material, Fisher, Alan, "The Jewish Electorate: California 1980–1986," in Seymour Martin Lipset, ed., *American Pluralism and the Jewish Community*, New Brunswick, Transaction, 1990, pp. 131–149.

2. Fuchs, Lawrence, *The Political Behavior of American Jews*, Glencoe, Free Press, 1956.

3. For an example of partisan Orthodox conservatism, see the *Jewish Press*.

4. Cohn, Werner, "The Politics of American Jews," in Marshall Sklare, ed., *The Jews*, New York, Free Press, 1958, pp. 615–626; Seymour Martin Lipset, *Political Man*, Garden City, Doubleday, 1960, pp. 243–244, 289.

5. Raab, Earl and Seymour Martin Lipset, "The Political Future of American Jews," New York, American Jewish Congress, March, 1985; Liebman, Arthur, *Jews and the Left: Genesis to Exodus*, New York, Wiley, 1979.

6. Lipset, Seymour Martin, and Everett Carl Ladd, "Jewish Academics in the United States: Their Achievement, Culture and Politics," *American Jewish Year Book*, 72 (1971), pp. 89–128.

7. Cohen, Steven M., *American Modernity and Jewish Identity*, New York, Tavistock, 1983.

8. Liebman, Charles S., *The Ambivalent American Jew*, Philadelphia, Jewish Publication Society, 1973; Cohen, Steven M., "1984 National Survey" and "Attitudes of American Jews 1988: A National Study in Comparative Perspective," New York, American Jewish Committee, 1989.

9. Helmreich, William, *The World of the Yeshiva*, New York, Free Press, 1982.

10. Cohen, *Jewish Modernity*, pp. 143–153.

11. See Cohen, "1984 National Survey" and "Attitudes of American Jews 1988."

12. Fisher, Alan M., "*Jewish Organizational Leaders, The Jewish Laity, and Non-Jewish Neighbors in Los Angeles: A Demographic and Socio-Political Comparison,*" Los Angeles, Wilstein Institute, Fall, 1993.

13. See Cohen, *Jewish Modernity*, "1984 National Survey," and "Attitudes of American Jews 1988"; Fisher, "*Jewish Organizational Leaders.*"

14. Cohen, *Jewish Modernity*, pp. 143–153.

15. Kosmin, Barry A., et al., *Highlights of the CJF 1990 National Jewish Population Survey*, New York, Council of Jewish Federations, 1991.

16. Fisher, *Jewish Organizational Leaders.*

17. ibid.

PART FOUR

Judaism and Gender

12

Women: Their Education, Work, and Jewish Communal Participation

Sylvia Barack Fishman

American Jewish Women: A Profile

Despite widespread Jewish communal anxiety about the impact of higher education and careerism upon the communal activities of American Jewish women today and tomorrow, this study finds that high levels of educational and occupational accomplishment are not in opposition to Jewish communal life. Instead, low levels of participation in Jewish communal causes, as members and as volunteers, are found among Jewish women who have generally weak ties to the Jewish community.

To put the matter in the simplest terms, the "enemy" of the dynamic involvement of Jewish women in American Jewish communal life is not higher education or careerist aspirations but a weak Jewish life socially, culturally, and religiously.

This study presents a profile of American Jewish women—their levels of education, participation in the labor force, and involvement in Jewish institutions such as synagogues and Jewish organizations, based on the data drawn from the 1990 National Jewish Population Survey. It can be viewed as a snapshot of the behaviors of Jewish female respondents during the time period in which the interviewing was conducted.[1]

The analysis focuses on the relationship between several background variables—age, levels of education, marital status (including Jewish or mixed-married households), stage of family formation, labor force participation, occupational status—and variables connected with Jewish institutional participation, such as belonging to synagogues and/or Jewish organizations, volunteering time for Jewish organizations (including a comparison with voluntarism for non-Jewish organizations), and serving in a leadership capacity in Jewish organizations. The study does not predict behaviors or assign cause and effect relationships between given factors. Thus, the analysis may state that a given percentage of women with Master's degrees volunteer time for Jewish organizations, but not that a particular level of educational attainment causes women to volunteer time.

Many of the survey questions on voluntarism and affiliation deal with the behavior of respondents only, rather than each member of the household. Therefore, this analysis does not include all Jewish females in the 1990 Jewish Population Survey but Jewish female respondents only. For most variables the data used are based on about 990 Jewish female respondents (born Jews and Jews by choice).[2]

Demographic Background on the Respondents

The Jewish female respondents included in this analysis are women who report that they were born Jewish and/or currently consider themselves to be Jewish. Thus, the sample includes both born Jews and Jews by choice. The following pages include background demographic data on the respondents studied: marital status, patterns of family formation, labor force participation, education, and occupational status. These briefly presented demographic data provide the backdrop for a more complete analysis of Jewish organizational activity by Jewish women.

Marital Status

Tables 12.1 and 12.1A show that Jewish respondent data clearly reflect the reduced percentage of American Jews currently living in married households, compared to the 1970 Jewish Population Survey. Fewer than two-thirds of Jewish female respondents in the 1990 survey are currently married: among the Jewish female respondents 16 percent have never been married, 64 percent are currently married, nine percent are divorced or separated, and 11 percent are widowed. Although Table 12.1A illustrates marital status by age and gender, for much of the analysis respondents are divided into two age groups: ages 18 to 44 and ages 45 and over.

Family Formation Status

Among Jewish female respondents, 28 percent have no children, 36 percent have children 18 and under, and 36 percent have children 19 and over. Reflecting the national trend toward postponed family formation, only seven percent of the women ages 18 to 24 have children; in the 25 to 34 age

TABLE 12.1
Marital Status of American Jewish Men and Women Surveys of Jewish
Populations in Individual Community Studies 1970 and 1990 National Jewish
Population Surveys (in percentages)

Location	Year Study Completed	Married	Single	Widowed	Divorced
Atlantic City	1985	67	13	13	6
Boston	1985	61	29	4	5
Baltimore	1985	68	19	9	5
Chicago	1982	65	23	6	6
Cleveland	1981	69	11	13	8
Denver	1981	64	23	4	9
Kansas City	1985	70	17	7	5
Los Angeles	1979	57	17	12	14
Miami	1982	61	7	23	8
Milwaukee	1983	67	14	9	10
Minneapolis	1981	66	22	7	5
Nashville	1982	70	17	8	5
New York	1981	65	15	11	9
Phoenix	1983	63	18	9	10
Richmond	1983	67	14	12	7
Rochester	1987	68	23	6	3
St. Louis	1982	68	9	17	6
St. Paul	1981	66	20	11	3
San Francisco	1988	69	19	4	7
Washington, D.C.	1983	61	27	4	7
Worcester	1987	69	14	—18—	
*NJPS	1990	65	17	10	9
U.S. Census	1989	64	21	8	8
NJPS	1970	78	6	10	5
U.S. Census	1970	72	16	9	3

*Based on respondents who were born or raised as Jews, 1990 National Jewish Population Survey.

TABLE 12.1A
Marital Status by Age and Gender (in percentages) 1990 National
Jewish Population Survey Jewish Respondents

	18–24 F	M	25–34 F	M	35–44 F	M	45–54 F	M	55–64 F	M	65+ F	M
Married	12	2	62	46	74	73	75	77	77	87	57	82
Never Married	88	96	30	50	11	17	7	9	2	6	2	3
Divorced (or separated)	1	1	7	3	14	10	14	11	14	6	4	3
Widowed	—	—	1	—	1	1	4	3	8	1	38	12

299

group, 45 percent have children; in the 35 to 44 age group, 76 percent have children; and in the 45 and older age groups, virtually all the respondents reported having some children, either biological or adopted.

Labor Force Participation

The prevalence of full-time work among contemporary American Jewish women is clearly illustrated by the Jewish female respondent data, despite differences between age and marital status groups. Full-time work was reported by 46 percent of all Jewish female respondents; that includes 59 percent of singles, 44 percent of married women, 72 percent of divorced women, and 22 percent of widows.

Among all Jewish female respondents, 17 percent call themselves home-makers, six percent are students, nine percent work part-time, 46 percent work full-time, and 20 percent are unemployed or retired. These labor force profiles differ substantially by marital status and by age. Among the never married Jewish female respondents almost one-third are students (31 percent), only five percent work part-time, 59 percent work full-time, and five percent are unemployed. In contrast, among married Jewish female respondents, more than one-quarter call themselves homemakers (26 per-

TABLE 12.2
Family Formation Status, Percentage by Age

AGES OF JEWISH FEMALE RESPONDENT	NO CHILDREN	CHILDREN 18 OR UNDER	CHILDREN 19 OR OVER	
Ages 18–24	93%	8%	—	101%
Ages 25–34	55%	45%	—	100%
Ages 35–44	24%	71%	5%	100%
Ages 45–54	—	40%	60%	100%
Ages 55–64	—	3%	97%	100%
Age 65 +	—	—	100%	100%

TABLE 12.3
Labor Force Participation of Women Jewish Respondents Percentages by Age Group

LABOR FORCE STATUS	WOMEN UNDER 45	45 AND OVER
Homemaker	17%	19%
Student	11%	1%
Work Part-time	11%	8%
Work Full-time	59%	31%
Unemployed/Retired	4%	44%

cent), only one percent are students, 12 percent work part-time, 44 percent work full-time, and 18 percent are unemployed.

Similar contrasts are seen in the age groups above and below 45: in the age 44 and under group of Jewish female respondents, 17 percent are homemakers, 11 percent are students, 11 percent work part-time, 59 percent work full-time, and only four percent are unemployed; among those age 45 and over, however, 19 percent are homemakers, fewer than one percent are students, eight percent work part-time, 31 percent work full-time, and 44 percent are unemployed or retired.

Background Profile of Jewish Female and Male Respondents
(Born and/or Raised Jewish)

Tables 12.4, 12.5, and 12.6 illustrate the increased levels of education and occupational status attained by Jewish men and women under age 45. For women especially, recent gains have been dramatic. These changes provide the backdrop for our study of organizational activity.

Reasons for Studying the Involvement of Women in American Jewish Organizations

One of the most burning practical issues for the contemporary organized Jewish community is that of attracting and retaining sufficient levels of Jewish communal activism to maintain institutional vitality. The issue of Jewish organizational participation is crucial not only for the institutions involved, however, but for the entire Jewish community for at least two reasons: First, members of and volunteers for Jewish organizations have higher levels of Jewish activism and involvement in other areas of Jewish life as well, and it seems likely that a process of mutual reinforcement may be at work; second, the vitality of the wider Jewish community is to a very real extent intertwined with the vitality of American Jewish organizations which provide the contexts for viable Jewish communal activity.

Voluntarism by both men and women is important to the Jewish communal world. However, voluntarism by women has historically had particular significance. For many decades American Jewish women viewed voluntarism as *their* Jewish activity, analogous in some ways to the communal role of men in the synagogue. For most of the twentieth century, the health of American Jewish organizational life was greatly enhanced by untold millions of hours of free labor and organizational ability donated by American Jewish women. Many of them were relatively highly educated for their socioeconomic and generational status; they had fewer children

TABLE 12.4

Educational Levels of Jewish Respondents Percentages by Age Group and Sex

	WOMEN		MEN	
ATTAINED	UNDER 45	45 AND OVER	UNDER 45	45 AND OVER
H.S. and Under	10%	36%	5%	19%
Some College (A.A.)	24%	24%	22%	19%
B.A.	38%	21%	42%	29%
M.A.	20%	14%	17%	15%
Ph. D. or Prof. Degree	8%	6%	14%	18%

TABLE 12.5

Occupational Status Levels of Jewish Respondents
Unweighted Percentages by Age Group and Sex

OCCUPATIONAL	WOMEN		MEN	
STATUS LEVEL	UNDER 45	45 AND OVER	UNDER 45	45 AND OVER
Hi-Prof.	14%	7%	22%	26%
Helping Prof.	29%	18%	18%	10%
Managerial	14%	15%	16%	20%
Cler./Tech.	31%	52%	27%	28%
Service	9%	5%	14%	14%
Other/Ref.	3%	2%	4%	3%

TABLE 12.6

Family Formation Status, Percentages by Professional Status

PROFESSIONAL STATUS	PERCENTAGE OF SAMPLE	NO CHILDREN	CHILDREN 18 & UNDER	CHILDREN 19 +
High Status Professions	11%	15%	11%	7%
Helping Professions	25%	24%	28%	16%
Managerial	14%	13%	13%	14%
Clerical/Technical	42%	35%	37%	56%
Service	8%	9%	9%	7%
Totals	100%	96%	98%	100%

than their gentile cohort; and, at least from the 1950's until relatively recently, they tended not to be labor force participants. They devoted themselves with professionalism and passion to Jewish organizations and often worked for several causes. These institutions, for their part, gave women a religiously and culturally approved non-threatening outlet for their intellectual, organizational, and social energies.[3]

Anecdotal evidence reveals that for many American Jewish women, meetings and other activities held on behalf of synagogues, Jewish schools, and other organizations provided a chance to get out of the house and socialize with like-minded women, as well as to engage in good works. The important role which Jewish organizations played in the social, cultural, and religious lives of women is documented by scholars[4] and veteran volunteers who describe not only hard work but friendship as well, plans mapped out, goals attained, and warm feelings of accomplishment. Even simple tasks such as preparing mailings and labor intensive tasks such as organizing bake sales and rummage sales could be experienced as enjoyable and worthwhile in such a context.

Female volunteers often worked for many years for the Jewish organizations of their choice, beginning with pedestrian tasks early in their organizational "careers" and proceeding up the ranks to more challenging and responsible positions as they gained experience and became more affluent. In many Jewish organizations, the most common pattern for volunteers was that positions of power and prestige went to those who donated substantial amounts of money and who had worked for years as foot soldiers for the cause. In other organizations, such as synagogue sisterhoods or school parent-teacher associations, however, hard work and competence often were more significant factors than affluence, and Jewish women of even modest means could attain leadership positions with diligence and dedication. These positions, in addition to providing satisfaction, were often an avenue to communal prestige. Thus, Jewish institutions thrived along with their female volunteers for many decades.

Jewish communal leaders have voiced great concerns about the potential impact of the American Jewish women's new life-styles upon the Jewish organizational world. Life has changed dramatically for today's American Jewish women. They receive more formal education, both secular and Jewish, than ever before. Almost one-third of respondents have completed their Bachelor's degrees, and one-quarter have earned post-graduate degrees as well. One out of four Jewish female respondents who work outside the home are employed in the helping professions (as teachers below the college level, social workers, librarians) and in other professional work. Many of them are connected with scientific technologies, such as engineers and computer programmers. In addition, increasing numbers of younger Jewish women are employed in high status, often more lucrative professions, working as physicians, dentists, lawyers, professors, and corporate executives.

American Jewish women today are more likely to be labor force participants than their counterparts at the mid-twentieth century. The majority continue to work outside the home for pay throughout their childbearing and childrearing years. Full-time work is far more widespread than part-time work among the Jewish female respondents in this study; thus, most women surveyed are unavailable during working hours. One can speculate that at the end of a day away from home they may often be resistant to—rather than grateful for—the invitation to leave the house to attend a Jewish organizational meeting. Moreover, increasing numbers of Jewish women do not have primarily Jewish friendship circles. Jewish friendship circles are closely related to being asked and agreeing to volunteer time for Jewish causes.

Given the sweep of socio-demographic changes, it is crucial for community planners to have an accurate picture of the Jewish organizational activities of today's women. Some results of the organizational profile of American Jewish women from the 1990 National Jewish Population Survey are surprising; others confirm the expectations of observers of the Jewish community. Together, they provide a profile of the contemporary female volunteer.

Who Volunteers Time for Jewish Organizations

Jewish female respondents with one or more of the following characteristics are among those likely to volunteer time for Jewish organizations:

- married or widowed (marital status);
- mothers (family formation);
- living in in-married or conversionary Jewish households, rather than in mixed-married households (in-intermarriage);
- age 44 or under (age);
- working part-time for pay outside the home (labor force participation);
- recipients of an educational degree beyond a B.A. (education).

In-marriage, Mixed Marriage, and Volunteering Time for Jewish Organizations

Perhaps the most startling outcome of the Jewish organizational profile of American women is that mixed marriage—rather than education, occupation, age, presence of children in the home, or any other factor—marks the single greatest difference in levels of female voluntarism for Jewish causes.

Forty percent of all married female respondents in the survey are born Jewish women married to born Jewish men. One-third of these in-married Jewish women say that they volunteer some time for Jewish causes. In contrast, among the 29 percent of married Jewish women who are married to non-Jewish men, levels of voluntarism for Jewish causes are very low: only six percent say they volunteer time for Jewish organizations.

Two percent of the married Jewish female respondents are born Jewish women married to men who have converted into Judaism, and three percent are women who have themselves converted into Judaism. While these cells are too small to make any definitive statements about levels of voluntarism among women in conversionary families, it is worth noting that one-third of Jewish women married to converted men say that they volunteer for Jewish causes, as do half of female converts. Thus, while the cells are very small, the patterns are clear—conversion makes a difference. Jewish women in conversionary households, whether the husband or the wife is the convert, are at least as likely as in-married women (or more likely) to volunteer time for Jewish causes.

Understandably, Jewish organizations are particularly concerned about levels of voluntarism among younger women, who must make up the next generation of volunteers—and younger Jewish women are far more likely to be involved in mixed marriage than are older cohorts. Among married female respondents age 44 and under, 24 percent were born Jewish women married to born Jewish men, two percent were born Jewish women married to men who converted into Judaism, and four percent were women who had themselves converted into Judaism; 38 percent of married born Jewish female respondents age 44 and under were married to non-Jewish men. Younger Jewish women in all-Jewish households (either in-marriages or conversionary marriages) were somewhat more likely to volunteer time than older women; however, in mixed-married households the rate of voluntarism for Jewish causes was equally low for both age groups.

For purposes of comparison, among married Jewish female respondents over age 45, 60 percent are born Jewish women married to born Jewish men, two percent are born Jewish women married to men who converted into Judaism, one percent are themselves converts into Judaism, and 18 percent are born Jewish women married to non-Jewish men. Of married Jewish female respondents over age 45, 29 percent of those married to Jewish men volunteer time for Jewish causes, as do 18 percent of women married to converted men, 48 percent of those who have themselves converted, and five percent of the Jewish women who are married to non-Jewish men.

As seen in Figure 1, the women now most frequently volunteering time for Jewish organizations are married, 44-years-old or younger, living in in-married and conversionary Jewish households. These data suggest that the prevalence of mixed marriage, rather than rising rates of careerism, provides the greatest single challenge to levels of Jewish voluntarism.

FIGURE 1

IN-INTERMARRIAGE AND JEWISH ORGANIZATION

Jewish Female Respondents Who Volunteer Time for Jewish
Organizations, by Religion of Spouse, Weighted Percentages
(Unweighted numbers indicated in parenthesis)

JEWISH WOMEN, BY MARRIAGE TYPE,
WHO DO VOLUNTEER TIME FOR JEWISH CAUSES

CATEGORY	PERCENT	(UNWGT. #)
All Jewish Women		
Jewish women married to born Jewish men	33	(321)
Jewish women married to converted Jewish men	31	(17)
Converted Jewish women married to born Jewish men	52	(26)
Jewish women married to non-Jewish men	6	(216)
By Marriage Type, Age 44 and Under		
Jewish women married to born Jewish men	42	(119)
Jewish women married to converted Jewish men	39	(14)
Converted Jewish women married to born Jewish men	53	(20)
Jewish women married to non-Jewish men	6	(157)
By Marriage Type, Age 45 and Over		
Jewish women married to born Jewish men	29	(200)
Jewish women married to converted Jewish men	18	(3)
Converted Jewish women married to born Jewish men	48	(6)
Jewish women married to non-Jewish men	5	(58)

FIGURE 2

MARITAL STATUS AND JEWISH ORGANIZATIONS

Female Jewish Respondents Who Volunteer Time for
Jewish Organizations, Weighted Percentages
(Unweighted numbers indicated in parentheses)

BY MARITAL STATUS (N = 975)	PERCENT
Never married	16
Married	23
Divorced	16
Widowed	23

Marital Status and Volunteering for Jewish Organizations

Other variables mark more modest—but still significant—differences. Within the rubric of marital status, 23 percent of both married Jewish women and widows volunteer time for Jewish causes, compared to 16 percent of both single Jewish women and divorcees.

Jewish Friendship Circles Make a Difference

Jewish women who do not have predominantly Jewish friendship circles are far less likely to volunteer than those who do. More than half of Jewish female respondents (51 percent) say they have few or some Jewish friends; only seven percent say they have no Jewish friends; and 43 percent say they have mostly Jewish friends.

Jewish women who say that none of their best friends are Jewish almost never volunteer for Jewish causes, although 40 percent of them volunteer for non-Jewish causes. Thirteen percent of Jewish women who have some Jewish friends volunteer for Jewish causes or a combination of Jewish and non-Jewish causes, and 40 percent volunteer for non-Jewish causes only. Among Jewish women who have mostly Jewish friends, however, 35 percent volunteer for Jewish causes or a combination of Jewish and non-Jewish causes, and 19 percent volunteer for non-Jewish causes only.

In the past, popular impressions were that the most traditional Jewish women would be at home with their children and have the most predominantly Jewish friendship circles, while less traditional Jewish women would work outside the home for pay and have more non-Jewish friends, presumably persons they may have met at work. However, data on younger American Jewish women do not bear out these stereotypes. The religious makeup of these friendship circles is not dependent on employment status. Within each of these groups, between half and two-thirds of the women are employed either full-time or part-time for pay. Indeed, labor force status remains relatively similar from volunteer group to volunteer group within each group of friendship circle types. Among women who have no Jewish friends 48 to 55 percent work; among women who have some Jewish friends 61 to 66 percent work; and among women who have mostly Jewish friends 48 to 57 percent work.

Perhaps contrary to expectations, part-time workers have the largest proportion of mostly Jewish friendship circles—50 percent. As might be expected, homemakers as a group have a larger proportion of mostly Jewish friendship circles (48 percent) than do full-time workers (34 percent). However, those homemakers who do not have primarily Jewish friendship circles are subject to the same trends as labor force participants who do not have mostly Jewish friends. For example, 19 percent of homemakers—the largest proportion of homemakers among women with some Jewish friends—is found among those who volunteer for non-Jewish causes only.

Thus, we can assume that factors other than the presence or absence of employment influence both the choice of friendship circles and the decision to volunteer for Jewish or non-Jewish causes.

Even in the youngest family units of the 1990 NJPS—that include

Jewish female respondents who are more likely to have grown up, been schooled, and currently reside in environments which are not densely Jewish—predominantly Jewish friendship circles are strongly associated with volunteering for Jewish causes. Women with mostly Jewish friendship circles make up from two-thirds to more than three-quarters of mothers of young children volunteering for Jewish causes.

Jewish communal leaders are understandably especially concerned about patterns of voluntarism among younger American Jewish women, the mothers of the next generation. It is widely accepted that the predominance of Jewish or non-Jewish friends is associated with age, generation, and life cycle status. Therefore we would expect to see—and do see—somewhat declining rates of all or mostly Jewish friendship circles among younger Jewish female respondents, who have largely been born and raised with access to the fullest opportunities and the least constricted friendship circles offered by the open American society.

Nevertheless, the pattern for Jewish mothers of children ages six and under is that the vast majority of those who volunteer time for Jewish organizations have mostly Jewish friends. The vast majority of those who volunteer time for non-Jewish causes only have few or some Jewish friends. Women who do not have Jewish friends almost never volunteer time for Jewish organizations.

Family Formation and Volunteering for Jewish Organizations

It has long been observed that American Jews are far more likely to affiliate themselves with Jewish organizations and to volunteer time for those organizations after they have children. Some observers have wondered, however, whether this would continue to be the case now that American Jewish women are so heavily involved in the work force. As Figure 3 illustrates, Jewish women with children are still much more likely to volunteer time for Jewish causes than those without children; furthermore, there is very little difference in overall rates of voluntarism among women with children age six and under (26 percent), age 18 and under (25 percent), and those with all children over 19 (27 percent).

When the age of children is combined with possible career demands, however, some suggestive data emerge. Although the cells are too small to make definitive assertions, the data indicate that women working outside the home in high status and inflexible time-demanding professions—such as law, medicine, dentistry, computers, and executive administration positions—are about twice as likely to volunteer time for Jewish organizations after their children are all age 19 or over (43 percent) than they are when their children are very young, age six or under (24 percent) or when

FIGURE 3

Mothers of Children Age Six and Rates of Volunteering/Not
Jewish Female Respondents, Percentages by Friendship Circles
(n = 165)

CATEGORY	PERCENT
Women Volunteering for Jewish Causes Only	
No Jewish Friends	—
Some Jewish Friends	21
Mostly Jewish Friends	79
Women Volunteering for Jewish and Non-Jewish Causes	
No Jewish Friends	—
Some Jewish Friends	36
Mostly Jewish Friends	65
Women Volunteering for Non-Jewish Causes Only	
No Jewish Friends	11
Some Jewish Friends	69
Mostly Jewish Friends	20
Women Not Volunteering At All	
No Jewish Friends	16
Some Jewish Friends	64
Mostly Jewish Friends	19

they have children 18 and under living at home (21 percent). Interestingly, these striking differences do not emerge among women in the helping professions, such as teaching below the college level, nursing, social work, and medium level computer programming, or among women in managerial positions.

We can speculate that Jewish organizations may ask women in the high status professions with older children to volunteer more often than other Jewish women because of their higher incomes and/or professional expertise. We know that Jews who are asked to volunteer have a much higher rate of voluntarism than any other group—and that being asked is in fact the single most important predictor of voluntarism.[5] One might also speculate that the dual stresses of high-power careers and young children effectively take such women out of the volunteer "market" until their children have left home. However, as Table 12.8 showing voluntarism for non-Jewish organizations will indicate later, even high status professional women with children under 18 volunteer more time for non-Jewish than for Jewish organizations. Additional research is needed to discover what makes such voluntarism more attractive to all strata of potential volunteers.

The vast majority of American Jewish women today are labor force

FIGURE 4
FAMILY FORMATION, CAREERS, AND
JEWISH ORGANIZATIONS
*Female Jewish Respondents Who do Volunteer Time for
Jewish Organizations, Weighted Percentages*

CATEGORY	PERCENT
Volunteering for Jewish Causes by Stages of Family Formation:	
By Family Formation	
No Children	14
Children Age 6 and Under	26
Children Age 18 and Under	24
Children Age 19 and Over	27
By Professional Status and Family Formation	
HI-STATUS PROFESSIONS	
No Children	—
Children Age 6 and Under	24
Children Age 18 and Under	21
Children Age 19 and Over	43
HELPING PROFESSIONS	
No Children	—
Children Age 6 and Under	24
Children Age 18 and Under	29
Children Age 19 and Over	31
MANAGERIAL	
No Children	—
Children Age 6 and Under	31
Children Age 18 and Under	32
Children Age 19 and Over	30
CLERICAL, TECHNICAL	
No Children	—
Children Age 6 and Under	20
Children Age 18 and Under	18
Children Age 19 and Over	25

participants, especially those up to age 44. Among all Jewish female respondents, 18 percent define themselves as homemakers, six percent as
students, nine percent say they work part-time, 46 percent say they work
full-time, and 21 percent are unemployed or retired. Significantly, rates of
full-time work far exceed rates of part-time work: among all respondents
age 44 and under, 59 percent said they work full-time, compared to only 11
percent part-time. Observers of the Jewish community often speculate that

the return of Jewish women to a more active, lifelong role in the labor force has a negative impact on the likelihood of Jewish women to volunteer their time for Jewish organizations. Following this line of reasoning, full-time homemakers and unemployed persons should be most likely to volunteer, and full-time labor force participants should be the group least likely to volunteer. When labor force participation is considered independently, part-time workers are the group most likely to volunteer for Jewish causes (32 percent), rather than homemakers (21 percent), students (13 percent), full-time workers (18 percent), or the unemployed (27 percent).

Among women under age 45, homemakers are somewhat more likely (29 percent) to volunteer time for Jewish causes than part-time workers (24 percent) and unemployed or retired persons (23 percent), and much more likely to volunteer for Jewish causes than either students or full-time workers. However, among women over age 45, part-time workers are by far the most likely to volunteer (45 percent), followed by unemployed or retired persons (27 percent).

When labor force participation is cross-tabulated with marital status, part-time workers continue to show the highest proportion of voluntarism for Jewish causes. Among the 367 married Jewish women interviewed, 21 percent of the homemakers, 19 percent of the students, 36 percent of the women working part-time outside the home, 18 percent of those working full-time outside the home, and 29 percent of the unemployed or retired report volunteering time for Jewish causes. Thus, well over one-third of married Jewish women who work part-time are volunteers, substantially greater than any other marital status category.

The Educational Profile of Jewish Female and Male Volunteers

Contemporary American Jewish women enjoy levels of secular education which are probably unmatched by Jewish women at any other time in history. Among the Jewish female respondents sampled, 22 percent had an educational level which did not go beyond high school, 23 percent had attended college or completed a two-year degree such as A.A., 30 percent had completed their B.A., and 24 percent had higher degrees—17 percent had a Master's degree or the equivalent, and seven percent had advanced degrees such as Ph.D., M.D., D.Ds., J.D., or the equivalent. Thus, the Jewish female respondent sample divides roughly into four groups: high school only, some college, finished college, and post-baccalaureate degrees, with the largest single group having completed a college degree.

Contrary to popular impressions that higher education for Jewish women is antithetical to voluntarism for Jewish causes, women with post-baccalaureate degrees are more likely than those with college alone to

FIGURE 5
**LABOR FORCE PARTICIPATION AND
JEWISH ORGANIZATIONS**
*Female Jewish Respondents Who Volunteer Time for
Jewish Organizations, Weighted Percentages*

CATEGORY	PERCENT
Homemaker	21
Student	13
Part-time worker	32
Full-time worker	18
Unemployed	27
Under Age 45	
Homemaker	29
Student	13
Part-time worker	24
Full-time worker	18
Unemployed	23
Over Age 45	
Homemaker	13
Student	★
Part-time worker	45
Full-time worker	18
Unemployed	27
Married Jewish Women, By Labor Force Participation	
Homemaker	21
Student	19
Part-time worker	36
Full-time worker	18
Unemployed	29

★ = Cell too small to include (n = 4)

volunteer time for Jewish causes. The group of Jewish women least likely to volunteer has never attended college; this is true of Jewish men as well as Jewish women. Yet Jewish women are much more likely to volunteer time for Jewish causes than Jewish men. Indeed, among those respondents with higher educational attainments, the discrepancy between men and women becomes more pronounced. Thus, women who have earned a Bachelor's or a higher degree are about 10 percent more likely than similar men to volunteer time for Jewish causes.

Comparing Voluntarism for Jewish and Non-Jewish Organizations

One of the most striking findings to emerge from the data on voluntarism among Jewish women in the 1990 NJPS is that many female Jewish re-

TABLE 12.7

Rates of Volunteering for Jewish Causes Female and Male Jewish Respondents by Highest Grades and Degrees Attained, Weighted Percentages

HIGHEST GRADE	JEWISH FEMALES VOLUNTEERING	JEWISH MALES VOLUNTEERING
High School or under	15%	11%
Attended college	22%	14%
Bachelor's degree	23%	13%
Master's degree*	27%	18%
Ph.D., Dr., D.D., Atty.	27%	19%

*includes nursing degree

spondents (who were born Jewish or currently consider themselves to be Jews) are more likely to volunteer for non-Jewish causes than for Jewish causes. This contradicts the findings for decades, in most city-based Jewish population studies, which showed that Jews were more likely to volunteer time for Jewish causes than non-Jewish causes.[6] The recent excellent analysis of "Jewish Women's Involvement in the Community's Organizational Structure" among Rhode Island Jewish women (A. Goldstein, *Contemporary Jewry* 11, No. 1, Spring 1990: 49–75), for example, notes that "involvement in non-Jewish activities does not substitute for involvement in Jewish activities" and that Jewish women are "more involved in the Jewish community than they are in the non-Jewish one."

These new data suggest an important and widespread shift in behavior which crosses almost all categorical lines. Among married Jewish female respondents, for example, 23 percent volunteered time for Jewish causes, compared to 41 percent for non-Jewish causes. The discrepancy was even more marked among younger women: among married Jewish women age 44 and under, 23 percent volunteered for Jewish causes and 46 percent for non-Jewish causes. Among both single and divorced Jewish women, only 16 percent volunteered for Jewish causes, compared to 47 percent of singles and 37 percent of divorced who volunteered for non-Jewish causes. Only widows are almost equally likely to work for Jewish causes (23 percent) as for non-Jewish causes (24 percent).

It is especially significant that even women with very low rates of Jewish voluntarism for Jewish causes, such as women who work full-time outside the home, have substantial rates of voluntarism for non-Jewish causes: only 18 percent of them volunteer for Jewish causes versus 43 percent for non-Jewish causes. Similarly, among women with high-status professions and children 18 or under living in the household, only 21 percent volunteered time for Jewish causes, compared to 49 percent for non-Jewish causes. Among women with high-status professions and older children (19 and over), all voluntarism was higher, with 43 percent volunteering for Jewish causes, compared to 60 percent for non-Jewish causes. Only 14 percent of respondents with no children volunteered for Jewish causes, compared to 44 percent for non-Jewish causes. As can be seen in the educational data, which compare rates of voluntarism for Jewish and

TABLE 12.8

Voluntarism for Jewish and Non-Jewish Causes
Jewish Female Respondents, Weighted Percentages

Category		Volunteer for	
		Jewish Causes	Non-Jewish Causes
Married		23%	41%
Under age 45		23%	46%
Over age 45		24%	36%
Never-married		16%	47%
Divorced		16%	37%
Widowed		23%	24%
No children born	(n = 240)	14%	44%
Children 6 and under	(n = 164)	22%	48%
Children 18 and under	(n = 304)	24%	46%
Children 19 and over	(n = 328)	27%	33%
Homemakers	(n = 161)	21%	41%
Under age 45	(n = 80)	29%	49%
Over age 45	(n = 79)	13%	32%
Students	(n = 52)	13%	54%
Work Part-time	(n = 102)	32%	39%
Under age 45	(n = 62)	24%	43%
Over age 45	(n = 40)	45%	32%
Work Full-time	(n = 474)	18%	43%
Under age 45	(n = 309)	18%	45%
Over age 45	(n = 164)	18%	39%
Unemployed	(n = 198)	27%	30%
Percentages of Jewish Women Volunteering by Educational Level			
High School or under	(n = 217)	15%	23%
Attended college	(n = 231)	22%	39%
Bachelor's degree	(n = 291)	23%	47%
Master's degree★	(n = 164)	27%	57%
Ph.D., Dr., DDs., Atty.	(n = 69)	27%	44%
Percentages of Jewish Men Volunteering by Educational Level			
High School or under	(n = 104)	11%	20%
Attended college	(n = 200)	14%	43%
Bachelor's degree	(n = 347)	13%	49%
Master's degree★	(n = 149)	18%	48%
Ph.D., Dr., DDs., J.D.	(n = 145)	19%	47%

★ Includes nursing degree

non-Jewish causes among female and male Jewish respondents, men and women exhibit a similar likelihood to volunteer for non-Jewish rather than Jewish causes. As has been previously noted, women as a group are somewhat more likely than men to volunteer time for Jewish organizations.

Were it not for the comparatively high rates of voluntarism for non-Jewish causes among many groups of Jewish women, the temptation would be to "excuse" low rates of voluntarism for Jewish causes as a result of the stresses created by lack of time or professional responsibilities. However, given the fact that among all groups, except for widows and/or older women, rates of voluntarism are substantially higher for non-Jewish causes than Jewish causes, time constraints alone cannot explain low rates of Jewish voluntarism. Clearly, further research, including qualitative research, is needed to determine the factors drawing comparatively low proportions of younger, highly educated, professionally active Jewish women into voluntarism for Jewish causes.

Once again, marriage between Jews is associated with Jewish voluntarism: among all female respondents (including those who were and were not born Jewish and those who currently did and did not consider themselves to be Jewish) in in-married or conversionary households, 34 percent volunteered for Jewish causes and 35 percent for non-Jewish causes; among female respondents in mixed-married households, however, only six percent volunteered for Jewish causes, compared to 51 percent for non-Jewish causes. This phenomenon persisted even when only female respondents age 44 and under were considered: among women in this age group who are in in-married and conversionary households, 44 percent volunteered for Jewish and 42 percent for non-Jewish causes; among those living in mixed-married households, only six percent volunteered for Jewish causes, compared to 51 percent for non-Jewish causes.

Female respondents age 44 and under living in in-married or conversionary Jewish households were the group most likely to volunteer for Jewish causes, and they were at least as likely to volunteer for Jewish causes as for non-Jewish causes.

Women Who Live in Households Affiliated with Synagogues

Synagogue membership, somewhat like Jewish organizational involvement, is most common among Jewish female respondents who fall into the following four categories: married, mothers, live in in-married or conversionary households, and part-time workers. With the exception of labor force participation, these categories are consistent with previous patterns

FIGURE 6
WOMEN WHO LIVE IN HOUSEHOLDS
WHICH BELONG TO SYNAGOGUES
Female Jewish Respondents, Weighted Percentages

CATEGORY	PERCENT
By Marital Status	
Never married	35
Married	40
Divorced	30
Widowed	37
By Family Formation	
No Children	26
Children under 18	45
Children over 19	44
By Marriage Type (includes all female respondents)	
In-married and Conversionary Jewish	57
Mixed Marriage	15
By Labor Force Participation	
Homemaker	43
Student	45
Part-time worker	48
Full-time worker	34
Unemployed	36
Under Age 45	
Homemaker	33
Student	46
Part-time worker	40
Full-time worker	31
Unemployed	29
Over Age 45	
Homemaker	52
Student*	—
Part-time worker	62
Full-time worker	40
Unemployed	37

*Cell too small to include

of affiliation among American Jews. Today, as in the past, women are most likely to join synagogues when they marry, establish Jewish homes, and have children. The prevalence of women who work part-time outside the home among synagogue members is probably due to two factors: first, married Jewish mothers as a group include a large proportion of women who are part-time labor force participants; second, the extra income provided by such work can ease the financial burdens of membership, while the limited number of hours imposed by part-time work enhances the possibility of Jewish activities.

Levels of affiliation with synagogues are, in general, considerably higher than affiliation with other Jewish organizations and institutions. Among

FIGURE 7

WHO BELONGS TO JEWISH ORGANIZATIONS
Female Jewish Respondents, Weighted Percentages

CATEGORY	PERCENT
By Marital Status	
Never married	21
Married	34
Divorced	34
Widowed	46
By Family Formation	
No Children	20
Children under 18	28
Children over 19	47
By Marriage Type	
In-married and conversionary Jewish	49
Mixed-married	13
By Labor Force Participation	
Homemaker	36
Student	23
Part-time worker	40
Full-time worker	26
Unemployed	46
Under age 45	
Homemaker	30
Student	23
Part-time worker	32
Full-time worker	22
Unemployed	44
Over age 45	
Homemaker	41
Student*	
Part-time worker	56
Full-time worker	36
Unemployed	46

* = Cell too small to include

married Jewish women, for example, 40 percent live in households which are affiliated with synagogues, compared to 34 percent who belong to another kind of Jewish organization. This pattern is, however, contradicted by widows: 37 percent of widows belong to synagogues, but 46 percent belong to other Jewish organizations.

Women Who Belong to Jewish Organizations

Belonging to Jewish organizations is a different, and in some ways a simpler issue than volunteering time or leading them. Jewish organizational members are more likely to be widowed, older, or unemployed, and to have children over age 18, than are women who volunteer or lead Jewish organizations. Almost half of Jewish widows (47 percent), married women in in-married or conversionary Jewish households (49 percent), unemployed women (46 percent), and mothers of children over 19 (47 percent) belong to Jewish organizations, as do about one-third of Jewish women who are married (34 percent), divorced (34 percent), and homemakers (36 percent). The groups of women least likely to belong to Jewish organizations are those living in mixed-married households (13 percent), never married (21 percent), and students (23 percent).

In an attempt to increase organizational affiliation levels among Jewish women, it would be very useful to know the current reasons women join organizations, their expectations, and the degree to which their expectations are being met. For example, among several areas which call for further research, women who define themselves as "unemployed" are substantially more likely to belong to Jewish organizations than women who define themselves as "homemakers." This is true of the age 44 and under group as well as the overall group of Jewish women. One out of every five Jewish female respondents sampled is unemployed (a projected 474,460 Jewish women), representing 18 percent of married, 19 percent of divorced, and 62 percent of widowed Jewish women. Are these women joining Jewish organizations with the idea of networking, leading to employment possibilities? If so, are these expectations being met?

Women Who Hold Leadership Positions
in Jewish Organizations

Even more crucial for the vitality of Jewish organizations than simple issues of affiliation are issues surrounding activism and leadership. A partial sample (module) of respondents was asked whether they had served in a leadership capacity for any Jewish organizations in the two years prior to the survey. Women who fall into one or more of the following categories are most likely to serve in leadership positions for Jewish causes: in-married or conversionary women, mothers to children under 18, women who work full-time, those who have a B.A. or Master's degree, mothers to children 19 or older, volunteers for Jewish organizations, and those who live in a household which belongs to a synagogue.

Although the cells in this section are rather small, due to the fact that information was collected through a module rather than from a complete sample, the data are highly suggestive. It should be noted that leaders, unlike volunteers, are more likely to be working full-time rather than part-time. It may be that leadership roles are more attractive to full-time workers than is simple volunteering. More than half of the women who volunteered time for Jewish causes also said they had served in a leadership capacity (indeed, rates of leadership reported in the most active groups in the module are about the same, and sometimes higher, than rates of volun-tarism reported in those same groups in the full sample).

We can speculate that unlike volunteers of the past, who were more content to rise slowly up the ranks through a progression of tasks, gradu-ally acquiring more responsibility and power, today's highly educated vol-unteers, most of whom have been labor force participants, are more likely to keep on volunteering if they have access to volunteer roles which are commensurate with their roles in the outside world. Given the high pro-portion of such women who do volunteer time for non-Jewish organiza-tions, it is well to keep in mind that such a woman has other options for her limited volunteer time. It is important for opportunities in Jewish volun-teering to be as attractive as possible. For today's Jewish woman, attractive voluntarism opportunities often imply access to decision-making, public prominence, and power.

The married mother with two children, aged nine and thirteen, who works part-time outside the home doing legal research, for example, is not likely to be attracted to a morning demonstration of kosher gourmet cook-ing or an evening session stuffing envelopes for an upcoming meeting, no matter how worthy the cause. If, however, she is asked to do legal research determining the feasibility of a public rally in support of Soviet Jewry, she may very well agree. The currently unemployed mother of two children under age six, formerly an advertising executive, may be uninterested in a rummage sale for the synagogue. The same woman may, however, enthu-siastically plan and supervise a telethon for her synagogue afternoon Hebrew school. A gastroenterologist whose last child has entered college may be quite willing to deliver a fascinating series of lectures on diseases which are prevalent in the Jewish community as part of a fundraiser for a Jewish hospital.

TABLE 12.9

WOMEN WHO HAVE HELD LEADERSHIP POSITIONS IN
JEWISH ORGANIZATIONS
Women Who Have Served in Leadership Capacities, Last 2 Years
Sample Module Only: Female Jewish Respondents, Weighted
Percentages (Unweighted numbers indicated in parenthesis)

Percentage of Each Group Holding Leadership Roles

By Marital Status

Never married	17%	(n = 26)
Married	28%	(n = 109)
Divorced	11%	(n = 15)
Widowed	22%	(n = 26)

By Age Group

Ages 44 and under	28%	(n = 78)
Ages 45 and over	23%	(n = 96)
Ages 18 to 24	14%	(n = 14)
Ages 25 to 34	31%	(n = 26)
Ages 35 to 44	32%	(n = 22)
Ages 45 to 54	19%	(n = 31)
Ages 55 to 64	21%	(n = 16)
Ages 65 or over	27%	(n = 37)

By Family Formation

No children	19%	(n = 30)
Children 18 or under	27%	(n = 55)
Children 19 or over	25%	(n = 79)

By Marriage Type

In-married and conversionary Jewish	30%	(n = 97)
Mixed-married	4%	(n = 12)
Two born Jews	27%	(n = 84)
Woman born Jew, man Jew by choice	40%	(n = 5)
Woman Jew by choice	57%	(n = 7)
Woman born Jew, man not Jewish	8%	(n = 12)

By Labor Force Participation

Homemakers	15%	(n = 33)
Students	25%	(n = 10)
Part-time workers	29%	(n = 25)
Full-time workers	18%	(n = 72)
Unemployed	40%	(n = 37)

By Education

High school or under	15%	(n = 39)
Some college	24%	(n = 37)
Finished college	23%	(n = 60)
Master's degree	45%	(n = 31)
Ph.D., professional degree	25%	(n = 8)

TABLE 12.10
WOMEN WHO ARE THE LEADERS OF
JEWISH ORGANIZATIONS
Characteristics of Jewish Female Respondents Who Lead Jewish Organizations, Percentages of Leaders Answering "Yes" to Indicated Variables (n = 45)

Currently volunteer for Jewish organization	87%
Currently don't volunteer for Jewish organization	11%
Have led non-Jewish organization past 2 years	51%
Haven't led non-Jewish organization past 2 years	49%
Age 44 and under	50%
Age 45 and over	50%
Married	69%
Never married	9%
Divorced	9%
Widowed	13%
No children	12%
Children 18 or under	39%
Children 19 or over	49%
High school or under	13%
Attended college	20%
B.A.	31%
M.A., etc.	31%
Ph.D., etc.	4%
High-status profession	13%
Helping profession	22%
Managerial	33%
Clerical/technical	31%
Homemaker	13%
Student	2%
Part-time worker	20%
Full-time worker	36%
Unemployed/retired	29%
Two born Jews	77%
Woman born Jew, man Jew by choice	7%
Woman Jew by choice	14%
Woman born Jew, man not Jewish	3%
Household synagogue members	89%
Household not synagogue members	11%
Never visited Israel	53%
Visited Israel once	24%
Visited Israel twice	7%
Visited Israel three times	2%
Visited Israel four or more times	13%

Significantly, women who said that they had served as leaders of non-Jewish organizations during the past two years also were more likely than those who had not served in such capacities to provide leadership for Jewish organizations. Thus, 30 percent of women who lead non-Jewish organizations also lead Jewish organizations, compared to 22 percent of women who do not lead non-Jewish organizations. Leadership may thus be a mutually reinforcing activity as voluntarism itself is. Jewish organizations do not need to make leadership of non-Jewish organizations unattractive, but to make Jewish leadership more attractive, in order to take advantage of the abilities of today's Jewish women.

In general, competent women who are fighting their way up occupational ladders may find it unpalatable to join and devote free hours to Jewish organizations in order to be told that the "Young Leadership Cabinet" is limited to men. As the profile of women serving in leadership capacities in Jewish organizations indicates, today's Jewish women are at least as willing to serve as leaders as they are to volunteer time for Jewish organizations. Indeed, learning how to provide such women with leadership opportunities and training them for these roles may be one of the outstanding challenges facing contemporary American Jewish organizations.

Not surprisingly, the vast majority of leaders of Jewish organizations said their households were affiliated with synagogues. More surprisingly, however, is the fact that more than half of female Jewish leaders have never visited Israel. One out of four female leaders have been to Israel once. A smaller, but no doubt highly involved minority—13 percent—have visited Israel four or more times.

Among the Study's Major Findings

* Jewish women who are married to non-Jewish men have drastically lower rates of voluntarism for Jewish causes than other married Jewish women: only six percent of women who were born Jewish and are married to non-Jewish men volunteer any time for Jewish causes—compared to one-third of Jewish women married to Jewish men (either born Jews or converts), and over half of the women who are themselves Jews by choice.
* Jewish women who do not have predominantly Jewish friendship circles are far less likely to volunteer than those who do. Those who say that none of their best friends are Jewish almost never volunteer for Jewish causes, although 40 percent of them volunteer for non-Jewish causes. Thirteen percent of Jewish women who have some Jewish friends volun-

teer for Jewish causes, and 40 percent volunteer for non-Jewish causes only. Among Jewish women who have mostly Jewish friends, however, 35 percent volunteer for Jewish causes and 19 percent volunteer exclusively for non-Jewish causes. (These friendship circles do not seem to be employment-related: within each of these groups, between half and two-thirds of the women are employed for pay outside the home.)

- Jewish women who hold post-baccalaureate degrees are proportionately more likely to volunteer for Jewish organizations than those who do not; similarly, Jewish women who have completed college are more likely to volunteer than those who have not. More education, in general, seems to mean more voluntarism for Jewish causes.
- Synagogue attendance among Jewish women is strongly associated with volunteering behavior. Half of Jewish women who attend synagogue services frequently also volunteer time for Jewish causes or a combination of Jewish and non-Jewish causes; only 12 percent of them volunteer exclusively for non-Jewish causes, and 18 percent do not volunteer at all. The picture of Jewish women who rarely attend synagogue services is almost the reverse of this pattern. Among Jewish women who never attend synagogue services, the negative picture is even more dramatic: fewer than five percent volunteer any time for Jewish causes, while 28 percent volunteer for non-Jewish causes only, and 24 percent do not volunteer at all.
- Jewish women who are synagogue members are twice as likely to volunteer for Jewish causes as those who are not. Two-thirds of women who volunteer for Jewish causes only are synagogue members, as are more than three-quarters of the women who volunteer for both Jewish and non-Jewish causes. Conversely, three-quarters of women who volunteer exclusively for non-Jewish causes are not synagogue members, and two-thirds of women who do not volunteer at all are also not synagogue members.
- Jewish women are more likely to volunteer time for Jewish causes than Jewish men. This is true of Jewish men and women on every educational level: 27 percent of Jewish women with M.A.s and Ph.D.s volunteer for Jewish causes, for example, compared to 18–19 percent of Jewish men with similar degrees. Among both men and women, Jews with higher levels of education are more likely to volunteer.
- Voluntarism for non-Jewish causes is more widespread among Jewish women than voluntarism for Jewish causes. Never-married Jewish women and students are much more likely to volunteer for non-Jewish causes than for Jewish causes. Moreover, even among more "settled" and/or older groups of Jewish women voluntarism for Jewish causes lags behind non-Jewish causes. Only part-time workers and women with

children age 19 and over are almost as likely to volunteer for Jewish as for non-Jewish causes.

- Women who work part-time are more likely than homemakers, full-time workers, unemployed or retired persons to live in households which belong to synagogues. The greater likelihood of the part-time worker to live in a synagogue affiliated household holds true across age lines, with 62 percent of part-time workers age 45 and over belonging to synagogues.
- The greatest differences in household synagogue membership are found between all Jewish households (born Jews and Jews by choice) and mixed-married households. Fifty-seven percent of women in all-Jewish households say the family has a synagogue membership, compared to only 15 percent of mixed-married households.
- Women who have children, no matter what age, are almost twice as likely as women without children to live in households which hold synagogue membership. Twenty-six percent of women without children live in households which belong to synagogues, compared to 45 percent of women with children ages 18 and under, and 44 percent of women with children ages 19 and over.
- Women who belong to Jewish organizations have a somewhat different profile than women who volunteer time for them. Although part-time workers are a significant population among both members and volunteers, members as compared to volunteers are more likely to be older, widowed, unemployed, or retired, and have children ages 19 or over.
- About half of the women who serve in leadership roles in Jewish organizations have also served in leadership capacities in non-Jewish organizations during the past two years. Two-thirds of them hold Bachelor's or Master's degrees.

Conclusion

Despite extraordinary changes in their life-styles, the willingness of American Jewish women to donate their time and energy for communal causes is still striking. Indeed, women with the highest levels of secular education, and women who work outside the home for pay and also have children, are among the most active in communal voluntarism.

However, the data make clear that American Jewish women no longer automatically choose the world of Jewish communal service for their volunteer activities. Large proportions of Jewish women volunteer time and serve in leadership capacities for non-Jewish causes and institutions. From the vantage point of Jewish communal life, a disturbingly large number of Jewish respondents under age 45 choose to volunteer only for non-Jewish causes.

The data do not reveal why Jewish voluntarism for non-Jewish causes is now greater than for Jewish causes, although it is certainly easy to speculate on what some of the reasons might be. Anecdotal evidence indicates that non-Jewish causes may be perceived as more conducive to professional networking activities, allowing women to further their careers while doing pro bono work for the community. It also indicates that many people have experienced greater emotional rewards in volunteering for the non-Jewish world. As one person put it: "If I give $1000 to the Girl Scouts I'm a heroine and people carry me around on their shoulders. If I give $1000 to my local Jewish Federation I barely merit a form thank-you letter."

It may also be true that for a large portion of the community, voluntarism for non-sectarian causes carries with it greater prestige, if for no other reason than that non-sectarian causes are more visible to the entire community. Thus, participating in a Federation "Super Sunday" phone-a-thon may be an enjoyable and very worthwhile experience, but volunteers do not appear on television like the Public Television phone-a-thon volunteers. And not least, American Jews are surely asked to participate in non-sectarian activities more often than they are asked to participate in Jewish activities. If one's name is in the phone book, one can be asked to volunteer for any cause, while Jewish causes depend on people whose names are already on affiliation lists.

Many of these factors are irrevocable aspects of American life. However, it is clear that further research is needed to determine which factors pulling people into non-Jewish voluntarism are actually tractable and can be changed. The 1990 NJPS data give a strong base from which to work, but new, targeted research is crucial in order to meet the challenge of creating a viable base of volunteers in the face of new life-styles and opportunities.

The data also indicate a strong association between broad-based Jewish involvements and Jewish voluntarism. Indeed, the more one works with the data, the clearer it becomes that for most younger American Jews, Jewish communal activism and religious or cultural Jewish activities often go together. The dense secularist Jewish socialist or Zionist neighborhoods which once produced Jews with a strong Jewish consciousness but little religious fervor no longer exist. The survey data tell us that American Jews between the ages of 18 and 44 who work for Jewish causes once thought of as "secular" are overwhelmingly likely to belong to synagogues and to have predominantly Jewish friendship circles and Jewish spouses (born Jews or Jews by choice). Anecdotal data tell us that these younger Jewish communal leaders often describe themselves as looking to the Jewish world for a sense of "community" and "spirituality."

Unlike older Jewish women, increased secular education and occupational opportunity among women ages 18 to 44 does not go hand in hand with increased assimilation. Highly educated, highly achieving young women are more, not less, likely to work for Jewish causes than their less educated and ambitious sisters. The intensity of Jewish social, cultural, and religious involvement is key to Jewish communal activism among Jewish women in the 18 to 44 age group. The long-range lesson to the Jewish communal world seems clear. Concern about increased education and careerism among women is misplaced, at least as regards Jewish communal activism. Instead, if American Jews wish to create the Jewish volunteers of tomorrow, it is necessary to strengthen the core of Jewish life today.

Notes

1. The author gratefully acknowledges the contributions of graduate research assistants Gila Diamond Shusterman and Miriam Hertz, who worked with the 1990 National Jewish Population Survey data sets, and Elizabeth Brandwein and Raquel Kosowski, who provided patient and diligent research assistance with a broad variety of research and clerical tasks.

2. The raw numbers responding to individual questions vary somewhat; these respondents are representative of approximately 2,315,000 Jewish women in the weighted population percentages. Household weighting was used throughout. Wherever percentages are given, numbers are rounded; as a result, totals may be slightly under or over 100 percent.

3. Some of these materials are explored in a different context in the author's book *A Breath of Life: Feminism in the American Jewish Community* (New York: Free Press/A Division of Macmillian, 1993). A more extensive examination of these issues can be found in *Changing Lifestyles of American Jewish Women and Men* (Albany: SUNY Press, forthcoming).

4. See especially Jenna Weissman Joselit, "The Special Sphere of the Middle-Class American Jewish Woman: The Synagogue Sisterhood, 1880–1940," in *The American Synagogue: A Sanctuary Transformed*, ed. Jack Wertheimer, New York, Cambridge University Press, 1987, pp. 206–230, for a discussion of the similar role which sisterhood activism played in all wings of American Judaism and an excellent bibliography; and Paula Hyman, "The Volunteer Organizations: Vanguard or Rearguard," in *Lilith*, 5 (1978), for an analysis of Jewish women's organizations in general.

5. G. Berger, *Voluntarism Among American Jews*, Brandeis University Cohen Center for Modern Jewish Studies Research Report, 1990.

6. There are only a few notable exceptions to this pattern, such as Tobin, Gary, *Bay Area Jewish Community Study: Philanthropy and Voluntarism*, 1988.

13

Helping Jewish Dual-Career Families Relieve the Overload

Rela Mintz Geffen

For younger Jewish women, labor force participation will not have any major impact on family size. To the extent that we can generalize further, the data imply that there is no conspicuous work-family role conflict for Jewish women.

(Goldscheider, 1986, p. 103)

Trying to make shabbas *and* yom tov *and have the family for each, continue to pursue a career, and keep a reasonably decent home without household help is difficult even with a supportive family. The community is only supportive in theory.*

Respondent, Jewish Women On The Way Up

Must-can-women now meet a standard of perfection in the work place set in the past by and for men who had wives to take care of all the details of living and—at the same time—meet a standard of performance at home and as mothers that was set in the past by women whose whole sense of worth, power and mastery had to come from being perfect, all-controlling housewives and mothers?

Betty Friedan, *The Second Stage* (p. 80)

The focus of this study is an analysis of role conflict and its potential resolution. The role conflict referred to is that of contemporary Jewish women who wish to combine careers with marriage and parenting during a transition generation. The potential resolution for them may be in the hands of the organized Jewish community. At the same time, the resolution of some of the dilemmas currently facing the American Jewish community may well be in the hands of these same women. Through an analysis of data from the National Jewish Population Survey (NJPS) of 1990 we shall first document the structural strains inherent in the situation of many Jewish career women and then suggest some policy implications for the organized Jewish community. For these women, Jewish identity has little effect on employment status, but does employment status have an effect on their Jewish identification? And how is this related, in turn, to their marital status? The intricate interaction of career, family, and Jewish identification and identity for today's employed Jewish women is at the heart of this analysis.

Who Are the Respondents?

The 526 women in this study are those who responded to the 1990 NJPS who, in 1989, were between the ages of 21 and 64, reported that they were employed, and were defined as Jewish. From time to time, they will be compared to the 175 Jewish women from the survey who are of like ages but who were not then employed outside the home for pay.

A combination of responses was utilized to define who would be considered Jewish for the purpose of this analysis. Any woman who was born Jewish and reported that she was currently Jewish by religion or ethnicity ("just Jewish" or "secular" or "agnostic"), and any woman who reported that she was not born Jewish but was currently Jewish "by religion" was considered Jewish. Thus, a sociological rather than a *halakhic* definition of membership in the community was used. For instance, even if a woman who was not born Jewish but who claimed to be Jewish now did not report undergoing formal conversion, she was included in the "Now Jewish" group.

The definition of employment included those who worked part-time as long as they defined themselves as employed. In fact, it is crucial to include women who are employed part-time in a study of role conflicts surrounding career, marriage, and parenting. If a woman thinks of herself as on a career track, then a short hiatus in employment, or even a more extended period of time during which she works part-time, does not remove her from the potential for severe role strain. On the contrary, part-time work is a coping mechanism fairly commonly employed by Jewish women who find themselves under stress because of role conflict.

The core Jewish population in the NJPS has a balanced sex ratio within an older population structure than the total population of the study. It is estimated that 1.5 million two-earner households are found in the total population of the NJPS (*Highlights*, 1991). Within the core Jewish population, the secular Jews are younger, more likely to be single, and a large proportion are students and employed women. Fifty-three percent of the female "Jews by Religion" and 64 percent of the secular Jewish women are currently employed. Just two percent of the women who consider themselves Jews by religion, and four percent of the secular women define themselves as unemployed. (Apparently the status of retired has greater value than that of homemaker. Therefore, currently unemployed older women who had worked at any time outside the home for pay tended to define themselves as retired.) The remaining 45 percent of the women who are Jewish by religion are split between: homemakers (18 percent), retirees (17 percent), students (seven percent), and disabled (two percent). Among the remaining 32 percent of secular women, 13 percent designated themselves as homemakers, seven percent as retired, 11 percent as students and two percent as disabled. The younger age structure of the secular women is reflected in this distribution. Clearly the overall trend among Jewish women is toward higher employment levels; fewer women define their primary status as homemakers. In fact, the proportion of currently employed Jewish women is nearing that of Jewish men. Among the Jews by religion 53 percent of the women and 68 percent of the men, and among the secular Jews 64 percent of the women and 73 percent of the men, are currently employed.

Education, Occupation, and Work Patterns

Jewish women are the most highly educated women in the United States. Of those under age 45 who say they are Jewish by religion, 85 percent have had at least some college education, 30 percent have Bachelors degrees, and 37 percent have graduate degrees. The comparable figures for women in the United States' white population are 11 percent with Bachelors degrees and six percent with any post-graduate studies. As one would expect (though it was not necessarily so in the past for women or minorities) these high educational levels are significantly related to occupational status (Table 13.1).

Nearly half (49 percent) of the employed Jewish women are in professional or managerial occupations. If those coded as semi-professional, such as teachers, nurses and others in the health professions are included, that figure rises to nearly two-thirds (63 percent) of the core Jewish population (Table 13.2).

Nearly one-fourth of employed Jewish women work under 30 hours a week (Table 13.3). This is a common strategy for those with young children—a "Mommy Track" for those juggling career and family. Table 13.4 reveals a significant relationship between the number of hours in the work week and the number of children the employed women have already had, thus confirming the existence of such a track. Nearly half of the employed women with two or more children work fewer than 40 hours a week. On the other hand, 54 percent of the women with two and 50 percent of those with three or more children work 40 or more hours a week.

For singles who have never been married, occupational status is significantly related to the number of hours they work, but the expected relationship between occupational status and hours worked does not operate for

TABLE 13.1

Occupational Status by Level of Educational Attainment of Employed Women (in percentages)

	EDUCATIONAL ATTAINMENT				
	HIGH SCHOOL	SOME COLLEGE	BA	MA	OTHER GRADUATE DEGREES
Occupational Status					
Professional	9	18	33	46	55
Managerial & Business	21	24	16	17	12
Semi-Professional	6	13	17	27	10
Sales	10	11	13	3	12
Clerical	39	26	14	5	4
Other	15	8	7	2	6
	26% (N = 135)	7% (N = 38)	34% (N = 176)	23% (N = 117)	10% (N = 49)

$X2 = 137.2$ Degrees of Freedom $= 20$ $p < .00000$. This means that there is less than one chance in ten thousand that the distribution in this table could have occurred by chance.

TABLE 13.2

Occupations of Currently Employed Jewish Women (in percentages)

Occupational Categories	
Professional	31
Managerial	18
Semi-Professional	15
Sales	9
Clerical	19
Other	8
	(N = 525)

TABLE 13.3

Number of Hours in Working Week Reported by
Currently Employed Jewish Women
(in percentages)

Number of Hours Per Working Week	
Under 30 hours	23
30–39 hours	17
40 hours	38
Over 40 hours	22
	(N = 525)

TABLE 13.4

Number of Hours in Work Week of Currently
Employed Jewish Women by Actual Number of
Children (in percentages)

	NUMBER OF CHILDREN			
	NONE	ONE	TWO	THREE OR MORE
Weekly Hours Worked				
Under 30	10	32	33	29
30–39 hours	14	17	19	21
40 hours	44	39	31	33
Over 40 Hours	32	12	17	18
N =	(201)	(89)	(156)	(80)

X = 49.97   df = 9, p < .00000

professional and managerial Jewish women. Perhaps for married or divorced women occupation is not related to the number of hours worked
because their parental status is more salient for them than career advance-
ment. In short, the number of hours worked is more related to the presence or absence of other social roles than to the type of occupation in which
a woman is employed.

Occupation and Fertility

For single and divorced Jewish women, whether currently employed or
not, there is no significant relationship between occupational status and the
number of children they expect to give birth to in their life. On the other
hand, employed married women do have lower completed fertility expectations than those who are currently unemployed. The most striking finding

from Table 13.5 is that 27 percent of the employed, single women do not expect to have any children. While this figure is actually on the low side for American career women generally, within the Jewish community it is quite high. Of course some of these women are young and their childbearing expectations may alter with changes in their age and/or marital status.

In contrast to the longer term expectations for completed fertility (which were lower for employed than unemployed married women), a look at a more short-term perspective, specifically, expectations of childbearing within the next three years, reveals no significant relationship between employment status and expected fertility for either single, divorced, or currently married women. Contrary to the general literature on American career women, there is not a significant relationship between the occupational status and the expected number of children for these employed Jewish women.

About three-fourths of professional and managerial women want to have at least two, and about one-fourth expect to have three or more children. This sets up the conditions of role conflict and resulting stress which define the "superwoman" syndrome. Analysis of the dilemmas which beset dual-career families can shed light on issues faced by those in dual earner, single parent, empty-nest, and even those in one-person households. The issues come most sharply into focus, however, in the households of the employed Jewish career women, who are the focus of this analysis.

Dilemmas of Dual Career Families

Perhaps the most profound familial factor affecting Jewish communal life today is the general realignment of the roles of men and women as reflected in intact families with children. These families, which appear "traditional" in structure, are in fact going through momentous adjustments. The dilemmas which they face highlight issues which confront all Jewish families in the community today. These dilemmas include, but are not limited to: "overload," normative and identity dilemmas, social networking problems, and the quintessential dual career family dilemma—"role-cycling" (Rapaport and Rapaport, 1976).

"Overload" refers to the assumption by society that there is one partner in the marketplace and another at home to manage household affairs for the family. This assumption is held not only by the plumber, moving companies, and the United States Postal Service, but also by Jewish institutions such as religious schools and women's divisions of organizations. Often, in addition to the stress caused by overload, families face emotional problems caused by a discrepancy between the way they have chosen to

TABLE 13.5

Expected Completed Family Size by Marital Status for Currently
Employed and Unemployed Jewish Women (in percentages)

	EXPECTED NUMBER OF CHILDREN							
	NONE		ONE		TWO		THREE OR MORE	
	EMP.	UNEM.	EMP.	UNEM.	EMP.	UNEM.	EMP.	UNEM.
Marital Status								
Single, Never Married	27	20	13	30	29	30	31	20 (106)
Single, Was Married	14	11	24	22	31	22	31	44 (58)
Married	8	3	19	8	52	43	22	47 (288)*

*The only statistically significant differences in expected fertility are found between employed and unemployed currently married women. The $x_2 = 19.898$ with 3 df p $<$ .00018.

live their lives and what is portrayed as normative by the media or expected by their immediate families. This problem has been termed the normative dilemma because it refers to a difference between the norms which have been adopted by the couple and those of various reference groups which are salient to them.

Closely related to normative dilemmas are those of identity. Here the discrepancy is between the rational and emotional sides of the same person (their heads versus their *kishkas!*). At various times a husband or wife feels that his or her own self-definition is threatened by the new role definitions they have assumed. These problems may begin before marriage when the couple begins to develop a future orientation toward childbearing, career development, sharing of household tasks, and decision-making. These dilemmas are, of course, greatest among intermarried and even conversionary couples. They tend to place stress primarily on women who are seen as the initiators of change and hence the "source" of the trouble. (After all, a rational man wouldn't object to a woman's role changing, as long as his life remained the same!)

The fourth dilemma, "role-cycling," refers to the situation which arises when one spouse has a chance to move on or up in a sphere of life while the other has a contradictory opportunity. This may involve the timing of their career, study, or childbearing. This feeling and the actual instances of being unsynchronized in life cycle stages applies not only to couples under the age of forty-five, but also to many in their middle years. Successful male executives in their fifties may "come home" to be with their wives and children now that they are financially secure, only to discover, to their chagrin, that spouses and children have left the nest—the wives to outside employment and the children to college and graduate school.

Finally, rigid time priorities create the social networking problems faced by many families today. Leisure time is as structured and prioritized as work time. Spontaneity is often abandoned for careful planning, to provide for and enhance private family time. It is very difficult to get adults in this stage of life—particularly if they are parents of young children—to participate in any activity which is not directed toward enhancement of family life or career achievement.

Some resolve this stress by setting up "sacred" times and commitments. ("We always spend Sunday mornings as a family and have dinner together on Wednesday nights.") These are often linked to the creation of high quality intensive family experiences and career achievement. For traditional Jews, these sacred family times are tied in with the rhythm of the Jewish calendar. However, those who were not raised in a family setting in which the Sabbath and festivals provided special family moments tend to perceive observance of the sacred times marked off in the Jewish calendar only as a source of extra work. Even those Jews, especially the women, who remember such family meals and ceremonies fondly, rapidly become aware that preparation for them, especially at the levels of elegance of their own mothers, will be difficult at best. These same Jewish adults will also cut down or entirely eliminate voluntary activities for the general or Jewish community unless these are perceived as career (such as involvement in a professional division of Federation) or family related (working on the board or in the parents' association of the school which their child attends).

One example of a family related involvement which enhanced the community was documented by Feldman (1989) in a study of the impact of Jewish day care on the Jewish identity of parents, conducted in Philadelphia. She found that parents of children in Jewish day care centers, compared to a control group of Jewish parents of children in non-sectarian day care centers, increased their observance of home rituals and their financial contributions to the Jewish community. If excellent childcare is provided in a Jewish environment such as a synagogue or Jewish community center, and thus endorsed by the Jewish establishment, not only is there relief of overload, but normative and identity dilemmas are also dealt with. If the rabbi praises the day care center, if the teachers include friends and neighbors, and the curriculum stresses the Jewish calendar and Jewish values, then the feeling about using such a service is positive.

Each of the delineated dilemmas has ramifications for a variety of institutional spheres within the Jewish community. After all, if the Jewish community and its institutional structures—whether the synagogue or the board of a Jewish agency—are perceived as adding to the overload, then it is unlikely that couples with young children will want to join it (this scenario is even more apt for single parents). However, if appropriate institutional services can be developed to meet parents' needs, then the Jewish community will be strengthened by their participation and will become part of the solution rather than the problem.

The Jewish Identifications of Career Women—a First Look

The Jewish identifications and affiliations of women may be separated into homebound and public familial and personal ritual connections, and formal religious and secular organizational ties and time commitments.

Since the Lakeville studies of the 1950's, sociologists and demographers have been documenting the home ritual observance patterns of American Jews. Sklare (1967) theorized in those important community studies that home ritual observance in America was tied to: aesthetics, child orientation, annual or infrequent occurrence, values in accord with American ideology, and/or the provision of an alternative to a concurrent Christian observance. The typology of home ritual observance developed by Sklare has remained remarkably apt, with the exception of the relatively small (less than 10 percent) Orthodox segment of the American Jewish community.

For the employed women respondents to the NJPS, observance of home ritual, whether annual (lighting Hanukkah candles) or weekly (lighting candles on Friday night), is more the province of married than single women. An example is the lighting of Sabbath candles, which though designated in the survey as a household variable, has been perceived traditionally, and still is seen by most Jews, as a women's ritual. Candle lighting may be the only household ritual outside of those related to the dietary laws which can be understood to reflect a direct action by the woman herself (Table 13.6).

Overall, 41 percent of employed women between the ages of 21 and 64 light Sabbath candles at least sometimes, and just 16 percent usually or always light them. Of the 84 women who usually or always light these candles, 76 percent are currently married, while just 12 percent are singles who never married, and 12 percent are divorced or separated. While a much higher percentage of employed women live in households where Hanukkah candles are regularly lit (73 percent) than are Sabbath candles (only 16 percent), the strong relationship to marital status is analogous. While about three quarters (79 percent) of the currently married women light Hanukkah candles, two-thirds of the divorced (66 percent) and 61 percent of the singles who never married do so.

TABLE 13.6
Ritual Observance by Marital Status of Employed Jewish Women
(in percentages)

	CURRENT MARITAL STATUS		
	NEVER MARRIED N = (108)	EVER MARRIED (97)	CURRENTLY MARRIED (321)
Ritual Observance			
a. Lighting Hanukkah Candles*			
Never	18	19	13
Sometimes	21	16	9
Usually or always	61	66	79
b. Lighting Shabbat Candles*			
Never	71	59	55
Sometimes	19	31	25
Usually or always	9	10	20
c. Fasting on Yom Kippur			
Yes	57	61	62
No	43	39	38
d. Celebrating Purim*			
Yes	16	17	29
No	84	83	71
e. Celebrating Israel Independence Day*			
Yes	7	21	21
No	93	79	79
f. Has Christmas Tree in Household*			
Never	76	64	65
Sometimes	8	10	5
Usually or always	16	26	30

* = statistically significant at < .001

Having a Christmas tree in the house is a family-oriented home ritual similar to Hanukkah candles. As can be seen from Table 13.6, somewhat ironically, for employed women this observance follows the same pattern as Jewish home rituals. Thus, overall, about one-fourth (27 percent) report usually or always having a Christmas tree in their households, but of these 139 women, 70 percent are currently married, 18 percent divorced, and 16 percent single, never married. (This is a remarkably similar distribution to that for Sabbath candles, though more homes have Christmas trees!) Apparently, the push for Jews to have Christmas trees when living alone or with their Jewish families of orientation has not increased much over the findings of the community-based demographic studies of the 1970's and 1980's. However, the impact of mixed marriage on this observance has been dramatic. The reasons for—and certainly the meaning of—the Christmas tree in a household with an adult Jew in it, may have shifted from an expression of assimilation into the majority American culture to a religious symbol set next to the Menorah, symbolizing mixed religious origins and perhaps current allegiances of spouses.

A second category of family-oriented rituals also shown in Table 13.6 is primarily observed outside the home. Purim is an example of a minor holiday in the Jewish calendar, which is observed to some extent by 25 percent of the employed women. However, among the 127 who report its observance, three-fourths (74 percent) are currently married. Purim observance is different from Hanukkah or Sabbath candle-lighting in that it most often takes place in the synagogue setting at a *Megillah* reading or synagogue, school, or Jewish community center sponsored carnivals. In American synagogues both have been targeted to families with children. In general, family oriented, child-centered publicly celebrated rituals are most likely to be celebrated by currently married women.

Another publicly celebrated holiday is *Yom Ha'atzmaut*, Israel Independence Day. Few employed women celebrate Israel Independence Day in any way (18 percent), but of those who do, 71 percent are currently married and another 21 percent are formerly married women who probably have children studying in synagogue or day schools. Israel Independence Day is ostensibly celebrated with community-wide parades, but the units making up the marching groups are most often synagogue or school-based, thus being comprised predominantly of married people with children of school age.

In contrast to the rituals discussed above, all of which are group and life-cycle related, fasting on Yom Kippur is intensely personal and private. Thus, we could not expect it to be related to marital status. A look at the rates of fasting for employed women confirm this theory (Table 13.6). Nearly two-thirds (61 percent) of employed women fast on Yom Kippur, and the rates are about the same for women of every marital status.

Synagogue Membership and Home Ritual Observance by Occupation

In contrast to fasting on Yom Kippur, synagogue membership is known to be a life-cycle related status for most American Jews. Over their lifetimes, the vast majority of American Jews affiliate with a synagogue for some period of time. And, while at any one point in time, the affiliation rates are much lower (about 40 percent of households), it is still true that more Jews are affiliated with a synagogue at any one point in time than with any other single Jewish institution or organization.

One might speculate that women of higher occupational status would be less likely to affiliate with synagogues or to celebrate home rituals than those in more traditional "women's occupations" such as in the clerical and sales fields. As in the case of expected fertility, this supposition is not substantiated. In fact the relationship is in the opposite direction (Table 13.7).

Of the 41 percent of employed women who report that someone in their household is currently a synagogue member, the highest proportion of members is found among those in managerial and semi-professional occupations. (This could be related to the high cost of synagogue membership and the higher income levels of those households, a matter which deserves further exploration.)

The pattern for synagogue membership is similar to that for the most popular home ritual observances, lighting Hanukkah candles and attending a Passover Seder (Table 13.8).

Women with higher status occupations are significantly more likely than those with lower status occupations to be living in households where at least someone lights Hanukkah candles and attends a Seder.

Jewish Communal Planning

What are we to make of the patterns of observance uncovered in this report? Clearly the employed Jewish women who are most highly educated, work in high status occupations, and who are struggling with the dual-career family dilemmas, are also the very women who incorporate Jewish home and public ritual and synagogue affiliation into their lives. I believe that this fact is what Goldscheider was referring to in the quote which appears at the beginning of this study ". . . there is no conspicuous work-family role conflict for Jewish women." What he (admiringly) documented from an analysis of the Boston Demographic Survey of 1975 (1986, p. 103) was that these women were maintaining unexpected patterns of childbearing compared to other white American women with similarly high levels of education, occupational attainment, and labor force participation. What he was really uncovering was the fact that the younger employed Jewish women were coping, and persisting in anomalous behavior, a pattern documented even more broadly by the analysis of the data from the NJPS. However, though they were—and are—coping, the emotional

TABLE 13.7

*Current Synagogue Membership by Occupation of
Employed Jewish Women
(in percentages)*

OCCUPATION	MEMBER IN HOUSEHOLD	NO. MEMBER IN HOUSEHOLD
Professional	40	60
Managerial	52	48
Semi-Professional	49	51
Sales	35	65
Clerical	40	60
Other	20	80
N =	(216)	(308)

X = 15.7, DF = 5   p < .008

TABLE 13.8

*Home Ritual Observance by Occupation of Employed Jewish Women
(in percentages)*

	Occupation					
N =	Profes. (159)	Manag. (91)	Semi-Prof. (81)	Sales (49)	Clerical (100)	Other (45)
Home Ritual Observance						
Hanukkah Candles*						
Never	14	7	7	14	22	33
Sometimes	17	11	9	14	9	13
Usually or Always	69	82	84	71	60	53
Seder Attendance*						
Never	10	6	4	4	11	27
Sometimes	20	12	10	16	21	13
Usually or Always	70	82	86	80	68	60

*These tables are statistically significant at p < than .001

and psychological cost to the women, their children, and their spouses, most of whom are supportive in the dual career enterprise, may be great.

The organized Jewish community must take these findings into account in its planning for the year 2000 and beyond. Jewish identity is transmitted to the next generation largely through families and other primary group relationships. The families described in this chapter are already, and will continue to be, the predominant model of intact Jewish families, whether from first marriages or remarriages. Therefore, we are speaking of reciprocal relationships. An investment in rhetorical and institutional support of Jewish career women, particularly of the majority who seek to combine marriage, parenting, and careers, will pay off in a more vibrant Jewish community for all American Jews now and in the next generation.

Specific Policies To Be Considered

- The redesign or expansion of services to Jewish families to include "well family" care. This would include support groups for employed women contemplating marriage, for dual-career couples contemplating child-bearing, and for those in the full throes of juggling multiple roles. These groups might emanate from a variety of institutions including synagogues, organizations, Federation young leadership or business and professional groups, Jewish community centers, and the Jewish family service itself.
- Further development of programs which bring together future parents to combine Jewish and general education, and create "fictive" kin or pseudo primary group ties among them, leading to the building of Jewish social circles. A concrete example of this is the "Lamazeltov" groups combining Jewish life-cycle education with Lamaze training for expectant parents. The couples then celebrate the births together and often bond into *Havurah*-like groups that continue. Such groups have been joint projects of Jewish family services and educational agencies. In some cases they have grown out of rabbinic initiatives within larger synagogues.
- Agency, organizational, and synagogue leadership cannot be based on the parents of young and school-aged children. They should not be made to feel guilty for not coming to meetings. Stereotypes which make them the most desirable Jews to head committees and the like have to be done away with. For example, singles, empty-nesters, and young seniors (65–80) should be better utilized in community work.
- The rhetoric of the community should be supportive and appreciative of dual-career families. Women, in particular, should be told what a terrific job they are doing, rather than how guilty they should feel because their patterns are different from those of their mothers. (This will change automatically by the next generation when the mothers along with the fathers will have become occupational and "juggling" role models for their daughters.) Taking into account the Friedan quote at the beginning of this study about the stresses inherent in becoming high achievers in careers and perfect wives and mothers, this rhetoric will stress learning about—and participation in—the sacred times of the Jewish calendar within primary groups, without relying on high levels of personal prepa-

ration. An example of such rhetoric, to be found in the rabbis column of the synagogue bulletin or in an article in *Hadassah* or *Outlook* magazines might be . . . "Take out food is okay for a Sabbath meal—the important thing is to be together regularly to share the happenings of the week in a Jewish framework. You or your spouse don't have to personally bake the *hallah* or even be the ones who buy it—it just has to be there with you and some friends on Friday night." In the terminology of dual-career family dilemmas—Jewish celebration should enhance family life, while only minimally adding to the overload.

- The community should sponsor family activities and reward Jewish fathers for their participation. The community should be prepared to support and encourage fathers even when they decline to come to meetings and events in the evenings and on weekends.
- Attention will have to be paid, both on the levels of ideology, rhetoric, and institutional support, to single Jewish women who cannot find Jewish men to marry, whose biological clocks are ticking away, and who don't want to be deprived of motherhood.
- With all of this attention to intact and single parent families, employed single women of all ages, particularly those who have never married, need to feel that the community thinks of them as worthwhile Jewish adults and offers them tasks and rewards commensurate with that worth.

In sum, we are talking about nothing less than a revolution in definitions of age-appropriate, gender-appropriate, and marital-status related social roles. These kinds of social changes entail enormous investments of time, and human and financial resources. The NJPS data have uncovered many momentous changes in the Jewish community related to the future quality of persistence of a distinctively Jewish way of life in America. Nothing less than a revolutionary response based on great vision will begin to be adequate.

References

Feldman, Ruth Pinkenson, *Proceedings Of A Consultation On Jewish Day Care*, New York, American Jewish Committee, 1989.

Friedan, Betty, *The Second Stage*, New York, Summit Books, 1981.

Goldscheider, Calvin, *Jewish Continuity and Change*, Bloomington, Indiana University Press, 1986.

Kosmin, Barry and Jeff Scheckner, *Highlights of the National Jewish Population Survey of 1990*, New York, Council of Jewish Federations, 1991.

Monson, Rela Geffen, *Jewish Women On The Way Up. The Challenge Of Family*

Career & Community, New York, American Jewish Committee, 1987.

Monson, Rela Geffen and Ruth Pinkenson Feldman, "The Cost of Living Jewishly in Philadelphia," *Journal of Jewish Communal Service*, Volume 68 (2), (Winter 1991–1992), pp. 148–159.

Rapaport, Rhona and Robert, *Dual-Career Families Re-Examined*, New York, Harper & Row, Harper Colophon Books, 1976.

Schwartz, Felice N., "Management Women and the New Facts of Life," *Harvard Business Review*, (1), (January–February 1989), pp. 65–76.

Sklare, Marshall and J. Greenblum, *Jewish Identity on the Suburban Frontier*, New York, Basic Books, 1967.

Tobin, Gary and Alvin Chenkin, "Recent Jewish Community Studies: A Round-Up," *American Jewish Year Book*, New York, American Jewish Committee and Jewish Publication Society, 1985.

14

Gender, Class, and Identity Among the Jewish Aged

Allen Glicksman and Tanya Koropeckyj-Cox

American Jews over 65 are often perceived as the best understood age group of Jews in this country, based on a sense of familiarity with parents, grandparents, or older relatives. But nostalgia and sentimental feelings cloud an accurate portrayal of this group.

The common image of elderly American Jews is that of the *bubbe* and *zeyde*—an immigrant generation that provides a nurturing Jewish environment for their children and grandchildren, and has little social contact with the non-Jewish world. This image is featured in literature and art—from Sophie Portnoy to the aging grandmother in "Crossing Delancey," and from "Molly Goldberg" to "Brooklyn Bridge"—and pervades the professional community that takes care of older Jews as well.

American Jewish sociology has paid little attention to the aged. This is due to a concern over the Jewishness of coming generations rather than passing ones and the stereotypical portrayal of older Jews in scientific literature. American Jewish history has adopted the image of the older generation as pious and traditional in behavior from such books as *Children of the Gilded Ghetto* (Kramer & Leventman, 1961).

Directors of Jewish centers lament that many do not attend their programs for the elderly. These programs are designed for traditional Jews who either speak Yiddish or are nostalgic for Yiddish culture. Literature appearing in the last 20 years that describes the changing nature of the elderly has hardly changed perceptions (Guttmann, 1973).

Explaining the persistence of these images is difficult and must be done elsewhere. But certainly a few reasons should be mentioned. First, never before has there been a generation in which the majority of grandparents are American-born. This has reinforced the connection between old age and immigrant status in the minds of many. Since we know many of these immigrants in their old age, we blend the two, age and immigrant, into a single image.

But one could question if indeed such a generation of pious immigrants ever existed. Beneath the Yiddish language and old world attitudes, many immigrants felt a tension between desiring to continue the Jewish tradition and becoming part of the new environment. This tension was passed on to their children. The image of a traditional and quaint generation of Jewish immigrants is in itself problematic and prevents us from understanding the development of the American Jewish community. In her classic work, *Number Our Days*, Myerhoff (1978) describes how the immigrants in her sample had broken with traditional Judaism before coming to the United States. She identifies this break as part of a life-long process of assimilation and change. As we will see, our respondents are the children of these immigrants and, in part, products of this conflict between new and old values.

If the image is accurate, then there is no harm in it. But if the image is mistaken, then there are gaps both in our understanding of the dynamics of the American Jewish community and in our future planning for the elderly in communal agencies. Planning based on assumptions of immigrant status and traditional values could lead to programs and services not meeting real needs, interests, and preferences of most older Jews. This study examines who the Jewish elderly really are and how realistic the popular image is.

Sample and Methods

Of the 2,441 respondents to the NJPS, 391 were 65 or older. Since we were only interested in the Jewish elderly, a criteria for Jewish status was set. A respondent was Jewish if he or she answered "Jewish" to the question about current religion, was affiliated with a Jewish denomination, or did not belong to any other religious group. Also, if the respondent answered the question of current religious affiliation as "none" but answered the affiliation question with a Jewish denomination, the respondent was coded as Jewish. For those who listed no religion or denomination, we examined each case for other identifying information, such as religion of parent's household, and made individual decisions. Using these criteria, 356 of the 391 respondents to the NJPS, or 91 percent of the aged, were considered Jewish.

Unfortunately, the data contain some limitations that affect the analysis. First, it was collected to represent a random sample of all American Jews, not only elderly ones. Generalizing from such a sub-population must be done carefully.[1]

The respondents were 65 to 95 years old with a median age of 71. There were 233 respondents 65 to 74 (65 percent) and 123 respondents 75 years and older (35 percent), lower than most estimates of age distribution (Schmelz, 1985). The low median age reflects the community-based nature of the sample. In fact, the younger and healthier elderly, those 65 to 74, are probably over-represented relative to their older and more impaired peers. Our analysis will then be less applicable to older and more impaired Jews.[2]

The most important finding from the analysis is that Jewish elderly are American both by birth and life-style. They resemble their children and grandchildren more than their immigrant parents and "old country" grandparents. Eighty-six percent of the sample were born in the U.S.—48 percent in New York State, 11 percent in Pennsylvania, and six percent in both Massachusetts and Illinois. Of those born overseas, 62 percent came to the U.S. before 1940, and 96 percent before 1960, so most of them have been in this country for a long time. Here falls the first traditional image of the Jewish elderly: they are no longer a generation of immigrants.

These people are, however, the children of immigrants. Eighty-three percent have at least one parent born outside the United States and 94 percent have all four grandparents born outside the U.S. This is then the first generation of American-born grandparents in the Jewish community. It is also a generation which remained with the ethnic/religious community into which it was born. Ninety-eight percent of those currently Jewish were born Jewish. Only 1.3 percent of the sample were born Jewish and now practice another religion, as compared to 7.8 percent of the entire American Jewish community.

In the 1990 NJPS sample, 54 percent of the respondents are female and 46 percent are male. Fifty-eight percent of the entire sample are married and 33 percent are widowed. Five percent are divorced, three percent were never married, and one percent are separated. It is noteworthy that 60 percent of those under age 65 in the sample are married, exactly the same percentage as in the over 65 group. Only three percent of the aged have never been married as compared to 20 percent of the Jewish respondents 25 to 64 years of age. These facts point to the longevity of marriages in the older generation, as well as the tendency of young people today to marry late, in their mid-thirties.

Differences exist between males and females in predictable areas. The males have higher educational achievement, both in secular and Jewish education, higher status occupations, are more likely to still work after age 65, and are more likely to be married. Women are more likely to marry a Jew and observe Jewish rituals than Jewish males of the same age, and are less likely to have a Christmas tree in the home. Jewish women are also more likely to be concerned about the Jewish character of their neighborhood. In sum, women fare worse than men in terms of material and educational success, but show greater fidelity to their cultural heritage.

The study found that this generation of older Jews is better educated than previously assumed. Forty percent of the respondents finished high school, 17 percent have some college education, 20 percent completed a B.A. degree, and 11 percent have more advanced training. Overall, 48 percent have at least some college education, as compared to about 20 percent of the general American population of the same age (Statistical Abstract of the United States, 1988).

The occupational distribution of Jewish elderly is similar to their gentile peers, and reflects the overwhelming concentration of women in professions traditionally regarded as "women's work" (see Appendix). The largest category is "clerical" (19.9 percent) followed by "administration" (11.7 percent) and "salaried sales" (10.9 percent), together adding to 42.5 percent of the total. Seventy-one percent work for others and only 19 percent are self-employed, which disproves the traditional image of the self-employed Jewish immigrant. Of the 22 percent of respondents who are currently employed, 66 percent are men, with members of higher status professions more likely to work past the age of 65.

Regarding income distribution among the elderly, the data show two major stereotypes to be false—that of the poor and abandoned Jewish elderly, and that of the very rich one. The first stereotype is a staple in what has been written about American Jewry (Kramer & Leventman, 1961), while the second developed recently as part of a growing resentment toward the elderly in American society. The majority of household incomes fall between $12,500 and $40,000—from low to middle class. Eight percent are very poor, and another eight percent are very rich (see Appendix). While both rich and poor exist, the majority of Jewish elderly are in the middle class. But these figures reflect a fixed, post-retirement income that may not allow for long-term medical care or other major expenses which can occur in old age. Therefore we should not assume that the Jewish elderly are "well-off."

Duplicating a national trend, older Jews have moved south and west from their states of origin. Thirty-seven percent live alone, while 55 percent live with one other person, for a total of 91 percent. Sixty-three percent are home owners and 37 percent are renters, while only 20 years ago about two-thirds were renters (Glicksman, 1991). Sixteen percent spend at least two months away from their homes annually, but it is debatable whether there is a special Jewish "snowbird" or if this is a phenomenon among all healthy and wealthy elderly.

Several questions about personal beliefs were also asked. Half the sample said they were "liberal" or "very liberal," with the rest split between "middle of the road" and "conservative" or "very conservative." The image of the Jewish elderly as liberal is confirmed here, while a more recent image of older Jews as more conservative is shown to be exaggerated. It is still problematic to identify what the respondents actually meant by the word "liberal." For the older generation, commitment to liberalism means concern for the underdog, either in caring for the poor or in the struggle against threats such as Nazism or Communism.

Regarding religious beliefs, 13 percent of respondents say the Torah was the "Actual word of God." This low figure is significant since authorship of the Torah is the basic issue separating the Orthodox from other Jewish denominations.

In their attitudes toward intermarriage, 51 percent accept it or are neutral, while the rest split equally between supporting and opposing it. These elderly have modified their views to accommodate non-traditional attitudes toward belief and behavior either by choice or by a desire to maintain relations with family members.

Ninety-one percent of the respondents believe anti-Semitism is a serious problem in the United States. Yet only one question dealt with the actual experience of anti-Semitism and it focused on job discrimination in the last five years. Therefore, it is not surprising that almost the entire sample, 97.2 percent, answered "no" to the question concerning job discrimination. On the other hand, this generation lived when public display of anti-Semitism was more acceptable than today, not to mention being alive during the Holocaust. Such concerns about anti-Semitism arise from a lifetime of experience.

The image of older Jews as isolated from the mainstream is also disproved by the study. About a quarter are volunteers for various organizations, but the number that volunteer for non-Jewish organizations is higher than those volunteering for Jewish organizations. Such activism also shows that the integration that has characterized the lives of Jews born in the postwar era has in fact been part of the lives of all American Jews. The experience of the Jewish aged is not significantly different from that of their children in this case.

In terms of religious behavior, most Jewish elderly identify as either Conservative (46.9 percent) or Reform (31.2 percent). Eighty-one percent of males and 59 percent of females received some Jewish education and participate in the rituals most associated with American Jewry, such as attending a Passover Seder or lighting Hanukkah candles. These holidays are both child-centered and coincide with Christian holidays. Interestingly, 12 percent sometimes have a Christmas tree in their home. We suspect that the tree is an attempt to maintain a link with younger members of the family who have married Christians and may now be raising their children as Christians. There is evidence, as we shall see, for this conclusion in the different ways women and men conceptualize their religious behavior.

The examination of how these ritual behaviors relate to one another and to the lives of older Jews was performed by examining 10 rituals which included the following: lighting Sabbath candles, attending a Passover Seder, buying kosher meat, separating meat and dairy, lighting Hanukkah candles, attending a Purim celebration, celebrating Israel Independence Day, fasting on Yom Kippur, refraining from handling money on the Sabbath, and having a Christmas tree at home.

We were interested in knowing how the individual items listed above relate to one another. That is, if one is likely to have a Passover Seder, what other rituals is one likely to follow? The answer would also allow us to understand how people conceptualize these ritual behaviors. If certain rituals form a single group in the minds of our subjects, then we assume that there is some underlying common theme that binds them. The statistical procedure that allows us to examine such relations is called Factor Analysis.

When we conducted such an analysis using all the items and all the subjects, the results were difficult to understand and interpret. We then conducted separate analyses for men and women. The results made more sense in the real world, and pointed to sharp differences between the sexes. This should not come as a surprise since Judaism identifies different roles for men and women.

There were three groups of items, called factors, for the men: community and family rituals, issues concerning Kashrut, and behaviors that might be considered extreme, such as not carrying money on the Sabbath and having a Christmas tree. If one does not carry money on the Sabbath, one does not have a Christmas tree either. This also might indicate that more religious men are less likely to accept their children's intermarriage, which, we believe, leads to having a Christmas tree in the house.

The results are quite different for women. The first group of items (factors) includes family oriented rituals such as Passover and Hanukkah, as well as fasting on Yom Kippur and having a Christmas tree. Those familiar with contemporary American Jewish ritual know that Yom Kippur has become a family holiday with a big "break the fast" meal involving close and extended kin. The presence of the Christmas tree in this group signifies that for older women rituals that bring the family together—even when they are outside Judaism—form a single unit because of the significance of their role as "kin keeper." Men, on the other hand, do not have a separate "family factor."

The second group includes personal rituals that involve the woman herself and not the entire family, such as lighting Sabbath candles. The final group includes two ethnic/national celebrations, Purim and Israel Independence Day. These holidays do not include significant home ritual, and so are neither family nor personal based observance.

Women, therefore, seem to separate the personal, familial, and communal in terms of the way they conceptualize ritual behavior. For men, most rituals seem to fall in one group—community and family rituals—with two residual groups, kashrut and extreme behaviors. (The appendix shows the major correlates of the ritual factors.)

If gender is a key to understanding ritual behavior, then socioeconomic status (SES) plays an equally important role in defining other aspects of Jewish identity for the elderly. That is, SES is an important predictor of life-style, including decisions about ethnic and religious identification.[3] The results show that identification with the Jewish community as well as participation in non-Jewish organizations is tied to socioeconomic-status. The first three (1–3) of these items are not significantly correlated with income, while the next three (4–6) are correlated more with socioeconomic status than income. The last five (7–11) are correlated more with income than with socioeconomic status. None of these items were correlated with the SES scale that Hollingshead devised.

The results can be summarized as follows:

Correlated with SES Scale But Not with Income
1. Giving to Jewish charity because of the Jewish tradition of giving (q127bd)
2. Going to adult education programs in the Jewish community (q76)
3. Not being Orthodox

Correlation with SES Scale Stronger than Correlation with Income
4. Donations to non-Jewish groups (q126)
5. Higher number of Jewish friends (q117)
6. Membership in a Jewish organization (q111)

Correlation with SES Scale Weaker than Correlation with Income
7. Gender (being male)(q3a)
8. Membership in a non-Jewish organization (q109)
9. Donations to a Jewish group (q122)
10. Spending more than 2 months away from home each year (q67)
11. Being an officer in a non-Jewish organization (q111b)

These are measures of communal association. The first item is particularly interesting because it indicates that among Jews, giving to charity is related to socioeconomic status. Therefore, socioeconomic status plays an important role in defining the meaning and displays of Jewish communal identity among the elderly. This difference between the influence of income and SES makes sense if one remembers that post-retirement income is not usually a measure of the SES of an individual or family over its working lifetime. Also, some high-status positions, such as being a professor or psychologist, are not necessarily related to the higher incomes of other high-status professionals. A wide diversity of incomes exists within and across SES categories. This diversity helps explain why SES rather than income is a better predictor of communal membership. But these measures of communal behaviors and attitudes are not strongly correlated with gender.

When the older respondents were compared to the younger ones (under age 65), there were significant differences in predictable areas, such as education, income, mobility, and employment status. The older group had higher levels of Jewish identification, but certain holidays, such as Hanukkah and Passover, which have become child-centered, were more often observed by those age groups likely to have children living at home. It seems that in the groups born and socialized before the Second World War, age 55, and not 65, is when ritual practices and other measures of Jewish identity begin to appear differently. Because of this, it may be said that the differences in the statistics are a result of both age and generational effects. In other words, part of the explanation lies in the life cycle stage of the respondent and whether or not they still have children living at home and part lies in the experience of socialization of Jews born before the Second World War.

Conclusions

This analysis of the data from the 1990 NJPS shows that the American Jewish elderly are well integrated into American life in many ways. They are economically successful, integrated into the Christian community, and have a continued sense of ethnic identity that does not segregate them from society. While this population is more connected with their Jewish heritage than their children and grandchildren, they appear more like their children in their social integration, economic status, and religious observance than like their ancestors.

It should be stressed that a national sample like the one used here does not allow for the consideration of special groups within the community.

There are Orthodox elderly who want the traditional services offered by some agencies within the Jewish community. There are Holocaust survivors, recently arrived Jews from the republics of the former Soviet Union, aging Israelis, and other special populations to whom generalizations concerning the American Jewish elderly cannot be extended. Since most American Jews were born here, these special populations are minorities within a larger minority group of aging Jews. The absence of these groups from the sample should not be used as an excuse to forget about them in community planning.

If the elderly are indeed well integrated within the general population, the question arises whether they should continue to receive special services. The data collected do not provide information on who the American Jewish elderly wish to receive services from or if indeed they want a strong Jewish content in the services they receive. This lack of information, and the fact that most elderly are well integrated into the general population, should not be a call for reducing services to this population. On the contrary, the study shows that the American Jewish elderly are concerned with the fate of their community, and in turn, they expect that the community will be concerned with their fate. Planning for this population must take these concerns into account.

Notes

1. Population weights were constructed for the sample in order to describe the universe, although we chose not to use weighted data or claim that our findings can be generalized over the entire population of American Jewish elderly. The weights for the population sample were constructed by assuming that there are 70,000 older Jews in institutions that were not counted by the study since it is a community based (non-institutionalized) sample. The gender and age distribution of elderly Jews who are homebound and in nursing homes is quite different from the sample's distributions. These under-represented groups are more likely to be older and female. Using the weighted data would distort the findings significantly.

2. The analysis was completed using percentages and cross-tabulations with chi-square statistics. Some factor analyses were also performed. Statistical significance was measured at the .05 level.

3. SES was examined using Hollingshead's Four Factor Index of Social Status (Hollingshead n.d.). The SES measures were then tested for correlations with the questions about Jewish life-style or belief. Using educational level and job description, a score was determined for each respondent. Years of education were measured on a scale of 1 to 7, with 1 being less than 7th grade and 7 being a graduate degree. Occupations were assigned the numbers 9 (highest) to 1 (lowest), using the Census Bureaus' Standard Occupational Classification. In Hollingshead's scheme, each employed person in the household is assigned a score, and then these scores

are averaged by the number of people in the household. Following Hollingshead's scheme, few items were found to be correlated at a significant level with the scale score.

The authors modified the household SES scores by using the highest score of any individual in the household to represent the household score. It was reasoned that Hollingshead's method of averaging the scores within a household had depressed the higher scores. Especially for this older cohort in which the husband was likely to have had a much higher status occupation than his wife, it was the husband's occupation which could be expected to define the family's SES. With this revised scale, significant correlations with the SES could now be seen. Higher SES as measured by the revised scale was significantly correlated with the following items at the .05 level.

Appendix
The Aged American Jewish Population: 1990

TOTAL NUMBER OF JEWISH SUBJECTS AGE 65 AND OLDER: 356

PROPORTION BORN JEWISH: 98%

GENDER BREAKDOWN:
Females: 54%
Males: 46%

MEAN AGE: 72.7
MEDIAN AGE: 71

PERCENT BORN IN UNITED STATES: 86%

WHERE BORN IN UNITED STATES:
New York 48%
Pennsylvania 11%
Massachusetts 6%
Illinois 6%

PROPORTION OF ANCESTORS BORN OUTSIDE UNITED STATES:
Parents: 83%
Grandparents: 94%

YEAR CAME TO UNITED STATES:
(For Immigrants)
62% Before 1940
96% Before 1960

MARITAL STATUS:
Married 58%
Widowed 33%
Divorced 5%
Never Married 3%
Separated 1%

NUMBER OF CHILDREN (ONLY ASKED OF WOMEN):
None: 9.4%
One: 17.2%
Two: 42.7%
Three: 21.4%
Four or More: 9.4%

WHERE EMPLOYED:
71% Work For Others
19% Self Employed

OF THOSE EMPLOYED BY OTHERS:
68% Employed In Private Business
9% In Not-for-Profit
19% For Government
4% Something Else

INCOME (HOUSEHOLD FOR THE YEAR):

Less Than $7,500:	7.8%
7,500–12,499:	9.6%
12,500–19,999:	17.4%
20,000–29,999:	21.9%
30,000–39,999:	15.6%
40,000–49,999:	10.0%
50,000–59,999:	4.4%
60,000–79,999:	5.2%
80,000–124,999:	5.2%
125,000–149,999:	.7%
150,000–199,999:	1.5%
200,000 +	.7%

OCCUPATIONAL BREAKDOWN:

Clerical	19.9%
Administration	11.7%
Salaried Sales	10.9%
Secretarial	7.9%
Helping	5.9%
Sales	5.0%
Professional	3.8%
Scientific-technical	3.5%
Art	3.5%
Health Care	3.2%
Manufacture	3.2%
Laborers	2.9%
Finance	2.6%
Sales Managers	2.6%
Legal	2.3%
Health	2.1%
Educational-help	2.1%
Academic	1.8%
Delivery	1.8%
Other	1.5%
Machines	.9%
Technicians	.9%

LIVING ARRANGEMENTS:
37% Live In One Person Household
55% Live In Two Person Household

CURRENT STATE OF RESIDENCE:
New York: 28.4%
Florida: 14.6%
California: 12.1%
New Jersey: 7.3%
Massachusetts: 6.2%
Pennsylvania: 5.1%
Illinois: 3.9%

63% OWN THEIR HOMES
37% RENT

16% SPEND AT LEAST TWO MONTHS AWAY
FROM CURRENT RESIDENCE

BELIEFS:

POLITICAL:
49% "Liberal Or Very Liberal"
27% "Middle Of The Road"
24% "Conservative Or Very Conservative"

AUTHORSHIP OF TORAH:
Actual Word of God: 13.9%
Inspired Word of God: 29.5%
History Written By Humans: 45.9%
Can't Select An Answer: 10.7%

ATTITUDES TOWARD OWN CHILD'S INTERMARRIAGE:
Strongly Support: 3.4%
Support: 17.7%
Accept Or Neutral: 51.1%
Oppose: 13.5%
Strongly Oppose: 6.5%
Don't Know: 6.2%

ANTI-SEMITISM A SERIOUS PROBLEM IN THE UNITED STATES:
Strongly Disagree: 1.7%
Somewhat Disagree: 7.6%
Somewhat Agree: 29.7%
Strongly Agree: 61.0%

DENOMINATIONAL AFFILIATION:
Conservative: 46.9%
Reform: 31.2%
Orthodox: 9.3%

RECEIVED JEWISH EDUCATION:
Males: 80.7%
Females: 58.9%

PERCENT OBSERVING JEWISH RITUALS (AT LEAST SOMETIME):

Attend Seder:	80.2%
Attend Synagogue At Least Once A Year:	75.0%
Light Hanukkah Candles:	73.6%
Fast On Yom Kippur:	51.8%
Light Sabbath Candles:	47.0%
Buy Kosher Meat:	45.3%
Separate Meat and Dairy Dishes:	23.7%
Attend Purim Celebration:	19.9%
Celebrate Israel Independence Day:	17.1%
Not Handle Money on Sabbath:	12.7%
Fast On Fast Of Esther:	2.0%

CHRISTIAN RITUAL OBSERVANCE:
Have Christmas Tree: 11.7%

VOLUNTEER ACTIVITY (IN PAST YEAR):
Volunteer For Jewish Organizations: 20.3%
Volunteer For Other Organizations: 27.6%

Officer In Jewish Organization: 25.0%
Officer In Other Organization: 22.0%

AREAS OF GENDER DIFFERENCES:
Males Had/Were More . . .

Years Of Education, Secular And Jewish
Likely To Be Married
High Status Occupations
Likely To Be Working After Age 65

Females Were More Likely To . . .

Be Married To A Jew
Be Married Only Once
Observe Rituals
Be Concerned With The "Jewishness" Of The Neighborhood

DIFFERENCES BY AGE GROUPS:
Aged Less Likely To . . .

Have High Socioeconomic Status And Education
Work For Non-profit Organization
Move
Observe Hanukkah Or Passover
Approve Of Intermarriage

FACTOR STRUCTURE FOR RITUAL ITEMS:
JEWISH RESPONDENTS 65 + YEARS OF AGE

Everyone	*Men*	*Women*
Factor One	*Factor One*	*Factor One*
Seder	Seder	Seder
Hanukkah	Hanukkah	Hanukkah
Yom Kippur	Yom Kippur	Yom Kippur
Sabbath Candles	Sabbath Candles	
Christmas Tree★		Christmas Tree
Israel Independence★	Israel Independence	
Purim★	Purim	
Factor Two	*Factor Two*	*Factor Two*
Milk & Meat Dishes	Milk & Meat Dishes	Milk & Meat Dishes
Kosher Meat	Kosher Meat	Kosher Meat
Money on Sabbath		Money on Sabbath
		Sabbath Candles
	Factor Three	*Factor Three*
	Money on Sabbath	Purim
	Christmas★	Israel Independence

★ = Item loads negatively on factor

MAJOR CORRELATES OF RITUAL ITEM FACTORS

Women

Factor One
  Number of Times in Synagogue in Year
  Synagogue Membership
  Belief in Revelation of Torah
  Number of Jewish Friends
  Conservative Jew

Factor Two
  Belief in Revelation of Torah
  Number of Times in Synagogue in Year
  Orthodox Jew
  Synagogue Membership
  Importance of Jewishness of Neighborhood

Factor Three
  Number of Times in Synagogue in Year
  Synagogue Membership
  Belief in Revelation of Torah
  Volunteering for Jewish Organization
  Lack of Physical or Cognitive Disability

Men

Factor One
  Number of Times in Synagogue in Year
  Synagogue Membership
  Conservative Jew
  Importance of Jewishness of Neighborhood
  Number of Jewish Friends

Factor Two
  Number of Times in Synagogue in Year
  Importance of Jewishness of Neighborhood
  Synagogue Membership
  Number of Jewish Friends
  Belief in Revelation of Torah

(We did not examine correlates of Factor Three.)

References

Glicksman, Allen, *The New Jewish Elderly: A Literature Review*, New York, The American Jewish Committee, 1991.

Guttmann, David, "Leisure-time Activity Interests of Jewish Aged," *The Gerontologist*, Volume 13(4), (1973), pp. 219–33.

Hollingshead, A. Irving, *Four Factor Index of Social Status*, New Haven, Privately Printer.

Kramer, Judith R. and Seymour Leventman, *Children of the Gilded Ghetto: Conflict Resolution of Three Generations of American Jews*, New Haven, Yale, 1961.

Myerhoff, Barbara G., *Number Our Days*, New York, Dutton, 1978.

Schmelz, Uziel, "The Aging of World Jewry," *Papers on Aging in the Jewish World*, Second Edition, Jerusalem, Brookdale, 1985.

PART FIVE

Looking Ahead

15

Jewish Giving and Strategies for Strengthening Campaigns

J. Alan Winter

The tradition of Jews giving of their financial resources to campaigns for Jewish causes is longstanding. Indeed, Moshe Rabbenu himself was perhaps the first campaign chair. Recall the opening verses of Shemot (Exodus) chapter 25 "And God spoke to Moses saying, 'Speak unto the Children of Israel, that they take for Me an offering, of every person whose heart is willing, you shall take my offering.' "

This study focuses on the current state of Jewish giving to Federation or United Jewish Appeal campaigns, and on prospects for future donations, based on data from the 1990 National Jewish Population Survey (NJPS). In light of those insights, some strategies for strengthening campaign will be suggested.

Who Are the Donors

Research[1] has shown that donating to campaign is primarily a function of three sets of factors: the level of Jewish activities; family affluence or disposable income, that is, income remaining after basic needs and taxes are paid for; and accessibility to campaign solicitation. These factors are, in turn, based on two simple tenets: people donate to causes in which they are interested and with which they can identify; and the amount they give is a function of both how interested or identified they are, and how much disposable income they have. It is usually assumed that those interested in and identified with things Jewish tend to give to Jewish causes, in this case to the UJA/Federation campaign. Furthermore, it is assumed that the more Jewish and the more affluent people are, the more they tend to give, if only they can be reached and asked to do so.

This study tests whether these simple ideas are supported by the 1990 NJPS data and whether or not knowledge of demographic factors such as age, generation-in-the-US, gender, secular education, and Jewish education improves the understanding of who the donors are.

The information concerning campaign donations is based on the following question in the 1990 NJPS: "In 1989, did you and/or other members of your household together contribute or give gifts to the Jewish Federation or UJA?" Consequently, the unit discussed is not the individual donor, but a household in which one or more unspecified members donate to campaign. Thus, questions asked only of respondents, such as "Do you fast on Yom Kippur?" are of limited, if any, use here since it is quite possible that the respondent is not the donor. Similarly, standard demographic variables such as age, for which information is available on each household member, cannot be used without some additional assumptions, as these are properties of individuals, not households.

The study's basic assumption is that the characteristic of a head of the household can be considered that of the household itself. For example, the analysis shall examine the donations of households whose head is self-employed compared to those whose head is not self-employed, or households whose head only recently moved to town as compared to those who moved much earlier.[2]

The head of the household fits one of the following definitions: any respondent living alone or with persons who are neither a parent, child, in-law, spouse, or partner of the respondent; the respondent, if he or she works as many or more hours than their spouse or partner; or the parent, whether respondent or not, if she or he works as many or more hours than an adult child with whom the household is shared.

The three basic sets of factors, Jewish activities, affluence, and accessibility to campaign solicitation, are first examined separately and then in combination as they relate to whether or not a household contributes to a Federation or UJA campaign and, if so, how much.

Household "Jewishness" and Campaign Donations

Whether or not a household is considered "Jewish," or even one with a Jew or Jews in it, was assessed by how many core Jews, if any, are in it, and by whether or not the respondent indicates that the household has a non-Jewish denominational orientation. As seen in Table 15.1, each indicator is

TABLE 15.1

Percent of Households Donating Or Not By
Household "Jewishness"

MEASURE OF "JEWISHNESS"	DONATION		
	% NONE	% SOME	N[a]
Core Jews			
All	58.5	41.5	1253
Some	88.6	11.4	641
None	97.0	3.0	382
Totals	73.5	26.5	2276
Denomination			
Jewish	58.7	42.2	1249
None, but Jews	79.9	20.1	156
Jewish & other	88.0	12.0	164
Non-Jewish	97.7	2.3	513
Totals	71.7	28.3	2082

[a] Number is adjusted by "relative weight" (weight/average weight) so as to reflect the population as a whole of 3.19 million households, but yet not inflate numbers used for statistical analysis beyond the total number of 2441 actual respondents. Totals vary due to varying non-response rates.

indeed quite closely related to the likelihood of a household's making a donation to a Federation/UJA campaign.[3] On each measure, within the category that indicates that the household is "not Jewish," the rate of donations to campaign is virtually nil: only three percent where no member is a core Jew, and just slightly over two percent in households described as having a non-Jewish denominational orientation. Among so-called "mixed households," those consisting of core Jews and non-core Jews, only 11 percent donate to campaign. Furthermore, tables not shown here reveal that where the household is "mixed" in its Jewish composition and has a non-Jewish denominational orientation, the rate of donation dips to about one percent.

In light of these findings, subsequent analyses will exclude those households in which there are no core Jews and those "mixed" households which have a non-Jewish denominational orientation.[4]

Jewish Activities

Three different indicators of Jewish activity of a household are used in this study: the celebration of Yom Ha'atzmaut (Israel Independence Day), annual decisions such as synagogue membership, and weekly decisions such as lighting candles on Friday night.[5]

As seen in Table 15.2, each of the three indicators is strongly related to whether the household is among the 34.4 percent that make a campaign donation or the 65.6 percent that do not. For example, among the 15 percent households which do celebrate Yom Ha'atzmaut, nearly two-thirds donate to Jewish campaigns, while only about a quarter of those who do not celebrate the holiday make a donation. Among those who perform the annual activities, just over 64 percent donate in contrast to 15.6 percent among those who perform none of these activities. The differences in Jewish giving among those who engage in weekly Jewish activities are somewhat less sharp, but still considerable: 57.6 percent among those who are involved in contrast to only 21.6 percent among those who are not.

In sum, the Jewish activities of a household, its "Jewish Identity," does indeed have a relationship to whether or not it donates to a Federation/UJA campaign. Households in which there are no core Jews, and those with a non-Jewish denominational orientation, are quite unlikely to donate. Households which celebrate Yom Ha'atzmaut are more likely to donate than those which do not. As the number of Jewish activities increases, so does the tendency to donate to campaign.

Affluence and Donations

The extent to which a household engages in Jewish activities is not the only factor that determines whether it will donate to campaign and, if so, how much. In addition, there has to be the disposable income to pay for it. The level of affluence is understood to be a function of three factors: household income, its source, and the presence of non-adult children whose needs must be met. The significance of the first and last factors is obvious, but the second may require some explanation. As Cohen suggests (1980:33), it is "not overly cynical" to believe that the self-employed and those working for a family business have a greater ability to shelter their income from taxes and thus have a greater disposable income than salaried employees. Moreover, it is likely that the self-employed may, in fact, pay their campaign donations out of business income. Those working in a family business may, in some cases, be able to do likewise. However, salaried employees most likely make donations from their paycheck.

In any case, it is not surprising, as shown in Table 15.2, that household income[6] is related to the decision as to whether or not to donate to campaign. Nevertheless, the relationship is only a weak one. The source of the head of the household's income, whether through self-employment, a

TABLE 15.2

Percent of Households Donating Or Not By
Jewish Activities

JEWISH	DONATION		
ACTIVITY	% NONE	% SOME	N [a]
Yom Ha'atzmaut			
No Celebration	71.2	28.8	1457
Did Celebrate	34.0	66.0	258
Gamma = .66		p < .0001 (one-tail)	
Annual Activity			
None	84.4	15.6	564
One	71.0	29.0	360
Two	62.6	37.4	409
Three	35.9	64.1	382
Gamma = .54		p < .0001 (one-tail)	
Weekly Activity			
None	78.4	21.6	758
One	63.3	36.7	515
Two	49.7	50.3	235
Three	42.4	57.6	208
Gamma = .44		p < .0001 (one-tail)	
Income Level			
Under $30,000	71.9	28.1	476
$30,000–$49,999	67.2	32.8	436
$50,000 & over	60.9	39.1	618
Gamma = .17		p < 005 (one-tail)	
Source of Income			
Salary	66.8	33.2	1212
Family Business	47.2	52.8	66
Self-employment	63.3	36.7	346
Gamma = .11		Not significant	
Presence of Children			
None under 18	62.7	37.3	1221
Some under 18	72.7	27.3	495
Gamma = −.22		p < .005	
When Moved To City Or Address			
Both 1985 or Since	77.0	23.0	460
Address 1985 or Since	74.6	25.4	349
Both Before 1985	56.0	44.0	868
Gamma = .37		p < .0001	
Nature of Occupation			
Non-Professional	66.4	33.6	1258
Professional	61.5	38.5	379
Gamma = .11		Not significant	

[a] N is adjusted by "relative weight" (weight/average weight) so as to reflect entire population without inflating N used in statistical analysis beyond N of actual respondents. Totals vary due to varying non-response rates.

family business, or working for others, is also weakly related, if at all, to whether or not the household donates to campaign. The presence or absence of children under age 18 is, however, more strongly, albeit only moderately, related to whether or not a donation is made.

Accessibility to Campaign Solicitation

To this point, it appears that an individual's level of activity in Jewish life and affluence are both related to decisions concerning donations to campaign. However, being ready and able to donate may not be enough. It is likely that one has to be asked as well and, if asked, be amenable to whatever pressure the solicitor can muster to persuade one to give or to give more. Thus, two indicators of accessibility are employed here.

First, the recency with which the household has moved to its present address or city is taken into account. It is assumed that the more recent the move, the more difficult it is for campaign personnel to locate and solicit potential donors.

Not surprisingly, this factor is moderately related to the propensity to donate to campaign. Thus, as seen in Table 15.2, 44 percent of donors have been at their current address for five years or more. In contrast, only 25.4 percent of donors have been at their current address less than five years, but have been in the city longer than that, and 22 percent have been in the city less than five years.

The second indicator of accessibility is the nature of one's employment. Cohen (1980:33) has suggested that professionals are less amenable to "the social and economic pressures that can be brought to bear on potential contributors." Moreover, he notes (pp. 33–34), "certain professions . . . can become a way of life and thus . . . individuals in these professions may feel less of a need to link themselves to the Jewish community through charitable giving." Contrary to Cohen's suggestion, the difference between professionals and non-professionals with respect to the propensity to donate is not statistically significant.

In sum, when each indicator is examined separately, the decision as to whether or not to donate to a Federation/UJA campaign is strongly related to whether or not the household celebrates Yom Ha'atzmaut and to its level of such annual Jewish activities as maintaining a synagogue or temple membership, attending a Seder, and lighting Hanukkah candles. The decision to donate is only moderately related to a household's level of more frequent decisions such as whether or not to light candles on Friday night, buy kosher meat, or use separate dishes for meat and dairy; the recency with which the household moved to its current address or city; and the presence of children under 18 in the home. Interestingly, the decision to

TABLE 15.3

Regression Coefficients: On Donating Or Not

VARIABLE	B	SE B	BETA	p <
Yom Ha'atzmaut	21	.03	.16	.0001
Annual Activity	.11	.01	.26	.0001
Weekly Activity	.05	.01	.11	.0001
Income Level	.05	.01	.09	.0004
Source of Income	.00	.01	−.01	NS
Presence of Children	−.17	.03	−.16	.0001
When Moved	.07	.01	.13	.0001
Nature of Occupation	.02	.03	.01	NS
Constant	−.31	.05		.0001

R = .47   R² = .22

donate is only weakly related to the level and source of household income, and is not related, at a statistically significant level, to whether or not the household head is a professional.

Overall, the decision whether or not to donate to campaign is most strongly related to the level of Jewish activity,[7] moderately related to accessibility to campaign solicitation, and related the least of all to an individual's level of income.

How Much Do People Contribute

A somewhat different pattern of relationships is found between the amount donated, on the one hand, and activity, affluence, and accessibility, on the other.[8] The level of a household's donation is strongly related to the level of its annual income and to its source, whether from self-employment, a family business or otherwise, and moderately related to celebration of Yom Ha'atzmaut, the level of annual Jewish activities, and to whether or not the household head is a professional (see Table 15.4). The level of donation is not related, at a statistically significant level, to the recency of the household move to its present address or city, the presence or absence of children under 18, or the level of weekly Jewish activities.

Table 15.5 reveals a similar, but not quite identical, pattern. Again, the level of household income and its source are shown to be most strongly related to the level of donation. However, the presence or absence of children under 18 in the home emerges as an indicator related to the level of donation. The celebration of Yom Ha'atzmaut and the level of annual Jewish activity are also shown to be related to the level of donation, as is whether or not the household head is a professional. The relationship between weekly Jewish activities is, surprisingly, not related to the level of

TABLE 15.4
Percent Donating Given Amounts By Jewish Activity

JEWISH ACTIVITY	DONATION LEVEL			
	UNDER $100	$100–499	$500 & UP	N[a]
Yom Ha'atzmaut				
No Celebration	58.6	29.9	11.6	420
Did Celebrate	39.6	39.5	21.0	171
Gamma = .33	p < .001			
Annual Activity				
None	66.4	26.7	6.9	88
One	58.8	27.1	14.1	105
Two	57.7	33.4	8.9	153
Three	42.9	36.7	20.4	244
Gamma = .26	p < .005			
Weekly Activity				
None	53.1	37.2	9.7	163
One	52.7	33.0	14.3	189
Two	50.4	30.1	19.5	118
Three	56.2	28.4	15.4	120
Gamma = .02	Not significant			
Income Level				
Under $30,000	68.2	26.2	5.5	133
$30,000–$49,999	59.9	32.9	7.2	143
$50,000 & over	36.7	40.7	23.2	230
Gamma = .44	p < .0001			
Source of Income				
Salary	58.5	33.4	8.1	403
Family Business	29.8	27.2	43.0	35
Self-employment	38.2	35.7	26.1	127
Gamma = .40	p < .0001			
Presence of Children				
None under 18	54.3	31.9	13.8	455
Some under 18	49.0	35.2	15.8	135
Gamma = .09	Not significant			
When Moved To City Or Address				
Both 1985 or Since	56.7	34.3	8.9	105
Address 1985 or Since	54.5	34.5	11.0	89
Both Before 1985	51.5	32.1	16.4	383
Gamma = .11	Not significant			
Nature Of Occupation				
Non-Professional	56.8	32.8	10.4	422
Professional	42.8	34.7	22.6	146
Gamma = .29	p < .01			

[a]N is adjusted by "relative weight" (weight/average weight) so as to reflect entire population without inflating N used in statistical analysis beyond N of actual respondents. Totals vary due to varying non-response rates.

TABLE 15.5
Regression Coefficients: On Amount Donated

VARIABLE	B	SE B	BETA	p <
Yom Ha'atzmaut	.21	.07	.13	.0054
Annual Activity	.07	.03	.11	.0249
Weekly Activity	− .03	.03	− .04	NS
Income Level	.24	.04	.27	.0001
Source of Income	.17	.04	.20	.0001
Presence of Children	− .20	.08	− .12	.0111
When Moved	.07	.04	.07	NS
Nature of Occupation	.15	.07	.09	.0332
Constant	.31	.16		.0479

$R = .43$ $R^2 = .19$

donation to a statistically significant degree, nor is the recency of the household's move to its current address or city. Apparently, if a recently moved household can be found and solicited, all other things being equal, it is as likely to donate as much as more established households.

In sum, whether or not a donation is made is most strongly related to the level of Jewish activity, followed by accessibility and then affluence. The importance of activity, affluence, and accessibility to campaign solicitation may be illustrated by looking at two sets of extreme cases: among the few (97 people, 5.6 percent of total studied) who exhibit the highest rate of annual Jewish activity and income level, nearly 69.1 percent donate and over a quarter (25.8 percent) contribute $500 or more annually. Among the even fewer Jews who showed the lowest amount of Jewish involvement and income (32 people, 1.9 percent of interviewees), fewer than one in five (18.8 percent) donate at all, and none donates $500 or more.

Once the decision to donate is made, affluence, or the level of disposable income, emerges as the dominant factor in determining the sum donated. The level of Jewish activity, while still a prominent factor, is somewhat less dominant. Of course, as important as activity, affluence, and accessibility are together (as shown in the regression analysis in Tables 15.3 and 15.5), they account for only a fifth or so of the variance in donating behavior. Thus, it is quite possible that an examination of such variables as age, generation-in-the-US, gender, secular education, and Jewish education would add to our understanding.

The Influence of Demographic Variables

Among the demographic variables, age, generation-in-the-US, and secular education are related to whether or not a donation is made (see

Table 15.6), while gender, secular education, and Jewish education are related to the amount donated (see Table 15.7).

Interestingly, however, when the eight variables defining activity, affluence, and accessibility are combined (see Table 15.8) they account for more of the variance than do the five demographic variables. Of course, using all the variables does improve the ability to predict whether a house-

TABLE 15.6

Percent Donating By Actuarial Characteristics of HH Head

	% NONE	% SOME	N[a]
Age			
18–24	92.5	7.5	70
25–34	81.6	18.4	381
35–44	74.1	25.9	432
45–54	66.1	33.9	241
55–64	54.1	45.9	195
65 & +	41.1	58.9	385
Gamma = .48		p < .0001 (one-tail)	
Generation-In USA			
Foreign-born	53.1	46.9	139
Native: Two For'n Parents	47.6	52.4	408
Native: One For'n Parent	64.6	35.4	180
3–4 Foreign Grandparent	71.3	28.7	643
0–2 Foreign Grandparent	83.2	16.8	263
Gamma = − .39		p < .0001 (one-tail)	
Gender			
Male	66.5	33.5	946
Female	64.4	35.6	762
Gamma = .05		Not significant	
Education			
HS, VoTech or Less	67.3	32.7	650
AA, BA, RN	70.5	29.5	572
MA	58.4	41.6	248
PhD, or Prof. Degree	54.8	45.2	203
Gamma = .13		p < .05 (one-tail)	
Formal Jewish Education			
None	76.7	23.3	602
Six yrs. or less	62.5	37.5	584
Seven yrs. or more	55.0	45.0	431
Gamma = .31		p < .0001 (one-tail)	

[a]N is adjusted by "relative weight" (weight/average weight) so as to reflect entire population without inflating N used in statistical analysis beyond N of actual respondents. Totals vary due to varying non-response rates.

TABLE 15.7
Percent Donating Given Amounts By Actuarial Characteristics

	Under $100	$100–$499	$500 & up	N[a]
Age				
18–34*	55.5	36.3	8.2	75
35–44	53.0	33.5	13.5	112
45–54	54.1	25.7	20.3	82
55–64	43.7	43.4	12.9	89
65 & up	55.0	30.0	15.0	227
Gamma = .01		Not significant		
Generation-In-USA				
Foreign born	50.3	32.0	17.7	65
Native: Two For'n Parents	57.5	27.5	15.0	214
Native: One For'n Parent	44.6	39.2	16.2	64
3–4 Foreign Grandparent	51.7	37.6	10.7	185
0–2 Foreign Grandparent	51.5	28.3	20.1	44
Gamma = .02		Not significant		
Gender				
Male	47.2	35.4	17.4	317
Female	59.9	29.6	10.5	271
Gamma = −.24		$p < .05$ (one-tail)		
Secular Education				
HS, VoTech or Less	63.8	28.2	8.1	212
AA, BA, RN	48.1	36.1	15.8	169
MA	49.7	38.2	12.0	103
PhD or Prof. Degree	39.8	30.9	29.2	92
Gamma = .25		$p < .005$ (one-tail)		
Formal Jewish Education				
None	59.9	28.5	11.6	140
Six Yrs. or Less	59.2	31.9	8.9	219
Seven Yrs. or More	44.4	37.1	18.5	194
Gamma = .20		$p < .05$ (one-tail)		

*18–24 combined with 25–34 due to low N of 18 to 24-year-old donors.

[a]N is adjusted by "relative weight" (weight/average weight) so as to reflect entire population without inflating N used in statistical analysis beyond N of actual respondents. Totals vary due to varying non-response rates.

TABLE 15.8
Standardized Beta Coefficients On Donating Activity

	ON DONATING OR NOT		
	ALL VARIABLES	ACTUARIAL VARIABLES	NON- ACTUARIAL
Variable			
Yom Ha'atzmaut	.14e	—	.16e
Annual Activity	.23e	—	.26e
Weekly Activity	.09d	—	.11e
Income Level	.10e	—	.09d
Source of Income	−.03	—	−.01
Presence of Children	−.06a	—	−.16e
When Moved	.01	—	.13e
Nature of Occupation	−.01	—	.01
Age	.30e	.32e	—
Generation-in-USA	−.04	−.08c	—
Gender	.03	.04	—
Secular Education	.08b	.12e	—
Jewish Education	.07b	.18e	—
Constant	−.59e	−.22c	−.31e
R	.54	.41	.47
R^2	.30	.17	.22
	ON AMOUNT DONATED		
Variable			
Yom Ha'atzmaut	.12b	—	.13b
Annual Activity	.10a	—	.11a
Weekly Activity	−.04	—	−.04
Income Level	.27e	—	.27e
Source of Income	.18e	—	.20e
Presence of Children	−.07	—	−.12a
When Moved	.04	—	.07
Nature of Occupation	−.05	—	.09a
Age	.14a	.12a	—
Generation-in-USA	−.01	−.01	—
Gender	−.03	−.09a	—
Secular Education	.07	.19e	—
Jewish Education	.06	.10a	—
Constant	.02	−1.15e	−.31a
R	.45	.26	.43
R^2	.20	.07	.19

^{a}:$p<.05$ ^{b}:$p<.01$ ^{c}:$p<.005$ ^{d}:$p<.001$ ^{e}:$p<.000$

hold will donate and, albeit to a lesser degree, how much it will contribute. However, that improvement is largely a function of the addition of the age of the head of household, which is the single best predictor of whether a household will donate and one of the better predictors of how much is donated. Little, if any, improvement comes from knowledge of generation-in-the-US, gender, secular education, or Jewish education. Moreover, some of the predictive power of age is due to its impact on two measures: when the person last moved to a new house and the presence of children under 18 in the home. Both measures are reduced in importance when age is included in the analysis. It is age that counts here and not cohort, youth and not the historical context in which they live. That is, "age" here reflects factors such as mobility and the presence of young children, associated with being a young, not-yet-firmly-established adult. Age does not appear to reflect factors such as, for example, attitudes towards Israel, affected by the fact that those under 45, who are less likely to donate to UJA, grew up with the establishment of Israel and its victories in wars more as historical facts than as something they lived through personally as adults.[9]

In any case, those responsible for developing strategies for strengthening future campaigns might do well to take these findings into account.

Strategies For the Future

In broadest terms, the selection of a future strategy will be greatly influenced by whether the campaign is seen primarily as a fundraising mechanism in support of Israel, which it so obviously has been, or more as an instrument for Jewish community building, which may well be its most basic accomplishment, whether such is a deliberate aim or not. Whatever the relative emphasis placed on fundraising and community building, several obvious basic strategies suggest themselves. They are:

* Pay Careful Attention to Locating Jewish Households

Stronger campaigns are known to engage in ongoing, consistent efforts to locate new Jewish households. Once located, efforts should be made to bring them into the active community. The more personal the initial contacts, the better. Data from NJPS not reviewed here indicate that the great majority believe they would respond favorably to a request to donate by somebody they know well. In addition, more believe they would respond better to appeals at work or at some activity or event they attend than to appeals in the mass media. The value of such outreach is underscored by the fact that once reached, newly arrived households donate at levels comparable to that of "old-timers."

* Broaden Understanding and Contact with Young Adults

The future of campaign is bleak if women and men under age 45 continue their relatively low rate of donations. We need to increase our contact with them and understand if their distance from campaign is a matter of youth, which will pass as they become established in the community and their children age, or a matter of cohort, of different historical context, which will be very difficult to overcome. Obviously, there is a need to continue and strengthen Young Leadership programs.

* Go Where the Money Is

Despite efforts to broaden the base of the campaign, it is likely that in any given community, as is true nationally, 1.5 percent of the total number of contributions will provide about 60 percent of the money raised. New gift development and upgrade are obvious components of any strategy. Fortunately, NJPS indicates there are quite a few such households where upgrade may be possible. There are slightly over 140,000 households with annual incomes of $125,000 or more in the population examined by this study.

* Work to Strengthen Jewish Identity

The maintenance of a strong Jewish identity is clearly a key factor to the long-term success of campaign. Where that identity has atrophied, as in households in which no core Jews remain or where a "mixed" Jewish and non-Jewish household has adopted the denominational outlook of the latter, campaign is almost a complete failure.

Unfortunately, there is no easy formula for increasing Jewish identity. However, I suggest efforts be extended to strengthen three aspects of Jewish identity: a religious identity, a sense of peoplehood, and a sense of uniqueness as Jews.

It may well be far from easy to find ways to strengthen the religious identity of American Jewry. We are, after all, the most secular of the three major faiths of North America; we affiliate with religious organizations less often and attend religious services less frequently than others. Indeed, many Jews are secular, even atheistic. NJPS suggests that more American Jews perceive their Jewishness today as an affiliation with a cultural rather than a religious group. Nevertheless, North American Jewry may well have developed, or at least be in the process of developing, a form of Judaism with which it is comfortable. Federation should seek ways to aid this process.

Whatever form it takes, a strong Jewish religion is good for campaign and for Jewish survival. So, too, is a sense of peoplehood. If, and only if, we see ourselves as members of one people, is it possible to understand how and why we are all responsible to and for each other, that *"kol yisrael arevim zeh b'zeh."*

Finally, we must take pride in our uniqueness. In our free and open society, anybody can, and some do, reject the heritage and tradition of one's parents. Therefore, we are all, even if not consciously so, Jews by choice. If we learn to take such pride, and if in doing so we strengthen our Jewish identity, then not only will campaigns thrive, but it will truly be said, *Am Yisrael chai v'kayam,* the Jewish People survive and thrive.

Notes

1. Cohen 1980; Dashefsky 1990; Rimor & Tobin 1990; Ritterband & Silberstein 1988; Silberstein et al., 1987; Winter 1989, 1991.

2. In cases of dual income homes, the head of the household is determined by comparing the number of hours that the respondent and the second adult in the household worked, unless that second adult is unrelated to the first by birth or marriage, with or without benefit of clergy. In all but two of the 1,491 cases *with a mate in the household,* of the total 2,441 sample population, the mate (spouse or partner) of the respondent was mentioned second. Such comparison is necessary since some respondents are young adults living at home with their parents, others are elderly parents living with a middle-aged child, and some are unemployed homemakers. In short, the respondent may well not be a head of the household. In any case, for purposes of the comparison, the adults in the household are categorized as: a) not employed, b) employed part-time, that is, working less than 35 hours a week, or c) employed full-time, that is, working 35 hours a week or more.

3. Households ($N = 68$) which indicate that a donation has been made but which did not specify the amount donated are excluded from these analyses in order to insure comparability, by using the same study population, with analyses of correlates of amounts donated. The inclusion of those who donated an unspecified amount does not alter the finds to any noticeable degree. Neither the gammas or the beta weights reported below are altered by more than /.02/ except in the case of the gamma for whether or not the head of the household is a professional when the gamma drops to .07 from .11.

4. These analyses shall employ gamma as their basic statistic. Gamma is a measure of the strength and direction of the relationship between sets of ordinal

scaled variables. Following standard practice, I shall regard gammas with an absolute value under .10 as "marginal," those between .10 and .19, as "weak," between .20 and .39 as "moderate," and those .40 or more as "strong."

5. These indicators are constituted by scores on scales constructed for the study on the basis of a factor analysis. On the first scale that covers decisions made annually, one point is given if anybody in the household is currently a member of a temple or synagogue, and one point each if the household attends a Seder or lights Hanukkah candles, respectively, all the time. On the second scale, understood as a scale of weekly or more frequent decisions about whether or not to undertake the activity in question, one point is given for each of the following activities the household ever engages in: lighting candles on Friday night, buying kosher meat for home use, or using separate dishes for meat and dairy.

6. As in most studies, the non-response rate with respect to questions about income is relatively high, about 12.6 percent or one respondent in eight.

7. When regression analysis is employed (see Table 15.3) to indicate the relationship between a given measure and whether or not a donation is made while simultaneously controlling for the influence of all the other measures, the level of Annual Jewish Activity emerges as the strongest single correlate, followed by the inhibiting presence of children under 18 (indicated by a negative beta coefficient) and the celebration of Yom Ha'atzmaut. The recency of moving to the household's current city or address as well as its level of Weekly Jewish Activities and its income are also related to the decision to donate or not, albeit only weakly so. The source of household income and whether the head of the household is a professional are not, according to the regression analysis, related to the decision to donate at a statistically significant level.

8. Household donations are categorized as "small," i.e., under $100 (53.1 percent), "moderate," i.e., between $100 and $499 (32.6 percent), and "large," i.e., $500 or more (14.3 percent).

9. Further indication that "age" is a matter of "youth," i.e., of not being established, rather than of being a member of a cohort with distinctive experiences, is found in a factor analysis of the 13 independent variables used in this study. After rotation, the analysis yields four factors. When only variables with loadings (in parentheses) of an absolute value of .35 or more are considered, these factors are: I: age (.88), generation-in-U.S. (−.71), presence of children under 18 (−.63), and when moved (.61); II: Annual Jewish Activity (.80), Weekly Jewish Activity (.75), Yom Ha'atzmaut Celebration (.66), and Jewish Education (.40); III: Secular Education (.81), Occupation (.80), and Income Level (.54); and IV: Source of Income (.73) and Gender (−.73).

References

Cohen, Steven M., "Trends in Jewish Philanthropy," *American Jewish Yearbook: 1980*, Volume 80, pp. 29–51.

Dashefsky, Arnold, "Sources of Jewish Charitable Giving: Incentives and Barriers," in *American Pluralism and the Jewish Community*, Lipset, Seymour M. (ed.), New Brunswick, NJ & London, Transaction, 1990.

Rimor, Mordechai and Gary A. Tobin, "Jewish Giving Patterns to Jewish and Non-Jewish Philanthropy," in *Faith and Philanthropy in America*, Wuthnow, Robert, and Virginia Hodgkinson (eds.), San Francisco, Jossey-Bass, 1990.

Ritterband, Paul and Richard Silberstein, "Generation, Age and Income Variability," *Jewish Philanthropy in Contemporary America*, New York, North American Data Bank, Information Series, No.2, (1988), pp. 44–63.

Silberstein, Richard, Paul Ritterband, Jonathan Rabinowitz, and Barry Kosmin, "Giving to Jewish Philanthropic Causes: A Preliminary Reconnaissance," New York, North American Jewish Data Bank, Reprint Series, No. 2, (1987).

Winter, J. Alan, "Income, Identity and Involvement in the Jewish Community," *Journal of Jewish Communal Service*, Volume 66, (1989), pp 149–156.

————, "Income and Involvement in the Jewish Community: Do Identity, Marital Status or a Child in the House Matter?" *Journal of Jewish Communal Service*, Volume 68, (1991), pp. 17–33.

16

Self Interest, Common Interest, and Public Interest

Barry A. Kosmin

The 1990 National Jewish Population Survey (NJPS) revealed a diverse population of Jews in the United States. In fact, depending on the criteria used, a number of different populations could be isolated. While about 4.4 million people claim to practice some form of Judaism, there are 1.1 million secular or ethnic Jews who do not report having a religion, another 1.3 million (the majority are children) who are from Jewish parentage and ancestry but currently follow a variety of non-Jewish religions, and almost 1.4 million gentiles who live with Jews, most commonly non-Jewish spouses. An accurate population figure could therefore range from 4.4 to 8.2 million members of the American Jewish community.

The fact that these findings lack precision and certainty may frustrate some people who require simple and clear-cut answers to questions. The totals represent a contemporary reality of fluidity and complexity based upon the self-reports of thousands of individuals or potential Jewish consumers. It is obvious to the food industry that the regular weekly market for *glatt* kosher cookies is much smaller than that for *matzoth* at Passover. There are different markets or populations for different purposes; that is the reality of a free market society, particularly in the American case where religion and ethnicity are voluntary identities.

Which population figure should be used? Communal organizations view as their constituency the 5.5 million who are religious or ethnic-secular Jewish. It is the natural market for their services. However, the *Highlights* report on the NJPS[1] reveals that many of those of Jewish descent who presently practice other religions share many views and values with Jews:

they are very concerned about anti-Semitism; nearly half say that being Jewish is important to their lives; they are emotionally attached to Israel (pp. 28–30); they endorse the organized Jewish community's public agenda; they exhibit a high degree of political participation, with more than 80 percent of adults registered to vote; more than a third of their households donate to political campaigns (pp. 35–36); they are socially active, have high levels of philanthropy and volunteerism to secular organizations, and tend to be liberal.

And what about the gentiles in Jewish households? NJPS data show that they resemble Jews in terms of education, occupation, and income, more than average Americans (pp. 10, 11, 19). Moreover, they are highly sympathetic to the concerns of their Jewish family members.

I suggest that the 8.2 million people who identify themselves in some way as part of the Jewish community should be considered the Jewish "political population." This enlarged group, whose size might even be regarded as a positive result of the increasing rates of assimilation and intermarriage revealed by NJPS, is the one that could suffer anti-Semitism; at the same time, it could also be a potential source of increased attachment to Judaism.

Obviously, the population figures have important implications for the Jewish community since, in this case, the internal political agenda may well cut across the external one. However, "population politics" are of growing significance in this country. Of course, Jews are not the only contemporary group affected by a penumbra population. In 1980, the United States Census reported an American-Indian population of 1.4 million, based on a question about race. However, when asked about their ancestry or ethnicity, another 4.6 million who reported their race as white responded "American-Indian." The "white Indians" were relatively prosperous as compared to the smaller group of "red Indians" largely concentrated on reservations.[2] The increasing identification by Americans with their American-Indian ancestors led Native American groups during the 1990 Census to encourage more "Indians" to reveal themselves, and presumably increase the group's political clout, by advertising on Los Angeles buses. A further complication, and an indication of how subjective and political rather than biological the Census tends to be, is the fact that probably a very high proportion of the American-Hispanic population originating in Mexico, Central America, Peru, etc., are in fact American-Indians by race.

The United States Census operates under an unstated assumption that results in the need for the NJPS in the first place: The Jewish organizations believe that religious questions in the United States Census are dangerous, if not illegal, although the latter point has never been tested in court.

Moreover, they have forced the Census Bureau to censor the response of citizens who wish to reveal their Jewish identification in the ancestry question. Jewish organizations have also insisted on the inclusion of a Census note saying that religious identity is not an acceptable response. A policy of negating Jewish identity in all official, public data sends a clear message to the Jewish community to keep a low public profile. This mentality contrasts with the situation in Canada where the category "Jew" is listed alongside "Roman Catholic" and "Sikh" as potential answers to the question of religious identity in the national census. In addition, the response "Jew" appears alongside such options as "French" and "Ukrainian" as answers to the question of ethnic origin.

National events such as the Census have an important educational function for the citizenry. The Jews of Canada fit comfortably within a policy of multiculturalism. Most observers would agree that the Jews of Toronto seem to survive the dangers supposedly inherent in revealing themselves as a collectivity, and that they even thrive as a community. In the United States, Jewish organizations must become aware of the message they send when they advocate a taboo on the use of the term "Jew," and actively pursue a policy of invisibility in the pluralistic American society.

The reality today is that Judaism no longer enjoys a captive market. Rising levels of assimilation, evident in the NJPS, such as increases in intermarriage and diminishing levels of Jewish association by fourth-generation American Jews, make patently clear that a battle for hearts and minds is needed to reverse these negative trends. The dominant Protestant religious influence together with secularizing tendencies have made religion highly privatized in our society. Individuals have much more freedom to choose among religious practices than ever before. The NJPS demonstrates that religion is no longer inevitably passed down from parent to child; rather, religious switching is more common. More Jews are exploring different religions than is commonly believed, and individual preference now outweighs family tradition. These trends seem to have passed by many of our leaders and rabbis. They fail to realize that even the best products have to be promoted and marketed today. The best ideas still require active advocacy to obtain a hearing in a crowded marketplace.

The present condition of American Jewry suggests that we need to convey the message that being Jewish is worthwhile and enjoyable. We must persuade Jews to take pride in the differences between them and other Americans. Perhaps we might talk about our distinctive beliefs. We need to show people that to be Jewish is to be different although not necessarily better. To have Jews marry other Jews and raise Jewish families they must be persuaded that it benefits them. To achieve any of this will require our organizations to look beyond the present affiliated minority. Reaching intermarried, single, and unaffiliated Jews means entering the competitive American marketplace of ideas with a strong and distinctive message geared to a highly segmented audience. American Jews are among the best educated and most affluent groups in the nation inevitably, and in a consumer society, there are numerous other competing products vying for their attention and time. Nevertheless if we believe we have the right product for them, then effective communication is crucial in attaining our agenda.

Egon Mayer has long advocated for our community to "take Judaism as a religion and Jewishness as a culture and civilization public, and stake its claim to a fair share of the public's attention." He suggests that we could learn from the struggle of blacks and Hispanics to improve the public image of their communities in education and the media. Undoubtedly, reaching our potential constituency will require a more positive image of Jews in the media. We must assert ourselves when negative images and detrimental role models are shown. This much-needed initiative requires a more subtle approach than fighting outright prejudice. We seek to rectify here a bias towards presenting intermarried Jews as the norm on Hollywood shows. Hasidic or even Orthodox Jews are often presented as typical religious American Jews, when Conservative and Reform Jews comprise 80 percent of the synagogue-affiliated population. Elderly Holocaust victims are often presented as the voice of the Jewish public, when over 90 percent are American born. We must also actively protest against negative jokes and depictions of Jewish women as "JAPS" or *"Yiddisher Mammas"* when today's average American Jewish woman is a lawyer, nurse or teacher.

An additional complication in such a campaign is that reversing the social invisibility and unrealistic stereotyping of Jews will involve persuading many Jews in the media and entertainment industries to change their outlook and confront their own emotions and loyalties. I foresee greater resistance from them than from gentiles. Nevertheless, we should apply the experience gained from our lobbying and interest-group activities in the political sphere to this crucial social and psychological issue in order to improve our self-esteem as a collectivity.

Getting the message across is also the function of Jewish education. The NJPS reveals that about one-third of students currently receiving any sort of Jewish education are in day school. In total, about 20 percent of young American Jews who have had any Jewish education attended day school. If this form of Jewish education is as effective in reinforcing Jewish identity as its advocates claim, then it is an important asset. This belief motivates the current policy of offering day schooling to refugee children from the former Soviet Union. Such a policy should be extended to other "at risk" groups like the children of intermarried or one-parent families.

However, day school is an expensive option. A logical alternative is to alter the present Jewish position on Church-State relations. It makes sense to try and obtain income tax relief for educational fees or, even better, to join forces with the Catholic Church, which has a similar interest in its parochial schools, in order to obtain legislation providing educational vouchers for parents. Many Jewish dollars would be saved, and should be spent on offering Jewish education to any child who wants it.

The NJPS will hopefully help Jewish community leaders realize that they must understand the makeup of today's Jewish population. American Jews resemble Scandinavians rather than their fellow American citizens, and like them they have low marriage and fertility rates. However, American Jews live in a growing country. Unless we rapidly and successfully convince our penumbra to join us as full-fledged members, we shall become a fast diminishing minority. Jewish interest requires a reversal of the current negative demographic trends such as low marriage rates, low fertility, and the increasing rates of divorce. NJPS data reveal that Jews have the largest proportion of households without children as well as the largest proportion of persons living alone. Rationally, our condition requires a pro-family and pro-natalist stance and inevitably involves coming to terms with women's issues.

The revolution that has transformed family roles in advanced societies has progressed further among American Jews than any other group. New definitions of a woman's place in society, more flexible gender roles due to declining family size and longer life expectancy, which diminish the proportion of the life cycle devoted to child rearing, have particularly affected our community. The dramatic rise in the socioeconomic status of Jewish women has been due to a remarkable level of educational attainment. Among Jewish women age 25–44, two-thirds are college graduates and most of them have postgraduate qualifications. The comparable figure for all white American women is under 18 percent. Moreover, the tendency for Americans to marry within their class reinforces the elite status of Jews. Gentile women in the same age group who are married to Jewish men exhibit "Jewish" levels of education—49 percent are college graduates. On the other hand, Jewish women who left Judaism have only average levels of education.

The Jewish community leadership, both professional and lay, must realize the importance of these social trends and their consequences. The growing gender equality is beginning to affect marital decision-making in areas as diverse as philanthropy and synagogue membership. Jewish women have increased the options open to them. It is in the self-interest of our organizational establishment to support their career goals and life aspirations. Likewise, the Jewish community has clear economic interests to guarantee equal rights for women in professional and managerial employment, and to fight against "glass ceilings" and other inhibiting employment practices.

A crucial aspect of encouraging families is children. NJPS data on current births show that the American Jewish population is increasing and will continue to grow during the next few years. This is because 40 percent of adult American Jews are baby boomers, a generation which is now settling down and having families. Therefore, supporting all forms of day care is in the interest of the Jewish community due to the high proportion of working mothers. Tax credits or relief for day care, as well as funding programs for parochial child-care facilities, make good sense in trying to convince young families to affiliate with Jewish organizations. Our interest in assisting Jewish women in combining careers with marriage and having children also requires us to sponsor programs for flextime and part-time employment, job sharing, and maternity leave.

In regards to a very controversial women's issue such as abortion, an objective assessment of the NJPS data suggests it is not necessarily a vital Jewish issue. American Jews have been using contraceptives effectively for over 60 years. Jews have very few unwed teenage mothers. Nevertheless, Jewish women and Jewish women's organizations are over-represented in the Pro-Choice movement. But, as might be expected of a population that marries late, Jews have below-average rates of fertility. Thus, the need for adoption has become a significant Jewish issue. Currently, three percent of children in Jewish homes are adopted, of which a quarter are brought to the United States from overseas. Fully 13 percent of couples who said they would like to have a child during the next three years are expected to adopt. Past data indicate that only a small proportion of these anticipated adoptions will be realized. Any assistance in easing the legal restrictions, lowering the expenses, and helping to make more babies available for adoption by these families would be a *mitzvah*.

Although the Jewish birthrate is temporarily increasing, the community is altogether getting older. The Jewish demographic profile shows that there is a larger proportion of elderly Jews over age 65 than the U.S. norm—17 to 13 percent, respectively. This means that retirees, their issues and gerontology should particularly concern Jews. Moreover, as a community, Jews pride themselves on exemplary treatment and care of the elderly. The result is that 12 percent of Jewish elderly—a greater than average proportion—are institutionalized. Thus, Medicare, Medicaid, catastrophic health care, and government support of elderly care and housing, are of prime interest to Jewish organizations and Federations which deal with the elderly. Yet the complex communal infrastructure of Jewish social welfare services cannot be financed solely by voluntary contributions; it requires public funds. At the same time, the diminishing pool of women volunteers undermines the formal and informal social support mechanisms. Thus, for Jews, it is clearly in the self-interest, community interest, and national public interest to fight for a government that will put more financial muscle behind calls for a "kinder and gentler America," through increased funding of social services.

Notes

1. Kosmin, Barry A. et al., *Highlights of the CJF 1990 National Jewish Population Survey*, Council of Jewish Federations, New York, 1991. All subsequent page numbers refer to this publication.

2. Farley, Reynolds, "The New Census Questions About Ancestry: What Did It Tell Us?", *Demography*, Volume 28, No. 3, (August 1991).

17

Inreach and Outreach

Donald Feldstein

The 1987 Hollander Colloquium, titled "The Emerging Continental Jewish Community," was an impressive success because for the first time Federations agreed to assume collective responsibility for settling Soviet Jews in the U.S. A short time later, 11 major Federations pooled their allocations to four national agencies. More important, this collective effort enabled the Federations to agree in April 1991 to participate jointly in a $900 million loan guarantee program to resettle Russian Jews emigrating to Israel.

The colloquium, however, failed to address the equally important question of how to strengthen the organized Jewish communal system now that the mobility of Jews in the United States is high. A number of excellent suggestions were raised, including the sharing of names across communities, a "Jewish Express" credit card transferable anywhere in the U.S., and outreach programs for newcomers. Since then, however, no substantial progress has been made to implement such programs and today we are in the same situation as we were in 1987.

Jewish concerns, however, extend well beyond demography. They include the most shocking statistic in the 1990 National Jewish Population Survey, the high intermarriage rate. By now many people have heard of the 50 percent plus intermarriage rate estimated by the survey, and they want to know how the Jewish leadership plans to lower that average. Three courses of action were suggested at the 1991 Hollander Colloquium.

The first was presented by Samuel Klausner, who said that the Jewish community should "draw the wagons into a tight circle" and weed out significant numbers of people that in the largest sense are part of the Jewish community in favor of a bipolar community with a smaller but stronger core.

The second view was presented by Jack Ukeles and Rela M. Geffen, who argued that the Jewish community should stop spending large sums on outreach programs to intermarried couples and their children. Instead, community efforts must concentrate on serving those who remain Jewish. There would be a greater payoff from this strategy even at the risk of losing certain groups, they concluded.

The third and contradicting viewpoint, expressed by Egon Mayer and others, was that the amount of money used for outreach to intermarrieds is not vast, and thus such spending should not be an issue in contention. Mayer believes that working to bring intermarried couples and their children into the community could be successful with some, and benefit Jews in the long run. My sense is that most of those present at the 1991 colloquium favored this view.

I believe, however, that Professor Mayer went a step further: he took a social problem which we cannot solve and declared that it was not a problem. This is a common American trait. Russell Baker wrote a column once about the evolution of the term "disabled" to "physically challenged," and the term "retarded" to "mentally challenged." He noted that Americans tend to think that if one finds inoffensive terminology with which to discuss a problem, the problem will disappear. Mayer suggested that intermarriage is so prevalent today that we should stop considering it a problem to be prevented, accept it as a reality, and deal with it. I have not felt any consensus with that viewpoint.

I think that most of the organized Jewish community wants to continue emphasizing programs which could reduce the intermarriage rate, since there is evidence that it is lower among Jews who were brought up in homes where marrying outside the religion was considered outrageous.

The NJPS results indicate that association with fellow Jews, more than attendance in day schools, at least through elementary grades, is most strongly correlated with the rate of in-marriage. These findings contradict data from other studies, particularly local ones, which show that the rate of intermarriage is lower among Jews with a strong Jewish background and education than among those who associate with fellow Jews but lack a strong Jewish background.

Whatever the final analysis of the data shows, I think that a focus on association with fellow Jews is very important and should be given a high priority by the organized Jewish community. I wish every Jewish college student in America could be exposed twice a year to a lox and bagel breakfast with other Jewish men and women at their local Hillel on campus. I wish our Jewish Community Centers could return to the kind of programming they had in the 1930's, 40's, and 50's, when they served large percentages of Jewish children and teenagers. I wish every Jew who relocates would be invited to a tea with other Jewish residents of his or her new community. We should learn from the Evangelical and Fundamentalist Christians how powerful and important fellowship can be. Fellowship counts, and it ought to be at the top of our priorities.

Outreach efforts should be directed towards Jews who are only marginally involved in the community; the Memorial Foundation for Jewish Culture has helped sponsor such programs in St. Louis and MetroWest and reports dramatic results. The general finding is that in a year an outreach worker can heavily involve about 300 Jewish families that were hardly involved before.

In addition, I hope we can also learn from segments in the Orthodox community how to make outreach to affiliated Jewish families a central part of our agenda. The 1990 NJPS found that about 12 percent of those calling themselves Orthodox said their parents or families of origin were not Orthodox. Most of them are probably *ba'alei t'shuva*.

Some studies suggest that visits by youths to Israel can be critical to their Jewish identity. These programs need not be expensive. Most large Federations have the resources to guarantee that any Jewish youth who wants to can visit the Jewish state. It should be made possible for every child to spend a year, six months, or at least a summer in Israel. Such programs will strengthen Jewish identity and I would make them a major priority. (This recommendation has been taken up since the 1991 colloquium.)

A fourth priority is to get the Jewish community back into providing infertile couples with adoption services. Adoption, which used to be the bread-and-butter service of the Jewish Family Agency system, has in the last 30 years been handed over to attorneys. Some of them do wonderful—although expensive—work in this area, but others, who are motivated solely by greed, can cause much harm. In either case, there is no reason why the Jewish Agency system cannot provide cheaper and better adoption services, while still making them a profit center for the agency.

To sum up, I suggest that our Federations should place an emphasis on outreach and associational programs to core and marginal Jews; should outreach to new Jewish residents, in order to integrate them into the community; should actively encourage visits by Jewish youths to Israel; and should offer adoption services again.

There is a growing consensus that there will be a slow but significant decline in the Jewish population in the United States in the coming years, particularly as the baby boomers get beyond their childbearing years.

Still, I am very optimistic about the future of Jews in the United States. Historically many of the greatest contributions of Jews were made where the Jewish community had to clash or integrate with other communities outside of Israel, such as in Spain during the Golden Age of Maimonides and Yehuda Halevi, in the France of Rashi, during the time of the great Yeshivot of Eastern Europe, and in the writing of the Torah and Talmud. These have been the creative ages of the Jewish people. When the final book is written, I am convinced that the American experience will go down as one of the most significant chapters in the glorious history of the Jews.

18

The Marketing of Judaism

Steven Huberman

A sage once said, "The Jews are like everyone else, except more so." The implication of this statement is clear. As Jews increasingly enter the mainstream of North American society, they take on the attributes of the larger community. They have done it with gusto. Just as the general community assimilates, becomes older, divorces, so does the Jewish community of North America.

The 1990 National Jewish Population Survey demonstrates critical trends in the changing demography of North American Jewry including: economic marginality, intermarriage, residential mobility, the breakdown of Jewish identity, and the need for new fundraising strategies.

The Persistence of Jewish Economic Marginality

Although Jews have a profile comparable to high socioeconomic status groups, low income persists. In many communities almost 20 percent of the Jews have low incomes bordering on poverty. In order to deal with this increasing strain, Jewish communities throughout North America have to bolster their social service structures. Since the New Deal, Jews came to fundamentally rely on the federal government for social welfare help. New realities dictate a change in communal priorities.

As a result of federal, state, and local government reductions for human services, Jewish community agencies are going to have to make up the gap, especially for the elderly. Doing so will require expansion of employment help, housing and support services for the elderly, food distribution programs, counseling, cash assistance, child care, and related activities. I believe the synagogue system is an untapped resource in this effort.

Although Federations and social service agencies may not be able to provide adequate financial resources to deal with the persistence of economic distress, they can mobilize their synagogue partners to provide an increasing share of the people power to deploy. One recent illustration in a community tells of a Jewish high school mobilizing a group of volunteers to provide food distribution to the homeless on evenings in the center city area. Such efforts can provide meaningful learning experiences and substantive assistance to needy Jews. They will require systematic coordination among synagogues and agencies to avoid duplication.

Intermarriage Continues to Rise

Since the mid 1980's, less than half of Jewish marriages involve two partners who were born Jewish. Increasingly Jews have come to accept intermarriage. Conversion to Judaism is also with us, but going down. It is estimated that there are currently about 185,000 Jews by choice.

The social psychologist Chaim Ginot observed that even though we may not approve of an action, we need to validate the actors. In the case of intermarriage, we may not approve of intermarriage, but we need to reach out to the persons involved in an intermarriage in a loving, caring fashion. As intermarriage increases within the community, efforts must be mounted to integrate these persons within the fabric of our social groups. Synagogues may need to reconsider their admissions procedures so that this growing group is not excluded from religious life. Programs which are developed to reach out to intermarried families will need to be sensitive to the unique makeup of the extended families. Programs which are a success among endogamous Jewish partners may not have the same likelihood of success within the intermarried situation.

There have been many Jews by choice over the past 20 years. Converts have a particular type of Jewish identity. Whereas most born Jews identify as cultural or ethnic Jews, Jews by choice define themselves as a religious group. This will invariably cause tension as we seek to integrate Jews by choice into our communities.

Jews Are On the Move

American Jews are an extraordinarily mobile population: nearly half changed residence in the last six years. The recent migration of Jews from overseas, particularly from the former Soviet Union, has added yet a new element to the transplanting population.

It is essential that we bring all of these newcomers into organized communal life. We should not expect them to come to us. It will, therefore, be incumbent upon us to reach out to these persons in a warm and personal way. Recent attempts to provide acculturation services to Russian Jews are a good model for outreach. Such programs as "adopt a family," mentoring newcomers, and providing free or reduced synagogue and center memberships are expressions of how to integrate these persons into the mainstream of Jewish life.

Our increasingly mobile America and immigrant Jewish populations necessitate that we work across denominational and organizational lines. This will require that we join together to provide a more human touch to our outreach activities.

Dor L'Dor

Judaism stresses *dor L'dor*, the need to transmit Jewish identity from one generation to the next. Although Jewish observance is down, there is a surprising level of residual behavior. Many continue to observe the Passover Seder, fast on Yom Kippur, light Hanukkah candles, and never have a Christmas tree. Despite this seasonal Jewish activity which is holiday related, the more weekly aspects of Jewish religious behavior are on the decline.

Judaism has been defined as the evolving religious culture of the Jewish people. Dr. Robert Gordis, who postulated this concept based on the work of Mordecai Kaplan, noted that this definition means that Judaism consists of three elements: religion, culture, and Jewish peoplehood or ethnicity. Until the Emancipation and Englightenment in Europe, Jews embodied all of these elements. We had an organic Jewish community and a good Jew incorporated all of these aspects in his identity. Judaism was like a beautiful vase in a home. It was passed down from generation to generation until an earthquake occurred and the vase fell from its sacred place and was shattered into hundreds of pieces.

Judaism today is like this shattered vase. Jews pick up one shattered piece or another. They pick up a piece of religion, a piece of culture, or a piece of ethnicity. Our goal should be to put the beautiful vase back together again and create organic Jews who care about the totality of Jewish life and *Klal Yisrael*.

How may we achieve this? I believe the solution lies in creating an orchestrated marketing plan with synagogues of every persuasion, plus the federated system of agencies. Such a plan will require bringing Judaism into the marketplace. It means having rabbis and educators teach Jews in their places of employment, in legal and medical offices throughout North America, wherever significant numbers of Jews gather in the corporate and professional world. I was recently invited to the office of a prominent attorney in a magnificent office building. When I approached the receptionist, who was clearly non-Jewish in appearance, I inquired, "Where is the study group?" She replied, "The rebbe is in the conference room." There in the conference room were 30 men and women attorneys, all appropriately dressed in three piece business suits, studying *Tanya*, a famous esoteric text. There was Rabbi Shusterman from the Yeshiva, who was serving salmon kugel and leading this corporate study group. These kinds of efforts to bring Judaism into the workplace must be reinforced.

Although formal Jewish education is essential, many Jews will unfortunately never belong to a synagogue. In addition to promoting synagogue affiliation, we must nurture the other contact points for entry into Jewish life. The following types of endeavors must be fortified: informal Jewish education at Jewish community centers, Hillel and college courses in Judaism, and Judaic content programming for future lay leadership. The efforts of the Wexner Foundation to create a new generation of Judaicly informed Jewish lay leadership is an excellent illustration of this orientation.

Although most Jews are linked to Israel, many have never visited the country. Empirical research has consistently shown that an effective way to promote Jewish identification is through a systematic learning experience in Israel. It is essential that every young person be afforded an Israel experience. Many communities have established Israel-incentive savings programs. The family, school, and community work together and set aside dollars each year so that each student may participate in an identity building project in Israel. These approaches must be multiplied.

Although dollars are scarce today, we can finance all of these endeavors. It is estimated that Jews give over $2 billion per year to charitable undertakings. The challenge is to redirect these dollars from general communal concerns to programs which specifically bolster the social and identity needs of Jews. In order to provide the financial undergirding, key institutions of the Jewish community must collaborate.

Will the Well Run Dry?

A famous article by Steven Cohen and Paul Ritterband asked the question "Will the well run dry?" The authors wanted to know if Jewish philanthropic resources would be adequate to finance the totality of communal endeavors. In my judgment, the increasing Jewish affluence in North

America should provide an adequate "well." The challenge is how to increase the Jewish philanthropic share.

Elie Weisel has stated, "Jews alone are vulnerable. But Jews must not be alone." Weisel meant that Jews function most effectively in organized groups. This insight undergirds much successful fundraising. Research has shown that in order for a federated campaign to work effectively, it must have the following attributes:

- The organization should be perceived as a central address of the organized Jewish community. Good public relations should be reinforced by good performance.
- Veteran leadership has to continue to be prominent in the campaign activity and in critical decisions.
- Systematic training needs to be conducted for all age groups. Potential leaders should receive special targeting.
- Past leaders should be held in high regard and given special developmental tasks.
- Board members should be constantly recruited and rewarded for excellence.
- High quality staff should be identified and cultivated.

In order to provide the necessary resources to finance programs, we need to look towards these types of strategies. To raise the philanthropic base we must involve more individuals in annual campaigns and seek to establish a higher standard of giving. In 1993, exclusive of Operation Exodus, Jewish Federation campaigns raised approximately 722 million dollars. We can do even better.

I believe it is imperative that the Jewish community of North America must confront the issues which are set forth in the National Jewish Population Survey. It must deal with the persistence of Jewish economic distress, the increasing incidence of intermarriage, high residential mobility, low observance, and undergiving to annual campaigns. Given the tremendous human resources in Jewish communal agencies, we have the personnel and the imagination to solve all of these problems. Our credo was best stated by Theodor Herzl, who noted, "If you will it, it is not a dream." It is time to move on with Herzl's vision.

19

Enhancing Jewish Identity: Form and Content

Steven Bayme

The release of the National Jewish Population Survey by the Council of Jewish Federations has elicited widespread comment in the Jewish community. Some have questioned its conclusions, claiming that the report understates the Jewish identity of American Jews. Others have boldly cited the report in order to challenge communal norms, priorities, and policies. For example, upon release of the survey, the *New York Times* cited one prominent opinion leader and social scientist to the effect that "The battle against intermarriage is now over—the time is for a new focus upon outreach." To date, however, the most widespread response has been increased anxiety among Jewish communal leaders, often accompanied by hysteria and communal paralysis.

Two themes have, thus far, dominated much of the initial communal discussion: the first is the perception that American Jews are, indeed, assimilating, and the second is a call for outreach to intermarried couples. These reactions, in and of themselves, are noteworthy and deserve broader comment. The report confirms what many have long expected: American Jews do, indeed, have strong concerns regarding future Jewish vitality and continuity. Intermarriage connotes declining Jewish identity—especially when measured and studied over several generations. Attempts to portray intermarriage as an opportunity rather than a crisis for the Jewish community amount to little more than wishful thinking. The much-heralded debate over the quality of Jewish life in America, for the moment, favors those who stress the forebodings of American Jews.

In the past few years, much discussion within the Jewish community concerning the quality of Jewish life has focused on the twin poles of form and content. Those who underscore the forms of Jewish life are generally optimistic. They perceive a vital American Jewish institutional structure and assume that this structure and enterprise are underpinned and propelled by sufficient quality and force to keep the enterprise viable. For them the cup is half full rather than half empty.

In contrast, those who emphasize the content of Jewish life worry about the Judaic commitments of American Jews. They focus upon a declining Jewish literacy, a low rate of communal affiliation, and a high level of intermarriage. For them the cup is half empty rather than half full.

Steven Cohen explains this dichotomy as a commitment to continuity versus a commitment to content. In an American Jewish Committee survey of American Jews, Cohen defines 10 to 15 percent of the community as totally unaffiliated. At the opposite end, he identifies a core group of 20 to 25 percent who are committed to content. The vast middle of American Jewry, however, manifests a commitment to continuity—they want to have Jewish grandchildren—but few commitments to ideological content.[1]

This debate between optimists and pessimists is by no means strictly academic. Rather, actual policy will turn on whether we choose to emphasize form or content when discussing ways to strengthen the Jewish identity of American Jews.

One policy question concerns our target populations. Do we seek to strengthen the periphery of Jewish life, the marginals, or do we strengthen the core in the belief that more effective leadership will build a community attractive enough so that others will wish to join us? Some will argue that we should emphasize the periphery because programs geared towards the Jewish core will often be irrelevant to the marginals. Programs directed to the core are likely to be strong on content, e.g., the leadership programs conducted by the Wexner Foundations. Conversely, programs targeted to the periphery are more likely designed primarily to bring individual Jews into communal institutions.

Related to this is the obvious economic question of how we should best utilize limited resources in the most productive ways. In other words, where will we get the biggest bang for the buck: in programs that seek to impart ideological content or programs that seek to bring Jews into contact with other Jews?

Then there is the philosophical question of content and ideology: Programs geared to strengthen the periphery of Jewish life may require significant dilution of content to the point of ideological vacuity. To date, much of the programmatic and policy discussion within the Jewish community has emphasized Jewish socialization experiences, vehicles for strengthening the community and enhancing existing structures, rather than focusing upon the ideological content of such programs. I think this is true for several reasons.

First, and most obviously, the debate has been led by sociologists and social historians. These scholars tend to underscore the structural bases of Jewish life. Norms, religious and cultural values often play a secondary role at most in their outlook or methods.

Second, and more important, the advocates of structure have captured the attention and approval of Jewish lay leadership. Although many suggest that we are a people that does not wish to hear good news, in actuality the argument for structure has struck a very resonant chord. It assures Jewish lay leadership that even if young people are intermarrying, there is no need to fear for the future of the Jewish people. Intermarriage, in this view, poses little or no danger to future Jewish continuity; programs of outreach will, in all likelihood, maintain the Jewish identity of the mixed-married household. To put it most starkly, the problem is said to be not that of the mixed-married but of a Jewish community that does not welcome them in its midst. In other words, advocates of structure, on the basis of social science research, articulate a message that Jewish communal leaders—given their personal involvement in intermarriages and their difficulty in articulating a language of endogamy to their children—are eager to hear and accept. Rather than the people that refuse to listen to good news, we are becoming the people eager to receive a message of consolation.[2]

Conversely, we are unclear as to the precise role of ideology in Jewish life. Does the power and persuasiveness of Jewish ideas compel Judaic commitment and identity? Or can ideas only contribute to an overall Jewish identity formation, perhaps merely part of a superstructure that is essentially grounded in social and economic factors? In other words, we are unsure whether we are motivated as Jews by the power of Jewish ideas or by a desire for contact with fellow Jews.

I believe we emphasize structure because of its historical significance. In medieval times, it was the capacity of the community to impose authority and compel behavior. The question before us today is whether strong and vibrant Jewish communal structures can elicit voluntary conformity.

Moreover, we emphasize structure at least in part to avoid ideological conflict within the community and to preserve a consensus that enables us to fulfill our functions. In other words, the absence of ideology frequently makes for sound communal politics. The contrast between the approaches of different elements of the community are significant in this regard. Outreach programs on the right are heavily dominated by content. Our Orthodox colleagues emphasize ideological maximalism in the belief that people will respond only to a message that is ideologically compelling and authentic. Non-Orthodox outreach tends to be as inclusive as possible. It minimizes the role of ideology and emphasizes the forms of Jewish life more than its content.

Finally, in emphasizing structure I believe that we are making a statement to our Israeli friends concerning the vitality of American Jewry. They underscore our assimilation and predict our eventual disappearance. In emphasizing structure, our message is far more upbeat. In the words of a telecast of *thirtysomething*, when Michael Steadman visited a synagogue and asked how things were going, the rabbi responded: "We are doing fine," a remarkable statement to the effect that the structures of Jewish life appear to be thriving even if, as *thirtysomething* so painfully revealed, the contents of Jewish life are often virtually absent.

The second major focus of communal attention emanating from the 1990 National Jewish Population Survey concerns the rising tide of intermarriage and the consequent human and demographic imperatives of outreach to mixed-marrieds. The human imperatives are obvious: Gentile family members are human beings, all created in the image of God, and therefore ought to be warmly welcomed by all family members. The demographic imperatives are also clear: Given the rising tide of interfaith marriages and low and declining rates of conversion to Judaism, we face the spectre of considerable population loss over the next generation. Advocates of outreach argue that we now have our single "window of opportunity" to transform the map of the Jewish community by increased investment in outreach programs designed to secure the Jewishness of the mixed-married home.

These statements are, of course, understandable and, in considerable measure, justified. Certainly one ought not quarrel either with the human imperatives of outreach or with the demographic realities. However, all too often communal policy is guided by the anxiety of Jewish leaders that their grandchildren remain Jews, paying little attention to the content and effectiveness of outreach, its overall message to the Jewish community, and the real financial cost involved in funding outreach activities. Such a heated and emotional climate (at times individuals insist that their grandchildren are Jewish even if outwardly practicing Christianity) is not very conducive to rational policy formulation and analysis. Advocates of outreach must, however, confront difficult questions: Does outreach, where successful, make it difficult if not impossible to discourage interfaith marriage? Moreover, are we diverting sorely-needed funds from those target populations that hold out the greatest promise for leading a creative Jewish life to programs targeted to those outside of the Jewish community whom we hope to attract? Finally, are outreach initiatives likely to succeed in building strong and stable Jewish homes given the long-term presence of gentile partners?

Most importantly, we must confront the reality that the primary weakness of Jewish life is our lack of commitment to content and our incapacity to articulate compelling ideological norms. Here lie our policy imperatives, for pragmatic as well as philosophical reasons.

Philosophically, it is ideas that have made us distinctive as a people. Judaic ideas inform us as to the purpose of our survival. Continuity for the sheer sake of continuity not only fails to excite the imagination, but also fails to hold out any transcendental imperative for survival beyond crude tribalism and the maintenance of the race. As Michael Rosenak argues, "Jewishness without an anchor in ultimate concern is apt to lead to sterile nostalgia or provincial particularism."[3] Furthermore, it is the mandate of Jewish communal leaders to set norms, provide leadership, and articulate values that will inspire others. We cannot and should not define as Jewishly authentic anything that Jews happen to do.

On a pragmatic level, I doubt that a focus on structural factors alone can ensure continuity; at best, they offer a snapshot in time. Yet, as historians have reminded us, the processes of assimilation are multi-generational. In the absence of ideological commitment, it is questionable whether assimilation can be checked in the second and third generations. Todd Endelman has written that the gradual nature of the assimilatory process often masks how extensive and corrosive that process actually is. In the past, he observes, ongoing immigration functioned as a brake upon the process. However, given the gradual nature of assimilation and the accompanying immigration trends, we fail to notice that each succeeding generation has been "progressively more distant from traditional practices and loyalties."[4]

Much can be learned from the experience of the Presbyterian Church. Its recent report on sexuality was motivated, according to the report's supporters and framers, by the concern that the Church, as it existed, was losing many of its members. Yet, to date, the report has not been adopted because it seeks to redefine Church teachings on sexuality in such a radical way as to be offensive to the core Church population. In other words, church leaders are discovering that their effort to reach out to those on the periphery entails so great a change of content that religious distinctiveness and ideological principle are forfeited.

Finally, I believe that some level of ideological conflict in the community is desirable; it indicates, at least, that people care. Pluralism should enable us to state firmly what we believe even as we reach out in an attempt to attract others to our beliefs. Judaic truths and ideals should emerge in a free marketplace of expression.

Conversely, those who advocate strengthening the structures of Jewish life often ignore how discussions of structure can spill over into the area of norms and values. A constant focus on the present situation easily translates into norms that should be expected. For example, in the name of realism, we often mute the ideological debate on intermarriage. With the emphasis upon the need for outreach, little focus has been directed to the ideological content of outreach: Do we engage intermarrieds in a spirit of true pluralism or in a spirit in which we dress up our tradition to make it palatable to them? Moreover, sociological pronouncements that the battle against intermarriage has already been forfeited, in and of themselves help create a cultural climate in which intermarriage becomes more normative. The community, in turn, struggles to redefine that which is problematic in normative language.

The distinguished Reform Rabbi David Polish has pinpointed this dilemma. He argues that outreach to mixed-marrieds, where successful, will have a transforming effect upon Jewish institutions, possibly diluting Jewish content. The danger of such successful outreach is the merging of Jewish and Christian identities into a meaningless hybrid, as well as the overall legitimation of intermarriage.[5] Thus, a well-intentioned effort to broaden the institutional bases of Jewish life can result in undermining Jewish distinctiveness in favor of ideological blandness.

In short, I believe that without ideas we have little to go on. Ethnic solidarity and the structural forces of community will lose their salience over time. Perhaps, in the short run, social networks of Jews can sustain Jewishness. However, without ideology, all that we have to go on is a combination of vague pro-Israelism, nostalgia, fear of anti-Semitism, and a liberal universalism that we dress up in Jewish garb. These, to me, are flimsy and unrealistic bases on which to guarantee the Jewish future.

Therefore, the challenge to our community is to unite form and content, to build the content of Jewish life within our quest for Jewish continuity and not lose sight of our ideological imperatives in a desire to ensure structural survival. Form requires content and content requires form. One cannot expect continuity if Jews know little about what they wish to continue. Conversely, we cannot continue unless we have the structures and institutions that enable us to be Jews. Absent community, we are unable to implement Judaic norms in a concrete and practical way that gives our beliefs and principles a "plausibility structure."[6]

In terms of specific suggestions, we have much to learn from the right-wing Orthodox who have been successful when measured by rates of inmarriage, observance of holidays and rituals, visits to Israel, and Judaic literacy. The rest of the community shares these goals of content. We should not be afraid to articulate them publicly.

Secondly, we must identify target groups that are most amenable to a unity of content and continuity—those who have demonstrated a commitment to Judaic survival that must now be enhanced ideologically. This means that one of the most popular slogans of Jewish life, the "outreach to the unaffiliated," is misdirected. Those who are truly unaffiliated are difficult to find. Moreover, we have no evidence that they wish to be pursued. Finally, the blessing of freedom in America does mean the freedom to opt out, and that is a choice we should respect.

Thirdly, we require an evaluation of existing programs from the perspective of both form and content. Quite often, when we see a program that is structurally sound in terms of numbers of people involved, we are reluctant to analyze its content and ideological message. This is particularly true in the case of programs of outreach to interfaith couples.

Finally, unity of content and structure means maintaining the capacity of Jewish organizations and institutions to say meaningful things. Institutional viability should never be allowed to come at the price of ideological blandness.

Where, then, does this analysis take us? First, we must be honest in recognizing that our failure to take normative positions seriously constitutes a critical weakness in Jewish life today. As a result, being Jewish is all too often an instinctual matter, an emotional response to perceived anti-Semitism or threats to Israel's existence. We lack serious incentives of a theological or spiritual nature. What we need are programmatic initiatives that will underscore and communicate the spiritual and intellectual bases of contemporary Jewish identity. Perhaps Yosef Yerushalmi is correct in arguing that Jewish scholarship cannot redeem "the faith of fallen Jews."[7] Academic research is clearly no substitute for collective memory. Conversely, however, institutional structures are an even poorer substitute for the content and meaning of being Jewish. Our policy imperative is to restore that content and meaning, to translate it to the minds and hearts of American Jews.

Much has been made in recent years of using a "language of resource" rather than a "language of reproach." That is sound tactical advice. Most Jews consider themselves to be "good Jews." They do not wish to be told otherwise. It is both inappropriate and impractical to communicate the values of being Jewish in a language that condemns those who do not share those values.[8] However, in using a language of resource, let us not delude ourselves into thinking that all is well in the Jewish community or that content is irrelevant to the Jewish future. Unfortunately, that message has all too often been blurred within the community by pronouncements of the optimistic social scientists.[9]

Moreover, content is critical in terms of core leadership for the future. Let us therefore acknowledge and strengthen the successful initiatives that have been taken in this area. It is particularly necessary to overcome whatever remaining communal ambivalence exists concerning Jewish day schools, the single most intensive and successful initiative to enhance the content of Jewish identity. To be sure, we are unrealistic if we think that the goals of content can be achieved in the dominant forms of Jewish education today. It is for that reason that content must be accompanied by socialization experiences such as Jewish camping, youth movements, and trips to Israel. This qualification, however, articulates the need for balance between programs designed to strengthen the core and programs designed to bring the periphery closer to the core.

Much of this discussion concerning form and content points to a re-definition of our relationship with Israel. The Jewish state represents the public agenda of American Jews, yet that is probably the least important role it plays in ensuring Jewish continuity. Where Israel is successful as an experience is in the sense that it addresses the private identity of American Jews. Israel communicates a sense of history and homecoming; it brings us into contact both with the intellectual treasures of the Jewish heritage and the emotional experiences of being among Jews. The Israeli fascination with archaeology, for example, is a powerful statement concerning the importance of roots.

To enrich the content of Jewish life, we will have to address this private side of Israel and its meaning for American Jews. Our problem is that within Jewish leadership circles, the Israel that is discussed is the political one; it is the opportunity to meet a Prime Minister that Jewish leaders find exciting; they would do well to underscore publicly not only the political questions but the meaning of Israel to contemporary Jewish identity as well.

Conversely, our Israeli friends must also look beyond the structural side of American Jewry. Their own experience demonstrates that it is not enough to live in a land that is structurally Jewish and to expect to remain Jewish simply by osmosis. On the contrary, the future of Jewish identity among Israelis is not guaranteed either. Thus, researcher Simon Herman warns that a strong Israeli identity that is not rooted in the Jewish heritage risks becoming a shallow nationalism, alienated from Diaspora Jewish culture and community.[10]

Will Herberg's thesis in his book *Protestant-Catholic-Jew*, that Jews have indeed arrived in American society, is still relevant today. Still, the other side of Herberg's thesis, that this triple melting pot does not really mean very much because all three faiths have become bland, is often ignored.[11] Efforts to ensure continuity without content will guarantee that continuing blandness. Our job as communal leaders is not only one of outreach. Rather, we must have authentic Judaism inform our outreach initiatives to the point that we stand for something that is clear, coherent, and meaning-ful. As Arthur Hertzberg has so eloquently stated, invoking anti-Semitism and preaching togetherness as techniques to preserve Jewish identity will undoubtedly fail. "A community cannot survive on what it remembers; it will persist only because of what it affirms and believes," he claims.[12]

The critical challenge for us today is therefore to explore what Judaism actually says in the modern world, what it affirms to us as modern men and women, and what values it conveys.

My own conclusions, heavily indebted to Mordecai Kaplan, is that Jewish teachings are quite salient when seen in comparison with and in contrast to dominant American norms. Without question, this country can and does offer us enormous opportunities. What makes Jewish life in America particularly exciting is the challenge to grab that opportunity, to think through what the areas are in which Judaic and American values complement one another and, more importantly, to wrestle with the conflicts and contradictions between American liberalism and Jewish tradition. In this respect, we are all disciples of Kaplan. Our challenge is to create a culture and a civilization that absorbs the best of American society, fused and integrated with the enduring values of Jewish heritage. The challenge of synthesis is not the monopoly of those few committed to content and ideology. Rather, it is the imperative of all committed to living in both civilizations, Jewish and American, but who are not prepared to sacrifice one for the sake of the other.

Notes

1. Cohen, Steven M., *Content or Continuity? Alternative Bases for Commitment*, New York: (American Jewish Committee, 1991), esp. pp. 40–42.

2. See for example, Goldscheider, Calvin, *Jewish Continuity and Change: Emerging Patterns in America*, Bloomington, Indiana University Press, 1986, p. 28, and more generally, Bayme, Steven, "Changing Perceptions of Intermarriage," *Journal of Jewish Communal Service*, Vol. 66, No. 3 (Spring, 1990), p. 221. By far the most popular and influential work of the "optimists" school is Silberman, Charles, *A Certain People: American Jews and Their Lives Today*, New York, Summit Books, 1985. It would be highly instructive to study the response to Silberman within Jewish leadership circles. For my own critique see, "Crisis in American Jewry," *Contemporary Jewry*, Vol. 8 (1987), pp. 125–128.

3. Rosenak, Michael, *Commandments and Concerns*, Philadelphia, Jewish Publications Society of America, 1987, page 104.

4. Endelman, Todd, "Response to Paula Hyman, 'The Ideological Transformation of Modern Jewish Historiography,' " in Cohen, Shaye, and Edward Greenstein (eds.), *The State of Jewish Studies*, Detroit, Wayne State University Press, 1990, pp. 161–162. See also, more generally, Endelman, Todd, *Radical Assimilation in English Jewish History, 1656–1945*, Bloomington and Indianapolis, Indiana University Press, 1990, ch. 1.

5. Polish, David, "What Is The Track Record of Intermarriage?," *Chicago Sentinel*, June 6, 1991.

6. Rosenak, op. cit., p. 253.

7. Yerushalmi, Yosef, *Zakhor: Jewish History and Jewish Memory*, Seattle and London, University of Washington Press, 1982, pp. 86–98.

8. Cohen, Steven M., "Outreach to the Marginally Affiliated: Evidence and Implications for Policymakers in Jewish Education," *Journal of Jewish Communal Service*, Vol. 62 No. 2 (Winter 1985), pp. 154–156.

9. See the critique of the optimistic sociologists by Liebman, Charles, "The Quality of American Jewish Life: A Grim Outlook," in *Facing the Future: Essays on Contemporary Jewish Life*, Bayme, Steven (ed.), New York, Ktav, 1989, esp. p. 69.

10. Herman, Simon, "The Study of Contemporary Jewish Identity," in *Facing the Future: Essays on Contemporary Jewish Life*, Steven Bayme, ed., New York, Ktav, 1989, p. 212.

11. Sarna, Jonathan, "Jewish Identity in the Changing World of American Religion," in *Jewish Identity in America*, Gordis, David and Yoav Ben-Horin, eds., Los Angeles, Wilstein Institute of Jewish Policy Studies, 1991, pp. 94–96, and Herberg, Will, *Protestant-Catholic-Jew*, Garden City, Revised edition, Anchor Books, 1960, esp. pp. 27–41 and 193–198.

12. Hertzberg, Arthur, *The Jews in America*, New York, Simon and Schuster, 1989, pp. 381–386.

Postscript
Structural Challenges to Jewish Continuity

Jonathan D. Sarna

A s I read through the outline of this volume, beginning with "Demographics" and ending with "Looking Ahead," I was struck by how traditional our approach to problems in Jewish life continues to be. Like the Passover *Haggadah*, which begins with slavery and idolatry and ends with redemption ("next year in Jerusalem"), our analyses too move from negative to positive, from challenge to response, from gloom and doom to creativity and hope. This may, at first glance, seem to reflect the continuing power of a traditional formula (what would today be called a literary trope). On a deeper reflection, however, it seems to me that this formula accurately depicts a critical dynamic in Jewish history generally, and American Jewish history in particular.

The great energizing force in American Jewish history has been external challenges: Christian missions, anti-Semitism, fear for Jewish survival. In each case, American Jews have been, in Salo Baron's phrase, "steeled by adversity." They have responded forcefully and effectively to communal challenges—so effectively, indeed, that the community has often emerged from them stronger than before. Jewish educational institutions, Jewish newspapers, Jewish hospitals, and Jewish defense agencies are prime examples of innovations pioneered by the American Jewish community as responses to external challenges. This suggests a profound and important historical paradox, pointed out years ago in a somewhat different way by Professor Simon Rawidowicz, and then again by Professor Marshall Sklare. If I may restate this paradox in terms relevant to our own agenda, it is that the most effective way to ensure Jewish continuity in America is to predict that Jews will *not* survive. That, more than anything else, stimulates our best minds to prove us wrong.

The widespread concern today with the issue of Jewish continuity—a new term for what used to be called Jewish survivalism—indicates that the strategies devised over the past century to ensure the Jewish future have not worked out as well as we had hoped. These strategies include: The study of Jewish history; the revolution in Jewish education; the emphasis on acquiring a Jewish language—Hebrew, and to a lesser extent, Yiddish; the many efforts aimed at revitalizing Jewish religious and spiritual life, as well as the synagogue; programs aimed at deepening the wellsprings of Jewish culture; the movement to strengthen the bonds of Jewish community (the *kehillah* experiments early in the 20th century, and more recently the development of *havurot*); the call to embrace a Jewish mission of social justice or *tikkun olam;* the attempt to strengthen feelings of shared Jewish ethnicity; the raising of Holocaust consciousness and a commitment to "no posthumous victories for Hitler"; and finally, of course, Zionism and deepening Jewish attachments to the State of Israel. All of these strategies have proved highly persuasive and, alas, all have turned out to be only somewhat effective. Whatever their promise, not one has fully succeeded in practice. The proof, if any is needed, is that today continuity is back at the very top of our American Jewish communal agenda.

All of us are aware, I think, of the structural challenges to Jewish continuity, the obstacles rooted in the very marrow of American Jewish life that so often prevent effective communal responses to the problems that we face. Some will argue that it is these structural challenges that have stymied strategies like those enumerated above that might otherwise have succeeded.

Take, for example, the problem of fragmentation and divisiveness. Notwithstanding the mantra "we are one," we know that on any given issue we are not one but many: many competing ideologies, many diverse interest groups, many different social, political, economic, cultural, and religious backgrounds. Jewish unity, it has been said, is an oxymoron. On most issues, and especially those bearing on survival and continuity, Jews remain fiercely divided, with a range of different constituencies that have to be satisfied. Consensus proves extremely difficult to achieve.

Another problem that we face involves lack of resources. Wealthy as the American Jewish community is in comparison to many others, we do not have anywhere near the money to afford all of the many highly creative survival strategies that different segments of the community propose. Indeed, at the moment we are, as a community, overcommitted: the unprecedent growth in the number of Jewish educational, cultural, religious, and philanthropic institutions here and abroad has largely outstripped our ability to pay for them. To fund programs for Jewish continuity we need to cut back on other programs. That, as everybody knows, is much easier said than done.

There are, in addition, political and organizational problems that beset the American Jewish community, as well as utterly irresolvable ideological tensions that infuse the continuity debate: tensions concerning assimilation and identity, tradition and change, unity and diversity, and so on. Taken together, all of these limit what we, as a community, can do in the face of challenges, and they account for the slow pace of change in American Jewish communal life that is so frequently criticized.

At the same time, these structural limitations (our American Jewish version of checks and balances) have at least one great benefit: they ensure that we do not put all of our communal eggs in one highly-touted continuity basket. However much we may believe that "Jewish education" or "the synagogue" or "trips to Israel" are our last best hope to keep Judaism going for the next generation, we know in advance (for most of us have sat on allocations committees) that in the end we shall offer inadequate support to satisfy everyone. That is what the politics of Jewish consensus are all about, and history suggests that we are better off this way. In a pluralistic Jewish community like ours, a range of programs appealing to different segments of the community almost always works better than a single program that leaves many on the outside.

There are two additional points that, as far as I can tell, are not well known and have been largely overlooked in recent discussions of Jewish continuity, although to my mind they are extraordinarily important.

First, despite our intuitive sense that Jewish continuity depends upon communal cooperation, it is a curious fact that historically American Jewish continuity owes an enormous debt to the forces of discontinuity and dissent. (Apparently, it is sometimes better not to be one.) Think of three great movements that have contributed heavily to Jewish continuity in this country: Reform Judaism (which opened the door to Jewish pluralism), Zionism, and—although usually overlooked—the day school movement. Each of these was at one time bitterly divisive. Each was charged with being either anti-Jewish or anti-American, or both. And each, in retrospect, did as much or more for Jewish continuity in America as the consensus strategies advocated by well-established leaders. I suspect that Jewish feminism, in our own day, will fall into this same category—what might be called divisive movements that ultimately strengthen us. There is a paradox here: Jewish continuity in America has been secured to a considerable degree by movements that have promoted discontinuity and discord. This is not a brief for communal dissent, since by no means have all revolutionary movements in Jewish life been salutary; some, indeed, have proved catastrophic. But at least let us remember that the potential for contributing to Jewish continuity is there. Dissent can prove to be a blessing in disguise.

The second observation is that discussions of Jewish continuity today take place within an entirely different intellectual climate than existed before. Following Werner Sollors, we might term the transition that has taken place as a move from descent to consent.

For much of the 20th century, the question of Jewish continuity was discussed in America within the context of Jewish ethnicity—what was often called Jewishness (as distinct from Judaism). Jews pioneered the study of ethnicity in this country, and many of them believed (as Horace Kallen who helped to shape so many of our ideas of cultural pluralism certainly did) that ethnicity is destiny, it is innate and immutable, passed on from one generation to the next ("descent"). However much self-hating Jews might deny their Jewishness, and however dormant an individual's own Jewishness might be, it was believed that it could not be eradicated, only sublimated. This was the secular equivalent of the traditional Jewish folk-belief in *das pintele yid*, a Jewish homunculus that all Jews inherit as part of their genetic legacy and can never be exorcised.

Today, this basic assumption of American Jewish life is under attack from two fronts. First of all, the larger society no longer recognizes Jewishness as an ethnic category at all. The United States Census Bureau does not recognize it (Jews themselves are partly responsible for that), and proponents of diversity no longer recognize it. In the eyes of many, we are just one more subcategory of white males and females.

Second, and to my mind much more significant, the idea of Jewishness-by-descent has been replaced in our day by the idea of Jewishness-by-consent. Where once we spoke of Judaism as our destiny (meaning that it was predestined), now we speak of Judaism as a choice. Indeed, we are told by leading thinkers that we are "*all* Jews by choice." Where once we confidently believed that we were the chosen people, today we are described as the "choosing people." This conforms to everyday reality where we see non-Jews choosing to become Jewish and born-Jews choosing other faiths. It also conforms with changing views of ethnicity and identity in American thought. Many scholars today consider ethnicity and identity to be social inventions rather than biologically or even culturally determined destinies.

This transformation from Jewishness-by-descent to Jewishness-by-consent has tremendous policy implications for Jewish continuity and, especially, for our sense of peoplehood. Jewishness by descent, for example, is irrevocable, as much a part of us as our nose; Jewishness by consent, on the other hand, is completely revocable, purely a matter of choice. Jewishness by descent suggests a genealogical metaphor; it relates one to another through ties of blood. Jewishness by consent implies a marital metaphor: committed today, divorced tomorrow. Jewishness by descent ties the future largely to propinquity, the number of children that Jews give birth to; Jewishness by consent links the Jewish future to conversion and adhesion, the ability to attract adherents and hold on to them.

Let me close, then, by returning to the paradox with which I began. Given what the past teaches us about the most effective way to ensure Jewish continuity in America, it is best for us to take an exceedingly gloomy view of our prospects. For if history is any guide, gloom and doom will put us in just the right frame of mind to go out and work aggressively and diligently to prove ourselves wrong yet again.

Contributors

Steven Bayme, Ph.D., is the national director of Jewish communal affairs for the American Jewish Committee, New York, and director of its Institute on American Jewish-Israeli Relations.

Barry R. Chiswick is a professor of economics at the University of Illinois in Chicago.

Donald Feldstein, Ph.D., is past associate executive vice president, Council of Jewish Federations, New York.

Alan M. Fisher is a professor of political science at California State University Dominguez Hills and a senior fellow at the Wilstein Institute.

Sylvia Fishman, Ph.D., is the assistant director and senior research associate of the Cohen Center for Modern Jewish Studies at Brandeis University, Waltham, Massachusetts.

Rela Mintz Geffen is a professor of sociology and the coordinator of the program in Jewish communal studies at Gratz College, Pennsylvania.

David M. Gordis is the president of Hebrew College, Boston, and the director of the Wilstein Institute of Jewish Policy Studies in Los Angeles and Boston.

Allen Glicksman, Ph.D., is the senior research sociologist of the Polisher Research Institute, Philadelphia Geriatric Center.

Calvin Goldscheider is a professor of sociology and Judaic studies and chair of the department of sociology at Brown University.

Sidney Goldstein is a professor of sociology at the Population Studies and Training Center at Brown University. He is also chairman of the Council of Jewish Federations National Technical Advisory Committee on Jewish Population Studies.

Steven Huberman, Ph.D., is the executive director of planning and research, Joint Distribution Committee, New York.

Ariela Keysar, Ph.D., is a researcher at the Mandell L. Berman Institute, the North American Jewish Data Bank, CUNY Graduate Center, New York.

Samuel Z. Klausner is a professor of sociology at the University of Pennsylvania.

Tanya Koropeckyj-Cox is a research associate at the Polisher Research Institute, Philadelphia Geriatric Center.

Barry A. Kosmin, Ph.D., is the director of research at the Council of Jewish Federations and co-director of the 1990 National Jewish Population Survey. He is also director of the Berman Institute, City University of New York Graduate Center.

Bernard Lazerwitz is a professor of sociology at Bar Ilan University, Israel.

Nava Lerer, Ph.D., is a researcher at the Mandell L. Berman Institute, the North American Jewish Data Bank, City University of New York Graduate Center.

Seymour Martin Lipset is a professor of public policy at George Mason University, Virginia. He is also a senior fellow of the Hoover Institution, Stanford University, and a senior scholar at the Wilstein Institute.

Egon Mayer is a professor of sociology at Brooklyn College, City University, New York.

Bruce A. Phillips is a professor of Jewish communal studies at Hebrew Union College, Los Angeles, and a senior fellow at the Wilstein Institute.

Jonathan D. Sarna is a professor of American Jewish history at Brandeis University, Waltham, Massachusetts.

J. Alan Winter is a professor of sociology at Connecticut College.